Shaping Suburbia

Pitt Series in Policy and Institutional Studies

Bert A. Rockman, Editor

Shaping
Suburbia

How Political Institutions
Organize Urban Development

PAUL G. LEWIS

University of Pittsburgh Press

Published by the University of Pittsburgh Press, Pittsburgh, Pa., 15260
Copyright © 1996, University of Pittsburgh Press
All rights reserved
Manufactured in the United States of America
Printed on acid-free paper
10   9   8   7   6   5   4   3   2   1

Library of Congress Cataloging-in-Publication Data

Lewis, Paul G.
   Shaping suburbia : how political institutions organize urban
development / Paul G. Lewis.
      p. cm.
   Includes bibliographical references and index.
ISBN 0-8229-3938-x (cl. : alk. paper). — ISBN 0-8229-5595-4 (pbk.
 : alk. paper)
   1. City planning—United States.   2. Suburbs—United States.
   3. Urbanization—United States.   4. Local government—United States.
   I. Title.
   HT167.L48 1996
   307.74'0973—dc20   95-52088

A CIP catalog record for this book is available from the British Library.

For August Kunst
and the memory of
Margaret Kunst
(1906–1992)

Contents

Figures

Tables

Abbreviations and Acronyms

CBD	central business district
CCDA	Clackamas County (Oregon) Development Agency
CMSA	Consolidated Metropolitan Statistical Area
CRAG	Columbia Region Association of Governments (Portland area)
DRCOG	Denver Regional Council of Governments
DTC	Denver Technological Center (in Greenwood Village, Colorado)
ISTEA	Intermodal Surface Transportation Efficiency Act
JPACT	Joint Policy Advisory Committee on Transportation (at Metro, Portland)
LCDC	Land Conservation and Development Commission (state of Oregon)
MHR	Metropolitan Housing Rule (Portland area)
MPO	metropolitan planning organization
MSA	Metropolitan Statistical Area
MSD	Metropolitan Service District (Portland area), now called "Metro"
MSDD	Metropolitan Sewage Disposal District No. 1 (Denver area)
PMSA	Primary Metropolitan Statistical Area
RTD	Regional Transportation District (Denver area)
RUGGOs	Regional Urban Growth Goals and Objectives (Portland area)
SMSA	Standard Metropolitan Statistical Area
Tri-Met	Tri-County Metropolitan Transportation District (Portland area)
UGB	Urban Growth Boundary (Oregon)

Acknowledgments

Numerous kind souls helped me avoid getting lost in my research trek through the metropolis. Michael Danielson, Jennifer Hochschild, and Thomas Romer provided close guidance and support throughout this project, and their useful comments and criticisms improved the final product beyond measure. Helpful suggestions on previous versions of this material were also made by Jameson Doig, Fred Greenstein, Paul Teske, and anonymous reviewers.

In Denver and Portland, the patient cooperation and honesty of 25 local government officials and developers in interviews provided some of my most rewarding research experiences. In addition to those cited in the endnotes, I thank the numerous unnamed people who furnished leads, suggestions, or information about these intriguing regions. Academic urbanists in each metropolitan area provided useful perspectives and advice: Peter Schaeffer and Allan Wallis at the University of Colorado at Denver, Susan Clarke of CU-Boulder, and particularly Scott Moore of Colorado State University; in Portland, Ethan Seltzer and Carl Abbott of Portland State University. (A glance at the endnotes will also reveal my debt to Abbott's excellent scholarship.) Government bodies, particularly the Denver Regional Council of Governments and the Regional Transportation District in Denver, and Metro and the Tri County Metropolitan Transportation District in Portland, provided rich data that inform the text, tables, and figures. Most of the figures were prepared for publication by the Graphics Department at Florida International University.

For support that was essential to my research, I thank the Center of Domestic and Comparative Policy Studies at the Woodrow Wilson School, Princeton University; and the Mellon Foundation (for a dissertation completion fellowship). I alone bear responsibility for the weaknesses of this work.

My family, immediate and extended, has given me far more kindness than I can repay. I dedicate this book to my grandparents, German immigrants who not only urged me as a youth to "make my homework," but also (unwittingly perhaps) encouraged my fascination with places, transportation, and things urban.

1

Shaping the New Suburbia:
An Introduction

This book asks why American metropolitan areas look the way they do and examines the political organization of these areas as one important piece of the puzzle. Do local and regional political institutions have any systematic role in shaping urban form and the "built landscape"? Some argue that economic restructuring has made these government institutions dependent on forces beyond their control. In this view, local politics, particularly in the suburbs, is largely irrelevant for understanding and interpreting the urban landscape. My argument, however, is that local political institutions do indeed play an important role in shaping urban growth.

The issue is timely, and not only for academic urbanists. Urban America is undergoing a substantial transformation. While the industrial cities of the Northeast and Midwest have battled rising fiscal and social mayhem, newer urban places have emerged rapidly and dramatically—in the outer orbs of the older urban regions of the Rust Belt, in blossoming expanses in the newer southern and western areas of the nation, and in countless locations well beyond the former peripheries of metropolitan areas. While generally labeled "suburban," these new formations defy easy categorization. Indeed, in the past decade they have acquired a dizzying variety of labels from scholars and popular commentators: "urban villages," "outer cities," "new downtowns," "postsuburbia," "technoburbs," "urban realms," and a host of other appellations. And in 1991, journalist Joel Garreau published his five-hundred-page opus *Edge City: Life on the New Frontier*, coining a term and drawing the most extensive public attention the topic has received to date.

Each of these terms has a different range of meaning but each emphasizes the continuing dispersal of population and business to suburbia, and (sometimes) its reconcentration there into multiple nodes. In particular, an explosion of economic activity has reordered the appearance, lifestyle, and marketplace of what were once clearly *sub*ordinate urban places, or *sub*urbs. Early in the 1970s, central cities were overtaken by their suburban rings in one key

1

measure of economic livelihood: the number of jobs. This suburban dominance took on even greater proportions during the rapid-fire growth of the
1980s. During this period, the formerly peripheral areas increasingly took on a
different appearance. In many locations, clusters of office buildings, often
high-rises, sprouted among shopping centers and a variety of types of housing, redefining the suburban skyline.

To many, suburbia's image may remain one of sleepy residential neighborhoods dotted with crabgrass. But a large and growing cohort of professionals
and service or office workers know suburbia as something else: a focus of
employment and commercial activity. Following economist Thomas Stanback
(1991), I refer to the burgeoning economic development of formerly peripheral areas as "the new suburbanization" and call areas developed since 1970
"the new suburbia." The new suburbia is distinguishable from earlier periods
of suburban development, which were more residential in character and less
purely automobile oriented.

In this book, I ask why some suburban regions are developing differently
from others, and argue that a fundamental political logic underlies the patterns taken by this new growth. Why, for example, do dense, clustered "new
downtowns" emerge in some places, while elsewhere, similarly situated places
experience low-density, formless sprawl? Why must clerical and service workers commute for long distances to some suburban employment centers, while
other centers are situated adjacent to large quantities of affordable apartments
and townhouses? One key to answering these questions, I suggest, is to discern
how public-sector institutions shape the interaction of public and private
elites involved in the development process. These elites, in turn, shape land-
use patterns, using their powers to *enable* and *regulate* new growth.

In particular, I will argue that the *institutional configuration* of a region's
local governance influences the perceptions, opportunities, and actions of
elites. Most notably, this configuration involves the relative fragmentation or
unity of the public sector. This factor organizes interests and structures the
incentives that face actors who make authoritative decisions about land use. In
short, suburban development is distinctively patterned or "organized" by
urban-regional political arrangements. I employ a number of methods in
testing this hypothesis at work: a series of aggregate quantitative analyses of
development in metropolitan areas, and two detailed comparative case studies
of growth and institutions in the Denver, Colorado, and Portland, Oregon,
regions.

If the ever-increasing ranks of Americans who live and work in the suburbs
are to understand their emerging landscape and use political channels to try to
change or master it, they must come to terms with the forces underlying

suburban development. For political scientists, this study presents new perspectives on the relationships among institutional arrangements, elite behavior, and policy outcomes. In particular, it counsels caution to those analysts who argue that decentralized institutions can routinely find solutions to the problem of "governing the commons."

The theoretical model underlying the analysis will be developed in detail in chapter 2. First, however, we need to tackle some preliminary tasks: defining some key terms used in the study, exploring the development of "the new suburbia" in greater detail, and assessing its political content. We also need to consider whether existing theoretical approaches from the literature on industrial location and on urban politics can explain the variations that America's suburban areas manifest.

What Is Urban?
A Note on Terminology and the Study of Urban Politics

For the purposes of this study, *urban politics* refers to the interrelationship of politics and urbanization, *wherever that urbanization occurs*. Urbanization is a social and geographic process whereby human settlements acquire great size and high levels of density, heterogeneity, specialization, and interdependence (Wirth 1938; Mumford 1961; Gans 1962; Castells 1976). Note that this process may occur in central cities and in places that were recently rural, within municipal boundaries or in unincorporated areas. By extension, *urban political economy* includes the economic behavior of individuals, firms, and governments in our analysis.

Indeed, it is difficult to justify a scholarly conceptualization of *urban politics* merely as politics that happens to occur within large cities. Urbanization does not cease at the city limits. It spills into contiguous and even noncontiguous land areas—whatever prejudices analysts might have regarding the "urbanity" of those areas. This study and others *do* indicate clearly that the boundary between a central city and its suburbs, and for that matter metropolitan political geography more generally, are important objects of study, and should often be addressed as potentially major explanatory factors in urban development.[1] But the mere presence of a city's "limits" rarely justifies confining one's attention exclusively to a single jurisdiction. City boundaries are often a product of political struggles or administrative conveniences of a century or more ago (Jackson 1972; Teaford 1979). The political pressures manifested on city political actors are rarely independent of a larger metropolitan context. This environment shapes each city's political and economic perceptions and prospects.

These contextual considerations for city politics assume even greater significance if the issue in question is urban development and growth. People, goods, and capital do not remain tied forever to one jurisdiction. The linkages and interdependencies among places should not be severed in an attempt to concentrate on one place, even if it is the largest, the most important, and the most colorful. Urban political science, in particular, has been hampered and perhaps misled by a nearly exclusive focus on development and redevelopment in large central cities (Danielson and Lewis 1996).

We also need to clearly define several other key concepts. The terms *metropolis*, *metropolitan*, and *metropolitan area* refer to places within Metropolitan Statistical Areas (MSAs), as defined by the United States Census Bureau. In Census Bureau terms, an MSA is a county or group of contiguous counties containing a central city or cities with a population of at least fifty thousand, significant economic and social integration, and a "metropolitan character."

The term *suburban*, as used in this study, refers to any areas of an MSA that have developed predominantly during the automobile era (generally since 1920). Suburban portions of the metropolis grew at densities much lower than that characteristic of the industrial era city, and usually at a distance of at least a few miles from the regional central business district (CBD).[2] So defined, *suburban* areas may exist both inside *and* outside central city boundaries, though the latter case is more typical.

In contrast, the Census Bureau and many scholars working with aggregate census data generally speak of a *suburban ring*, which is simply all the land within a metropolitan area that is outside the boundaries of the central city (or cities). Given the wide differences in central city annexation patterns, however, this "ring" varies extensively from one metropolitan area to another. The suburban ring is the residual concept of what is "left over" in metro areas when the area inside the central city boundaries is excluded. Such a concept, therefore, is in a very real sense a political artifact. My concept of suburbia, in contrast, relies on a more generic ecological conception of metropolitan development. It allows one to isolate the effects of political structure, and thereby avoid spurious arguments.

Sometimes it is necessary to refer more generally to specific or generic urban spatial units. Where not specified with actual place names, the terms *urban area* or *(sub)urban region* denote contiguous, usually multijurisdiction areas that have some interdependent qualities and are subsets of some metropolitan area. For example, California's "Silicon Valley" is such an urban area, as is "eastern Long Island." Both areas contain numerous local governments and are part of larger MSAs.

I use the words *municipality*, *city*, *locality*, and *town* (all synonyms) to indicate incorporated local jurisdictions in metro areas. These are primary units of local government, and have mayors and other elected officials. A *local government* or a *jurisdiction* may refer to such an entity, or to other relatively autonomous local political units, such as counties, school districts, and special districts. Finally, a suburban *place* is just that—an identifiable location, neighborhood, or small area, which may or may not possess its own government.

The New Suburbia

In the 1970s and 1980s, American metropolitan areas "turned inside out," in the words of one urbanist (Muller 1981, x). At paces that varied widely from one MSA to another, major central cities were challenged and frequently overtaken by the emerging economic power of their suburbs. Frequently, areas well removed into the "exurban" periphery anchored this change. This dramatic spatial restructuring was made possible in large part by nearly universal auto ownership by households in the United States, coupled with an interstate highway program reaching maturity.

Several seminal pieces of scholarship in urban history and economic geography made clear that at the heart of the new suburbia was the movement of large-scale office, commercial, and service functions away from their previously almost exclusive downtown focus (Muller 1981; Hartshorn 1973; Hartshorn 1976; Manners 1974; Vance 1977; Fishman 1987). While a large national sample of suburban municipalities showed 13 manufacturing jobs for every 1 service job in 1972, the ratio a decade later was 2.2 to 1 (Schneider 1989, 151). Office space in particular has come to represent suburban economic vitality. For example, Joel Garreau develops his concept of an "edge city" around a five-part definition that includes, first, a minimum of 5 million square feet of leasable office space (Garreau 1991, 6–7).[3] Similarly, when a leading urban planning scholar wanted to investigate "America's suburban centers," he identified such employment nodes by using as a lower threshold centers with two thousand workers and 1 million square feet of office space (Cervero 1989, 18).

Thus the locus of white-collar activities that had been at the heart of the century-long economic, intellectual, and cultural domination of the central cities has gradually shifted. Accordingly, metropolitan residents have reoriented their lives around suburban jobs, leisure, and lifestyles. Urbanists have noted with particular interest "business, retail, housing, and entertainment focal points amidst a low-density cityscape. Each urban village has a core—a kind of new downtown—where the buildings are tallest, the daytime population largest, and the traffic congestion most severe" (Leinberger and Lockwood 1986, 43; see also Leinberger 1990). One of the purposes of this study is to determine which characteristics of urban areas are most conducive to these "kind of" new downtowns, and under what circumstances the "low-density cityscape" lacking such cores is more likely to prevail.

Suburbanization's Third Wave

While suburban downtowns may be new, suburbanization itself is not. Kenneth Jackson, a premier contemporary historian of suburban America who has written the best one-volume comprehensive history of suburbia, finds evidence that dispersal was well under way in the largest United States cities by the early decades of the nineteenth century (Jackson 1985, chap. 2). The first wave was initially an upper and upper-middle income migration, as higher-status people showed their willingness to pay to escape the crowded conditions at the core of emerging industrial cities. Gradually, they were joined by out-migrants of lower socioeconomic status, as transport innovations, particularly the electric trolley, made the costs of daily commuting less onerous. By the early part of this century, suburbia was becoming more and more representative of the population as a whole. Suburbanization accelerated after World War II in the wake of rising affluence, automobile ownership, and government mortgage subsidies.

Thus, the residential growth of suburbia was not really unprecedented. What was new in the early twentieth century was the failure of central city boundaries to follow the new growth. The emerging political and social consciousness of suburbanites led to the desire to wall themselves off politically from the central cities (Teaford 1979).

During and after World War II, suburbanization's second wave began to emerge. Manufacturing, and later large commercial facilities, followed residents out of the older downtowns at a rapid pace. Some firms entered the newer areas because they were chasing after potential customers or skilled workers. Others were lured by the emergence of trucking as a superior alternative to rail freight shipment. The national government played a major role in underwriting such dispersal, first by locating war plants in peripheral areas for defense purposes, and then by providing a major source of infrastructure for the new areas: the interstate highway network. These developments made centrality of location less fundamental to a firm's access to suppliers, markets, and workers. And once a "critical mass" was attained in any given suburban region, business and professional services were sure to follow—albeit in small numbers at first.

Today's office-based growth is the third and most mature wave of suburbanization. The professional, technical, administrative, and clerical workers who fill America's office buildings are representative of the most specialized and "high order" activities that a service-oriented economy has to offer. Theoretical knowledge, writes Daniel Bell, has become the "axial principle" around which the emerging postindustrial society takes shape (Bell 1973, 115; see also Reich 1992). Thus, office work plays an essential role in defining American economic and cultural life in the late twentieth century. In recent decades, moreover, not only office employment, but the amount of office space per worker has climbed.

The explosion of office work has made an impact not merely on the amount and type of economic activity, but also on its geographic distribution. Once bound to central locations so that they would have ready access to financial markets, clients, competitors, and consultants, many firms have found that at least parts of their organizations can be moved to suburban locations. In particular, divisions engaged in functions that are more routine or that require less administrative oversight have been candidates for such a shift. The entry of large numbers of skilled suburban female workers into the American labor force has made peripheral location particularly advantageous for many firms.

On the other hand, it is not merely "back offices" that have left the city. The so-called FIRE sector (finance, insurance, real estate), which made up a large proportion of recent employment growth, has been a major force behind the office boom in both CBDs and suburban regions. Many corporate headquarters in larger MSAs have also sought out suburban locations. By 1979, 22 percent of Fortune 500 firm headquarters in the New York region were located outside Manhattan; in MSAs such as Boston and Detroit, the suburban percentage was at 50 percent or above (Armstrong 1979, 86). Thus, nearly all segments of office-oriented firms can be considered candidates for suburbanization.[4]

In sum, the proportion of total office space located outside central cities rose from 25 percent in 1970 to 57 percent in 1984 (Feagin and Parker 1990, 168–69). In the first half of the 1980s, the square footage of office inventory in the ten largest CBD markets increased 25 percent, while the corresponding suburban markets registered more than three times that gain (Brazes 1986a, RE2).

That period was the culmination of a flurry of building activity that shaped contemporary suburbia. In the late 1960s and early 1970s, real estate interests began turning more attention to the speculative possibilities of "rapid return" items like office parks, apartments, and motels (Baerwald 1978, 313–15). Until the 1986 tax reforms, the tax code was very favorable toward these types of investment. Moreover, developers found many sources of capital—including pension funds, syndicates, insurance companies, and foreign investors—willing to underwrite their suburban projects. Financing became much more difficult to come by in the real estate recession of the late 1980s and early 1990s, and much office space sat vacant. But the development pattern had already been set in the boom years, and suburban office markets in many MSAs proved quicker to rebound than downtown districts.

Taken together, these trends created a revolutionary change in the structure of the city, according to Garreau:

> An old-fashioned downtown—sporting tall concrete-and-steel buildings with walls that touch each other, laid out on a rectangular grid, accented by sidewalks, surrounded by political boundaries, and lorded over by a mayor—is only one way to think of a city. In fact, it is only the nineteenth-century version. These sorts of cities, epitomized in the United States by Manhattan and San Francisco, are proud places that will always be cherished. But they are relics of a time past. They are aberrations. We built cities that way for less than a century. (1991, 25)

Garreau is not the only witness to the new suburbia. For scholarly analysts, too, the new suburbanization represents a challenge to the central city (Stanback 1991).[5] Perhaps the most notable symbol of this challenge is the sixty-five-story skyscraper anchoring the Post Oak development in suburban Houston. Even a high-rise skyline, it would seem, is no longer the exclusive perquisite of cities.

In short, there has been a breakdown of the traditional hierarchy of places in metropolitan areas. Historian and urbanist Carl Abbott refers to "outer cities" or "outtowns," which he identifies as "loosely connected and substantially self-sufficient suburban realms in which hundreds of thousands of residents may focus on concentrations of employment, retailing, and services" (Abbott 1990, 65). Clearly, traditional social science models of the metropolis, which identified a single urban center, are not as useful as they were the past. Urbanism is now a factor of accessibility in terms of time rather than distance. Robert Fishman concludes that "as the automobile gives rise to a complex pattern of multi-directional travel that largely by-passes the old central cities, the very concept of 'center' and 'periphery' becomes obsolete" (Fishman 1990, 29; see also Hughes 1993).

Suburban Clusters and Subcenters

Location in central city CBDs may continue to be mandatory for some office functions of some firms. Analysts have stressed the importance of face-to-face, interpersonal contact for certain administrative, trading, informational, and command-and-control functions (Gottman 1979). But for many activities, the use of telephones, overnight mail, fax, and computer communications is more than sufficient. These new technologies are analogous to earlier rounds of technological advancement, from trollies to interstate highways, that promoted the dispersal of urban society. The most recent innovations have freed many office functions to locate far from their traditional settings.

To the extent that business activity is not merely deconcentrating to suburbia, but also *recentralizing* into distinctive nodes or subcenters there ("new downtowns"), some of the advantages of face-to-face contact can be maintained or regained. Many organizations, particularly high-level administrative units, require agglomeration economies to thrive (Stanback 1991; Oakey and Cooper 1989); advances in knowledge and technology and astute financial decisions often depend on frequent interactions with competitors, consultants, and associates. In addition, a specialized labor pool can provide major competitive advantages.

Thus, geographer David Greene (1980, 34–35) finds that "within the trend of population and employment suburbanization, there is a trend toward concentration of employment and population occurring in certain suburban areas. . . . Employment growth outside the central city is concentrated in a relatively small number of zones." Many claim that the suburban business nodes serve as the hubs of cities in their own right. As geographer Thomas Baerwald writes:

> The list of activities found in large suburban concentrations is an inventory of traditional downtown land uses—all types of retail, service, and entertainment establishments; office buildings; hotels and meeting places; governmental and institutional activities; medical facilities; industrial and warehousing operations; and higher-density residences. The only downtown activities not likely to be in suburban concentrations are low-rent transient housing and the highest-level financial exchanges. (1982, 7)

To the extent that agglomeration economies can take shape, true competition between city and suburban downtowns may result. While the potentialities of agglomeration are perhaps not yet widely appreciated by suburban interests, "there is considerable evidence that economic growth in the suburbs is increasingly focussed on a restricted number of magnet areas in which locational advantages associated with agglomeration play a key role" (Stanback 1991, 60).

Clearly, we might expect many office users to seek convenient agglomerations in their new suburban locations. In that way, they could receive the amenities that suburban location provides, but retain the conveniences and business advantage associated with the old CBDs. One would expect office developers to try to cash in on these proclivities by developing a great deal of

office space at relatively high densities in the most accessible suburban locations. These entrepreneurs have an incentive to place as much square footage
on a given site as is practicable and marketable, in order to increase the ratio
of future rents to land, labor, and carrying costs. At the same time, for policy makers, "office growth enables burgeoning suburbs to concentrate nonresidential development in clusters that introduce urban form and amenity,
require less land consumption, and create less auto-dependent urban regions"
(Armstrong 1979, 61).

As this study will show, however, sometimes these expectations of agglomeration are borne out, and sometimes not. For example, one recent
analysis contrasts the relatively formless shape of Westchester County, New
York, and Marin County, California, to what is posited as the archetypal new
suburban region, Orange County, California. Orange County is a multicentered region with "a hodgepodge of specialized centers built miles apart and
separated by large suburban-style housing tracts." Orange County "differs
from the traditional suburb by having lively commercial and cultural centers
for residents" (Kling, Olin, and Poster 1991, 8). A broader empirical project by
sociologist Holly L. Hughes (1993) examines commuting patterns in metropolitan areas and finds varying hierarchy "networks" among suburban places.
Some MSAs show multiple strong subcenters, while others have none.

This finding highlights the variety of spatial forms that suburban growth
can take on. Geographers and planning scholars differentiate between *clusters*,
relatively high-density, centered areas, and *corridors*, linear strips of development along major transportation arteries (Baerwald 1982; Cervero 1989). In
the most extensive empirical analysis to date, Robert Cervero further classifies
these phenomena into several subcategories (1989, 4). But while these classification studies are useful, Baerwald notes that descriptions and case studies of
suburban concentrations "do not explain why clusters and corridors develop
as they do. Many factors affect land use patterns in these concentrations,
including locational tendencies of specific land uses, characteristics of the
transportation system, historical factors and the timing of development, and
other factors" (1982, 9).

Subsumed under his "other factors" category are the actions of local government. Baerwald quickly dismisses these as relatively unimportant within
the American context, noting that clusters and corridors in the Twin Cities
region closely resemble those in the Houston area, despite the highly different
government structure and ethos of Minnesota and Texas. But he does not
attempt to show that MSAs have systematically similar suburban forms. Nor
does Baerwald satisfactorily explain why clusters and corridors within given
regions arise in some places and not others. Regional scientist Rodney Erick-

son puzzles over an "emerging randomness in the patterning of suburban nucleations" (1986, 343).

Are suburban growth patterns random? Theoretical guidance is needed in understanding the circumstances under which reconcentration or formlessness might be expected to prevail. Given the unexplained variations, local government structure ought to be considered more thoughtfully as a potential systematic influence.

The Shortcomings of Traditional Location Theory

To hear many writers tell the story, one would think that economic analysis is the only key necessary for analyzing the patterns of the new suburban development. Garreau sees various public-sector entities "swirling around like gnats" in edge cities. But according to Garreau, these swarms of government fiefdoms only obscure the reality that such places take shape due to "the historical force of commerce more than governance" (1991, 46–47).

If this is the case, however, analysis rooted purely in economic theory has had surprisingly little to offer. Few economists have attempted to grapple with the office location question—and for good reason. Gerald Manners recognized early on that "deductive economic and geographical principles offer very little assistance to anyone seeking to understand the locational characteristics of the industry." He explains that "traditional partial location theory, for example, is rooted in such concepts as the minimization of physical inputs and the maximization of revenue output, concepts that are completely alien to the process and nature of locating office activities" (Manners 1974, 103).

In the case of traditional factories and warehouses, industrial location theories based on the input and output movement of discrete, bulky goods have proven instructive. But where knowledge and expertise is the primary "product," such optimization techniques are far less enlightening. In the technical vocabulary of economic geography, "non-market-sensitive location has little relationship to transportation costs because for most firms these costs have become a relatively small part of total costs" (Giuliano 1986, 257; see also Erickson 1986, 343).

In all but the very largest MSAs, moreover, office rents, as well as labor costs for office jobholders, do not vary significantly within the region. In this situation, economist Manners is put in the extreme position of concluding, "The benefits of alternative locations are apparently deemed by most office managements to be either incapable or unworthy of measurement" (1974, 105). It may be more reasonable to assert, as does British office-location analyst Peter Daniels, that "a suboptimal location in economic terms may well possess non-economic attributes which counterbalance any economic disadvantages, while it is also equally likely that location decision-making incorporates social, psychological and environmental variables as well as more objective economic appraisal of alternatives" (Daniels 1979, 5).

One such consideration is the convenience of various land site options to heavily indebted, time-conscious and politically savvy office developers. After all, office development is not usually the outcome of an exhaustive search by a new or moving company, but is a speculative process by people and firms who make a living by taking gambles. Developers normally attempt to build quickly and keep a watchful eye for financially disruptive and time-consuming opposition, in an attempt to minimize the interest charges they incur between the time land is acquired and the time completed buildings are rented to tenant business firms.

Office-based firms or organizations normally decide to move in "after the fact," when a decision to develop on a particular site has already been made (Daniels 1979, 14–15).[6] Thus, what should normally capture our attention is the behavior of developers rather than that of the occupying tenants. Accordingly, the typical economic studies of firm location decisions, and political science studies of policies that jurisdictions use to recruit firms, are not as useful for studying development patterns in a metropolitan, information-based economy as they are for studying old industrial cities.

The Political Nature of Suburban Development

Thus, the public sector's role has most often been viewed as residual: Government activity is one of several factors in the location process of firms that has not been accounted for. But this residual factor may well overwhelm the quantifiable variables that have long been the economic geographer's tools of the trade. As we have seen, traditional economic location models have not proven satisfactory in explaining metropolitan office location. While the speculative nature of such development may make developers less than predictable economic agents, the local political system may constitute an additional intervening force in the process. Economic geographers recognize that the viability of their theories is "reduced to the degree that the public sector can control or regulate the land market" (Giuliano 1986, 257).

There is good reason to suspect that there is a political character to suburban growth patterns. The development process clearly generates identifiable costs and benefits, but is not purely a market transaction. Would-be developers must ordinarily work for public-sector approval, a process likely to include hearings before planning agencies and sometimes legislative votes at the municipal and/or county levels.[7] Builders must also conform to the local zoning code—often a very political set of regulations (Babcock 1966; Danielson 1976; Fischel 1985)—or obtain a variance from it, which often involves negotiation. Increasingly, new state, county, or regional regulations govern large-scale development as well. It should come as little surprise that a survey of 22,000 builders identified "zoning and regulation" as "the toughest problem the homebuilding/development business faces." That factor was cited by 54 percent of respondents ("Zoning" 1988, 28).

In short, types of *regulatory* policies, not traditionally measured in models of how "politics matters" to urban growth, may be of key importance in the location of suburban economic activity. Normally, measures of local taxation, expenditure patterns, or service delivery have been used as independent variables in empirical models of firm location. But such an approach omits a crucial intervening step whereby local governments help shape land use, rather than economic development per se.[8]

In a totally "free" land market, activists who oppose growth in a given location would have to buy the land in question to prevent its development. But the realities of local political discretion over land use mean that opponents are not forced to take such expensive measures. Like the legislative process in Congress, the land-use decision-making process in most suburban regions provides numerous access points, enabling opponents of an action several options for blocking it.

Sometimes, however, public-sector authority and resources are necessary to *enable* or to aid urban development projects. A given site will probably be undevelopable from the start without substantial public involvement in providing the necessary infrastructure to the area—roads, sewers, and water supply. "Jurisdictions build infrastructure not only to accommodate recent growth but also to compete for new growth" (Taylor 1991, 60). This infrastructure provides access and basic services that help create demand for a potential office or mall site. Moreover, government intervention is of key importance in successfully producing large, ambitious, or unusual projects. Consider Joe R. Feagin and Robert Parker's discussion of "mixed-use developments," or MXDs, projects that involve combinations of housing, retail shops, offices, and hotels:

> One important reason for MXD viability is the assistance frequently provided by local government officials. A ULI [Urban Land Institute] survey of 131 MXDs revealed significant governmental involvement, with nearly 50 percent of them requiring some local code or ordinance change, 36 percent receiving indirect economic incentives or infrastructure improvements, 34 percent including governmental investment in supporting projects, and 16

percent involving direct governmental ownership or shared risk. (Feagin and Parker 1990, 119)

One of my purposes in this book is to determine the institutional conditions under which public authority is likely to be used in this more "creative" sense.[9]

In general, growth is a pressing issue to suburban residents, and thus to their representatives. Activist citizen groups regularly organize to fight or shape growth. On the other side of the controversy, development interests have also formed lobbying organizations and professional associations, and are known in many locales to be generous campaign contributors. Survey research also illustrates the issue's salience, as do a variety of case studies in the urban development literature.[10]

Policy Implications of a Changing Urban Geography

Moreover, a number of interrelated clusters of key public policy issues surround the suburban development process. Some of these will be featured in the course of the empirical analysis, and the concluding chapter will take up these issues in a more sustained manner and will offer some recommendations. For now, it is enough to briefly introduce the controversies involved.

Recall that what is at issue in suburban development is not merely the *fact* that metropolitan areas are decentralizing from their cores, but the *form* such decentralized economic activity takes. If jobs and housing both flee to suburbia, but even there are relatively inaccessible to one another, congestion and costly journey-to-work patterns may result. Ever-increasing reliance on the automobile—particularly single-occupant cars—also raises concerns about air quality. In the early 1990s, amendments to the federal Clean Air Act brought new attention and urgency to these issues, as did the new Intermodal Surface Transportation Efficiency Act. Taken together, these laws required assurances from states and metropolitan planning organizations that all federally subsidized transportation improvements would conform to regional transportation plans aimed at reducing air pollution. States and metro areas were also given new flexibility in using federal highway funds on public transit projects and "demand management" measures. The ultimate issue in policy discussions that link transportation and land use is the overall efficiency of the emerging patterns of settlement and commerce. This set of policy considerations has become a key concern in most rapidly growing metropolitan areas.

More broadly, a heated debate emerged in the 1980s over the extent to which the growth of suburban entry-level jobs left economic advancement out of reach of the transit-dependent central city poor. This is the "spatial mismatch" hypothesis, promulgated most notably by sociologist William Julius Wilson, as part of an explanation of inner-city impoverishment. While *Shaping Suburbia* will not venture into this debate, its findings may point to institutional arrangements under which such mismatches are especially likely, or under which local governments might be more amenable to linking economic need with economic opportunity.

Additional policy considerations concern the levels of amenity and quality of life in the rapidly changing suburbs. Recent patterns of spread-out development raise the specter of dirty air and the disappearance of open space, diminishing the supposed selling points of suburbia. Development that fails to stay compact in form can lead to tremendous despoliation of recently rural areas, and perhaps to a loss of productive farmland. As a fiscal consideration, growth nearly always burdens public infrastructure. To the extent that new growth leapfrogs over more established inner areas, the problem is exacerbated. Even at the micro scale of the new projects themselves, there are architectural and design features that have raised political controversies. At issue here are concerns about pedestrian access and landscape preservation.

Ultimately, questions of aesthetics and community character are central to suburban growth regions: Is the proper scale to be more traditionally "urban" or "suburban"? Who will pay for the impact of change? Should growth be controlled or managed, and if so, in what way, and by what level of government? Is the built landscape disorienting, or does it provide residents with a sense of place?[11] Should suburban officials heed the admonitions of professional planners? In considering these questions, policy analysis and political analysis necessarily become blurred.

The Politics of Urban Development: The Case of the Unexplained Variance

Given the prominent policy implications and the *political* forces shaping much office development, we might expect that the literature on urban political science would provide an appropriate and convincing approach to understanding development in the suburbs. But this is not the case. Three of the most fashionable schools of contemporary urban political science have fallen short as instruments of *comparative* and *metropolitan* research. A fourth approach, the "urban regime" perspective, will be evaluated in chapter 2.

Economic Approaches to Urban Politics

In a thoughtful review, Bryan Jones argues that recent work in the study of American urban politics demonstrates rapid theoretical advances, but lacks integration as a field. In comparison to the "mainstream" of political science in the United States, urban politics has engaged in more theoretical debate about fundamental constraints and possibilities of political action, and has shown a keen appreciation for historical and economic context. Nevertheless, it is something of an empirical weakling as a subfield of political science (Jones 1989).

Part of the explanation for this state of affairs lies in the framework of recent theories that view economic factors—namely, interjurisdictional competition under conditions of international capitalism—as *the* central fact of urban political systems. In the wake of dramatic fiscal crises in American cities in the 1970s, political scientists became attuned to the prime importance of capital investment patterns and intergovernmental grants for urban political vitality, and also noted the responsiveness to these capital flows that public officials clearly display.

I do not dispute assertions of the centrality of economic forces to urban politics. These considerations introduced insights that substantially reinvigorated urban political science and made researchers aware of basic external factors affecting local governance. But while what might be called the "economic hypothesis" accurately characterizes political and policy *continuities* across cities, it provides distressingly little leverage for explaining differences among cities, except as residual "noise." Casual observation, not to mention comparative case study, shows considerable variance in the politics of jurisdictions in the United States. While the politics of all cities may look similar in theory, Frederick Wirt writes, "practice has made local government a diverse, thriving aspect of urban democracy" (Wirt 1985, 83; see also Clarke 1987). In short, the economic hypothesis is significant but not definitive (but see Swanstrom 1993).

To this point, I have treated the economic hypothesis as if it were a unified school of thought, when in fact it includes two methodological and ideological traditions at opposite ends of the spectrum: public choice and neo-Marxism. Nevertheless, the justification for speaking of these paradigms in the same terms is that both represent "economistic" approaches to political economy, drawing on neoclassical and Marxian economic traditions respectively. In urban studies as elsewhere, both schools ultimately use economic concepts to account for political behavior.

Public Choice Models

The public choice approach to local politics draws on the power of the "exit option," by which residents and firms in local jurisdictions are supposed to signal preferences to public officials (Tiebout 1956; Teske et al. 1993). In this formulation, local public goods are "club goods," with municipalities acting as clubs that set the terms of membership, and mobile citizens as the members who distribute themselves among the municipalities by "voting with the feet." Each set of actors seeks optimal outcomes in a fluid, market-approximating mechanism (Mueller 1979, chap. 7). As extended to the context of American federalism by Paul Peterson (1981), jurisdictions compete for capital investment so as to optimize the position of their respective average taxpayers.

There is much that is useful in the public choice approach, and elements of its rationality assumptions will be employed in this book. I will not elaborate upon the usual litany of charges of obfuscation directed at the public choice model.[12] Rather, I am struck by the shortcomings of the model for comparative work: *Relative efficiency in pursuing investment must be made to explain all.* It is hard to establish any congruence between this formulation and reality (Neiman 1975, 16).

Some variants of public choice theory itself provide hints of contextual factors, apart from which the mechanism of competition cannot be analyzed. For instance, models of bounded rationality, frequently deployed in the study of organizations, demonstrate an appreciation for the circumstances and decision rules that guide rational behavior (Simon 1955; see also March and Olsen 1989). The institutional arrangements of metropolitan areas can be considered "organizational." Moreover, the "Arrow problem," situated more squarely within the public choice tradition, provides a deductive proof that most schemes for aggregating preferences (including, one would imagine, "voting with the feet") must include some nondemocratic, coercive element if they are to produce definitive and workable outcomes rather than voting cycles (Arrow 1951). Arrow's theorem implies that political institutions are not neutral aspects of the choice environment.[13] That is to say, on public choice theory's own terms, institutional arrangements matter, and are themselves political.

Neo-Marxist Models

Contemporary Marxist practitioners of urban analysis also stress the competitive position of cities, but in a quite different fashion. Generally following Althusserian "structuralist" variants of Marxism, they see the internationalization of capital flows, and cities' relative place in this world system, as begetting urban outcomes. Capitalism's capacity to reproduce itself generates economic restructuring, with differential opportunities for places to successfully capture new economic growth. Cities' fates depend on their ability to rapidly alter land uses—usually in a socially regressive manner. This is presented as a universal "logic of capital investment." (Judd 1988, 376; see also

Fainstein et al. 1983; Smith and Feagin 1987). With no viable alternatives to participation in the competition for new investment, "even the most resolute and avant-garde municipal socialists will find themselves, in the end, playing the capitalist game" (Harvey 1989, 7).[14] Given the conflict between these constraints on redistributive action and the realities of local political demands, urban governments tend to oscillate between political and fiscal crises (Shefter 1985).

Marxist scholarship has been valuable in showing the importance of spatial factors to the study of urban political economy, demonstrating the importance of the broader economic context and the often privileged position of business. But frequently, the Marxists' view of local politics as implicated in the reproduction of capital merely substitutes a world-systemic structural functionalism for the public choice analysts' reductionism. Trying to explain the behavior of city governments by the "needs" of capitalism is methodologically precarious (Peterson 1981, preface).

Neo-Marxism is no better at accounting for variance in urban development than is deductive public choice. A macrolevel process is supposed to inform us about a variety of local outcomes. This perspective can be persuasive where the communities being examined are sites of capital flight, such as Detroit, but is less informative in more typical jurisdictions. Little is written, for example, about the varieties of *suburban* experience, yet suburbs are increasingly heterogeneous and cannot be viewed merely as affluent exile communities.[15]

For neo-Marxists, in short, "cities are dependent on global and national trends that shape their fate" (M. Smith et al. 1985). Clearly, this perspective shares much with the "dependency" approach to the international political economy, which stresses the asymmetrical economic relationships between developing countries and the corporations and governments of the developed world. Dependency theory has been attacked for overemphasizing external influences on developing nations while blurring the authentic political choices made by government actors. The urban studies version of dependency theory can be criticized on similar grounds. The claims of this line of thinking often fail to be borne out by comparative empirical tests (Clark 1985).[16] They also obscure the political meaning of the growth and development that *does* manage to occur in the economically peripheral polities. Is development in America's poorer towns and cities an epiphenomenon of some larger, malignant process, or is it the outcome of local and national political struggles over growth? (See Mollenkopf 1983; Logan and Molotch 1987.)

As neo-Marxists carry out detailed empirical case studies, they sometimes come to modify the more rigid structuralist position. In particular, they are apt to assert the importance of the "local State." This may introduce an irresolvable dilemma, however. How can a paradigm deduced from economic principles come to terms with the centrality of intrastate conflict to urban development? Thus neo-Marxists who feel a need to account for the state's importance come to verbose and puzzling conclusions such as the following:

> Territorial structure is a necessary property of the State. It is equally restrictive to assert the necessary territoriality of the State without some recognition that capital and labor are themselves dependent on the circulation of value through specific territories. This does not mean that capital "requires" a particular territorial structure in the State. It is to acknowledge that changes in territorial organization cannot occur without a simultaneous reorganization of the interests of territorially dependent citizens and States. This is a very political process driven ultimately by economic conditions. (Jonas 1991)

In many of these studies, then, we are left with little more than an assertion that the local political environment, seemingly something purely contextual, colors the fundamental process of capital accumulation. Case studies portray an elaborate economic superstructure and a great deal of local "noise" that, though fascinating perhaps, is ultimately not the most important thing.

Summary: Urban Politics Redux

Both public choice studies and work in the Marxist tradition have had excessively single-minded views of urban politics. Both derive their approaches to urban politics from grand economic theories of history or of human behavior, employing essentially a single variable, competitive capitalism. Perhaps not surprisingly, cities appear to be more *deduced* than studied. As Jones argues, the urban affairs field "has suffered from the assertion of intellectual certainty" (Jones 1989, 36).

A Response to Economism: The "Growth Machine"

Some would have us fill the impersonal void left by these deterministic approaches with an analysis of local "growth machines." This approach to urban development offers an elite-centered sociological theory that is posited as a more nuanced alternative.

Harvey Molotch, the leading "growth machine" theorist, critiques both the public choice advocates and the neo-Marxists. Of the former's rationalist assumptions, he writes: "Because neither a rational bureaucracy nor a rational market organizes what happens, cities can be overdeveloped, deserted, or inconveniently arranged. Cities are 'designed' primarily to maximize returns for the organizationally successful entrepreneurs" (Molotch 1988, 27). Thus, Molotch would have us look more closely at the local elite structure than economistic analysts do. The "organizationally successful entrepreneurs" he refers to are locally powerful individuals with parochial, profit-oriented interests. They wish to see ever-increasing economic activity in the particular "place" in which they have a stake.[17] For example, real estate interests, local retailers, and owners of local mass media all have profits tied directly to local growth. Thus these entrepreneurs, normally with the help or acquiescence of local government, attempt to secure a favorable "business climate" for development in their municipality by using political power to manipulate land-use regulation, weaken organized labor, or restrain redistributive spending.

Molotch agrees with the structuralists that the capitalist system is hegemonic over localities, but maintains, "Within the local realm, it is the growth elites who are hegemonic." In this sense Molotch is nevertheless in accord with the neo-Marxists in putting the brunt of the explanatory burden on private-sector forces, neglecting a sophisticated perspective on the institutions of the local political system. "Politicians, like geography, do matter," Molotch concludes. "But at least at the local level, it is the growth machine system that determines how they matter" (Molotch 1988, 38).

Thus, although Molotch presents the beginnings of a sophisticated organizational perspective on private-sector actors, the public sector is granted no such detailed analysis. "In both ideological and structural terms," Molotch concludes, "[the growth elites'] dominance over the development process is felt across a wide array of political, economic, and cultural institutions" (1988, 42). Yet, as William Form takes care to stress in this context, "Struggles between businessmen and government do not always work out in favor of the former" (Form 1954, 322).

Molotch is quite unclear about the geopolitical composition of "place." To date, the "growth machine" model has been applied to only one jurisdiction at a time. Molotch tends to select supporting evidence wherever available, shifting from one case to another for juicy quotes and illuminating events. But it is difficult to see how far we might go with "the growth machine system" as a tool for comparative analysis of metropolitan areas.

An Outline of the Study

In recent years, all three methodological and ideological schools have made more or less the same admission—that "politics matters," that "the local state is important," that "Tiebout needs politics." What remains is the somewhat more daunting task of demonstrating more precisely *under what conditions* and *how* local politics matters to urban development.

Another fundamental shortcoming has plagued the explanatory capabilities of research on the politics of urban development: the lack of an attempt to place the phenomenon or case selected within the wider context of the metropolitan political structure. Central cities are studied in isolation. If, as has been argued, urban development ought to be studied in a regional rather than purely local context, the analyst must make note of the multijurisdiction character of the region in question. We cannot assume that every suburb is an Atlanta or New Haven in miniature. Similarly, techniques developed, assumptions made, and results generated in the study of big cities cannot be transferred wholesale to the larger metropolitan context.

Perhaps political science's lack of attention to suburbs is understandable, given that any particular suburb is not a well-bounded unit of analysis. But neither is the central city well bounded. Today, many efforts at redeveloping the downtowns of central cities are simply defensive, an attempt to stave off the decline of the central jurisdiction in the face of suburban economic growth. These strategies clearly demonstrate that city politics is not self-contained. The lack of a metropolitan focus precludes attempts to build comparative empirical theories of urban development.

This book sets forth such a theory. It will explore and test the hypothesis that urban development patterns are neither predetermined and given, nor completely contextual; rather, development is in some sense *organized* in each MSA. Metropolitan growth is organized by the institutional makeup of the public sector, and thus varies as that configuration varies. I certainly do not argue that political organization is the *only* systematic variable operating to shape urban development. Clearly, age and historical evolution, industry mix, growth rate, and transportation system, among other powerful factors, operate so as to affect the location, clustering, and dispersion of the new suburban growth. Many of these factors will be introduced as the study proceeds, and where possible, I shall try to "hold constant" for such factors, in both case studies and statistical analyses.

Chapter 2 is the central theoretical chapter of the book. It presents the institutional model in some detail, drawing on two "ideal type" cases of political organization. This framework suggests three hypotheses, linking political fragmentation to metropolitan deconcentration, sharp intrasuburban disparities in development, and sprawl. After examining the ways in which the suburban institutional context differs from that of central cities, I look at one additional theoretical school of urban political economy—"regime politics"—and evaluate its usefulness as an explanatory tool for suburban development politics.

Chapter 3 tests the specific hypotheses advanced in chapter 2, describing the formal organization of the governance of land use in the United States, and illustrating patterns of political fragmentation in a sample of eighty met-ropolitan areas. It offers a multivariate analysis of the likely effects of this institutional characteristic on a variety of characteristics associated with ur-ban development outcomes in the sample MSAs.

In chapters 4 through 6, the model is grounded in the actual preferences of elite actors operating in different institutional environments. I present ac-counts of two emerging postindustrial regions that grew rapidly in the 1980s, the metropolitan areas of Denver and Portland. Chapters 5 and 6 relate the in-stitutional arrangements of the metropolitan areas to their urban develop-ment patterns. The case studies (which are actually composed of multiple case studies of particular places and events in each MSA) draw upon inter-views, fieldwork observation, and historical analysis of political structure and growth dynamics in the two metro areas.

Finally, chapter 7 brings together and evaluates the aggregate analysis and comparative case study material, in light of current policy debates over trans-portation, land use, and urban form. It offers a set of general conclusions and some lessons and questions for further research.

The study asks big questions, and I have tried to proceed carefully. In particular, I bear in mind the warnings raised by the authors of a 1961 study of the Syracuse metropolitan area, who noted two potential problems with re-search into metropolitan decision structures. First, they argued, care must be taken that case studies are actually comparable. Second, "since by definition [such studies] will treat of extraordinary decisions in the metropolitan area, they will provide an imperfect picture of the day-to-day forces of influence at work within the metropolis" (Martin et al. 1961, 16). I attempt to avoid both pitfalls. First, I use implicit or explicit "controls" in comparing metropoli-tan areas. Second, I emphasize recurring patterns of metropolitan decisions, rather than isolated incidents. Instead of focusing on individual decisions to determine who exercised power, I examine the biases of the decision rules themselves.

Actors, Preferences, and
Political Institutions in Urban Development

The first step is to analyze the social forces operating in the land market. Obviously, the image of a free and unorganized market in which individuals compete impersonally for land must be abandoned. The reason for this is that the land market is highly organized and dominated by a number of interacting organizations. Most of the latter are formally organized, highly self-conscious, and purposeful in character —William Form

There is . . . one very striking omission in this rich literature: there has been no serious effort to relate the patterns of influence within the community to the institutional structures of the community government. It is a commonplace of political science that institutional arrangements have something to do with who gets what, when, and how. —Roscoe Martin et al.

The degree to which Phoenix can insist on adherence to strict locational criteria [in its plan for several clustered "urban villages" within the city] is greatly restricted by the real possibility of losing development and its attendant tax base, to Mesa, Tempe, Scottsdale, or other surrounding communities offering developers more attractive opportunities. The institutional backdrop has real implications in terms of physical design. —David Plane

The passages cited above indicate that institutional characteristics of regional political economies can be viewed as a key explanatory "backdrop" for urban development. If these institutional patterns are of any significance, one would expect them to be implicated in the interactions among suburban elites in government and business, and in the land-use outcomes shaped by those elites. Can the organization of governance in metropolitan areas account for much of the variation in the location of economic development within those areas?

In this chapter, I wish to highlight the potential for a theoretically grounded *political-economic* analysis of metropolitan growth patterns, particularly those related to speculative office and commercial development. It is the strategic behavior of developers and local governments, rather than individual firms or households, that should occupy our attention as we examine the nonresidential development process. I present a new explanatory framework for development politics and focus on the way differences in local government organization create different incentives for public and private elites during the land-use decision-making process.

I certainly do not argue that the institutional factors analyzed here are the *only* systematic variables operating to shape urban development. Clearly, the age, industry mix, growth rates, transportation system, culture, and ethos of a given region, among other powerful factors, shape the new suburban growth. Moreover, the scale and integration of the development industry itself plays a role. My main question, however, is whether the political organization of a metropolitan area has its own significant effect, and if so, what that effect might be.

What Is Institutional Analysis?

Unlike individual- or firm-level approaches to urban development, institutional analysis considers organizational features of each region in attempting to understand land-use differences among metropolitan areas. It takes into account the institutional context in which key land-use decision makers operate. My conception of *institutions* draws on comparative studies of national policy making, as well as the somewhat different approach normally labeled "positive political economy" or the "positive theory of institutions."[1] In both these approaches, the term *institutions* refers to the formal and informal organizations, structures, rules, conventions, and standard operating practices "that structure the relationship between individuals in various units of the polity and economy" (Hall 1986, 18–19; see also Katzenstein 1985; Heclo 1978; March and Olsen 1989). These organizational arrangements delimit the set of choices available—and imaginable—to political and economic actors.

Why are these concepts relevant to growth patterns in metropolitan areas? In some contexts, the urban landscape may take shape as a cumulative product of a multitude of isolated, disconnected decisions in a number of spheres. In other situations, a few public actors and private interests, who with sufficient resources or proper organization have disproportionate impact over a relatively small number of arenas, may effectively determine futures for numerous communities (cp. Warner 1962; Caro 1974; Danielson and Doig 1982). In short, for urban-regional political economy, the ways in which the local public and private sectors are organized are central. Such comparative features of urban political-economic systems have thus far rarely been appreciated.

At the comparative *sub*national level of my analysis, it should be possible to identify and measure more specific institutional relationships than analysts typically can muster at the cross-national level.[2] I refrain from asserting that institutions are themselves causal; ultimately, of course, it is people who act. Nevertheless, it is important to study the incentives created by the nexus of public and private institutions operating at the local and regional levels. Unlike the more economistic theorizing associated with neo-Marxism or the more deductive variants of public choice, my approach is designed to make comparative research on urban development politics practicable. After all, institutions differ widely across metropolitan areas. "Capitalism" and "self-interest" do not.

Actors and Preferences

The aim, then, is to evaluate the effects of political organization on a region's development. Let us first posit several simplifying assumptions regarding the behavior of key actors. The five assumptions discussed below seem intuitively reasonable, which is not to say they will hold up uniformly well in all cases. I will assume that each of the five stated preferences is uniform in *direction*, if not *intensity*, in all urban areas.

1. *Developers of suburban properties seek to maximize the return on their investment.* This assumption posits a relatively straightforward notion of economic rationality. Given their resources and capabilities, developers will seek to build a project with a site, design, and size that will allow them maximal profits. Since developers normally operate on borrowed money, *time* is also a key consideration. The carrying charges associated with drawn-out battles for local regulatory approval may prove prohibitive.

2. *Other private elites with parochial interests—i.e., business people closely tied to the local rather than national economy—similarly seek increased profits, and will favor any growth that is consistent with that motive.* This assumption reflects the motivations of local "growth elites" who do not make their living specifically from development: for example, retailers, construction trade unions, and real estate brokers. By the phrase "consistent with that motive," I mean that the parochial elites may on occasion be opposed to new growth that they see as potentially compromising to the ultimate viability of their businesses, due to excessive congestion, degradation of amenities, or increased competition.

3. *Municipal elected officials, within the constraints of limited resources, try to maximize their approval levels among those constituencies who are most*

important in the short term to their successful reelection. In other words, urban politicians seek supportive coalitions and financial backers to help them return to office. As students of Congress have noted, elected officials who seek to achieve programmatic goals must first ensure they will remain in office; thus, reelection is often the most proximate objective. And in central cities, as Clarence Stone has shown, a mayor's reelection is predicated in part on pleasing key constituencies—notably business interests—in order to muster some of the resources these interests can offer the mayor while in office. These resources are necessary if the mayor is to be perceived as a success (Stone 1989). Such resources may include favorable investment, location, and employment decisions, as well as campaign contributions. Pleasing these constituencies, then, is an immediate concern for incumbent officials in large cities. However, for reasons that will become more obvious, the key constituencies in a small, residential suburb are much less likely to include corporate capital. Rather, homeowners and their associations are probably the central coalition in such an environment.

4. *Some types of special-district governments also take actions that can affect land use. The (typically unelected) officials who control these special-purpose units attempt to maximize the revenues feeding their domain and seek to increase the size, clientele, and power of their organizations.* While perhaps an overly simplistic rational choice perspective on bureaucracies (but see Niskanen 1971; Schneider 1989), this assumption takes into account the motivations of special-district officials. Special-purpose governments with an especially important impact on land use and development include water and sewer districts, housing and community development districts, road and infrastructure agencies, and public transit authorities.

5. *Residents seek some optimal balance or combination of: (a) increased property values or an increase in the ratio of local public services to local taxes (in the suburban context, generally the property tax);³ (b) the preservation or enhancement in their neighborhood or immediate area of amenities, stability, lifestyle advantages, lack of urban ills, and other quality-of-life considerations; and (c) an economically robust urban region, as measured by high average wages and low unemployment, in order to minimize economic anxiety and increase opportunity.* This complex set of assumptions posited for residents requires some brief explanation. Which of the three goals (5a, 5b, or 5c) will a resident value most? Obviously, this depends on the individual; presumably, the distribution of such opinions can be established empirically through survey research or the like. For now, it seems safe to assume that most residents desire most of these three outcomes most of the time.⁴ (Renters, however, will rarely be concerned with property values.)

Economists may look askance at goal 5b, an inelegant assumption which, on the surface at least, may not be an economically rational preference. After all, residents who resist an intensification of land uses in order to preserve their neighborhoods willingly forgo a likely rise in property values. But sociologists and political scientists, who are less likely to make simplifying assumptions about "tastes," will not be as troubled by the assumption. Slow-growth movements and numerous other manifestations of suburban disgruntlement over rapid change provide empirical evidence of the pervasiveness and intensity of such attitudes (Baldassare 1986). Moreover, "citizens associations concentrate most attention on zoning decisions, and they usually seek rulings that preserve the status quo. Citizens groups support strong controls and restrictions on land development" (Linowes and Allensworth 1973, 15; see also Davis 1990, chap. 3; Wirt et al. 1972, 135).

Urban residents worry about losing valued social contacts or about having to make unwanted changes in lifestyle (B. Williams 1988). Moreover, powerful economic incentives do often underlie these motivations, to the extent that high property values are predicated on the amenity, ambiance, or low-density residential character of a neighborhood. For tenants, low rents or lack of displacement may depend on retaining the neighborhood's existing qualities.

In the language developed by sociologists John Logan and Harvey Molotch (1987), goal 5b represents a resident's "use value"—the psychic value placed on maintaining a familiar, nonthreatening, and rewarding social environment conducive to one's daily rounds.[5] In contrast, goals 5a and 5c are related to "exchange values"—the preference of those with a financial stake in some place for transactions that will intensify land uses and thus increase the potential profit opportunities of that place. The two preferences (5a and 5c) are quite different, however. The desire for regional economic vitality is likely to be widely shared, but normally will not be among a resident's most intensely held preferences. The preference for favorable property values and service/tax ratios, on the other hand, can be expected to vary widely in intensity.

In many situations, it can be expected that there will be trade-offs between advancing goals 5a and 5b. This conflict between localized use values and exchange values is central to Logan and Molotch's analysis of urban development in *Urban Fortunes*. Such a conflict involves a parochial political debate over the fate of particular pieces of turf, and thus is taken up in most cases at the most local levels of government.

The economic vitality goal 5c, however, is played out on a different geographic scale. The region as a whole normally cannot sustain itself in the absence of commercial and industrial growth, which are the most obvious tickets to sustained or improved employment and wage levels.[6] But at the

neighborhood level, these considerations are usually secondary; "job creation" is rarely a primary concern of small suburban municipalities. In fragmented urban areas, most residents do not work in the political jurisdiction in
which they live.[7]

Thus there exists a distinction among various "exchange values," a distinction that has not been adequately explored by Logan and Molotch. Within
the region as a whole, the preference for goal 5c may well trump the more
neighborhood-oriented goals (5a and 5b). That is, suburbanites have a basic
need for a healthy economy, but may have little desire for busy firms in their
own "neck of the woods." The political organization of the region will therefore have a great deal to say about how preferences for the three goals are
aggregated into the public policies that will shape land use.

The assumptions about elite actors' preferences (1–4 above) are simpler
and less varied than the residents' preferences (5a, 5b, and 5c). But once again,
the institutional configuration of the region will affect the elites' perceptions
of the optimal means to achieve their goals.

Finally, note that to avoid excessive complexity, I have left some major local
players out of the set of assumptions. For instance, land speculators, farmer-
owners, and landholders of large, developable parcels, can probably safely be
grouped with the developers under assumption 1. Their existence is not especially important here, except inasmuch as it provides continuity to development interests, even in periods when regional growth pressures are low.[8]

I have also disregarded persons who might be called "cosmopolitan elites"—
executives of national corporations with local facilities, for example. This may
seem surprising since the great push of growth and much of the office construction in suburban regions has been designed to capture their business. But
especially to the extent that their firms *are* footloose, and they are tenants
rather than owners of local facilities, these people have few incentives to be
politically active in local land-use debates, except in their role as residents.
Having often been recruited on the basis of amenities or quality of life, they
probably are as likely to side with the residents for goal 5b as to side with
parochial growth elites (goal 2).

The Organization of Municipal Power

I have noted that residents' goals are multiple and that the manner in which
these preferences are manifested and aggregated has key implications for
policy choices. At this point, it is therefore useful to introduce the institutional
backdrop which, I suggest, may profoundly affect outcomes. Most central is
the question of how the region's land-use governance is organized.

The Degree of Municipal Political Fragmentation

The concept of political fragmentation has been addressed frequently in the literature of urban politics. In this study, I am particularly concerned with the fragmentation of authority as it pertains to the regulation or supervision of nonresidential development in a given region. For now, the discussion can be simplified by considering only municipalities. These are generally the local governments with the broadest range of land-use powers. Through their zoning powers and subdivision requirements, municipalities have in effect been granted the power to *ration* land for various uses. Municipal politicians can use this tool to help assemble and reward coalitions of local interests.

A fairly straightforward political science theorem lies behind the importance of municipal organization. As William Riker and others remind us, a region's "social choice" will be dependent upon the *method* by which that choice is generated (Riker 1980; see also Riker 1986). In the case of metropolitan land use, this method depends on the geopolitical arrangement of space in the metropolitan area. For social choice theorists such as Riker, there is no "will of the people"—in fact, there is no will of any large group, such as development interests—outside the institutional context in which that "people" or group operates politically. Thus, as Norton Long writes of the metropolitan context, "The common interest, if such there be, is to be realized through institutional interactions rather than through the self-conscious rationality of a determinate group charged with its formulation and attainment. . . . The general business of the metropolitan area is scarcely anybody's business" (Long 1958, 255).

To envision the significance of the division of municipal power in the metropolis, we need to conduct a thought experiment. Imagine an urban region, with pressures for commercial growth, carved up into dozens or hundreds of municipalities, as opposed to the same region under one unitary government. We might label the first entity a "fragmented metropolis" and the second a "regional city." These ideal types can begin to suggest some of the general tendencies of actors under alternative institutional arrangements.

In the fragmented metropolis, the existence of many separate territorial spheres of governance will have a profound effect on the land-use outcomes of the region. Each little polity's current land-use policy will reflect some combination of its past political and geographical "legacy," its current public opinion, and its own institutions and decision rules. Moreover, the character, status, and strategic advantages of municipalities in a differentiated region will differ significantly. To the extent that each municipality is at all a power-political unit, its political values will shape the built landscape through the

process of land-use regulation. These political values will differ, often significantly, from those of other municipalities.

In short, if we take a given urban region, put a border around it, and call it
a city, its government will be likely to act on one set of concerns. If we
partition that region into several different cities, its governance and policy
making will be likely to reflect some other set of concerns. Each municipality,
given its particular constituency, locational (dis)advantages, and other characteristics, will manifest a cluster of preferences different from those of the
other towns. In other words, the relative proportion of residents identifying
with preferences 1 through 5c will vary across municipalities. If there is any relationship whatever between residents' preferences and elected officials' preferences, suburban public policies will reflect that variation.

One way of conceptualizing the problem is in terms of median voters in
given municipalities. Urban economist William Fischel writes that "almost all
observers agree that if the median voter model applies anywhere, it is in the
suburban and exurban towns that account for most new real estate development" (Fischel 1992, 174). Each municipality may reflect in its public policy
the preferences of its median voter; this voter will differ from town to town.
The median voter in the metropolitan region taken as a whole may not see his
or her preferences reflected in any government's policies. In short, metropolitan residents may not act politically on the basis of widely shared values,
given the institutional machinery of the fragmented metropolis, unless those
regional preferences are also intense at the municipal level. This is true by
definition if *political integration* is conceptualized as the capacity of citizens to
act on the basis of shared values (Jacob and Teune 1964).

Consider the perspective of an individual citizen. At any given time, individual preferences among the three goals may be relatively equal. But the
structure of governance may make it more or less easy to effectively voice a
given preference—for, say, a "quiet neighborhood" (preference 5b)—through
local politics.

Moreover, the institutional context faced by each citizen or elite actor will
tend to lead to shared and reinforced attitudes as to what the proper or
expected scope of public decision making is, which issues can fruitfully be
addressed by local government, and which are more properly the province of
more inclusive layers of government. Based on their own experience and that
of others in their "home" municipality, citizens make strategic choices about
how and under what circumstances they can profitably attempt to influence
public policy, and what "access points" in the policy process might be most
useful to them. In the fragmented region, one of the barriers to collective

action on the neighborhood level has been eased, since the community is already in one sense a formally organized group: a municipal corporation.

Alternatively, we can conceive of the difference between fragmented and unitary political organization not in terms of median voters or access points, but in terms of the likely *dominant political constituency*. In the fragmented region, the dominant local coalition will differ from municipality to municipality—it may be wealthy homeowners in one town, tenant groups in another, farmer-landowners in a third, and tax-generating local industry in a fourth. But in the regional city, the group holding greatest sway will probably be the development elites who can mobilize significant resources important to public officials under goal 3. This conclusion reflects the findings of many analysts of central city development politics. It also is echoed by Fischel, who writes:

> Effective fiscal zoning [i.e., zoning that protects homeowners and keeps out lower-status land uses] is least likely to be implemented where the political interests of developers and their allies balance that of homeowners. Development interests are most likely to have an important voice in large and heterogeneous jurisdictions such as states and large central cities. (Fischel 1992, 174)

Adopting this perspective, we may conclude that if the region is governed by a large single unit, goals 1, 2, and 5c will be more central to the motivations of rational public officials. In this situation, the health of the regional economy and the character of regional development are much more firmly within the purview of the local public sector; any particular neighborhood-level dispute is less likely to trump the citywide concern among high-level elected officials. Conceivably, goal 5c, employment and wages, can override the more localized citizen goals 5a and 5b in a wide enough polity. A regional city has a "political market" available to allocate the costs of growth among places; it has at least the potential of dealing with what is a collective action problem in the fragmented region.

In essence, there are three interrelated facets of the institutional configuration of local politics that may influence political behavior in a metropolitan region (see table 2.1). First, the institutional arrangement serves as a *perceptual filter* for residents, developers, and politicians, as it shapes the way "our city (or town)"—its politics, history, and the impacts of growth upon it—are understood. Second, municipal boundaries also function, almost by definition, as a *geographic organizer* of *interests*. Third, the municipal system offers *rules for decision making*, as it sets regulatory authority over any given property, and provides access points and veto opportunities for interested parties. Thus, even if we accept assumptions 1 through 5 as "constant" motivations for

TABLE 2.1

Political Institutions and Urban-Regional Politics

Institutional Dimension	Effects
Organization of interests	Each polity constitutes shared interest in a given geographic area; it includes some actors and interests and excludes others, in greater or lesser proportions, and thus helps determine political majority and minority in given places.
Rules of decision	Rules may be biased for or against certain types of regional policies in requiring multiple or supermajoritarian decisions; may be oriented toward incremental or synoptic policy change; may or may not be organizationally insulated or informed by technocratic "expertise."
Filter of perceptions	Sense of political (dis)advantage shapes political tactics, feelings of efficacy and of what is properly a "local, political" issue; geopolitical divisions create perceptions of shared experiences and of legacies or inheritances of given places.

political actors, the optimal means of seeking those goals and the likely success of various actors are influenced by the degree of political fragmentation.

Fragmentation and Land-Use Policy

What are the implications for land-use decision making? For a variety of reasons, a given region with a *highly fragmented* political system is likely: first, to experience *more spread-out* urban development at a given growth rate than is the same area governed as a regional city; second, to show *starker disparities* in development among suburban places; and third, to have a *less dominant central business district.*

To see how these effects might occur, let us assume that our hypothetical region has a given distribution of citizen preferences across the three options of 5a, 5b, and 5c (property values, amenity, and regional economic vitality). We can also assume that the relative intensity of each individual's preference varies geographically within the region in some nonrandom way—a realistic assumption, given the spatial differentiation of classes and other social groups. The proclivity to want to give priority to 5a over 5b is likely to vary as a function of several characteristics distributed unevenly across the urban landscape. Such factors include social class, the amount of potential exchange-value gains from a change in land use, and perceptions of the neighborhood's existing quality of life and of the marginal effect of the proposed change in that quality of life. These perceptions would seem to rest in part on the age of the community and the length of time that the individual in question has lived there (Pelissero and Fasenfest 1989, 303).

Consider first the case of the highly fragmented region. To the extent that municipal power can protect or reinforce existing patterns, the variety and disparity that distinguish places will also tend to be reinforced. A fragmented decision process in any given polity or area thus makes it more likely that a regional status quo will be preserved. The multiple decision points make it easier to block a proposal for some fundamental, regionwide change than to enable such a change. Even policies or development projects that might maximize regional economic vitality (goal 5c), are not likely to override this logic, since

> suburbs, exurbs, and small towns rarely encompass a sufficient portion of a differentiated urban region to value highly the purely economic benefits of development. Most new jobs in a community are filled by residents of other localities; commercial, professional, and leisure facilities typically service populations beyond the boundaries of their particular locale. (Danielson and Wolpert 1991, 394; see also Schneider 1992, 228; Abbott 1987c, 287)

A high level of political fragmentation permits the resolution of land-use disputes at the neighborhood level, because neighborhoods will constitute nearly entire municipalities. Thus, "use value" (goal 5b) will probably be reflected more in municipal policies than in many of the jurisdictions that Molotch and others use as evidence of growth machine politics. In the fragmented metropolis, then, municipal decision making is likely to be protective or obstructive, rather than creative.

The existence of preservationist suburbs operating under goal 5b means that during regional growth spurts, new jobs or residences will probably be forced farther out, toward the metropolitan periphery. Only marginal alterations to existing land-use patterns are tolerated in these municipalities. As noted earlier, the typical suburban elected official in a fragmented region is probably more likely to be oriented toward the desires of resident homeowners and their associations than toward regionwide capitalists or land developers.[9] And in cases of rezoning, suburbs' governing bodies tend to follow the recommendation of the local planning commission, particularly if that recommendation is for a denial (Fleischmann and Pierannunzi 1990). Therefore, more and smaller suburbs will imply a greater spread of the MSA—in other words, sprawl.[10]

In the unitary regional city, on the other hand, spatial disparities in preferences and status are not ensconced in a similar variety of political units. The decision process must integrate many demands, and thus has the potential to invoke values other than localism. In a regional city, therefore, it is not out of the question for government action to mitigate some existing disparities among neighborhoods.[11] A different scheme of preference aggregation, internal to a single political system, is at work. Localized opposition to certain land uses may be overwhelmed by a more widespread, if less intense, preference for other goals in the rest of the city: economic vitality, for example, or regional transportation mobility, or an equalization of living conditions. Such regional issues as job creation and transportation problems will now have a political outlet.[12]

In reality, such ideal types as the regional city do not exist.[13] But in terms of general tendencies, the theory suggests that more fragmented metropolitan regions are likely to show greater territorial disparities in development. There is little incentive for a small community in a wide urban region to try to match new jobs and housing opportunities. Depending upon its circumstances, constituency preferences, and political mechanisms, any given municipality in a fragmented region might decide to maximize goal 5a or 5b. For example, it might seek to zone for a large proportion of commercial or luxury residential land uses in order to increase property values or service/tax ratios for its existing residents. If an economic growth boom in a nearby community accelerates the demand for residences, it might well refuse to allow more dense subdivision of available residential property. Why admit more residents than necessary and thereby compromise the ratio of tax base to residents?

On the other hand, if an adventurous developer has found a way to dominate a municipality politically, or to convince municipal officials of the fiscal benefits of extensive building, the town may become rapidly and haphazardly overbuilt. This outcome seems especially likely in lower-status municipalities or those with little political or technical competence. And regardless of any given municipality's level of strength or sophistication, a wide variety of municipalities in a region will allow for a wide variety of land-use strategies.[14]

Overall, a region organized in a fragmented fashion simply presents *more* sets of preferences to be maximized. And normally, local governments in such a region have been given some of the ammunition they need to pursue strategies of local maximization, through their regulatory powers over land use. (Highly fragmented urban regions also tend to be in states with strong "home rule" traditions.) Municipalities differ widely in their success in employing such strategies, but that should not surprise us. As several empirical studies show, municipal fragmentation stratifies communities, and that stratification tends to increase during periods of rapid growth (R. Hill 1974; Logan 1978; Danielson and Wolpert 1991; Weiher 1991).[15]

Finally, the institutions of the fragmented metropolis are less likely to protect the dominance of an existing CBD. Downtown elites may be the dominant political constituency in the central city, but with that city's boundaries constrained, their influence will not stand in the way of progrowth coalitions seeking to form competing business nodes. The multiplicity of municipalities provides a wide array of options for would-be developers of business centers. In a regional city, by contrast, public authority over land is relatively monopolistic, and regulators are more likely to be deferential to the CBD and its defenders. A regional city may associate preservation of the CBD with maintaining the economic vitality of its region (goal 5c). As we have seen, this goal is less likely to be acted upon by a suburban municipality in the fragmented metropolis.

Extending the Framework: Other Forms of Land-Use Governance

The basic framework laid out thus far has dealt in a very simple fashion with the political organization of the metropolis. But MSAs display widely varying forms of governance. For example, some suburban regions are governed by counties with few or no municipalities; others are dotted by an array of small-area or regional special-purpose districts; and many suburban regions are partially encompassed within central city boundaries. I shall consider the impact of these factors, "all other things being equal."

The Role of Special-Purpose Governments

Recall that assumption 4 posits maximizing behavior on the part of officials of special districts, such as sewer or water districts. What does such behavior portend for the predictions generated by the model thus far? Will increases in the number and power of such limited-function governments *reinforce* the anticipated impacts of fragmentation among general-purpose governments? Or will they *alter* the expected relationship?

In general, I expect that the effect will be reinforcement. Special districts are often established to subsidize developers indirectly or to fuel growth, particularly at the outer frontiers of metropolitan areas. Drawing on the literature on collective action, Nancy Burns notes that any efforts to form a new government are problematic; to succeed, proponents require organizational and financial backing, or a very small, cohesive group. Most formations of special districts, Burns finds, fulfill both these requirements: "The most systematically present source of sustenance is a small group composed of a single developer with clear motives for forming a special district" (Burns 1994, 31).

Many special districts, by employing a system of user fees for new residents or developments, effectively remove the issue of growth from municipal budgetary politics. Such financing conceals some of the direct costs of growth from existing residents. In general, special districts serve to increase the infrastructure capacity of peripheral areas without broad public debate over the issue. A proliferation of such districts at the suburban fringe can thus have the effect of promoting uncoordinated sprawl.[16] As Burns concludes:

> [Development politics] are played out largely in the realm of special districts. These special districts lower the risk and the cost of development immensely, arguably encouraging more speculative efforts where special districts are easier to form. Developers clearly win more easily in this realm; often they create the realm precisely for that reason. (Burns 1994, 115)

However, there are prominent cases in which a more regionally oriented special district can serve to integrate the development decision process and underwrite more regional planning. This is especially the case with regional transit authorities, regionwide sewer or pollution control authorities, some port authorities with broad mandates (Doig forthcoming), and metro service districts. While not nearly as common as the more limited special districts, these integrative districts have been known to shape the relative costs and benefits of potential project locations in such a way as to increase the likelihood of more "balanced" development. For example, Bellevue, Washington, was able to redesign its auto-oriented business area into a more high-density "activity center" largely through the flexibility, encouragement, and resources of the Seattle metropolitan transit authority's policies.[17] It is possible that creating an additional special-purpose government will not have a "fragmenting" effect on regional governance, if the district captures authoritative policy-making prerogative for functions with areawide spillovers, rather than leaving these functions to localities.

Thus, there are both *fragmenting* special districts and *integrating* special districts. The former are ubiquitous in many metropolitan areas, and as noted, are often easy to manipulate. These hidden governments constitute one of the most fluid features of the institutional configuration of metropolitan areas. Moreover, they are powerful; they are created because they can get things done. As R. Robert Linowes and Don T. Allensworth write, "The planning that is done by such special-function units is 'meaningful'—that is, it is planning that has a good chance of being carried out, a good chance of becoming program reality" (1973, 37).

The Role of Urban Counties

Metropolitan reform advocates have long touted the promise of urban counties, strengthened vis-à-vis the governments within them, as a government form deserving attention. Such strong counties, they argue, can more truly serve the regional commonweal.

In many metropolitan areas, county governments have only a marginal effect on our model. With their land area largely or totally subdivided into municipalities that have strong home rule powers, such counties constitute weak oversight units, sometimes only exacerbating fragmenting tendencies. But in other areas of the country, particularly in southern and newer urban regions, there are strong county governments that hold much greater sway— often retaining direct regulatory control over land use. The scant literature on county governments in metropolitan areas, however, particularly with respect to land-use issues, does not allow decisive generalizations to be drawn about the role of such institutions. Drawing instead on the theoretical reasoning laid out in this chapter, I would expect that where only one or relatively few counties exist in an urban region, and where those counties have primary land-use authority over a substantial portion of the region's land area, they will tend to approximate the patterns expected of a regional city, rather than a fragmented metropolis. Suburban protectionism is less likely to prevail. Counties that are more rural or administratively weaker may find it difficult to cope with rapid urbanization, but are unlikely to restrain it very much (Sokolow 1981, 185).

Still, the scope and organization of municipal power within the county remains a key factor. Few urban county governments enjoy a total lack of competition from municipal subunits; Baltimore County, an inner-tier suburban county in the Baltimore metropolitan area, is one rare example. Two other patterns appear more common: first, a strong metropolitan county with one major city within it, and few or no smaller suburban municipalities; or second, a county with strong land-use powers in unincorporated areas, but little power within the several incorporated municipalities it contains.

In the first scenario, the county and the city will constitute the two major power bases in the area, and the two governments may be drawn into more competition than collusion regarding development and land-use regulation. Relevant interests may be able to play one government against the other, particularly if their land-use powers are coextensive in parts of the county. In rare cases, counties and their dominant cities have merged into consolidated city-counties, as in Lexington-Fayette, Kentucky.

The second pattern is typical in parts of the Middle and Far West, and in parts of the South Atlantic region. In these cases, the county becomes the "residual" government for the region, governing what is "left over" outside municipal boundaries. The territory in question will tend to be of more recent settlement and much less dense than the municipal territory. Again, the county does not closely enough approximate monopoly control of land to serve as a proactive regulator of development.

Even in the absence of municipalities, strong counties have to contend with special districts. A large number of special districts may erode some of a county's monopoly of control over the supply of improved, serviced land.

Suburbia as Part of a Region's Central City

In the nineteenth century, central city boundaries normally expanded as the urban area expanded. In this way, cities were able to encompass most new growth. This phenomenon came to an end in most of the nation's older industrial cities by 1920. With innovations in infrastructure and service delivery, the advent of special districts, and the increasing desire for tax advantages and social exclusion, new suburban areas incorporated as separate municipalities, or stayed under the purview of county governments, rather than asking for or allowing annexation by central cities.

Some urban regions, however, particularly in the newer areas of the Sun Belt, have retained a political pattern more closely approximating the nineteenth-century standard. Liberal state annexation laws, extreme growth boosterism by city elites, and a relative lack of social problems associated with the central city have all contributed to the extensive size of cities such as San Antonio, Orlando, and Albuquerque. Since these cities' boundaries have been adjusted to encompass a large proportion of the phenomenal growth taking place at their peripheries, huge amounts of territory that appear "suburban" are now administered by central city governments. It is no wonder that most of the "fastest growing" American cities are those that annex liberally.[18] Even where the central city has stopped expanding rapidly, as in many western cities, a significant portion of attractive suburban turf is often still part of the city. Many of these cities are new enough that their urban form—with the exception of a small downtown area—has been auto dominated and suburban in character for most of their histories. Houston and Los Angeles are notable, but hardly atypical, examples. And even some of the nation's older cities, such as Indianapolis and Lexington, gained city control of much suburban land through city-county consolidation.

The suburban areas within these cities are governed by relatively unitary governments. As such, their development patterns may be expected to parallel a regional city much more closely than a fragmented metropolis. Preserving the land-use status quo in residential neighborhoods, or blocking all new growth, are not likely policy outcomes from such jurisdictions in any event.

In cities that encompass a great deal of suburban territory, institutional characteristics internal to a single polity take on special significance. In the

American Sun Belt, for example, many cities have traits that limit their ability to offer coordinated public policies. For example, quasi-independent civil service bureaucracies in southwestern cities, and "reformed" weak-mayor arrangements, mean that some of the unity and coordination of a singular public sector have been compromised. Special districts also tend to be more prominent in and around cities in parts of the Sun Belt (notably Houston), again deflating the unitary characteristics of the cities. Thus, although they tend toward extensive physical size, they may lack some of the integrative potential of a regional city.[19] Moreover, there remains a great deal of suburbanizing land located outside the city limits in most of these metropolitan areas. In this way, these cities' regulatory leverage is curtailed, compared to the leverage of a regional city.

Nevertheless, cities encompassing suburbia are able to contain within a single political system the natural tension between peripheral growth and the strength of the existing central business district. Downtown business elites acting under assumption 2 (profit maximization) may oppose plans for an outlying business node if they see it competing with their own enterprise. The organizational strength of developers and boosters of outlying areas, in comparison to downtown business people, can thus have particularly important consequences in these extensive cities. Overall, it is likely that the legacy of downtown economic and political power will be carried on to some degree in such cities; therefore, defense of the existing center of commerce will receive more regionwide attention in an extensive city than in the fragmented metropolis.

State and Federal Roles in Local Land Use

The federal nature of governance in the United States also complicates analysis to some degree. Land use, though primarily in the hands of local governments, is also influenced by state and national politics. Although the states and the nation obviously operate at a more unitary geographic level than any unit of local government, it is difficult to predict in any general way the implications of their involvement in land-use politics.

On the one hand, states and the nation can act politically on behalf of wide interests. Local maximization strategies are not as dominant in determining the policy agenda. Thus, some states have delegated relatively fewer of their land-use and other powers to the localities that are their legal subdivisions. In other words, urban regions in such states may be either fragmented or unitary, but overall these organization patterns are somewhat muted by the larger share of activities performed and expenditures made at the state level.

Specific state and national policy initiatives may also blunt fragmentary proclivities. National environmental regulations have forced regional approaches and interlocal cooperation in several regions—notably southern California—where it was otherwise not forthcoming. An increasing number of states since the early 1970s have entered the land-use field in a more direct way, intervening by creating statewide plans or development restrictions, or by establishing regional regulatory or planning bodies. In particular, these are used to establish wider control over development patterns in environmentally sensitive areas.

On the other hand, the state and national governments have their own fragmentary tendencies. State and federal bureaucracies with rather narrow functional goals have exerted a great degree of influence over the nation's urban development patterns. This functional orientation, which rarely takes into account the wider impact of policies in terms of settlement patterns, is probably most notable in the case of transportation. Influential state highway departments (which normally do not have to follow municipal or regional land-use plans), to say nothing of the federal interstate highway program, have been among the most notable forces fueling (and subsidizing) suburban expansion.

The localism of federal politics and its tendency to distribute benefits widely also have an impact. Place-specific pork barrel legislation has tended in recent decades to improve the infrastructure of suburban and rural places disproportionately. At the state level, a common legislative alliance consists of rural and newer suburban interests against the representatives of central cities and older suburbs. These alliances can be expected to stress aid in infrastructure and economic development, rather than programs to boost the competitiveness of older commercial centers or the workforce skills of the poor.

The partisan characteristics of state and national governments are also worth considering. In the era of the New Deal Democratic coalition, the national government channeled much developmental aid to the older cities, which were bastions of Democratic strength. In particular, benefits were targeted to the CBDs, as urban renewal programs responded to an intergovernmental coalition of urban progrowth elites (Mollenkopf 1983). Later, the "New Federalisms" of Republican administrations under Nixon and Reagan spread federal aid more evenly across jurisdictions, placed fewer restrictions on the uses of that aid, and (under Reagan) heavily cut the level of aid to subnational governments. These actions probably heightened the capacity to provide governance and infrastructure in newer and more rapidly growing municipalities, compared to older central cities, thereby heightening metropolitan fragmentation in many regions.

Clearly, a measure of political organization in metropolitan areas should attempt to include some notion of state and national aid patterns. Are suburban municipalities highly subsidized by transfers from their states, for example, or do they get to control a relatively small slice of the expenditure pie? Numerous intergovernmental issues will be considered in the empirical portion of this book. But a full consideration of the comparative impact of federalism on land use in American metropolises lies beyond the scope of this project. In short, the framework developed in this chapter assumes "all other things being equal"—and for the most part, state and national interventions in local land use are among those exogenous factors.

The Role of the Development Industry

Organizational considerations in the development industry operate simultaneously with the variety of public-sector organizations described above. Thus, it is important to consider this element alongside the institutional framework.

At one time, numerous small entrepreneurs and homeowner/builders were collectively responsible for the general shape of suburban development (Warner 1978). Early in the century, however, the real estate market was reorganized and modernized. According to Marc A. Weiss, "Many of the large brokers and builders became 'developers,' providing the service of managing and linking together the varying stages of transforming parcels of unimproved land, from the initial subdividing process through the construction of improvements to the selling and renting of the completed structures" (Weiss 1987, 30). In the postwar era, the increasing scale economies of development implied a need for larger tracts of open land, and for smaller groups of elite actors, so that the suburban landscape could be more profitably developed (Judd 1988, 167–69; Giuliano 1986). This was the era when large builders constructed Levittowns and Park Forests. More recent decades have seen the emergence of complex, bureaucratized development corporations employing their own architects, lawyers, and managers, and operating nationally and internationally (Feagin and Parker 1990).

A highly capitalized, vertically integrated and cohesive commercial development sector may pursue goal 1—maximum rate of return—by building large, speculative, high-risk projects. This responds to the real and growing attraction of agglomeration economies in suburbia—clusters of high-intensity land uses that represent the most serious threat to traditional city downtowns (Stanback 1991). Emerging sectors of the economy often place a premium on access to specialized business services, professional contacts, restaurants and hotels, and employee housing. In suburbia, these aspirations can best be realized in mixed-use agglomerations—i.e., the more dense "edge cities." Potentially, large and well-financed development companies may pursue innovative mixed-use projects with elements of multifamily housing, hotels, and retail space, as well as office space. An extreme example of this type of enterprise is the Irvine Company in Orange County, California, which has planned and developed a fair-sized, multicentered, mixed-use suburban region, more or less on its own (Schiesl 1991). But numerous other development corporations have undertaken ambitious mixed-use projects in suburbia.

In short, larger, more established firms have a greater capacity to invest, plan, and innovate, and the networks in which their employees operate seem more likely to instill such a "professional" ethos, even if only as a pretense.[20] The larger firms are also better armed financially for battles with recalcitrant governments in suburbia, whether that battle takes the form of polished public relations and smooth presentations at planning board hearings, campaign contributions to key elected officials, or, if all else fails, litigation. What cannot be easily predicted is whether large firms will be more inclined to use such power to overload an area with housing or commercial buildings, or whether they are more likely to construct a well-rounded, mixed-use development.

Of course, not all development companies fit this powerful, well-organized stereotype. In some metropolitan areas during certain periods, an atomized, small-scale, precariously financed industry prevails. Firms that are less well financed, and marked more by entrepreneurialism than by organized research, planning, or marketing functions, would appear more likely to "play it safe." They will tend to build smaller, less ambitious projects. Such firms may lack expertise in building and financing something other than one type of development—office buildings, for example—so they are likely to stick with one type of project. With fewer sources of information for innovations, and less precise market predictions, smaller firms are likely to follow the "received wisdom" of builders.[21]

With less capacity to influence public land-use decisions in an authoritative manner, these smaller firms would seem more likely to choose a path of least resistance in selecting what to build and where. They can scarcely afford to continue to pay high interest and other holding costs for their land, while their would-be project is tied up in hearings, protests, or litigation. For that reason, if the location they desire for their project presents a regulatory or political thicket in a fragmented MSA, they may be more willing to "satisfice" by taking their plans down the road to the next jurisdiction, even if the new site is a less optimal or less accessible location. In a more unitary MSA, small firms may be inclined to follow the development agenda set by the most powerful municipal jurisdiction(s), rather than attempt to blaze new trails for growth in the area.

Other organizational aspects of the development sector, too numerous to detail here, also shape growth patterns. For example, developers with roots in, and commitment to, a given metro area may take a more long-term perspective toward it than absentee developers who have limited aspirations for the region. The structure of finance capital for the new projects also has an impact on the urban development process. Financial institutions in some areas specialize in loans for certain types of real estate projects—office buildings or single-family homes, for example—and are reluctant or unable to finance more ambitious mixed-use plans. For example, Garreau describes the problems of the Forrestal Village office/retail/hotel development near Princeton, New Jersey. The developer there "ended up with a consortium of eleven lenders, all of whom had to agree in order for him to correct any flaws that might crop up in his scheme. That turned out to be a recipe for rigidity. This division of expertise among financiers is a genuine problem for the mixed-use places" (Garreau 1991, 248; see also Whyte 1968, 253).

In other regions, the prevalence of foreign or institutional investors with deep pockets (insurance companies, for example) permits more flexibility. Increasingly, in slow markets, investors insist on equity in projects they fund, involving themselves more directly with development decisions. And of course, real estate investment patterns have both influenced and been influenced by the crisis in the savings and loan industry and other financial institutions. The redundant development that marks many areas of the southwestern United States is a testament to the freewheeling and cyclical characteristics of financing in those regions during the 1980s. In contrast, Canadian development companies interact closely with that nation's powerhouse banks; by the 1980s they had taken a leadership role in the construction of the largest and most sophisticated projects in North America.[22] Clearly, the fates of financiers and would-be developers are closely intertwined.

Suburban Development "Regimes"

The attention I have given to private development actors will be familiar to urbanists who devote their study to central city politics. There, the relationship between business elites and elected officials has long been thought to be central. In these large jurisdictions, elected officials (acting under assumption 3) may be most concerned with accomplishing spectacular development projects, achieving measurable growth, obtaining large amounts of campaign contributions, and establishing links to the regional business community, compared to their counterparts in smaller, more homogeneous or less dynamic jurisdictions. It is therefore no surprise that Clarence Stone and many others who have studied big cities have found large-scale development firms among the central actors in "governing regimes," with concomitant access to policy makers at the highest levels.

To Stone and his fellow regime theorists, urban regimes are the governing coalitions assembled by city leaders to effectively command resources in a policy environment characterized by a division of labor between state and market (Stone 1989; Stone and Sanders 1987; Elkin 1985; Elkin 1987). Emphasizing cooperation over domination, the regime analysts stress the close working arrangements between politicians and a limited, fairly exclusive set of resource-rich private-sector actors. In short, urban regimes are "the mediating agents between the goal of economic well-being and the particular development policies pursued" (Stone and Sanders 1987, 269).

The regime concept has been rightly praised for representing an advance over studies that locate the source of urban policy in forces outside politics. In that sense, it has moved urban political economy away from the determinism of the perspectives I criticized in chapter 1. Thus far, however, regime analysis has been used only to study single jurisdictions, almost always large central cities.[23] In the less "dependent" political economy that characterizes politically independent suburbs, regime analysis is likely to produce less clear-cut answers. Regimes are more fluid in suburbia, and their character and influence will depend heavily upon public-sector jurisdictional arrangements.

In case studies analyzing the redevelopment of central business districts in big cities, elected officials are seen as favoring large-scale development interests and financial elites because of a need for favorable investment and location decisions. Such close coordination, however, becomes problematic in a suburban context where there are highly fragmented public elites, a corporate sector without much at stake in any given jurisdiction, and no obvious center that symbolizes economic and civic vitality. In the diffuse and complex political economy of the suburbs, cooperative or competitive relationships among elites are likely to arise as much from the formal organization of public authority as from any other factor. Moreover, in small jurisdictions with relatively limited goals, the private resources of business elites may not be as necessary to governance, and governing regimes may in fact more closely resemble electoral coalitions.

Finally, it is far more costly for a development company to organize politically in ten separate suburban municipalities than in one city that encompasses its suburban turf. While development interests might find some small municipalities easy to infiltrate and dominate, sophisticated suburbs may need and heed such outside meddlers far less. Once again, political fragmentation points toward more development disparities among places in the region. But where developers can act through a central city to influence "suburban" growth patterns, as in some physically extensive cities, they are likely to be able to muster far greater private and public resources behind mixed-use and agglomerative developments—*if* they can overcome the privileged position of downtown interests.

At times, sophisticated elites can manipulate patterns of governance in a suburban region by working to alter the arrangement of public institutions. For example, they might attempt to bridge political fragmentation by making the case for a new, regional layer of government. Conversely, where it is to their advantage, elites in the region might add to fragmentation by creating new special districts to subsidize new growth and remove its cost consider-ations from the public agenda. What we see at any given time is a snapshot of an ongoing political process by which the parameters of governance are de-fined and redefined.

Conclusion

In his study of edge cities, Garreau finds a "patchwork" of governments "swirling like gnats" in one area, which makes him despair of detecting any authoritative action on the part of local government actors in shaping that area. Rather, "what really shapes the Edge City . . . is the historical force of commerce more than governance" (Garreau 1991, 46–47). I would argue that the very existence of the swarm of gnats, as opposed to a more Leviathan-like public entity, is itself the "historical force of governance" that Garreau cannot detect. In a politically fragmented region, the social, geographic, and power inequalities that mark a region inhere in governing institutions and serve to perpetuate disparities in development.

By making some realistic assumptions about the goals of politicians, de-velopers, and residents, I have been able to fix upon institutional structure, rather than ideology, as the factor underlying the variations in urban develop-ment interactions and outcomes. What differs across metro areas are not the goals, but the organization of the public sector. This variation, in turn, shapes the optimal means toward achieving the objectives of each group, and the viability of those goals. Of central significance is the organization of munici-pal power, which filters perceptions, organizes interests geographically, and sets decision rules for development.

In essence, the framework presented here suggests a three-step schema in which *interests* (taken here as given) are interpreted through political *insti-tutions*, which help determine development *outcomes*. The likely outcomes emerging from differences in public-sector organization can be summed up in three causal statements relating fragmentation to growth patterns. Political

TABLE 2.2

Likely Effects of Public-Sector Organization
on Elite Orientations and Interactions

Low Fragmentation	High Fragmentation
Longer time horizons	Shorter or conflicting time horizons
More public-sector coordination	Less public-sector coordination
More insulated political elites	More accessible political elites
More bureaucratic/routinized public decision making	More ad hoc public decision making
Norms of planning, professionalism	Norms vary by jurisdiction
Close networks and working relationships between public and private elites	Case-by-case negotiation with private sector
"Trustee" orientation of elected officials	"Delegate" orientation of elected officials

fragmentation is likely to: (1) spread growth out over the landscape, as developers bypass restrictive municipal environments; (2) lead to wide disparities across suburban places, as some local governments are overwhelmed by developers or are unusually enthusiastic about exchange-value goals, while others emphasize neighborhood use values; and (3) sap relatively more of the strength from the region's CBD, as multiple political settings provide more options for developers and serve to contain the influence of the downtown elite within the central city's boundaries.

For better or worse, a politically fragmented region allows for more definitive differences in character among the region's places. Moreover, based on its established pattern, a fragmented region would seem likely to incrementally "muddle through" issues that are metropolitan in scale. The most important characteristic of such a region is its lack of political accountability for regionwide concerns. These concerns may include the supply of affordable housing near agglomerative suburban downtowns, the proper location for edge city locations to compete with other regions, and regionwide issues of open space, traffic congestion, and sprawl. In fact, it is conceivable that attempts by localities to maximize *local* concerns about quality of life or use value systematically detract from *regional* quality of life.

Nevertheless, I do not wish to make a normative argument about the "proper" structure of local government, but rather to provide an explanatory framework to address an empirical question. This is not a call for metro government, or for turning urban life over to planners. In fact, some might argue that the economic advantages of providing varied tax/service/amenity

TABLE 2.3

Likely Effects of Public-Sector Organization
on Suburban Development Patterns

Low Fragmentation	High Fragmentation
New developments will tend to be located at highly accessible locations.	New developments will appear at a variety of locations, some with poor accessibility.
New developments will be proximate to, or combined with, housing and services.	There will be leapfrog development, sprawl, and a mismatch between jobs and housing.
Subregions will be relatively mixed-use.	Subregions will be single-use.
The viability of existing business centers will receive substantial public attention.	Existing centers will decline.
	Disparities in density and tax base will arise among jurisdictions.

bundles to mobile citizens and firms far outweigh the potential social benefits of "balanced" growth.[24] But any such analysis of potential costs and benefits of different forms of political organization in urban areas rests on the identification of the actual effects of such organization. Only when that task is complete will I offer prescriptions for metropolitan political organization.

3

Political Structure and Urban Outcomes: An Aggregate Analysis

In this chapter, I apply the theoretical framework of my institutional analysis to test the influence of political organization on urban development patterns in a variety of metropolitan areas. In particular, I provide a multivariate analysis of the effects of political fragmentation and other factors upon urban form.

The central issue is the aggregate-level connection between political structure and spatial structure. That statement is misleadingly simple, however, and aggregate quantitative research proves less straightforward than one might imagine at first. I will explore the methodological difficulties in attempting to "model" directly the complex political economy of metropolitan development, and will present some more practicable, albeit indirect, tests of the impact of political organization on spatial structure. These include regression models explaining the distribution of office employment, travel time for commuters, the frequency of "edge city" nodes, the concentration of journey-to-work flows, and metropolitan density gradients.

First, however, we need to seek an appropriate quantitative measure of urban political fragmentation, as it affects the regulation of land use, and establish the data set to be used and the patterns of political organization in metropolitan areas in the sample.

The Political Fragmentation of Land-Use Authority

If we are to conduct an aggregate analysis, the variations in government arrangements in urban areas require a well-conceptualized measure of political fragmentation. Previous studies have put forth a variety of scales, simple and complex, as appropriate measures of political fragmentation. For instance, some authors simply count up the local governments in metropolitan areas.[1] Other scholars use more sophisticated ratio measures, such as the number of governments per unit area or per capita.[2]

These attempts to measure political fragmentation are inadequate to the task at hand. They have two primary shortcomings. First, the indices fail to consider the variations in powers and capacity granted to local governments across metropolitan areas. The functions expected of local governments vary widely by state.[3] Second, in this study, we need only consider those governments that are likely to affect land-use patterns. For an examination of the role of fragmentation in shaping metropolitan growth, it is important to consider two variables in particular. First, the measure developed must communicate the extent to which land use authority is *divided* among government units in each metropolitan area. Second, it must in some way take into account the *total level* of land-use powers possessed by local governments, as opposed to state and national levels of government.

I have therefore devised a political fragmentation index, *PFI*, which incorporates these two factors. For each metropolitan area, the *PFI* is calculated as follows:

$$PFI = TE\,(1 - SSP)$$

where *TE* is total expenditures per capita (in thousands of dollars) by land use–related local governments in the metro area, and *SSP* is the sum of squared percentages of *TE* accounted for by each local government. The *SSP* measure is adapted from Douglas Rae's measure of the "fractionation" of party systems in Western democracies (Rae 1967).[4]

In effect, the term $(1 - SSP)$, which will range between zero and one, can be understood as *the probability that two randomly selected dollars of local public expenditure in a given metro area were not spent by the same local government.* For example, in a hypothetical metropolitan area where one government spent 90 percent of the MSA total, and a second spent the remaining 10 percent, $(1 - SSP) = 0.18$. In an MSA in which four units of local government each spent 25 percent of the total, $(1 - SSP) = 0.75$. In the first case, there is only an 18 percent probability that two dollars of local expenditure in the MSA, selected at random, will have been spent by different governments; in the second case, where there is greater fragmentation of government, that probability jumps to 75 percent.

Multiplying the term $(1 - SSP)$ by *TE* effectively weights this measure of fractionation by the level of government expenditure in the MSA. Thus, *PFI* satisfies the two desired properties specified above: It represents the division of local expenditures in each metropolis, and distinguishes metropolises by their total *levels* of local per capita expenditure. The *PFI* may then be taken as a measure (admittedly quite rough) of the power or capacity of local government to affect land-use patterns. By this measure, therefore, there is "more fragmentation" when, at a given level of division in local spending, there is more of such spending.

Critics might point out that measuring a municipality's expenditure is not the same thing as measuring its degree of land-use regulation. However, the more sophisticated types of such regulation, involving boards and commissions, expert studies, the hiring of consultants, and the use of detailed planning technologies, *do* indeed require notable expenditures. And in the case of special districts that provide infrastructure, expenditures *are* related to the capacity to influence growth patterns. Moreover, how else are we to reasonably measure fragmentation? Looking at the dispersion of *population* instead of the dispersion of expenditures is inadequate for several reasons. First, there are no "population" data for special districts, which are important to my argument. Ordinarily, people are governed by several overlapping local governments. Second, some citizens live in unincorporated county territory, which is not covered by any of the municipal statistics. Finally, local jurisdictions in some metro areas may be little more than administrative conveniences for higher levels of government that perform most "local" services. We have no way of knowing this from a population measure of fragmentation.

I am not interested in all units of local government. For example, mosquito-control districts and governments that administer cemeteries do not seem particularly relevant to the issue of land-use regulation, while districts that provide infrastructure to urban areas do. Fortunately, the Census of Governments codes each special-district government according to the functions it performs. Using this coding, I included the following types of local governments in my data: counties (parishes in Louisiana), municipalities, townships or towns,[5] highway districts, housing and community development districts, sewerage districts, water supply districts, transit districts, and districts that provide both sewer and water services (see table 3.1). Thus, in the context of this study, "political fragmentation" refers only to what I term "land-use" governments.

The census coding has its deficiencies, and thus, my *PFI* data are not as definitive as I might like. For example, there is no reliable coding that distinguishes metropolitan planning districts, port authorities, or such entities as the Regional Council in the Twin Cities area. Nevertheless, by taking into account expenditures by nearly every relevant local government, rather than merely dividing total population or expenditures by total number of governments, *PFI* represents an advance over previous measures. It incorporates counties, townships, and relevant special districts, as well as municipalities of all sizes, to create a more unified measure. In this way it can take into account how the *overlap* of land-use powers in a given place affects its governance.

TABLE 3.1

A Typology of Local Governments

LAND-USE GOVERNMENTS

Counties	Serve as primary units of local government for unincorporated areas; sometimes provide roads and infrastructure; frequently write plans, have planning boards; sometimes have veto power over certain types of developments (e.g., very large developments, those with cross-municipal impact, those along county roads).
Townships	Serve as primary units of local government in several states; frequently build roads; sometimes have concurrent jurisdiction over land use or infrastructure provision.
Municipalities	Primary unit of local government in most cases; delegated "police powers" by the states, including zoning, planning, subdivision controls; build roads; often provide other types of infrastructure.
Transportation and transit districts	Influence patterns and capacity of private and public transportation systems; sometimes have eminent domain powers.
Housing and community development districts	Plan and cause to be built housing and public facilities; often attempt to change patterns of existing land use; frequent contact with development industry elites; often have eminent domain powers.
Water and sewer districts	Plan and cause to be built infrastructure that encourages and serves new growth.

SOME EXAMPLES OF NON-LAND-USE GOVERNMENTS

School districts	Can attract families to move to an area; although they build new schools to accommodate population, they usually have no direct influence on land-use regulation; including school expenditures in fragmentation index data would result in severe bias, since schools often account for more than half of local expenditures, very little of which is land use–related.
Fire districts, school building authorities, cemetery districts	Follow growth, rather than shaping it.

For example, most southwestern MSAs appear to be fairly unitary urban regions, if examined purely on the basis of municipal boundaries or populations. However, in parts of the Southwest (Houston, for example), numerous small special districts provide much of the infrastructure of suburban areas, thereby taking some land-use prerogatives out of the hands of general-purpose cities. This "hidden" form of fragmentation is unmasked with the *PFI* measure. In another case, there might be several municipalities, but a strong county may dominate suburban expenditure. Since the *PFI* index implicitly weights the county government's relative influence, rather than merely counting the county as just another government, it is more sensitive to true patterns of political organization.

Political Fragmentation in a Sample of Metropolitan Areas

One difficulty with quantitative research in urban affairs has to do with the wide changes in the territory of many metropolitan areas with each decennial census. In order to capture the urbanization of new areas in the periods between censuses, the Census Bureau adjusts the boundaries of its Metropolitan Statistical Areas outward, so as to encompass urbanizing counties that have entered the sphere of influence of each metropolis since the last census. In other cases, the bureau has defined entire new metropolitan areas by carving them out of larger urban agglomerations, in order to reflect the growing importance of newer suburban areas as economic realms in their own right.[6] In short, the "units of analysis" for studies such as mine are redefined every decade.

In order to generate as much comparable data as possible, I have used the 1982 Census of Governments (which uses 1980 definitions of metropolitan areas), to calculate my measure of political fragmentation for each Standard Metropolitan Statistical Area (SMSA) in my sample.[7] I have also compiled a wide variety of economic and demographic "control" variables for these 1980 SMSAs.[8] I decided that, ultimately, it was wiser to develop a cross-sectional model to assess the effects of political fragmentation—a "snapshot" of each metropolis as of 1980—rather than a more complex time-series approach. In so doing, I avoid the dubious task of "correcting" for the changing geographical composition of metropolitan areas. The methodological pitfall of my choice is that it fails to recognize the time lag between elites' perceptions of their environment (in, say, the mid-1970s), their decisions regarding land use and development, and the physical outcomes of those decisions. One need not worry excessively over this point, however. In the vast majority of regions, broad patterns of political organization change only very slowly and incrementally (Epple and Romer 1989). Growing regions that have institutional rules allowing for easy annexation by central cities tend to continue to experience such annexation; those making special districts difficult to form will continue to see few special districts. Even though any single jurisdiction may undergo sizable boundary changes, the *overall* dispersion of land-use authority is little affected. Therefore, it is fair to assume that actors making development decisions in the mid-1970s encountered a political-institutional environment that was extremely similar to the one I have measured for 1980. Ultimately, the choice rested on practicality: Using cross-sectional data removes the fundamental and probably irreparable problem of having to adjust all data to account for the (sometimes vast) territorial differences in metropolitan areas from census to census.

My initial sample consisted of eighty-two Standard Metropolitan Statistical Areas. New York was subsequently dropped from the sample as an extreme outlier, and a very poorly defined SMSA, and Honolulu was omitted because its *PFI* score of zero represents a unique special case. These deletions leave a sample of eighty SMSAs, which together comprised 105.3 million residents, or 46.5 percent of the total United States population for 1980. To increase comparability, I chose in all cases metropolitan areas of the more "traditional" type; that is, those with an identifiable central city or cities along with adjacent urban areas. The sample includes most of the largest metropolitan areas of this type, and ranges in population size from metropolitan Lincoln, Nebraska (192,884), to Los Angeles (7.48 million). The sample excludes newer SMSAs of almost purely suburban character—relatively centerless realms such as the Nassau-Suffolk, New York, and Riverside–San Bernardino–Ontario, California, metro areas.[9]

Appendix 1 lists the SMSAs in the sample, their 1980 populations, number of land-use governments, local expenditures per capita, and values of *PFI*. Eight cases that lacked complete expenditure data for all land-use governments reduced the number of observations of that variable to seventy-two, though all eighty cases are used for analyses that do not incorporate *PFI*. The fragmentation index shows a relatively normal distribution around a mean of 0.64; the median is 0.57. The standard deviation is 0.27. The values of *PFI* range from 0.17 (Albuquerque, New Mexico, SMSA) to 1.61 (Washington, D.C./Maryland/Virginia SMSA). The city of Albuquerque, known for its extremely active annexation program, thoroughly dominates its region, which includes only two other small municipalities. In contrast, Washington is a heavily suburbanized region spanning large chunks of Maryland and Virginia as well as the District of Columbia. Not only is local governance highly divided in metro Washington, but per capita levels of local expenditure are the highest in the sample.[10]

Using the sample, we can see how *PFI* differs from some simpler ways of

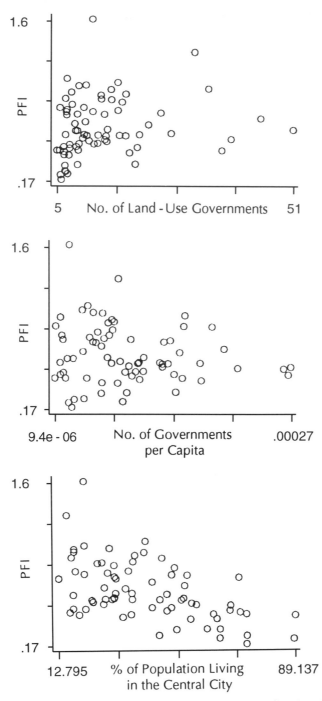

Figure 3.1 Political Fragmentation Index for Sample Metropolitan Areas Plotted Against the Number of Land-Use Governments, Governments per Capita, and Percentage of the Population Living in the Central City. *Key:* PFI = Political Fragmentation Index.

measuring political fragmentation (see figure 3.1). The first diagram plots the political fragmentation index against the number of land-use governments for each SMSA in the sample. Clearly, there is no obvious relationship between *PFI* and a "count" measure of land-use governments. What about a density measure of fragmentation, using land-use governments per capita? The second diagram plots *PFI* against the number of land-use governments per capita. Once again, there is no discernible pattern. Neither of these traditional measures shows a clear relation to *PFI*.

One even simpler conceptualization of urban political organization actually does a better job at approximating the information that *PFI* provides. If we think in terms of the central city/suburb dichotomy, what is the relative share of each metro area's population accounted for by the central city? In the third diagram *PFI* shows a relationship with the share of SMSA population contained in the central city. Although there is a fair degree of variation, larger values for the central city population share tend to be associated with smaller values in the fragmentation index. (In fact, the simple correlation is −0.55.) If we consider the mathematical relationships behind *PFI*, this relationship is intuitive, since the central city will in most cases have the largest single share of total local expenditures.

Keeping in mind the limitations of the index of political fragmentation, we shall move on to use *PFI* in a series of multivariate analyses. While in some instances missing data reduce the sample to a very small one, in every case the institutional variable shows interesting relationships with the dependent variable.

Proposition 1: Institutional Configuration and the Deconcentration of Employment

We expect highly fragmented areas to have weaker central business districts, more place-based disparities, and wider sprawl, all other things being equal. In this section, I discuss the first of these hypotheses. The first task at hand in testing this hypothesis is to specify an appropriate dependent variable for CBD strength.

The rise in employment in office-oriented occupations has been considered one of the defining characteristics of the postindustrial metropolis. And as a prominent force behind new construction, it has contributed mightily to the spatial reshaping of American cities and suburbs. Given the importance of office buildings and office work, which are the dominant activities of both old central business districts (CBDs) and new suburban business centers, one might examine the relative degree of spatial clustering of office facilities in the CBDs of each metropolitan area. Unfortunately, there is no systematic cataloguing of office space in the United States, and those private-sector entities that have collected data for some regions do not follow the metropolitan area categories used by the Census Bureau—categories that are the geographical basis for all the other variables in this data set. Moreover, such enumerations often prove to be of poor reliability, and incomparable across metropolitan areas.

A Test: The Deconcentration of Office Employment

The Census Bureau does, however, collect *employment* statistics at the level of central business districts, and that is the basis for the initial empirical test. How much office work has each metro area in the sample retained in its central city's downtown? "Office employment," for our purposes, is defined as work in the professional, technical, and clerical categories, minus the sub-category of sales. The spatial patterns of these employment categories correspond well to those of office square-footage statistics in a rigorous study of the New York region (Armstrong 1972).

The dependent variable for this model, "office share," is the percentage of a region's office employment that is contained within its central city's CBD. In the sample, office share ranges from a low of 2.4 percent (Gary) to a high of 33.2 percent (Des Moines), with a mean of 11.9 percent and a standard deviation of 5.2 percent.

The measure is a somewhat crude tool to capture the entire center-versus-periphery dynamic in office development, since in many cases other old business centers exist outside the main CBD. Thus I introduce a dummy variable, "extra CBD," for use as a control term. It takes a value of one for SMSAs with two or more large, traditional central business districts, and zero in all other cases. "Extra CBD" thus measures the presence of a close substitute for the central city's CBD—for example, Saint Paul in the Minneapolis metro area. The presence of a second CBD should be expected to have a sizable negative effect on office share.

Other potential estimators consist of the following variables, calculated for each SMSA as of 1980:

Population = Total SMSA population;
Age = number of decades elapsed since the census in which the SMSA's
    central city first achieved a population of fifty thousand;
Office = percentage of all metropolitan employment that is office
    employment (i.e., technical, clerical, and professional, excluding sales);
FIRE = the percentage of all metropolitan employment that is in the
    categories of finance, insurance, and real estate;

PFI = political fragmentation index;

Capital = a dummy variable, taking the value of one for state and national capitals, otherwise zero; and

Contiguity = a dummy variable, taking a value of one if the SMSA is contiguous to another SMSA, otherwise zero.

I introduce contiguity as an additional control, since proximity to another SMSA might be expected to generate more office employment at the metropolitan periphery, and thus reduce office share.

Among the other variables, increases in the age of the metropolitan area may be expected to generate increases in the office employment muscle of CBDs, since newer urban regions have developed in a dispersed, auto-oriented form from the start. The effects of a metro area's population are less clear. On the one hand, larger populations could generate economies of scale that would lead to increased needs for administrative and "command-and-control" functions; these are characteristic of firms that continue to locate in central business districts. On the other hand, urban economic theory suggests that large regions may find it inefficient to crowd more employment into a congested CBD, and would instead show a propensity to decentralize employment.

Three special characteristics of a metropolitan area's economy might also be expected to play a role in office deconcentration patterns. Specifically, to the extent that the workforce engages in activities that are typically associated with downtown patterns of face-to-face contact—most notably finance, insurance, and real estate—office concentration may be sustained. Thus FIRE, which measures the percentage of the labor force working for finance, insurance, and real estate companies, will probably be positively associated with office share. The overall prevalence of office work in the economy, represented here by "office," may also intensify CBD concentration. Finally, I have developed a dummy variable, capital, taking into account the special characteristics of state capitals (and Washington, D.C.), which may retain a disproportionate base of downtown office workers because of the fixed presence of government offices and the firms that serve them.

What is the hypothesized effect of a metro area's political characteristics on office concentration? I expect that a more unitary decision process will protect the viability of existing centers. This would seem especially the case where a dominant central city, with its political system geared toward economic vitality, defends its business core through favorable fiscal actions, zoning commitments, or redevelopment policies. An extensive central city seems less likely to allow overheated real estate activity in its suburban portions to threaten the health of its most prominent "neighborhood," the downtown. In addition,

TABLE 3.2

Multiple Regression Models:
Share of Office Employment Retained by the
Central Business Districts of Metropolitan Areas

Variables	Model 1	Model 2
Population	−7.10E-7	−5.36E-7
	(−1.80)*	(−1.30)
Age	0.516	0.678
	(3.20)***	(3.77)***
Office	−0.154	−0.126
	(−2.87)***	(−2.24)**
FIRE	1.180	1.155
	(4.01)***	(3.77)***
Capital	2.481	2.724
	(1.994)**	(2.17)**
Contiguity	−2.612	−2.328
	(−2.23)**	(−1.84)*
Extra CBD	−4.761	−3.876
	(−4.43)***	(−3.30)***
PFI	—	−4.297
		(−1.85)*
B_0	10.702	9.897
	(3.31)***	(3.06)***
Adj. R^2	0.46	0.50
Prob $>$ F	0.000	0.000
N	75[a]	68[b]

Sources: Bureau of the Census, *State and Metropolitan Area Data Book*, 1982; *Census of Governments*, 1982; and author's calculations.

Note: PFI = political fragmentation index; * = 0.10 significance; ** = 0.05 significance; *** = 0.01 significance.

a. The five observations missing in model 1 reflect the unavailability of reliable FIRE data.

b. Seven observations were lost in moving from model 1 to model 2 because of missing data for the fragmentation index variable.

central city politicians' most important short-term constituency tends to have a vested interest in CBD vitality. In contrast, a wider array of government units in the metropolis present a wider fiscal and political portfolio of choices for a strategic developer or a relocating firm. Thus, the theoretical framework gives us strong reason to suspect that the political fragmentation index should be negatively associated with office share.

I use two alternative regression models to measure these relationships (see table 3.2). Each of the models explains roughly half the variance in office share.

Most of the control variables are significant and take on the anticipated sign. An exception is "office," which has a negative sign. Population also shows negative coefficients. A possible explanation for both results is that large SMSAs experience inefficiencies if office and administrative functions are too centralized in CBDs.

A strictly economic and "urban ecology" explanation of office share, represented by model 1, accounts for 46 percent of the variance. Does the organization of metropolitan governance have anything to tell us about the strength of the CBD beyond what model 1 offers? Model 2 demonstrates that a careful measure of political fragmentation adds significant explanatory power. A version of the *F*-test may be used to determine the "marginal" contribution of an additional explanatory variable. Examining the difference between models 1 and 2, we find that the addition of the political fragmentation variable in model 2 improves the explanatory power at the .05 probability level.[11] (The fragmentation variable itself is significant in model 2 at the .10 level.) As predicted, political fragmentation detracts from the centralization of the metropolitan office market. The substantive interpretation of its coefficient indicates that, all other things being equal, a one-point increase in the fragmentation index (as, for example, between the Indianapolis and Boston metro areas, or between Philadelphia and Washington) leads to a reduction in the CBD's office share of over 4 percent. This is comparable to the negative influence of the extra CBD dummy variable.

Given these results, we can continue to maintain that more unified political decision structures will tend to boost the fortunes of the center in metropolitan areas, while fragmented institutions favor outer areas at the expense of the CBD. But a potential criticism of the above test is that it ignores the extent to which other, smaller CBDs beyond the central city anchor the metropolitan area with centers. As I have emphasized, significant nodes of activity are increasingly typical of outer areas. The next test explores a measure of "network centralization" in metropolitan areas, looking not only at the dominance of the central CBD but at the overall concentration of work.

A Test: Centralization of the Commuting Network

Sociologist Holly L. Hughes has developed an alternative approach to measuring the (de)centralization of metropolitan areas. Drawing upon network theory, which has often been applied to the study of communications, Hughes has analyzed the journey-to-work patterns of a sample of forty-one multicentered SMSAs (Hughes 1993; Irwin and Hughes 1992).[12] Her methodology

TABLE 3.3

Multiple Regression Models:
Network Centralization of Metropolitan Areas

Variable	Model 1	Model 2	Model 3
City Centrality	0.115	0.147	0.126
	(3.86)***	(5.12)***	(4.81)***
Population	−2.20E-8	−2.61E-8	−1.69E-8
	(−1.19)	(−1.55)	(−1.06)
Age	0.006	0.018	0.011
	(0.80)	(2.31)**	(1.56)
Office	−0.0004	0.003	—
	(−0.20)	(1.34)	
Contiguity	—	—	−0.129
			(−1.67)
PFI	—	−0.268	−0.167
		(−3.07)***	(−2.18)**
B_o	0.314	0.148	0.457
	(1.84)*	(0.899)	(4.17)***
Adj. R^2	0.34	0.50	0.52
Prob $> F$	0.002	0.000	0.000
N	36	34	34

Sources: Bureau of the Census, State and Metropolitan Area Data Book, 1982; Census of Governments, 1982; Holly L. Hughes, personal communication; and author's calculations.

Note: PFI = political fragmentation index; * = 0.10 significance; ** = 0.05 significance; *** = 0.01 significance.

involved compiling a matrix of commuter movements, which allowed her to determine the "centrality" of each central city, each suburb of over twenty-five thousand, and the "balance of SMSA" within each metropolitan "network." A single measure of "network centralization" was then computed for each metro area. This index "ranges from 0 (even distribution throughout the network) to 1.00 (complete domination of network flows by one city). High network centralization . . . indicates a dominant central city" (Hughes 1993, 426). More broadly, higher levels of network centralization, my dependent variable in this section, indicate that commuting flows are concentrated in a small number of cities, rather than being dispersed across the metropolitan area.

Thirty-six of Hughes's cases correspond to cases in my sample. For these SMSAs, the values of network centralization range from 0.26 (Jersey City SMSA) to 0.85 (Oklahoma City SMSA, the most centralized metro area in Hughes's full sample). The mean is 0.57, with a standard deviation of 0.14.

I present three models showing the influence of political fragmentation and other variables on centralization. In addition to the *PFI*, other independent variables considered include population, age, office, and contiguity. These are expected to have analogous effects on network centralization as predicted for office share. I also include Hughes's city centrality score for the central city of each metro area. Hughes notes that the centrality of the largest commuter magnet will have substantial effects on the overall measure of network centralization, since the latter is constructed from centrality scores for each city. Indeed, city centrality alone explains 36 percent of the variance in network centralization for the metropolitan areas in my sample. Results of the OLS regressions for three somewhat more complex models are shown in table 3.3.

In model 1, adding age, population, and office to city centrality appears to offer no additional explanatory leverage. However, the addition of the political fragmentation index in model 2 brings the situation into sharper focus: As age increases sharply in both substantive and statistical significance, population again shows a negative coefficient, and the *PFI* itself is strongly negative. Replacing office with contiguity in model 3 increases the explanatory power to 52 percent, and illustrates that proximity to another SMSA does appear to reduce network centralization. (Contiguity, at the 0.10 level, is not quite significant.) Again, the negative coefficient on the political fragmentation index is larger than the standard deviation of the dependent variable.

In short, political fragmentation appears to significantly reduce the overall concentration of employment locations within metropolitan areas. In combination with the office share test, this analysis bolsters the theoretical conclusion that divided local authority over land use detracts from the competitiveness of existing business centers.

Proposition 2:
Institutional Configuration and Intrametropolitan Disparities

I proposed that there would be wider disparities among places in a frag mented metropolis than in a unitary metropolis. Political fragmentation gives suburbanites the institutional ammunition to preserve land-use advantages, and provides little incentive for local politicians to consider the externality costs of their land-use decisions. Fragmentation also provides a setting in which some jurisdictions may be overrun with growth, while others may be able to deflect development. Thus we might expect to find greater mismatches between job areas and housing areas in fragmented SMSAs. In the new suburban era, fragmented regions could be expected to develop a greater number of employment-heavy districts outside the CBD; unitary political systems could be expected to retain the CBD's dominance while mixing suburban employment opportunities with suburban housing.

These theoretical predictions about intrametropolitan disparities are tested below. First, I model average commuting times for workers in each SMSA, which serve as a proxy for jobs/housing mismatches. The second test examines the number of "edge city" employment districts in each SMSA.

A Test: Metropolitan Commuting Times

Why focus on commuting? Average daily commuting times may be taken to represent the degree of accessibility of jobs to housing in metropolitan areas. There are persistent disparities between employment opportunities and housing options for some income groups in some metropolitan areas, particularly for people working in the new suburban centers.[13] Low commuting times are probably indicative of relatively well-balanced jobs to housing ratios in an urban region. Of course, as anyone who has cursed a rush hour traffic jam would attest, commuting times are of substantial importance in and of themselves. In short, commuting times can be taken as a rough measure of the overall "efficiency" of a metropolitan area's spatial patterns of settlement and commerce.[14] They also have the advantage of being measured at the SMSA level, which is not true of other variables we might use to represent metropolitan development patterns.

Theoretically, one might approach the problem more directly by computing a composite job/housing mismatch index for each metro area, using data for each subarea. In practice, however, the Census Bureau collects employment statistics only for counties (a level too large to be useful in calculating spatial mismatches) and large municipalities. This would artificially delete numerous small suburban places in most SMSAs. If one *could* collect data on jobs to housing ratios for each municipality in a metropolitan area, there would still be numerous problems in measurement. One problem is unincorporated territory—land outside any municipality. Another involves the tremendous variation in size among municipalities. Even if one tried to "correct for" the size of each municipality, the actual, substantive accessibility of residences to places of employment would remain uncertain. A very large municipality might appear "balanced"—but its huge scale might mask highly segregated land uses. A small residential municipality would appear "unbalanced," even if all its residents commuted to jobs in neighboring towns within a few miles of their homes. In short, we would have a classic ecological problem in trying to generalize about one level of analysis, the metropolis, on the basis of information collected at a different level of analysis, the municipality.

Thus I turn instead to the imperfect, but interesting, commuting-time measure. The dependent variable is the daily one-way commuting time, in minutes, spent by the average worker in each SMSA in the sample. This includes commuters using all modes of transportation. On the suspicion that the results might differ systematically for auto commuters, I ran a parallel series of regressions in which the dependent variable was limited to commuting times for those using a car, truck, or van.[15] However, the results were nearly identical to those below, and thus are not reported here. Average commuting times among the sample SMSAs vary from 16.3 minutes (Lincoln, Neb.) to 29.9 minutes (Washington, D.C./Md./Va.). The median is 20.8 minutes, with a standard deviation of 2.8 minutes.

Estimators used include population, extra CBD, age, contiguity, and *PFI*. New variables include:

Density = SMSA population per square mile;
Growth = average annual change in SMSA population, 1970–1979;
Drive = percentage of SMSA workers who commute to work by driving alone; and
CBD Size = an absolute measure of office employment in the SMSA's largest central business district.

The nature of the data made it advisable to carry two "control" variables through all equations: drive and extra CBD. The first measures the proportion of workers who commute by driving alone to work, as opposed to using other means. (This is the variable transportation planners call "modal split.") Small values for drive indicate that public transportation is taking proportionally more "competitors" for roadway space off the road. On the other hand, since public transit commuters tend to experience somewhat longer commutes, low values for drive could potentially increase commuting times. I include extra CBD, a dummy variable signaling SMSAs with more than one traditional central business district, because it is possible that a bifurcation of employment centers could reduce some of the congestion associated with a single, larger CBD. Thus extra CBD could potentially reduce commuting times. As it turns out, however, these two variables do not have significant effects.

I estimated several ordinary least-squares regression models that represent contrasting explanations of SMSA commuting times. The results of three interesting models, representing contrasting theoretical explanations, are displayed in table 3.4.

Model 1 tests the pure impact of *size* on accessibility. It reflects the simple economic theories of the monocentric city, in which workers trade off convenient transportation for more residential space. In the traditional theory,

TABLE 3.4

Multiple Regression Models:
Average One-Way Commuting Times in Metropolitan Areas
(*in minutes*)

Variable	Model 1	Model 2	Model 3
Population	3.83E–7	— —	
	(0.98)		
Density	0.0008	0.0014	0.0010
	(1.31)	(2.31)**	(1.53)
CBD size	0.00004	0.00005	0.00005
	(2.49)**	(5.07)***	(4.96)***
Age	—	0.227	0.247
		(1.92)*	(2.12)**
Growth	—	0.604	0.741
		(2.34)**	(2.77)***
Drive	−0.021	0.023	0.068
	(−0.39)	(0.44)	(1.10)
Extra CBD	−0.519	−0.271	−0.580
	(−0.97)	(−0.52)	(−1.07)
Contiguity	—	−0.428	−0.912
		(−0.76)	(−1.42)
PFI	—	—	2.795
			(2.31)**
B_o	20.821	15.423	10.895
	(5.49)***	(3.82)***	(2.26)**
Adj. R^2	0.50	0.52	0.57
Prob > F	0.000	0.000	0.000
N	79	79	70

Sources: Bureau of the Census, *State and Metropolitan Area Data Book*, 1982; *Census of Governments*, 1982; *1980 Census of Population—Subject Reports: Journey to Work*, 1984; and author's calculations.

Note: PFI = political fragmentation index; * = 0.10 significance; ** = 0.05 significance; *** = 0.01 significance.

urban areas that grow beyond an "efficient" size will begin to suffer decline. But as Peter Gordon and associates argue, the spatial decentralization of firms, not recognized in the monocentric model, in effect represents the market responding to congestion diseconomies in growing metropolises (Gordon and Wong 1985; Gordon et al. 1989a).[16] Thus model 1, like the results attained by Gordon and his colleagues, does not demonstrate a significant relationship between SMSA population and commuting times. However, a measure of the absolute size of the central city's CBD, where monocentric economies would be expected to come into play, does increase commuting times. Population density, another measure of size, is not significant in model 1, though it does figure in some alternative specifications (as we might intuitively expect if we consider what "congestion" means).

Model 2 represents a more complex explanation of commuting times. While retaining the density measure, it reflects such urban-system characteristics as the age and growth rate of the metropolitan area, and its contiguity with one or more other SMSAs. With these new variables introduced, CBD size increases in statistical and substantive significance. In addition, the disturbance that rapid growth might create for urban "equilibrium" is confirmed by its significant positive effects of growth on commuting times. The age variable indicates that the average one-way commute will increase by about 1.1 minutes for every 5 additional decades of a city's age.

Model 3 adds the political fragmentation index to model 2. As anticipated, fragmentation appears to lead to more disjunctures between work and housing. The coefficient indicates that an increase of 1.0 in the *PFI* adds about 2.8 minutes to the average one-way commute. This is nearly equal to the standard deviation in commute time. When this extra commuting time is combined across all commuters in a metro area for two commutes per day, it is a quite significant inefficiency in urban development patterns.

The adjusted *R*-square for model 3 indicates that 57 percent of the variance in commute time is explained. The addition of the political fragmentation variable again added significantly to the explanatory power of the model (using the variation of the *F*-test referred to earlier). Other statistically significant estimators in this model include CBD size, age, and growth.

Overall, then, the commuting time models make a strong case in favor of the institutional perspective on urban development. Metropolitan areas with a more fragmented organization of land-use authority are marked by greater difficulty in traveling from home to work.

A Test: The Frequency of "Edge Cities"

I have argued that more fragmented political institutions will lead to more competition with existing centers, and more varied development outcomes across suburban places. Some municipalities, responding to "use value" concerns, will defuse attempts to increase density; other towns (or, in unincorporated areas, counties), where property values and service/tax ratios are of greater importance, are likely to allow a great deal of development. At the same time, developers and their allies may be able to dominate some of these local jurisdictions politically, even though they may be unsuccessful suitors of other municipalities. Moreover, a greater array of political entities would seem likely to make for greater variation, even experimentation, in land-use strategies and outcomes.

Thus we might expect a larger number of suburban agglomerations in more fragmented metropolitan areas. Suburban interests there will have more control over resources necessary to compete with the CBD than they have in a unitary regional city. Suburban developers will have more arenas in which to attempt to launch large projects; in a regional city, in contrast, their desires must always be balanced against the "special relationship" political elites have with representatives of the existing CBD.

In an appendix to *Edge City*, Garreau enumerates all the "edge city" complexes—existing, emerging, and planned—within certain metropolitan areas (Garreau 1991, 423–39). For example, business agglomerations in the Kansas City region include downtown Kansas City, the College Boulevard-Overland Park edge city, and emerging complexes at Country Club Plaza, Crown Center, and the Kansas City International Airport.

It is unclear why Garreau chose the metro areas he did, since there are identifiable "edge cities" in some regions he does not list. Nevertheless, Garreau's count of edge cities does represent a measure of suburban nucleation in the metropolitan areas he discusses. Although not ideal, since Garreau's definition of an edge city is disputable, his enumeration does appear to be systematic for the MSAs covered. And since there are no real alternative measures of suburban business clusters at the present time, I have adopted Garreau's notion to use as a dependent variable.

Thirty metropolitan areas in Garreau's "sample" correspond to cases in my data set. I use these observations as my abbreviated sample in the following model. Given the small number of cases, it is important to limit the number of explanatory variables introduced in order to conserve degrees of freedom. One must also recognize that the small number of cases will tend to inflate the R^2 goodness-of-fit measure.

The dependent variable, "edge cities," is the number of edge city business nodes in each metropolitan area. I include in this figure all edge cities and the CBD, and count what Garreau labels "emerging" edge cities as one-half of a unit. Planned or "future" edge cities are not counted at all.[17] This variable takes on values ranging from 1.5 to 20.5, with a median of 3.5 and a mean of 5.1; the standard deviation is 4.0.

What factors might lead to the construction of more edge cities? One might hypothesize that since metro areas with greater populations have a greater "critical mass" in suburban areas, they would provide more of a market for such agglomerations. SMSAs with high growth rates tend to experience a great deal of peripheral development, and that should be reflected in a higher propensity for edge-city growth.

TABLE 3.5

Multiple Regression Models:

Number of "Edge City" Business Nodes in Metropolitan Areas

Variable	Model 1	Model 2	Model 3
Population	1.44E–6	1.47E–6	1.25E–6
	(3.74)***	(4.06)***	(4.13)***
Age	0.078	—	—
	(0.27)		
Growth	0.239	0.108	0.906
	(0.38)	(0.28)	(2.36)**
Office	0.154	0.155	0.086
	(3.10)***	(3.22)***	(2.00)*
PFI	—	—	8.887
			(4.04)***
B_o	–7.648	–6.899	–10.426
	(–1.89)*	(–2.92)**	(–4.02)***
Adj. R^2	0.42	0.44	0.65
Prob > F	0.001	0.000	0.000
N	30	30	28

Sources: Bureau of the Census, State and Metropolitan Area Data Book, 1982; Census of Governments, 1982; Garreau 1991, chap. 11; and author's calculations.

Note: PFI = political fragmentation index; * = 0.10 significance; ** = 0.05 significance; *** = 0.01 significance.

The effects of age are uncertain: Older central cities may create more disamenities and thus a demand for "fresh" business centers in their suburbs, but they also tend to have more strongly defined CBDs and less auto travel.

Finally, I introduce the office variable. Recall that it measures the percentage of SMSA employment that is accounted for by office occupations. Metropolitan areas with office-based economies can be expected to have more of a market for edge cities, and perhaps a greater propensity to cluster employment. In repeated estimations, the size of the main CBD had no systematic effect on the propensity to develop edge cities, nor did the density of the metropolitan area.

Table 3.5 provides three estimations of edge cities. I dropped the age variable in models 2 and 3 due to its lack of significance. Population and office have the expected signs and are significant, as is growth, once the PFI variable is introduced (model 3). The effect of political fragmentation is statistically significant and substantively striking: An increase of one point in the PFI is associated with nearly nine more edge cities, when we hold the other variables constant. In addition, model 3 is able to explain nearly two-thirds of the variance in "edge city."

Even if we allow for the small number of cases and for the limitations of the data, it certainly appears that political fragmentation tends to generate a greater number of employment-heavy suburban nodes. This probably occurs because a fragmented region gives developers more options, because a greater proportion of local governments engage in fiscal zoning, and because the central city's CBD is less well protected.[18]

Proposition 3: Institutional Configuration and Sprawl

A final implication of our theoretical framework is that political fragmentation leads to greater sprawl. Since many suburban jurisdictions will tend to block further growth in their areas, new residents and jobs are likely to be deflected instead toward the periphery of the metropolitan area. This leads to an expansion of the region, which implies a flattening of the urban density curve.

"Sprawl" is difficult to measure definitively, but the test below does examine the phenomenon. While hampered by a limited number of observations, this examination of the population density gradients of SMSAs provides useful insight.

A Test: Steepness of the Density Gradient

Over the past four decades, urban economists have worked to refine a formal descriptive model of urban structure, relating the population of a given tract of urban land to its distance from a dense center (McDonald 1989, 376–81).[19] Most of this work follows from Colin Clark's 1951 statement of the relationship between population densities and distance, which takes the following form:

$$d_x = d_o e^{-bx}$$

In this formula, d indicates density, o is the city center (actually, a location just outside the central business district where residential density is highest), x is distance from that center, and e is the natural log base. The variable of interest here is b, the so-called density gradient.[20] It measures the percentage decline in density per unit of distance from the center. The value of b can therefore be used as an index of the (de)concentration of the urban population (Berry and Horton 1970, 277).

While subsequent scholarship has found that Clark's equation misses some aspects of urban structure, such as sudden disjunctures or "shift points" in the density curve, the formula is flexible and accurate enough to remain in common use by urbanists. For the purposes of my analyses, the density gradient variable is useful to measure the steepness or "distance decay" of the density curve of metropolitan areas. In that sense it represents the compactness of an urban region. For example, historical analyses indicate that gradients generally remained unchanged in the United States for the period 1900–1930, increased during the Depression years as funds for suburbanization became more limited, and then flattened steadily from 1940 to 1970 (McDonald 1989). Higher levels of b indicate a steeper density curve and therefore a more compact, less decentralized, metropolitan population.

Unfortunately, calculating values for b is a tedious process involving detailed census tract–level analysis in each metropolitan area. Moreover, the literature has shifted from accumulating descriptive data to refining the econometric techniques involved. Accordingly, I found only one study that listed gradient values calculated for SMSAs as defined in 1980. An article by Molly Macauley (1985) presents the values of b for seventeen metropolitan areas as of 1980, also listing the 1940 gradient values for these areas.[21] All seventeen correspond to cases in my sample, but missing data for the *PFI* reduce the number of observations to fourteen for analyses using the fragmentation variable.

Given the tiny number of observations, multiple regression is a less valid method for drawing inferences. Collinearity among regressors becomes a serious hindrance to drawing inferences from regression results, and significance levels can be extremely sensitive to the inclusion and exclusion of variables. Probably the best way to proceed for such a sample is to investigate simple correlations between the density gradient and variables that may be associated with it. I also present regressions with a small number of parameters, as an exploratory exercise to examine the relative influence of some of the more important variables.

GRADIENT80 is Macauley's 1980 set of density gradient estimates. These ranged from a b value of 0.11 (San Diego) to a value of 0.47 (Albuquerque). The mean is 0.24, and the standard deviation 0.09.

McDonald's review of the literature suggests that age, population, and values of the gradient from a baseline year have tended to be the most consistently important independent variables in attempting to explain gradients using cross-sectional data (McDonald 1989). My variable GRADIENT40 is Macauley's measurement of density gradients for the same metropolitan areas as of 1940. Some studies also suggest that an urban area's income or its centralization of employment, along with population density, may provide some explanatory leverage. Thus I include some additional variables: density, income (1979 household income), office, and office share. We might also expect a relationship between density gradients and growth, since rapidly growing urban regions tend to have experienced more suburban-style development.

TABLE 3.6

Simple Correlations Between
GRADIENT80 and Other Variables

GRADIENT40	0.62
Population	−0.55
PFI	−0.51
Income	−0.33
Density	−0.32
Age	−0.26
Office share	0.23
Office	−0.16
Growth	−0.13

Sources: Bureau of the Census, *State and Metropolitan Area Data Book*, 1982; *Census of Governments*, 1982; Macauley 1985; and author's calculations.

Note: PFI = political fragmentation index; GRADIENT80 and GRADIENT40 = metropolitan area density gradients for 1980 and 1940, respectively.

Finally, I expect the political fragmentation index to be negatively related to GRADIENT80—that is, where land-use authority is more divided, there is likely to be more decentralization.

I thus measured the simple correlations of all these variables with GRADIENT80 (see table 3.6). The density gradient in 1940 varies most directly with GRADIENT80, and population shows a correlation of −0.55. But age has a surprisingly low correlation. Strikingly, the political fragmentation index is among the variables with the strongest correlation, and has the predicted negative sign.

I ran a number of OLS regressions for exploratory purposes, introducing only a few variables at a time. I focused on GRADIENT40, population, and age because of their *theoretically* strong connection to the density curve. With the exception of growth, the other demographic and economic variables consistently provided meager results, showing coefficients of effectively zero and no statistical significance. This was true even of income, which, according to urban economic theory, should have a strong effect.[22]

By itself, GRADIENT40 explains 35 percent of the variance in GRADIENT80, indicating the strong role of a region's historical growth legacy in driving subsequent land use.

The results of four somewhat more complex models are shown in table 3.7.

TABLE 3.7

Multiple Regression Models:
Density Gradients of Metropolitan Areas in 1980

Variable	Model 1	Model 2	Model 3	Model 4
GRADIENT40	0.215	0.181	—	0.150
	(2.07)*	(1.23)		(1.08)*
Population	—	−2.67E-8	−3.21E-8	−1.11E-8
		(−0.81)	(−1.67)	(−0.41)
Age	—	0.012	—	—
		(1.44)		
Growth	—	—	−0.033	−0.030
			(−2.19)*	(−1.96)*
PFI	−0.077	−0.163	−0.211	−0.170
	(−0.77)	−0.40)	(−2.14)*	(−1.62)
B_o	0.146	0.156	0.483	0.316
	(1.23)	(0.96)	(6.40)***	(1.85)*
Adj. R^2	0.37	0.37	0.45	0.46
Prob > F	0.032	0.083	0.029	0.046
N	14	14	14	14

Sources: Bureau of the Census, State and Metropolitan Area Data Book, 1982; Census of Governments, 1982; Macauley 1985; and author's calculations.

Note: PFI – political fragmentation index; GRADIENT40 = metropolitan area density gradients for 1940; * = 0.10 significance; ** = 0.05 significance; *** = 0.01 significance.

The adjusted R^2 levels should be discounted because of the tiny data set. However, in these as in other regressions I ran, it is comforting to note the small amount of volatility in the signs or coefficients of the independent variables. In model 1, PFI adds little to GRADIENT40 in explaining the compactness of metro areas, though its sign takes the appropriate (negative) direction. In model 2, PFI, age, population, and GRADIENT40 collectively account for 37 percent of the variance, though none is statistically significant. The signs of the coefficients indicate that metropolitan areas that are older and smaller in population size have steeper density gradients—that is, they are more compact. GRADIENT40, which individually shows a high correlation with GRADIENT80, tends to lose significance when other variables are introduced, though its direction is still strongly positive.

In model 3, PFI, population, and growth provide a relatively simple and powerful explanation of GRADIENT80. Growth, as expected, has a negative effect. The fragmentation variable is statistically significant and negative. Realistically, however, political fragmentation in model 3 is probably acting as a proxy for other variables with which it is correlated. In regressions where age, density, and/or population were introduced, *PFI* never quite achieved statistical significance, though its coefficient remained negative and generally exceeded the standard deviation of GRADIENT80 (see model 4, for example).

Because of the small number of observations in these models, we must be wary of drawing inferences. It would appear, however, that the organization of a region's governance may have an impact on urban deconcentration—though the results are far from clear. The results seem to comport with the earlier tests. But to be conservative, we ought not reject the null hypothesis that fragmentation has no effect in this case. At a minimum, scholars analyzing the determinants of urban density gradients would do well to consider the role of government in shaping settlement patterns.

Conclusion

The results of the tests presented lend support to my three hypotheses regarding urban development. Politically fragmented metropolitan areas appear to lose more office employment from their central cities' CBDs than do more unitary areas, and are marked overall by less centralized patterns of the journey to work. Politically fragmented areas are also apparently marked by greater spatial disparities among places: jobs/housing mismatches resulting in longer commutes, and more "edge-city" developments. Finally, while it cannot be conclusively stated that political fragmentation is associated with less compact urban areas, neither did the analysis of density gradients disprove such a thesis.

Of particular interest are the incremental effects of political fragmentation, with *PFI* showing an influence on most dependent variables even when a number of economic, demographic, and other urban-system variables are included. For example, there are many plausible reasons why it should take longer, on average, to commute to work in some regions than in others. The legacy of development patterns in an area (which is a factor of age), the degree of solo automobile use, and the size and density of the area and its core may all influence the ease or difficulty of the daily journey to work. I attempted to control for these variables and determine the additional role, if any, of political organization. Following the work of Scott Bollens on income inequality in metropolitan areas, we may term the equations that include *PFI* *political-ecological* models of urban spatial structure (Bollens 1986). The implication is that political organization needs to be more carefully considered in discussing the causes of urban development patterns than it has been in the past.

There are, however, limitations to these tests, which use proxies of varying quality for urban development patterns. The number of observations is also limited, and there is likely to be measurement error in some of the variables used. In addition, *PFI*, in spite of its advantages over prior indices, is still a somewhat crude representation of institutional configuration. While I presented the relationship between institutional structure and urban form as a continuous linear variable for the OLS regressions, it may be that it is much more complex, possibly involving a nonlinear relationship with negative or positive "returns to scale" for greater institutional unity. Given small-group theories of collective action (Olson 1965), for example, perhaps metropolitan areas with more than a very few units of government cannot hope to approximate a regional city's regulatory leverage (Plane 1986, 411).[23] In that case, the effects of fragmentation would escalate rapidly in the lower ranges of *PFI*, less so in the upper ranges. The techniques used in this chapter were not designed to deal with such "thresholds."

In any event, I have not yet shown a *direct* link between institutional configurations, political behavior, and economic outcomes. The burden of the quantitative evidence supports the theoretical expectations; but as in many aggregate studies, the politics that straddle the world of institutions and the world of policy outcomes remain a "black box." In the following chapters, I attempt to shed more light on the subject, detailing the specific political relationships involved in actual cases of urban regional development.

4

The Institutional Context for Development in Two Regions: Comparing Portland and Denver

Situated on a high plain about ten miles from the foothills of America's most significant mountain range, the city of Denver and its suburban areas have an appeal that has always been associated with the scenic landscape of the Rockies. Today, although the metropolis has spread out over huge areas of arid prairie to the east of Denver, the western mountain view remains the visual focus of the area, and undergirds a notably environmentalist political ethos. Despite that ethos, views of the Rockies have been obscured by office buildings, strip malls lurk beneath mountainsides, an extensive freeway network draws growth into recently rural areas, scarce water supplies are a perennial concern, and a fabled "brown cloud" of air pollutants sometimes hangs over the atmosphere. Meanwhile, Denver's downtown has had a difficult time competing with suburban business nodes. With one of the highest auto ownership rates in the country, Denver is in many ways a quintessential suburbanizing metropolis. Even with a marked slowdown in the region's growth in the mid to late 1980s, the explosive development at the urban periphery continued.

In short, quality of life and environmental preservation are always prominent political issues in the Denver metropolis, and have been responsible for drawing countless numbers of people and businesses to the area. Nevertheless, urban development there has often proceeded in patterns that do little to conserve these qualities.

In contrast, metropolitan Portland frequently makes headlines in land-use planning circles. Natural amenities are also the principal lure for new residents and firms in this area of rapid growth. But thus far, these newcomers have been accommodated without compromising Portland's central business district or stretching freeways throughout the periphery.

Portland's urbanization is limited at its edge by an "urban growth boundary." Suburbs share in the costs of growth—notably, by ensuring a supply of affordable housing—as well as in its benefits. The region's process for allocating federal funds for transportation projects has been held as a model of rationality and innovation. And downtown Portland—a destination for tourists as well as business travelers—is often cited as both remarkable on its own terms and successful in competing with suburban locations in an age of decentralization. Not surprisingly, the city won the "Planning Implementation Award" from the American Planning Association in 1990 (Friedman 1993, 17).

What can account for the differences between Denver, with its steady accretion of growth-related problems, and Portland, with well-received attempts at shaping metropolitan growth? While some writers suggest that ideology or state political cultures can explain the differences, I rest my argument instead on the formative impact of political-institutional arrangements for development decision making in the two metro areas. Stated most succinctly, the relatively insulated policy process in the Portland area, where suburban interests have weak institutions around which to coalesce, promotes a center-oriented and relatively technocratic approach to regional land use. In metropolitan Denver, in contrast, the number and scope of land use–related local institutions are greater, and governing arrangements are in greater flux. This political structure enables both progrowth and antigrowth interests to influence (and even create) local governments. Since Denver's institutions have relatively localized geographic scale, the metropolis as a whole shows more land-use disparities than Portland, and regionwide transportation and growth management issues seem literally "out of control" to residents. In this chapter, I examine the institutional, social, and economic environments of the two regions.

Comparing Denver and Portland

Conceivably, any metropolitan area might have been fair game for a case study based on the theoretical framework set out in chapter 2. One might, for example, decide to look at the "limiting cases" that come closest to the ideal types I have termed "regional city" and "fragmented metropolis." In my aggregate sample, this might involve comparing Honolulu or Albuquerque to Washington, D.C., or Boston.

In using comparative case studies as a research method, however, it is important to isolate the variables that differ among the cases. In this way, a fair (if still rough) account can be made of the influence of different factors on variance in the dependent variable. I chose metropolitan Portland and Denver as cases that minimize variance across potential independent variables. While every metro area has unique features, Denver and Portland exhibit striking similarities in an array of historical, demographic, and economic characteristics. At the same time, they differ significantly in their institutional political characteristics at the metropolitan level.

For each metro area, I examined the existing scholarly literature on its history and development, and then perused hundreds of newspaper and periodical articles (generally from the period 1980 to 1992) using an on-line news retrieval service. I consulted many government reports, maps, and demographic and economic analyses. After identifying urban development issues of regional significance, I contacted representatives from a variety of government entities and development firms that were active in these regions. During research trips to Denver in late 1992 and Portland in mid-1993, I conducted over two dozen interviews, many of which I cite.[1] During these periods of fieldwork, I also toured each metropolitan area extensively by auto, logging over eleven hundred miles in each. In the process, I recorded observations about growth patterns, particular municipalities and unincorporated areas, and specific development projects.

The Study Areas

Portland and Denver share some notable traits. First, the Census Bureau views each region as a "double" metropolitan area, each with two "primary" metro areas (PMSAs) making up a "consolidated" metro area (CMSA). The Portland PMSA and the Vancouver, Washington, PMSA make up the Portland-Vancouver CMSA; the Denver PMSA and the Boulder-Longmont PMSA are the analogous units in Colorado. My analysis will concern itself almost exclusively with the primary part of each urban region.

In the case of Portland, the focus is on the urbanized portion of the Oregon counties of Multnomah, Clackamas, and Washington.[2] The broader CMSA also includes Clark County, Washington, with the city of Vancouver. The shaded portion of the map (figure 4.1) represents the urbanized and urbanizing study area on the Oregon side. Clearly, the three Oregon counties all contain a substantial amount of rural territory as well. The PMSA's officially designated urban growth boundary and the area's principal roadways are shown in figure 4.2.

While Vancouver has long been viewed as the region's "second city," it remained a relatively self-contained urban world until quite recently. Until 1980, Clark County was connected to Oregon by a single bridge across the wide Columbia River, and the level of cross-commuting was low. In the 1980s, Clark County grew in part as a bedroom for Portland-area workers, though it has begun to spawn some suburban employment of its own.

In Colorado, the Denver metropolis is the dominant portion of the so-called Front Range—the territory along the base of the eastern side of the

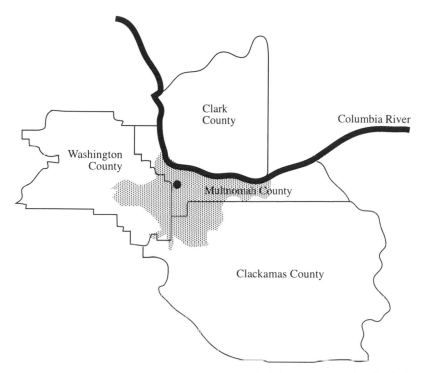

Figure 4.1 Metropolitan Portland-Vancouver. *Note:* The shaded area represents the urbanized area in the Oregon portion of the metropolis.

Rocky Mountains. The boundaries of the six-county Denver CMSA are shown in figure 4.3. The continuously developed portion of the metro area covers Denver, western Adams and Arapahoe Counties, and the part of Jefferson County located east of the Rocky Mountains. That portion of the CMSA is the major focus of my case study. The urbanized area also extends south into northern Douglas County, and northwest into a portion of Boulder County.

Denver and Portland as Social, Economic, and Geographical Units

Several characteristics are likely to affect development patterns in each of the two regions. For example, sheer population size is an important consideration. In the 1990 census, the Denver-Boulder CMSA (with 1.85 million persons) ranked twenty-second in population for the nation's metro areas; the Portland-Vancouver CMSA (1.48 million) ranked twenty-seventh. The two areas were twenty-first and twenty-sixth, respectively, in population *growth* during the 1980s. Overall, both at the CMSA and PMSA levels, Portland is

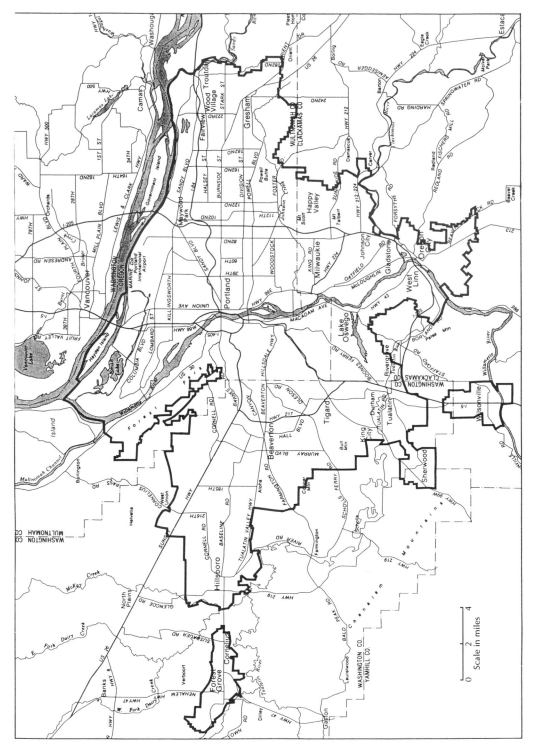

Figure 4.2 The Urban Growth Boundary in the Portland Metropolitan Area. *Source:* Metropolitan Service District, Portland.

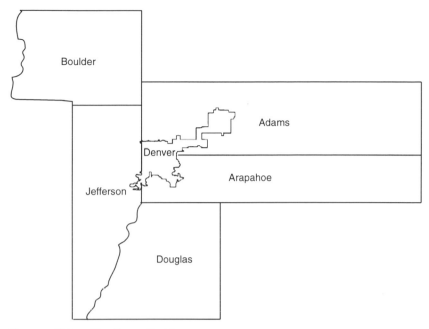

Figure 4.3 Metropolitan Denver-Boulder

about one-quarter smaller in population than Denver. Its average per capita personal income level is also slightly lower, though both Portland and Denver are within 5 percent of the national average. Part of the income disparity can be attributed to Portland's significantly higher share of population over age 65 (though both Portland and Denver are "young" metropolitan areas by national standards).

Within the overall distribution of large metropolitan areas, however, the two areas' demographic and economic characteristics are quite close. In his comparative study of five Sun Belt metropolitan areas representing the "new urban America," Carl Abbott writes:

> Denver and Portland show striking similarities in social status and ethnic composition. Both have a wide range of white-collar positions in banking, education, personal services, business administration, and public administration that result in levels of education and proportions of professional and managerial workers that are above the average for all metropolitan areas in the United States. Their commercial economies also support average family income levels and relatively low percentages of poverty families. High rankings on status indicators are also related to low minority populations. Portland is located off the main path of black and Hispanic migration in the twentieth century and Denver has been only a secondary target for minority migrants. (Abbott 1987, 48–49)

Certainly, race has been less influential in driving development than in most large metropolitan areas in the United States. In both regions, black populations were very low and were effectively marginalized in a small area of segregated housing until World War II. Wartime employment—particularly by the military—and the succeeding eras of rapid economic expansion brought more substantial African-American populations to both areas.[3] But with a makeup of 83 percent non-Hispanic whites, Portland is still one of the "whiter" metropolitan areas in the country, and Asians and Hispanics have in recent years had a higher rate of growth than African-Americans. Since the central city of Portland, unlike Denver, has not had to undergo mandatory school desegregation, it is possible that the flight of middle-class whites from the central area has been slowed.[4] The city of Portland in 1990 was 7.7 percent black, with 9.7 percent of the population belonging to other minority groups.

As some of the regression models in the last chapter illustrated, the age of an urban area can be one of the most important characteristics to examine. Historical trajectories play a major role in establishing patterns for urban development. While Portland was a recognized settlement slightly earlier than Denver, the Colorado city did attain the key threshold of fifty thousand in population one census earlier—1890 in Denver, 1900 in Portland. Still, growth histories are quite well matched. As is the case for nearly all western metropolises, both regions have seen by far the greatest portion of their growth during the age of the automobile, and have thus had to accommodate development that tends toward low densities. After the 1950 census, both *central cities* slowed to below the national rate of growth. This indicates that the suburban era had arrived in both Denver and Portland, since each MSA considered as a whole routinely exceeded the United States growth rate between censuses. Both metro areas have seen growth accelerate in recent decades.

Recent Development Histories

Since 1970, growth was fueled in both regions, for the most part by the type of development with which this book is most concerned: office and related work in the high-tech manufacturing, service, telecommunications, military-industrial, and research sectors. Both have also had a traditional role in head-quartering an extractive industry that operates in nearby hinterlands: energy and mining in Colorado, timber in Oregon.

Denver, as the dominant metropolis in the Mountain Time Zone, has played host to a large number of corporate relocations and expansions. "Indeed, Denver is the sunbelt city personified. Money and people for oil and gas development throughout the West are funnelled through the corporate offices which occupy the new aluminum cylinders" (Judd 1986, 167). The metropolis

TABLE 4.1
Non-Agricultural Employment in
Metropolitan Denver and Portland
(*in percent*)

Sector	Denver CMSA	Portland CMSA
Construction and mining	5.3	3.5
Finance, insurance, and real estate	7.3	7.7
Government	16.4	15.0
Manufacturing	11.9	17.6
Services	28.0	23.7
Transportation, communications, and public utilities	7.5	6.1
Wholesale and retail trade	23.6	26.6

Source: Data released by Colorado Department of Labor and Employment, 1992, and Metropolitan Service District, Portland, 1990.

underwent particularly rapid change during the oil boom of 1979–1982, when it "sustained a nearly mythic image, a place where entrepreneurs and developers, and not a few hucksters, came to town with billfolds open for quick profits" (Johnson 1991).

The office-related sectors of FIRE (finance, insurance, real estate), government, and services play a large role in the economy of metro Denver's employment market (see table 4.1). Office and information-based organizations tend to have a substantial choice of location, since they are not constrained by the cost of transporting goods. Accordingly, new recruits to the area tend to emphasize quality-of-life issues. As the CEO of an oil firm relocating to Greenwood Village, a suburb south of Denver, said, "We think from a business and professional standpoint the Rocky Mountain basins have long-term potential. And we have a house in Aspen that we don't get to use often enough" (quoted in Booth 1988). A Merrill Lynch executive explained why his division had moved to the area, despite its higher costs, compared to other potential locations. "It's such a tremendous working environment. People want to make this a place of choice" (quoted in "Top ten cities"). Similarly, by one account, "Colorado became the capital of cable [television] simply because Bill Daniels, who pioneered that medium, chose to live in the Rockies" (quoted in Leonard and Noel 1990, 418).

Many of these business movers chose suburban locations. As elsewhere, "corporate executives tended to locate their offices where they wanted to live" according to Larry Mugler, director of development services of the Denver

Regional Council of Governments (DRCOG) (quoted in Brimberg 1990). To accommodate the growth surge, huge areas of land became urbanized in the postwar era. Historical maps show that as of 1960, the basic urbanized area consisted of Denver, a small periphery, and several satellite communities. The 1960s saw growth spread along newly constructed highways that opened up additional areas. In the following decade, the region experienced the greatest number of tracts to become urbanized, as previously rural domains became large-lot subdivisions. In the 1980s, in-fill connected the core and satellite communities into a more continuous urbanized area (DRCOG 1992, 5).

For a time in the 1970s, residents of the Denver area registered political uneasiness with the out-of-state developers, the wheeler-dealer financing, and the general atmosphere of boosterism. An unprecedented referendum vote killed Colorado's decision to host the 1976 Olympics, an event growth interests had worked long and hard to recruit. State Representative Richard Lamm, who had led the anti-Olympics movement, was swept into office as governor, pledging a more thoughtful approach to growth and the environment. While Lamm's opponents came to dub him "Governor Gloom," it was clear to some that "preoccupation with the side effects of growth was a natural reaction to the runaway pace of development in the 1970s" (Judd and Ready 1986, 218). During the same introspective period, Denver's old neighborhoods began to attract gentrifiers and preservationists.

But it was difficult to maintain a political emphasis on measured, managed growth in a wildly cyclical economy, particularly one that was increasingly based on the energy sector. While the period of the late 1970s had seen huge amounts of development capital flow into the region, the trend reversed thereafter. Judd and Ready write:

> The national recession of 1981 and falling oil prices substituted disinvestment for the problems associated with development. Optimism about sustained regional growth had fueled downtown office construction that far exceeded demand once the recession hit. By 1984, Denver had the highest downtown office vacancy rate in the nation, 28.1 percent—more than double the national rate. (1986, 219)

A second crash in oil prices in the late 1980s hit Denver even harder, leading to net out-migration and a drop in construction jobs.

That bust ground real estate construction activity to a near halt, a situation that continued well into the early 1990s. Permits for new housing units in the CMSA shrank from 10,500 in 1987 to 5,940 in 1990 (RTD 1992a, 3:2). Of the 200 leading home-building firms of 1979, 177 were no longer active in the Den-

TABLE 4.2

Comparing Denver and Portland Area Demographics

	Denver-Boulder CMSA	Denver PMSA	Portland-Vancouver CMSA	Portland PMSA
Area (square miles)	4,503	3,761	4,371	3,743
Population, 1990	1,848,320	1,622,980	1,477,900	1,239,840
Labor force, 1989	1,005,400	870,900	797,900	675,000
% Growth, 1970–1990	49	47	41	35
Per capita income ($)	18,257	18,156	16,446	16,837
% Black	4.8	5.3	2.6	2.9
% Latino	10.9	11.5	2.3	2.4
% Elderly	7.9	8.0	11.8	12.1

Source: Bureau of the Census, *State and Metropolitan Area Data Book,* 1991.

ver market in 1992 (Rebchook 1992). With the collapse of savings and loans throughout the western United States, and a reported $900 million in foreclosures from 1984 to 1989, developers found that financing for more buildings was very hard to come by. The Resolution Trust Corporation became one of the area's largest landlords (McGraw-Hill, Inc. 1991, 5; Reed 1991a; Furlong 1991). Given the excess of capacity and the lack of new construction, metro Denver's physical structure was set for the foreseeable future.

Like Denver, Portland was helped along by its favorable location and level of amenities. Despite frequent clouds in Portland and occasionally heavy snows in Denver, both cities have pleasant climates that have helped draw migrants seeking quality of life. Portland's proximity to forests, ocean, mountains, and lush farmland "is clearly an extremely powerful locational incentive to businessmen who put a high premium on the quality of life" (Hamilton 1987, 185).

Portland has trailed a bit in comparison to Denver's explosive growth rate in the period since 1970 (see table 4.2). Part of the relative slowness is due to the serious recession (some label it a depression) experienced in Oregon in the early 1980s, when a timber industry crisis coincided with the national recession; for a time, more people were leaving the area than moving in. Still, the PMSA added over 320,000 persons from 1970 to 1990, enough to comprise a fair-sized city. Its rate of gain in the 1980s trailed the Denver PMSA's rate by only 2.5 percent.

To the Portland area's suburban residents, growth has seemed anything but slow. But it is possible that some of the excesses of peripheral development around Denver were exacerbated by its higher growth rate, and that development pressure at Portland's fringes has not been extreme enough to duplicate those problems on a large scale. One ought not take such an argument too far, however. Public-sector infrastructure decisions that made distant growth possible and profitable were clear and recurrent in Denver, while such actions have for the most part been studiously avoided in northwest Oregon.

The structure of the Portland-area economy, delineated by the traditional job categories, does not differ very markedly from Denver's (compare the figures in table 4.1). Neither metro area is overly dependent on a single sector, and both have most of their employment in small firms. The Portland economy is particularly diversified (Kale and Corcoran 1987; see also McDermott 1991). Both regions are above the national average for the categories of TCPU (transportation, communication, public utilities) and FIRE (finance, insurance, real estate) and are close to the national rate in construction, trade, and government. The major difference is in manufacturing, where Portland has a heavier concentration of employment—17.6 percent versus 11.9 percent in Denver—and is closer to the national average of 17.9 percent. Portland's corresponding deficiency is in the broad category of services, where it trails Denver by 4.3 percent.

These data indicate that Portland's economy is slightly less "postindustrial." But the aggregate data categories are a bit misleading. Much of the Portland area's new manufacturing employment in the 1970s and early 1980s was in the electronics and high-tech sectors, including jobs in management as well as assembly. These activities are closer to the amenity-driven model of postindustrialism than other types of manufacturing. One geographer writes of the electronics industry, "Innovators, mostly dedicated Oregonians or immigrants 'addicted' to Oregon, neither wanted nor needed to locate elsewhere in the U.S. . . . Their products were light, high value, and easily transportable by truck or air to other regions of the country and abroad" (Hamilton 1987, 182). High-tech industries employed about forty thousand workers by the mid-1980s, but then hit hard times.

The key characteristic of the region, as throughout the Pacific urban areas, has been rapid growth. Relatively inexpensive housing and proximity to problem-ravaged California stirred much of the in-migration. Occupied office space in multitenant buildings grew by about 7 percent per year in the late 1980s and early 1990s (Portland Metropolitan Association 1993, 22–24).

Geography and Metropolitan Growth

Topographically, there is one major difference between metropolitan Portland and Denver. With mile after mile of rolling hills and flat prairie, development around Denver is hindered only by the floodplains of the South Platte River north of the city, the Cherry Creek Recreation Area south of the city, a few military installations, and of course the Rockies at the western fringe of the region. In Portland, by contrast, the Tualatin Mountains (or "west hills") loom just west of the city's downtown area. While not very tall, they are steep enough to have made suburbanization *west* of the city a difficult proposition until the automobile era. The early suburbs ranged across the flat areas north and east of the CBD. Later highways have enabled urban growth to fill in the areas between downtown Portland and what were formerly small satellite towns west of the hills. The areas of highest elevation, however—many of them within the city limits—have mainly been the province of the wealthy. Thus, the major effects of topography around Portland have been to retain a preserve for the well-off quite close to the city center, and to form something of a barrier demarking eastern and western portions of the metro area—a barrier reinforced by the north-south Willamette River. The Columbia River, Oregon's northern border, has also served to section off Clark County, Washington, as a semi-independent satellite realm.

Topography does distinguish Portland from Denver. But overall, the two regions have enjoyed similar attractions and faced similar challenges. (For a capsule history and brief sketch of contemporary development patterns in Denver and Portland, see appendixes 2 and 3.)

Denver and Portland as Political Units: The Institutional Facts of Life

What difference, if any, have *political system characteristics*, that is, the "rules of the game" structuring political and economic behavior, made for development in these MSAs? If one looks at the specific institutional characteristics of interest to this study, the Portland area shows clear differences from Denver.

Geopolitics: The Relative Positions of Central City and Suburbs

The first contrast is apparent by a quick glance at a map of the municipalities in each PMSA. In Denver, suburban giants such as Aurora, Lakewood, and Arvada flank a medium-sized central city. Figure 4.4 shows municipal boundaries as they appeared until the late 1980s. Note the large size of several suburban cities. Later, Denver would be permitted to annex lands northeast of its existing boundary, in order to build a new regional airport. In exchange, Denver made a number of concessions to neighboring Adams County. The city of Portland, by contrast, is relatively dominant territorially in its region, expanding into small portions of Washington and Clackamas Counties from

TABLE 4.3

Comparing Governance in Metropolitan Denver and Portland

Urban Development Institution	Denver	Portland
Geographic scale of central city relative to metropolis	Moderate to small	Moderate to large
Population ratio of central city to second-largest city	2.1:1	6.5:1
Suburbs over 50,000 population	Arvada Aurora Lakewood Thornton Westminster [Boulder] [Longmont]	Gresham [Vancouver]
Special districts	Entrepreneurial, easy to form	Reactive, hard to form, and tending to consolidation
Regional government	Absent or minimal	Moderately strong
Development industry	Mixture of large and small firms	Small firms

Note: Brackets indicate cities in adjoining PMSA.

its base in Multnomah. Portland physically dwarfs the largest suburban cities of Gresham, Beaverton, and Hillsboro (see figure 4.5).

DENVER

The unenviable position Denver finds itself in requires some explanation, especially since Colorado, like many western states, has liberal annexation rules. Denver, in fact, was able to take advantage of this capacity for many years. As it witnessed the first flood of residents outward across its boundaries around the turn of the century, it often could use its unrivaled capacity to provide water as leverage for annexing unincorporated settlements. Some small suburban municipalities opted into Denver when, in a boom-and-bust economy, they could not meet the financial commitments that municipal service provision required.

To combat the remaining holdouts, Denver engaged in political machinations at the state level. These maneuvers allowed for the creation of a new, consolidated City and County of Denver by a state constitutional amendment in 1902. The so-called Rush Amendment expanded central city boundaries to fifty-nine square miles, abolishing some incorporated towns in the process; it also granted Denver home rule for the first time.

Denver's original proposal for the constitutional amendment had foreseen

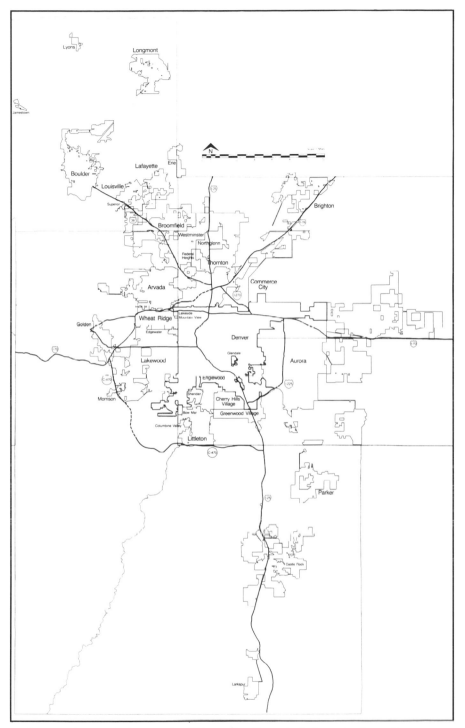

Figure 4.4 The Municipal Geography of Metropolitan Denver in the Late 1980s. *Source:* Denver Regional Council of Governments.

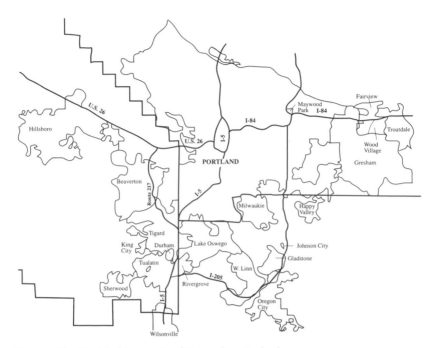

Figure 4.5 The Municipal Geography of Metropolitan Portland

an arrangement not unlike the ideal "regional city" discussed in chapter 2. The city-county, as envisioned, would have administered hundreds of square miles of territory. Political compromise forced the shrinking of the would-be Leviathan to a far more modest scale. Nevertheless, the consolidation of government responsibilities into a single entity alarmed many residents of outlying areas. In particular, the amendment created a school district with boundaries identical to Denver's. This triumvirate of coterminous city, county, and school system boundaries "was to a considerable degree responsible for resistance to the [later] geographical expansion of Denver" (Riethmayer 1971, 38). Subsequent annexations were doubly difficult because they threatened far more people than just the residents of the specific tracts to be encompassed. Rather, residents far removed from the annexed area saw a part of their county or school district—often a relatively affluent part—taken away from them. Annexation, then, became more of a zero-sum game among polities in the Denver area.

Thus, Denver City and County was viewed as a threat, and the state legislature enacted some overt restrictions on its annexation privileges in 1945 (Furniss 1973). Annexation proceeded more gradually in subsequent decades. By 1970, the central city was essentially "built out," and needed more land merely to maintain its population, given the national trend toward declining household size. Moreover, federal courts were pushing Denver hard to develop a more comprehensive school desegregation proposal. Nearby suburban areas had the open land and the white schoolchildren that were in increasingly short supply in Denver.

Under these circumstances, voters approved a state constitutional amendment in 1974, which was dubbed the Poundstone Amendment, after its architect Freda Poundstone, a conservative activist and state legislator from Greenwood Village. It required *counties* that sought to annex territory to obtain the permission of voters from the entire neighboring county, not merely the voters or landowners in the affected portion. Of course, the only county in the business of annexation was Denver City and County. The Poundstone Amendment obliged Denver to retain its boundaries, except under extraordinary circumstances.

Poundstone represented a profound change in the rules of the game. Denver's options for future expansion were literally circumscribed, and it began to experience absolute population declines. Public school enrollment had dipped sharply even before busing was ordered in 1974, and white Anglo students were in the minority by 1976 (Judd 1986). The imposition of fixed boundaries proved particularly untimely when the city was forced to respond to a collapse in oil prices later in the decade.

In 1987, voters in neighboring Adams County did approve an annexation by Denver to allow construction of a new regional airport. But this maneuver required a set of extraordinary and prescribed concessions on the part of the city and county, which negotiated in advance with Adams County's commissioners.

PORTLAND

In northwest Oregon, in contrast, Portland basically *was* the region until the last few decades. Today, the city's portion of the entire metropolitan population hardly seems overwhelming. But as of 1990 the city constituted 37 percent of the population in the three Oregon counties (down from 43 percent in 1970). It also included 42 percent of the people living within the area's state-designated urban growth boundary, which is a good approximation of the PMSA's urbanized area.

Many central cities in other metro areas can boast more impressive numbers. What has been more important to Portland's political primacy, however, is the relative lack of a separate institutional presence for its suburban areas. A map of the urbanized area from thirty years ago shows Portland smaller than today, but the handful of other cities appear as tiny satellites in orbit around the central city.[5]

Twenty years ago, while Portland was physically smaller by about a third, the main suburban municipalities were generally two to five times smaller in geographic size than they are now. The only suburbs in the PMSA with more than 15,000 residents in 1970 were Beaverton, at 18,577, and Milwaukie at 16,379; most were below 5,000. While Vancouver had over 40,000 residents in 1970, it was itself a central city, and was obviously not competing in the same state or county arenas as Portland. At the same time, in the Denver PMSA, seven suburbs exceeded the 25,000 population threshold.

Early in its history, the central city in Oregon had an easy time of annexation, using legislation in a Portland-friendly statehouse. As residential and industrial areas expanded in the north, northeast, and southeast portions of the city, its boundaries generally kept pace. In 1906, however, new provisions allowing local home rule were enacted, making an affirmative vote by affected citizens and property owners necessary for annexations (Poulsen 1987, 91).[6] These rules made expansion more difficult for both Portland *and* the suburban cities.

The upshot of the institutional provisions was that most growth was in unincorporated areas. With easily formed special districts providing water and minimal services at low cost, and with county governments picking up some of the slack, Portland's suburbanites were generally unwilling to assume the costs thought to be involved in attaining municipal status. The three decades following 1940 saw only 8,000 residents of the three Oregon counties incorporate into new municipalities, despite growth of 350,000 during the period. Meanwhile, a modest 57,000 were annexed by already established municipalities. Portland continued to expand at a slow, steady pace, picking up 15,262 new residents in the 1960s through annexation. The lack of a serious threat by Portland to the territorial integrity and school systems of outlying areas doubtless contributed to the lack of enthusiasm for suburban incorporations.[7]

In the 1980s, Portland began a more rapid expansion, annexing nearly all the mid-Multnomah County territory up to the Gresham city line. Unlike Denver, no suburban jurisdiction comes close to Portland territorially. Portland has an area and population over six times larger than its nearest PMSA rival, the city of Gresham. Portland also comprises 125 square miles of the 350 miles within the urban growth boundary.

Within its home county of Multnomah, Portland has always accounted for well over half the population. This provides the central city with additional political leverage, since the large county government (which has the second-largest budget of local governments in the PMSA) has been dominated by a Portland perspective. And with county government taking much of the burden of redistributive policy off Portland's hands, the city spends nearly two-thirds of its operating budget on the city-shaping infrastructure functions of sewer, water, planning, community development, and transportation. By contrast, the City and County of Denver spends a large share of its budget on "maintenance" and redistributive activities such as public safety and health and hospitals (*Financial World* 1991).

Thus, when the new suburban era began, Portland was well situated geopolitically. Today, Portland contains most of the older suburban-style neighborhoods in the region, much of the upper-class highlands, and a small but not insubstantial portion of the automobile-oriented suburbs, particularly in its southwestern and easternmost portions.[8] Compared to Denver, Portland has a higher proportion of suburban territory, as indicated by population density statistics. Roughly the same age and physical size as Denver in 1970, Portland had a population density that was 21 percent lower.[9]

Internal Structure of Central City Government

Since being landlocked by the Poundstone Amendment, *Denver* has had severe external restrictions on its capacity to respond to the environment of decentralization. But given those limitations, Denver at least has an internal institutional structure that allows it to make fairly clear (if not always effective) strategic responses to those pressures.

Its government is organized under a "strong-mayor" system, which allows it to avoid some of the challenges of divided authority and internal fragmentation that characterize many other western cities. Of the thirteen members of the city council, two are elected at large while eleven represent districts. Nevertheless, a council position is considered part-time, and the staff is small. With a few notable exceptions, the council has rarely hamstrung mayoral initiative. Aiding in this collaboration is Denver's strong Democratic partisanship. Although local races are officially nonpartisan, elected city officials in recent years have tended to be lopsidedly Democratic.

Portland's internal institutional arrangements—featuring a short ballot and at-large electoral system—also emphasize policy integration. The city's mayor and four commissioners, all elected at large, constitute the city council. Portland's commission form of government was chosen in a 1913 ballot measure. It is the largest American central city to use the commission form, and the largest whose legislative body is not elected from districts. The commissioners and the mayor each head a complex city department composed of numerous related agencies. Except for the auditor, they are the only elected city officials.

Although there is only anecdotal evidence to support the claim, it is likely that citywide elections have helped contribute to less of a NIMBY ("not in my backyard") attitude to land-use change within the city on the part of elected officials. City commissioners have been more inclined to establish power bases in the city agencies they oversee than to engage in sectional fights or neighborhood logrolling.[10] Portland's mayor lacks the independence of Denver's chief executive; the office's major power consists of assigning city bureaus and departments to the portfolios of the various commissioners. On the other hand, it is often easier for a mayor to push legislation through Portland's four commissioners than through Denver's thirteen city council members.

Suburban Governance: Municipalities

Beyond the boundaries of their respective central cities, both regions have multiple and varied general-purpose governments. But their influence is far more pronounced in the Denver metro area.

DENVER

While many areas outside Denver's borders remain unincorporated, municipal government became the norm for most suburbs in the postwar period. Over the last two decades, opposition to school busing for racial desegregation caused many whites to think twice about remaining in Denver (Denver Urban Observatory 1975), and on this count, politically independent suburbs had an advantage, since they were not subject to annexation. The last large-scale suburban incorporation, when 92,000 west-suburban residents banded their neighborhoods together as Lakewood in 1969, was prompted in part by fears of busing. Several major suburban cities with home rule, and a number of smaller towns, now share the political spotlight with Denver, while three major suburban counties have each developed a huge government apparatus.[11]

The political geography of metropolitan Denver is complex and difficult to comprehend without a knowledge of historical events and political rivalries. In addition to the counties, over two dozen municipalities are located within the study area, with several others not far distant. The metro area's political fragmentation index is 0.76, well above average for my sample.

The motivations behind suburban incorporations have varied enormously. Some cities, such as Aurora, Englewood, and Golden, had early origins as distinct towns. Other suburban areas followed more eclectic paths to independence. Edgewater, about one square mile in area, incorporated in 1901 when it was a red-light district adjoining Denver, in order to stay "wet" (Mehle 1992). Commerce City, then an agribusiness and hog-raising area, was founded in 1952 after "a 14-year-old boy allegedly mounted his horse and galloped around like Paul Revere, warning that Denverites were coming to annex the area" (Leonard and Noel 1990, 361). At the other end of the socioeconomic spectrum, Cherry Hills Village, a country-club suburb, went independent in 1945 in order to write a strict zoning ordinance barring anything but single-family, large-lot homes. At one point, it was the nation's third-richest municipality.

In the 1960s, the Colorado legislature tightened incorporation requirements, basically freezing what was by then a well-developed pattern of multiplicity. There were a few subsequent incorporations, most notably the large city of Lakewood in 1969. Today, the municipalities continue to display a tremendous variety in size, socioeconomic status, ideology, and endowment of natural amenities and development. Policy orientations vary widely as well, and local planners tend to toe the line set by their city councils (Ferdinandsen interview 1992).

While the flow of incorporations appears to have stopped, the existing suburban cities have used Colorado's annexation rules to increase their spatial and political influence. When municipalities are able to alter their boundaries, they are given new ammunition to encompass, regulate, and shape development. They can attempt to keep pace with decentralizing economic activity, or take advantage of new opportunities for tax base enhancement in attractive peripheral areas. As Denver's suburban cities attained substantial indigenous political capacity and increasing political muscle in the state legislature, Colorado liberalized its annexation provisions in the 1960s while somewhat tightening incorporation and special-district formation. The idea was that existing municipalities would be best equipped to provide for orderly development when growth pressures pushed beyond their boundaries. Many have availed themselves of opportunities to annex regularly and substantially.

In the 1980s, municipalities in the CMSA annexed more than two hundred square miles (see table 4.4). Despite Denver's unprecedented airport addition, the central city, restricted by the Poundstone rule, managed to grab less than a fifth of all annexed territory. The small cities of Castle Rock and Parker, both in rapidly developing Douglas County, together proved just as prodigious as Denver. The huge suburban city of Aurora nabbed a third of the new area. It now stretches to an eastern border that is roughly one-third of the way between downtown Denver and the Kansas state line. Other suburbs are also very extensive, with some now reaching into more than one county.

Observers describe annexation as an issue shaped largely by land speculators, who propose annexations and development scenarios to revenue-hungry municipalities:

> People with land want to be annexed. They come back every few years for another attempt. Colorado dumps all its tax burden on local government; it says, "You're on your own." Land speculators go to cities and say, "We'll get you a regional mall." And maybe they will. Whoever is lucky enough to get it gets a windfall. (Johnson interview 1992)

TABLE 4.4

Municipal Annexation in the Denver CMSA,

1980–1990

	% of Total Area Annexed
Aurora	32.0
Brighton	4.9
Broomfield	6.3
Castle Rock	12.9
Commerce City	4.4
Denver	18.1
Lakewood	2.4
Parker	5.4
All others	13.9

Source: Denver Regional Council of Governments 1991b, 6.

Developers with options to buy specific sites will play localities off against one another. But "zoned land popping up all over" often proves very difficult to service efficiently (Mugler interview 1992).[12] Overextended municipalities may later appeal to more unitary entities for relief. According to one critic of local land-use regulation, the tendency has been for suburbs to "annex and then come back and say, 'Give us roads.' They go to RTD [the regional transit district] and say, 'Give us buses.' But there are no centers." Thus, transit is not viable (Spitzer interview 1992).

PORTLAND

Portland's difference from Denver is based not so much on the number of suburban cities as on their type. As the city of Portland grew to dominance and maturity during the nineteenth and twentieth centuries, the major outlying cities—Gresham, Lake Oswego, Oregon City, Beaverton, and Hillsboro— were long-standing centers with their own downtowns. Smaller suburbs such as Tualatin, Troutdale, and Sherwood are also descendants of independent towns with small central business districts (Lycan 1987, 99; Seltzer interview 1993b).[13] Of the twenty-two municipalities in the urbanized study area, thirteen incorporated before 1920.[14] The preexistence of business nodes in these towns may have served to mute suburban tendencies toward residential exclusionism, since local merchants tended to lobby actively for new population growth to drum up business (Tobias interview 1993).

While several of the suburbs had long independent histories, a flurry of small upstarts joined the municipal ranks in the 1960s and early 1970s. At that time, Oregon rules required only that 20 percent of the residents of an area sign a resolution for a vote to be called on incorporation. Some areas saw benefits of incorporation in the ability to share state-gathered excise taxes, but for most, land-use control was the motivation.[15] The most substantial defensive incorporation was that of Tigard in 1964, though it hardly matches the weight of Lakewood's 92,000 residents escaping Denver. Tigard's 1990 population was 29,100.

While the number of suburban municipalities in Portland is not much lower than in Denver, the populations of most of the towns are very small. Only Gresham exceeded 50,000 in population as of 1990, and there were no cities in the league of Colorado's Aurora, Arvada, or Lakewood. Eight of the nine Portland-area cities that incorporated after 1950 have populations that are well below 1 percent of the total for the urbanized area. This lack of suburban institutional wherewithal helps explain the area's lower than average political fragmentation index score of 0.56.

Thus, not only is the geopolitical position of the central city somewhat stronger in Portland, but the position of the suburban cities is somewhat weaker. None of the other municipalities has the organizational capacity of Portland to shape urban growth. While cities in the tri-county area do have home rule powers, nearly all the suburban towns have a city manager form of government—and thus part-time elected officials. Only Beaverton has a full-time mayor.[16] Fiscally, too, these are not major league cities. Portland's 1992–1993 budget was $1.28 billion, about twelve times that of the second-largest city, Gresham.

Suburban Governance: Counties

DENVER

The evolving role of Colorado's suburban *county* governments deserves special mention. (Denver's county government, as noted, is the same as its city government.) On paper, the state's counties are little more than administrative areas. Their main stated functions are to oversee the traditional activities of policing and justice, roads, and welfare. "Suburban county governments operate with three elected county commissioners who direct overall policy. Other elected officials, typically an assessor, clerk and recorder, coroner, sheriff and treasurer, are responsible for directing specific parts of a county government's operations" (Greater Denver 1991, n.p.).

In reality, and despite their relatively anachronistic organizational form, county governments around Denver have stepped in to assume major significance. In each of the major suburban counties, the three commissioners oversee huge populations and budgets.[17] Perhaps their most notable decisions involve the response to growth pressures at the unincorporated urban fringe.

On this front, some counties have assumed a more active involvement in land use than others, with different effects. Recently, Adams and Boulder Counties have followed a strategy of trying to accommodate new growth in, or directly adjacent to, existing cities that have the capacity to provide services and infrastructure (Coney interview 1992; Mugler interview 1992). In that way, the county avoids the fiscal strains of servicing scattered pockets of unincorporated development. On the other hand, both Jefferson and Arapahoe Counties have embraced the activist, strong-government "urban county" concept often floated in the literature on metropolitan reform. These counties have tried to stimulate outlying development, and particularly, to pump up their property tax base. Douglas County, still largely rural, has until recently been too overwhelmed by growth to be able to muster a coherent response.

Colorado's large counties correspond superficially to the "regional city" ideal type. With larger, more diverse populations, it is true they have pursued less quirky and varied strategic paths than have municipalities. As land-use arbiters, they are more neutral middlemen, and according to one county planning director, "the corporate personality of the cities is much different from the county" (Coney interview 1992). Counties are less likely to allow job-producing commercial development to be quashed by the protests of individual neighborhoods. Rather, their interest is in stable growth to provide revenues for the public safety and social services needs of an expanding population. The counties that have allowed unincorporated growth have more laissez-faire attitudes regarding the types of growth, compared to the entrepreneurial suburban municipalities, which pursue specific development agendas (Mugler interview 1992; Ferdinandsen interview 1992). Not surprisingly, counties' land uses tend to be more mixed.

But counties have serious structural limitations, which makes the comparison to a regional city less than apt. With their three-person commissions, they are often quite unstable politically from election to election. Counties can lend technical assistance to the municipalities they contain, but they have no real regulatory oversight over cities (Johnson interview 1992; Coney interview 1992). Not controlling sewer, water, or utility resources directly, counties have less ammunition than some cities to bargain with developers (Coney interview 1992). In permitting a great deal of unincorporated growth, Arapahoe and Jefferson Counties have had to allow special districts to acquire substantial authority.

PORTLAND

In overseeing the growth of unincorporated area in the Portland region, two of the three Oregon counties have been granted home rule. This gives them the authority, unlike their counterparts in Colorado, to provide city-type services, and to move beyond the status of mere administrative areas of the state. But acting in such a full-service mode has proved fiscally straining, and Multnomah and Washington Counties have backed away from that role.

Multnomah County, with relatively little new population growth, attempts to maintain and bolster areas of older development. Washington County government has tended to maintain a highly progrowth attitude. In particular, it has done "what was needed to attract the new [electronics] industry's payrolls" (Dodds and Wollner 1990, 57, 150). Clackamas County has been more interested than the other two in being an urban service provider. Historically, it has had a much more substantial proportion of its population in unincorporated areas: In 1986, 35 percent of the county's residents lived in an incorporated city, 25 percent in unincorporated suburban areas, and 40 percent in unincorporated rural areas. Outnumbered, its cities have been either unwilling or (more likely) unable to overcome a system of county service provision that has been shown to result in significant double taxation of cities (Davis and Edner 1993; Seltzer interview 1993b).

Suburban Governance: Special Districts

DENVER

Analyzing development around Denver would be far simpler if counties and municipalities were the only local governments of relevance. But special-purpose governments have taken on a key role in underwriting and responding to growth. Under Colorado law, these entities are termed "metropolitan districts"—even when they are located in a rural setting—if they provide two or more functions.

Although financial requirements for special districts have recently been tightened by the state, these governments were for a long time simple to establish. Developers merely set the boundaries of their proposed district, gave a little land away to friendly parties in order to accumulate the requisite number of electors to vote for the district, approached the county with the district plan, and had it approved in court. These last two stages, interviewees maintain, were almost always pro forma, designed to ensure that the letter of the law had been followed with respect to the number of electors and the drawing of the boundaries.

One public official described the special-district law as "laissez-faire, minimal accountability, easy money. The safeguards weren't there. It was mostly a *procedural*, not a *substantive* requirement." Developers created districts to make possible the almost risk-free provision of streets, lighting, water connections, and other infrastructure. When the area's growth took a nosedive in the

1980s, many planned subdivisions and minicommunities failed to take shape; those districts often went bankrupt, and their bondholders were left holding the bag. But most residential and commercial developments were relatively successful, and creating the necessary districts became little more than another business deal for developers.

Metropolitan districts have become very popular, and politically very important, because of their unique powers to raise development capital in the tax-free bond market (Broderick interview 1992). Moreover, an increasing number of municipalities have almost forced the use of districts for outlying development by refusing to take on the front-end costs associated with new growth. In unincorporated areas, where counties have no real capacity to directly provide infrastructure other than roads, districts are especially necessary. Either way, to make growth "pay its own way" in Colorado frequently means creating additional limited-purpose, low-visibility governments.

These localized districts handle the *provision* of services, but typically must arrange with more inclusive entities (or private firms) for the actual *production* of services (see Advisory Council 1987). In a semiarid region, water supply has been the public good involving the most significant relationships among local and regional units. Water supply in Colorado (and throughout much of the West) features a maze-like system of century-old water rights, special water courts, and cartel-like groups of rural ranchers who control water sources. Specialized water developers attempt to induce rural areas to sell their supplies to serve distant urban areas. Water attorneys labor on behalf of either side (Fayhee 1986; Langfur 1989; Finley 1992; "Private water scheme" 1991).

Water rights can be purchased by public (or private) entities, but may not be condemned by governments for public purposes. This puts a premium on entrepreneurial behavior by the water suppliers of growing urban areas. The City and County of Denver purchased its water supply company in 1918 and "set it up as an independent city water agency, with the philosophy that it would be operated as a business and remain apart from political influences" (Denver Water Department 1990). This Progressivist philosophy was made explicit in the city charter.

Today, water is not truly a "metropolitan" service. But there is a relatively unitary nature to its supply, which grew out of Denver's early position of political dominance in the metropolis. No serious rival to the Denver Water Department has emerged, and its water serves more than half the metropolitan population. The numerous water providers serving suburban areas—sometimes municipal water departments, sometimes metropolitan districts—are generally middlemen, purchasing water from Denver supplies and selling it to residents.

The Denver Water Department has generally been consistent in maintaining its ethos of insulation from city elected officials and its businesslike entrepreneurship. With a staff of over one thousand, it is governed by the Denver Water Board (DWB), a recognized locus of political power in the region. DWB consists of five commissioners, appointed by the mayor for staggered six-year terms.

Before Poundstone, Denver mayors were sometimes able to link extensions of DWB service to annexation (Ferdinandsen interview 1992). But with few formal connections to city hall, the water board has had little incentive to pursue a "Denver first" strategy. Its insulation frees it to expand its bureaucratic domain as the board sees fit. After the completion of the massive Dillon Reservoir project in 1963, DWB eliminated the "blue line" that had delimited its service areas, and began providing water beyond those boundaries. This helped fuel expansion into more far-flung suburbs, leading to a less competitive position for Denver.

A former state senator, John Birmingham, said of DWB, "Those guys are developers by nature. They want to build things because that's what they do best. They prefer to solve problems by building their way out of them" (quoted in Fayhee 1986). In any event, the handful of suburban water providers that have tapped their own independent supply system, such as the city of Aurora, have been responsible for most recent extensions of service.

By comparison, treating the water that leaves Denver-area households has to date proved a less contentious process than supplying the water. The Metropolitan Denver Sewage Disposal District No. 1 (MSDD) provides sewage treatment for about three-quarters of the metro area, in essence the area north of Englewood. It is a federation of local general- and special-purpose governments, and is governed by a board of delegates from the member units.[18] Interview respondents indicated that MSDD—a far less visible entity in the region than DWB—has a primarily passive service role, responding to the demands created by urban growth rather than shaping that growth.

In addition to DWB, MSDD, and the localized districts, Colorado has created a number of public authorities to deal with transportation issues. These units—such as the W-470 Authority, set up to construct and find funding for a suburban freeway—are typically committed to specific projects. They react to perceived infrastructure deficiencies in some portion of the metropolis, rather than considering the full range of interrelated transport and land-use issues. Thus, they fit the mold of limited-purpose, fragmenting governments. Because no local or regional entity was geared toward considering the MSA's air pollution problems, the state has also created a Metro Air Quality Council, a planning agency appointed by the governor. The council has attempted to form regional strategies to attack the problem, but must rely on voluntary actions by the public (Dinner 1992; Knudson 1987).

PORTLAND

In suburban Portland, the picture is quite different. As noted, large suburban municipal governments were in short supply there until very recently. Rather, most growth was unincorporated. Given this context, special districts replaced municipalities as service providers to some degree. The districts flourished in the years after 1915, though recent efforts at consolidation have succeeded in decreasing their numbers. Abbott describes the emergence of a special-district undergrowth in metropolitan Portland, *reacting* to home-building activity rather than leading it:

> Because service districts were almost invisible governments, they were also easily controlled by cliques of suburban businessmen, crossroads cronies, and new householders eager to hold down property taxes. Between 1941 and 1967, the number of water districts in the three Oregon counties grew from 31 to 57, the number of fire districts from eight to 44, and the roster of sanitary districts from zero to 33. In nearly every case, the new districts had minimal influence on land-use patterns. (Abbott 1983, 235; see also Poulsen 1987, 91; MacColl 1979, 658)

Many districts were organized to provide fire protection, drainage, and the like, and thus are of little interest here. If we focus solely on the provision of growth-supporting infrastructure, the institutional picture becomes clearer. Sixty-five public entities deliver water to customers in the PMSA, but Portland's city department supplies about two-thirds of the population. Water (until very recently) has been perceived to be plentiful in this part of Oregon, and has not been the source of the geopolitical turf battles that marked Denver (Eisler 1993; Portland Bureau of Water Works 1989).

Sewer provision is somewhat more fragmented, and includes one departure from Abbott's conclusion of "minimal influence" on growth patterns. This exception came about in the wake of a state-imposed emergency moratorium on new growth in Washington County in 1969. Rapid development had overwhelmed the small sewer systems and septic arrangements in the area, and water quality was seriously threatened. As a result, the county was forced back to the drawing board, and, with input from the development industry, oversaw the establishment of a new Unified Sewerage Agency, governed by the county commissioners. The unified district covered all the county's urbanized area—and beyond. As 550 miles of new sewer lines were built by 1986, vast new stretches of farmland in the west suburbs were opened to development. For this and other reasons, Washington County became the locus of suburban growth in the period that followed.[19]

Since then, special-purpose governance has been further consolidated. The state of Oregon created Metropolitan Boundary Commissions for each of its metro areas in 1969. The boundary commission for the Portland area, though generally a quiet actor, has encouraged special districts to merge, and has generally forbidden the formation of new districts. The commission must ensure economical service provision and compliance with approved comprehensive plans, and is given veto authority over expansions of water and sewer services (Poulsen 1987, 94–95; Kelley interview 1993).

In recent decades, by and large, special districts in metropolitan Portland have been set up in reactive rather than proactive fashion. In short, they cannot be used as a mechanism to bypass municipalities in order to initiate fringe growth. Developers can build in areas that are serviced, but they cannot hope to create a new entity to service outlying areas. As one development firm executive puts it, "Here, if you're inside the Urban Growth Boundary, there's a service provider. . . . I don't know of any effect [of special districts on development]" (Cain interview 1993).

Integrative Institutions: Transit Districts

Districts performing one or two narrow functions do not have to consider the range of political debate that a general-purpose government does. However, the case of metropolitan transit districts is somewhat different from infrastructure districts, since the efficient provision of public transportation depends on supportive land uses. Thus, entrepreneurial water or sewer districts, even on a metropolitan scale, may see benefits in encouraging growth at the urban periphery; in contrast, transit districts, which have to serve the scattered growth likely to result from such a policy, are biased toward land-use policies that favor existing downtowns and dense neighborhoods. Thus, regional transit authorities may be considered integrative metropolitan institutions, though they lack the scope of multipurpose regional governments.

With *Denver's* private bus system a shambles in 1969, the area faced a potential urban transportation crisis. The Colorado General Assembly, at the prodding of Denver's Chamber of Commerce, created the Regional Transportation District in 1969. While the old bus system was taken over by Denver City and County and eked out an existence, the legislation required voter approval of a public transportation bond issue by July 1974 before RTD could commence operations. A 1973 referendum gave the go-ahead for RTD and allowed $425 million in debt to be issued, to be backed by a regionwide sales tax "to provide for the local share of designing, constructing and operating a $1.56 billion multi-modal transit system" (RTD n.d., 6). As the sole transit operator in its twenty-three hundred square mile district, RTD runs bus lines throughout the urbanized Denver/Boulder area, and also to a handful of small outlying communities. The legislation provided RTD with a dedicated sales tax, currently set at 0.6 percent.

The district originally had a twenty-one-member board, ten of whom were appointed by the mayor of Denver, reflecting the primacy of that city in the existing bus system. Nine other members were appointed by suburban county commissions, with two at-large members selected by the balance of the board (RTD n.d., 3). A 1980 election brought approval of a referendum that expressed some popular disgruntlement with the large agency by changing its governing structure. Henceforth, RTD was to be governed by an elected fifteen-member board representing districts. The new board initially overextended RTD financially by commencing new bus routes in growing suburban areas that lacked transit-supportive land-use patterns. It also experienced divisiveness, as various factions supported light rail construction in different geographic quadrants of the metro area. Interference by board members in staff activities caused agency morale to decline, and many staffers took advantage of a new early retirement plan to bail out in the late 1980s (Wells 1990b). Thus, the transit district began to replicate some of the fragmentation of local government in the metro area. Until quite recently, RTD was unable to muster much political credibility or to initiate transit modes that could potentially reshape development patterns in suburbia.[20]

In *Portland*, too, the dawn of the new suburban era found transit services financially strapped. Bus ridership hit a low of 16 million trips in 1969. Paralleling Denver, the state created a Tri-County Metropolitan Transportation District (or Tri-Met), to take over for crisis-ridden local and private providers. While Denver's RTD uses sales taxes for the local component of its revenue base, Portland lacked a sales tax precedent. Thus, Tri-Met was given access to a dedicated revenue stream that is perhaps more hidden from the view of the everyday public. It levies a payroll tax on employers, set at 0.62 percent of total payroll (Friedman 1993, 150). Tri-Met had a $395 million budget in 1992–1993, compared to RTD's estimated 1993 expenditures of $257 million.

Integrative Institutions: Regional Government

Regional government provides perhaps the clearest contrast in government structure between the Denver and Portland metro areas. Making the comparison all the more pointed was the 1975 decision of the National Academy of Public Administration to award each of these regions a small grant, funded by the Department of Housing and Urban Development. The grant's purpose was to underwrite a local panel's study of options for metropolitan reorganization. At the time, however, Portland already had extensive experience with regional entities, and the geopolitical patterns made it more predisposed to use the HUD-funded study as a springboard toward further experiments in regionalism. Denver's advocates of metro government, hampered in challenging institutionally strong local interests, were forced into compromises that did little to advance their cause.

DENVER

While Denver's multiple municipalities, annexation rules, sales taxes, and special districts reinforce localism and fragmentation, there have been several experiments with entities operating at a more unitary spatial scale. Most have been charged with a single task, such as funding and building a new baseball stadium or highway. These public authorities tended to muster less political opposition because their work was perceived in positive-sum terms. Less common is a type of public entity that deals with issues that have clearly perceived distributional consequences for development in the metro area. These units have by and large been seriously constrained in the ammunition that state legislators or suburban voters have been willing to grant them.

The Denver Regional Council of Governments, or DRCOG ("Doctor Cog" to locals), is the most significant of these units. The designated metropolitan planning organization (MPO) for the Denver region, it has its origins in the earlier Inter-County Regional Planning Commission, created by the legislature in 1956. As its name indicates, DRCOG is a membership organization of local governments (unlike some MPOs, which are freestanding in character). Each county and municipality selects one voting delegate to DRCOG's governing board—since Denver is both a city and a county, it is entitled to two. The board operates largely by committee. Membership dues of participating governments provide a financial base for the council, with state and federal funds (mostly federal transportation planning grants) providing its major funding (Mugler interview 1992).

Councils of governments have shown severe limitations since their heyday. Initially supported (and required) under the provisions of federal program planning grants, the nation's COGs cut back activity as those grants were cut back, beginning in the late Carter years. The requirement that they evaluate grant proposals by local governments (the so-called A-95 review) was dropped during the Reagan administration. By one account:

> The 1960s version of regionalism was largely mandated by the federal and
> state governments, and once the A-95 clearinghouse function was lost, the

COGs found they had little to do. Some of the more aggressive COGs developed new and responsive agendas; some became providers of technical assistance, primarily to small governments; and, some became empty shells.
(McCoy and Gallis 1993)

While DRCOG cannot be characterized as an empty shell, its direct service
responsibilities are few and minor. One of DRCOG's most useful activities is
the preparation of a substantial number of demographic, economic, and
environmental reports, and the related data collection.

DRCOG's most significant responsibility, however, has been the preparation of the region's transportation plan, including highway and transit projects. Any project for which a metro-area entity seeks federal funds must be
included in this Transportation Improvement Program. Designated by the
state as the regional planning commission in 1973, DRCOG also has responsibility for creating a master plan for physical development.

Nevertheless, DRCOG's political visibility is low, and it has been limited in
its capacity to influence land-use decision making in the counties and municipalities. More than one interviewee described the council as a "paper tiger."
(Or as one responded when asked about DRCOG's role, "Well, it's a great
place to hold meetings.") Nor has DRCOG been able to venture far into the
dangerous waters of *equity*—in fiscal health, service quality, and regional responsibilities—among the many jurisdictions. Given its constitutive membership, none of this is surprising politically. Denver, with only two of forty-five
votes, has at times complained that DRCOG is a forum for suburbs to gang up
on the central city. DRCOG's lack of efficacy in a metropolis that continues to
be rife with regional problems has not won it many outspoken admirers.
Former governor Richard Lamm complained in 1989, "For all the money
we've put into DRCOG, the results are marginal. When you try to list the
dynamic things DRCOG has done, nobody can think of anything" (quoted in
Leonard and Noel 1990, 475).

It is possible, however, that the council's profile will be boosted by new
federal transportation initiatives. But for now, DRCOG relies primarily on
persuasion. It cannot enforce its recent Metro Vision plan for the region's
development, but is instead "trying to make locals want to follow the plan"
(Mugler interview 1992).

Thus far, the Denver area has not developed a freestanding metropolitan
government. In 1972, the state legislature sanctioned the creation of a metropolitan service authority—in effect, a super-special district at the regional
level. According to the Service Authority Act of 1972, it was permitted to
provide services that could include water, sewage, solid waste disposal, transportation, fire protection, housing, cultural facilities, management services,

and others, in any combination (DRCOG 1988a). Regional planning and the preparation of a "comprehensive development guide" would be a mandatory function for such an authority, as would review of county and municipal plans and grant or loan applications. But proposals along these lines have been nixed or watered down by local officials, who feared a loss of home rule, or by DRCOG itself, which felt threatened with extinction. Other officials worried that a new metropolitan authority would hinder the regional service districts already functioning, such as MSDD and the Regional Transportation District. Compromise plans—including one developed under the National Academy of Public Administration grant—have proposed giving just a few minor powers to the proposed authority; these plans have twice been defeated in the re-quired referenda.

In the final analysis, these potential reforms foundered on the shoals of localism and distrust of government. But the proposals can also be faulted for a lack of purpose. The compromise proposals, developed by study committees composed in large part of local public officials, did not include key issue areas that made for the most conflict between existing local governments—air qual-ity, transportation, and water supply. In attempting to write politically palat-able proposals, these committees failed to address the main shortcomings of Denver's regional governance. Voters were being asked to add another unit, without clear areas of responsibility, to a complex system of metropolitan government.[21]

PORTLAND

A major departure from Denver is the presence in Portland of the nation's only directly elected regional government, Metro, which in 1990 had authority over an area of 1.03 million residents.[22] Metro was established as the Metro-politan Service District (MSD) in 1970. Given fairly open-ended powers, it expanded tentatively from its small early role. Portland officials had initially been uncomfortable with MSD, fearing the city might lose its profit-making regional water system to a metropolitan service provider. "In general, the creation of the MSD violated Portland's self-image as *the* governmental entity with regional interests and concerns" (Abbott 1987b, 200). But Portland was not to fear, as the service district felt its way along uneasily in an institutional environment where it lacked a clear role. It initially took over two thankless tasks—running the regional zoo and disposing of solid waste. It also had police powers, property and income tax authority, and the ability to issue bonds (Poulsen 1987, 94).

Meanwhile, an unelected council of governments, formed in 1969, worked alongside MSD. The Columbia Region Association of Governments (CRAG), created to meet federal requirements as a metropolitan planning organization, described itself as a "permanent forum" for raising regional issues and adopting regional plans. By referendum in 1973, CRAG was transformed into a regional planning district, with mandated membership of local governments. In stark contrast to the unit voting on DRCOG, voting in CRAG was *weighted by population*.

State legislation added to the picture with other important institutions of metropolitan governance. First, the Metropolitan Boundary Commission was chartered in 1969. Thereafter, incorporations, annexations, and special-district formation would be subject to close scrutiny. Second, the district funding the Port of Portland was expanded to the three-county area by state legislative action in 1974. Previously limited to Multnomah County, it had been "necessarily Portland-centered," and helped bring industrial jobs nearer to poor workers living there (Abbott 1983, 254). The state legislation enabled it to take on new industrial development activities at the regional level.[23] The Port of Portland's budget exceeds half a billion dollars. Third, in 1981, the state expanded the jurisdiction of the Portland Development Commission (PDC), formerly Portland's urban renewal authority. PDC was given the new responsibility of coordinating economic development in the tri-county area. Having a regional entity recruit business obviates some of the competitive instincts of counties and localities.[24]

If regional governments seemed to be proliferating in northwest Oregon, changes in the late 1970s brought important consolidation. The 1975 National Academy of Public Administration grant led to a study commission proposal for a two-tier system of local government (Harrigan 1993, 389–90). The result was the first of two referendum votes boosting the metropolitan government's power, as voters approved merging CRAG into MSD in 1978. At this stage, MSD had "broad planning authority to set goals through 'functional plans,' but not to supplant localities as a land regulator" (Abbott 1994, 212). In 1992, voters renamed MSD simply "Metro," and gave it broad new grants of authority as a home rule government. While it was always informally called "Metro," I refer to the regional government in its days prior to home rule as "MSD," in order to emphasize the distinction.

Names aside, the regional government has acquired a wide array of functions. Metro operates the area's zoo and its publicly owned sports and entertainment facilities, and it constructed and operated the $85 million Oregon Convention Center. It also manages garbage disposal and recycling; acquires "greenspaces" for preservation; plans for natural disasters; and collects and distributes extensive regional data. More important, its land-use powers are more extensive than most regional governments. It is given sole authority to establish and manage the region's urban growth boundary (subject to state oversight), and has the power to write functional plans that can override local comprehensive plans. MSD (and earlier, CRAG) did the region's water and sewer planning; local governments must make their plans consistent with Metro documents in order to receive state or federal funding. Metro also engages in a wide variety of transportation planning, which has had far more effect than DRCOG's planning efforts. In 1988, Metro assumed the authority to appoint members of the Metro Boundary Commission, consolidating its oversight of local land-related decisions.

Metro had an annual budget for 1992–1993 of $209 million—about fifty times that of DRCOG's. Its revenues come from federal and state grants and from per capita contributions by local governments, but also from excise taxes levied at Metro's garbage transfer stations, bonds, a lodger's tax, and admissions charged at its facilities. This broader revenue stream enhances its capabilities, compared to Denver's council of governments.

The contrast is immediately apparent to a visitor. DRCOG rents some space in an older office building north of downtown Denver. Metro, by comparison, bought a former Sears department store building in Portland's Lloyd District, and then spent $11.5 million to redesign and elaborately renovate it (Tax Supervising 1993; Metro n.d.; Portland Future 1990, 112; Seltzer interview 1993b). In short, metropolitan government is active and politically credible in the Portland area; it is minimal and pro forma in Denver.

The Fiscal System: Implications for Land Use

Up until this point, I have addressed the "political structure" considerations involved in measuring political fragmentation, as it was calculated in chapter 3. But taxing and spending arrangements among state and local governments are another facet of the organization of urban political economies, as field research in Portland and Denver have shown.

DENVER

Overlaid on the multiplicity of governments in the Denver area is a fiscal pattern that emphasizes local autonomy. Local governments in the region spend more per capita than in comparable western metropolitan areas, and receive more in redistributed revenues from their state. Expenditures by local governments are about a third higher per resident in the Denver area than in metropolitan Portland (see appendix 1).

However, Colorado's direct *state* spending is lower than many others. In 1990, Colorado spent $997 per capita, compared to an average for states in the United States of $1,141; Oregon spent $1,218.[25] Thus, the state is significantly weaker in Colorado in relation to localities than it is in Oregon. This can be expected to intensify fragmented land-use control in the Denver MSA.

Another aspect of the Denver fiscal environment is not captured in the political fragmentation index. Colorado municipalities differ from those in many other states by their heavy reliance on local *sales* taxes. The state grants them substantial discretion in setting sales tax rates. Total sales tax rates in 1992 varied from 3.8 percent to 7.8 percent in Denver-area localities (Greater Denver 1992).

In combination with annexation rules, the fiscal system makes outlying development more feasible for commercial developers, because local regulators see sales taxes as more politically palatable than property taxes. Sales taxes burden shoppers primarily, many of whom are nonresidents, while property taxes apply to politically active property owners. The favorable treatment of commercial development tends to inhibit orderly growth patterns, according to Steve Wilson, an official of the metropolitan area's Homebuilders Association, since cities often go into all-out competition to land a new retail center. "The communities will go to war for the opportunity to have creative ways to annex commercial property, whether or not it makes good land-use planning sense" (quoted in Wells 1991). Another critic claims the sales tax encourages "competing for the K-Mart on the outside of town" (Spitzer interview 1992). A former county commissioner says reliance on sales tax produces a "tremendous distortion," and encourages the overbuilding of roads and water lines in some locations. Municipalities, he said, respond to the anticipated revenue, and since the state shares in the kitty, "cities and the state are partners in this growth scenario around the sales tax" (Ferdinandsen interview 1992).

The city of Thornton, which stretches into the northern fringes of metro Denver, illustrates the pattern. In 1992, the owner of a "furniture warehouse store" in the north metro area sought incentives as he looked to relocate his business. Arvada and Thornton emerged in a competition in which the latter offered location subsidies amounting to about $3.5 million (Ferdinandsen interview 1992). Thornton has also developed a "Thornton Town Center." Despite its pretensions to being a cutting-edge "suburban activity center," the Town Center consists of a mall (half-empty in late 1992) and associated office development, and has no residential component. It was pursued, a respondent says, almost solely to enhance Thornton's sales tax base.

The situation is different for county governments, however. State rules require voter approval before a county may institute a sales tax. As a result, counties depend on property taxes for the lion's share of their revenue. Accordingly, they have pursued more industrial zoning than the retail-oriented cities (DRCOG 1980). Jefferson County, which has about half its property taxes generated by residential uses, and half by industrial or commercial uses, thus pursues a balance of land-use types. Its commissioners lured Martin Marietta decades ago to launch its military-industrial sector, and have more recently (in cooperation with Coors Brewing Company) pursued a Japanese sake manufacturing plant (Ferdinandsen interview 1992).

PORTLAND

In the Portland PMSA, there is no sales tax—local *or* state. While the Denver area gathered one-quarter of local taxes from levies on "sales and gross receipts" as of 1976–1977, the corresponding figure in Portland was 2.5 percent.[26] Rather than having an orientation toward sales taxes and retail development, the Portland area depends heavily on property taxes. Due to the eccentricities of Oregon tax law, however, municipal governments do not stand to gain revenue by attracting new businesses into their existing boundaries. Each Oregon city has a set total, confusingly referred to as its tax "base," which is the maximum it is permitted to collect in property taxes. The tax base is equal to the city's tax revenue in 1916 (or the date the city was incorporated, if more recent), plus a "natural" annual increase. The tax base can be increased only by referendum, or proportionally as new lands are annexed.[27] Thus, inducing a new factory or office building to locate in town will not increase the municipal treasury—though it probably will reduce the property tax rates of existing residents by a small amount. Overall, the local tax system appears to have a relatively neutral effect on development patterns in the PMSA.

However, a new complication appeared in the Oregon fiscal environment in 1990. After nineteen unsuccessful referenda seeking to reform local property taxation or school funding, a ballot measure enacting mandatory tax limitation passed with 52 percent approval. After a phase-in over several years, by 1995–1996 Ballot Measure 5 limited local property taxes (including all components—school and special districts, cities, and counties) to $15 per $1,000 of real market value. One-third of that amount goes to the local school district. For sake of comparison, the 1992–1993 rate in the city of Portland was $23.21 per $1,000. While the long-term effects of Measure 5 remain to be seen—some of the lost funds are being replaced by the state—the measure seems likely to place a greater impetus on recruiting new nonresidential growth to municipalities (see Friedman 1993, 149, 153–62).[28]

The States' Roles in Regulating Urbanization

We have seen the differences in *local* and *regional* institutional arrangements between Denver and Portland. An additional consideration is the role of state government, ostensibly the creator of the local public sector. Are the political

culture, partisan composition, or programmatic agendas of Oregon so notably different from Colorado as to systematically affect local land-use policy
preferences? The answer, I argue, is no. However, particular pieces of legislation in Oregon *have* created a different local regulatory process. Oregon's land
conservation laws set a framework of goals and guidelines for local land-use
decision making, while allowing substantial local discretion in addressing
those goals. Metropolitan political arrangements have distinctively shaped
Portland's response to the state land-use framework, as I show in chapter 6.

Comparing State Political Systems

Portland and Denver have each had ongoing traditions of both progressive
and conservative politics, based in large part on state initiative and referendum systems enabling frequent populist impulses of both varieties. In Daniel
Elazar's well-known categorization of state and local political culture, both the
Denver and Portland areas are given a dominant "moralistic" strain, though
in Denver it is mixed with elements of "individualism." As states, Oregon and
Colorado are both classified as moralistic. In both states, Elazar concludes,
political conflict is organized along axes that include sectionalism and a met-
ropolitan/rural split. Jack L. Walker's index of program innovation in the
states placed Oregon eighth and Colorado ninth. Klingman and Lammers's
index of state policy liberalism rates Oregon sixth and Colorado ninth (Elazar
1972, 106, 150, 194–95; Abbott 1994, 208).[29]

Political parties lack organizational strength in Colorado, and are even
weaker in Oregon. Maverick candidates have been common in both states.[30]
Oregon tends to vote like Colorado in presidential elections—in recent decades, generally Republican (though both went for Clinton in 1992, and Du-
kakis squeaked out a victory in Oregon in 1988). At the state level, when
Oregonians elected Barbara Roberts to succeed Neil Goldschmidt as governor
in 1990, it was the first time since 1883 that one Democrat had succeeded
another. Goldschmidt and Roberts reversed the traditional pattern of Democratic legislature and Republican governor. Colorado has tended in recent
decades toward Republican legislatures and Democratic governors.

In both states, parties are relatively weak and interest groups strong and
engaged. Brace and Straayer uncover a pattern of former state officials serving
as paid lobbyists in Colorado. In a companion essay, Hedrick and Zeigler see it
as "ironic that Oregonians, so immersed in the western populist ideals of
controlling government, have given impetus to a system that actually tends to
be most responsive to Madisonian factions" (Brace and Straayer 1987; Hedrick
and Zeigler 1987, 105, 111ff.). In both states, real estate interests are among the
most highly organized. All in all, programmatic action by state parties cannot

explain why land-use regulation takes such distinctive forms in the two metro areas under study.

State Planning in Oregon:
Setting Goals and Guidelines for Local Regulators

While the political environment in Oregon is not vastly different from that of Colorado, Oregon has enacted specific pieces of legislation that have important implications for land-use regulators in metropolitan Portland.[31]

As Knaap and Nelson note:

> Before 1973 land use was determined in Oregon as in every other state: land use changed when private developers purchased land and obtained building permits and urban services from local governments. After 1973 the process of land development in Oregon changed dramatically. . . . Every local government was required to prepare a comprehensive land use plan, every plan had to be approved by the State Land Conservation and Development Commission, and every local government had to make land use decisions consistent with its comprehensive plan. (Knaap and Nelson 1992, 39)

Indeed, the 1973 passage of Senate Bill 100, a major land conservation program, put the state in the business of establishing goals and guidelines for local land-use regulation. The debate in the Oregon legislature over the bill was not partisan, but rather divided along metropolitan/rural lines. Legislators from the Willamette Valley—the most highly urbanized part of the state, but also the section with the most productive farmland—used their superior numbers to defeat representatives from southern and eastern Oregon, who preferred the land-use status quo. The law's ultimate effects on governance and land development in the Portland PMSA have been significant.[32]

The law's origins lay in concerns about the loss of fertile farmland, and cases of untrammeled development in environmentally sensitive areas. Accordingly, the focus of Senate Bill 100 was on rural lands. Nevertheless, the emphasis on land use had tremendous implications for Oregon's urban areas. First, the new law required that every privately owned acre of land in the state be covered by a municipal or (in unincorporated areas) county comprehensive plan. This requirement meant that zoning would extend over the entire state, thereby forcing governments in rural areas to regulate land in advance of development pressures from a spreading metropolis. Second, the law mandated that *counties* would coordinate and reconcile local plans, except in the Portland area. There, no single county spanned the urbanized area, and the *metropolitan planning organization* was given the task instead. This initially meant CRAG, but the coordination process was completed by MSD when CRAG was merged with that unit in 1978.

Third, the act created a new state agency, the Land Conservation and Development Commission (LCDC) to formulate state land-use goals and guidelines and to determine whether local plans were in compliance. In other words, LCDC set standards, but Oregon's 36 counties and 241 cities wrote the actual plans, issued building permits, constructed water lines, and performed the other day-to-day duties involved in land-use regulation. The legislation established that the governor would appoint the LCDC's seven members. After much committee work and public forums, LCDC arrived at fourteen goals, later expanded to nineteen.

The most prominent and controversial goals were those stressing farmland preservation, housing opportunity, and "an orderly and efficient transition from rural to urban land uses." A major mechanism to attain these goals was the requirement that each metro area (and each freestanding city) establish an urban growth boundary (UGB). The UGB was to encircle a supply of land sufficient to serve twenty years of growth. Beyond the UGB, the vast majority of land had to be zoned for "exclusive use" farming or forestry. (Owners of exclusive use lands qualify for greatly reduced property tax assessments.) The flip side is that jurisdictions inside the UGB must demonstrate to the LCDC that their plans make sufficient accommodations for the anticipated level of residential and business growth. These UGB and exclusive use provisions, as part of the state goals, have been described as a "constitution" of sorts for local land-use decision making (Knaap and Nelson 1992, 25; Leonard 1983, 13).

The acceptance of a local plan by LCDC is referred to as *acknowledgment*. In the period before a plan was acknowledged, the state had the power to review each land-use decision of the local government in question—for example, rezonings. Lack of local progress toward acknowledgment could be punished by a cut-off in cigarette, liquor, and gas tax revenues, which the state normally shared with localities. After acknowledgment, the plan was self-enforcing, since the approved zoning determined land uses. Any local modifications of plans, or attempts to allow variances from approved zoning, would be subject to state oversight. In addition, the state periodically reviews each plan.[33]

Despite these substantial controls, we must not conclude that LCDC has a "slow growth" mentality. Rather, as Jeffrey Leonard explains, it is a growth *management* agency. "While the Oregon program attempts to ensure that urban development is contiguous and that rural land is preserved, it does not attempt to direct how much growth takes place—either statewide or in particular areas—or what kinds of development a locality may accommodate" (Leonard 1983, 13). The state system merely requires that lands be reserved for exclusive agricultural use, with other lands designated as urbanized or "urbanizable." In this last category are unserviced areas designated for future rezonings that will allow development, once the urbanized areas become "built out"—that is, once their supply of buildable land is exhausted (Knaap and Nelson 1992, 106). In this way, land values can accurately register the development potential of fringe lands. Developers seeking service extensions into urbanizable areas can build only on properties that are reasonably contiguous to existing built-up areas.

Although sometimes attacked as antibusiness, the urban growth boundary rule has withstood challengers. In the 1980s, the Portland metropolis was the fastest-growing area in the country for the electronics industry, and most of these firms were accommodated by suburban sites. Of particular interest is Washington County's "Sunset Corridor," which is sometimes cited as the most successfully planned high-tech corridor in the country. William Fulton writes: "Oregon was able to use the law to its advantage in actually encouraging high-tech businesses along the Sunset Corridor. The urban growth boundaries don't just require cities to determine where growth *won't* go. They also demand that they determine and plan for where growth *will* go" (Fulton 1986, 11). In fact, local growth moratoria within UGBs are illegal. The state also requires local governments to issue a decision on an application for a permit within one hundred and twenty days. By way of contrast, complex real estate projects often require one to two *years* to gain permits in the Seattle area (Cameron 1990). Developer Barry Cain, who works in both Oregon and Washington says, "We're not as purposely delayed here [the Portland area] as in Seattle" (Cain interview). Similarly, the state mandates that localities must have "consolidated" systems of development regulation. This rule has been an impetus for counties and municipalities to establish one-stop permitting and departments of community development (Rohse 1987, 20). Thus, while bounding urbanization geographically, LCDC also forces cities to maximize buildable, serviced land. So long as they respect these guidelines, LCDC generally has allowed cities "broad local play" (Pemble interview).

Overall, Gerrit Knaap and Arthur C. Nelson argue that state planning can be a "positive—though perhaps minor" force *favoring* economic development in Oregon, since it contributes to the preservation of amenities and provides a degree of "certainty in the regulatory environment" (Knaap and Nelson 1992, 5; see also S. Gordon 1988). Illustrating this point was former Republican governor Victor Atiyeh's attempts in the early 1980s to convince Japanese electronics firms to locate in his state. Atiyeh touted Oregon's land-use system as a comparative advantage, "promising them specific industrial sites for their plants that are near affordable housing and recreation, yet free from confrontations with angry homeowners" (Townslee 1985).

The political dynamics of the state land-use regime conjure up images of the differences between the regional city and fragmented metropolis. As Knaap and Nelson write:

> Compared to purely local systems of land use control, combined state and local systems of control enfranchise a wider geographic constituency. Perhaps, then, the major structural difference between planning in Oregon and planning in other states is the ability of nonlocal interests in Oregon to participate in local land use decision making throughout the state. (1992, 36)

The authors cite "exclusionists"—homeowners and neighborhood associations—as examples of groups less successful at the state than at the local level. "Because undesirable land uses wind up in somebody's backyard, NIMBY interests are much more difficult to mobilize at the state level. At the local level, it's we against them; at the state level, it's we against us" (Knaap and Nelson 1992, 205).

One "nonlocal interest" that positioned itself early to influence the land-use regulation system is a public interest law firm of environmental and planning advocates, calling itself 1000 Friends of Oregon. Created with the support of former governor Tom McCall, the group started with a staff of two, operating in the executive director's home. It consisted of volunteers and cooperating attorneys, and served as a watchdog group by issuing reports and bringing lawsuits under the provisions of state law and LCDC rules. By 1992, 1000 Friends had a twenty-two-person staff, a budget of $2 million, and a national leadership position among growth management activist organizations.

The group helped the state planning program overcome referendum challenges in 1976, 1978, and 1982. The first challenge was backed in part by developers unhappy about growth boundaries and exclusive agriculture zones. After a resounding loss, development interests switched sides, focusing their energies on the enforcement of antiexclusionary housing goals for areas within the UGBs. In so doing, they cemented a strong and unusual alliance between environmentalist and prodevelopment interest groups. In recent years, 1000 Friends and the Homebuilders Association of Metropolitan Portland have banded together to issue reports and to press Metro to take on a stronger land-use role (Law 1992).

Overall, it appears that Oregon's development interests are prepared to play by the rules, so long as those rules ensure that growth will be accommodated. Real estate and industry groups have set up an Oregon Business Planning Council to monitor local plans for compliance on *its* concerns. The group's spokesperson says, "We're basically LCDC groupies; we're prepared to go in there and use their goals when they work for us" (quoted in Leonard 1983, 24).

One business commentator explains the relative lack of controversy over Oregon's growth boundary this way: "Companies building new plants mainly want to know what the rules are" (quoted in Fulton 1986, 11). This neatly sums up not only the politics of the situation but also the manner in which institutional arrangements help shape development behavior.

With powerful interest groups arrayed against them at the state level, municipalities have learned to live within the state guidelines. Reportedly, there have been no subdivisions or shopping centers built in freestanding or "greenfield" locations in Oregon since the UGBs have taken effect (Kasowski n.d.). LCDC maintains its vigilance, reviewing local comprehensive plans at least once every seven years and requiring updates as necessary. Reflecting the position of Oregon with respect to its municipalities, L. B. Day, the first chair of LCDC, once said of local governments, "We've had some problems with them and had to whip them into line" (DeGrove 1984, 249–50) The contrast with Colorado's localism could not be sharper.

State Planning in Colorado:
Encouraging and Assisting Local Regulators

Colorado has also had a strong environmental movement. Conservationists helped turn back the decision to host the 1976 Olympic Games, and more recently helped force the cancellation of a planned massive water diversion project intended to supply the Denver area's future needs. In the 1960s, Colorado's Front Range experienced rapid growth, increased smog, and a boom in vacation homes. A majority of Coloradans were nonnatives by the early 1970s, and there was a sense among many new residents of the Front Range that land-use control by old-timer locals was not capable enough (DeGrove 1984, chap. 7).

With environmentalism growing, the state General Assembly felt pressure to do something about growth. In 1970, it passed the Colorado Land Use Act, which established a Land Use Commission. The commission was directed to study and develop legislation on land management and planning. Aiming primarily at marginal developments in low-service or environmentally fragile areas, the commission pushed localities and counties to plan and institute subdivision regulations.

However, the tradition of home rule in Colorado made more aggressive state policy difficult. Subsequent proposals for state land-use control were defeated in the legislature in the mid-1970s, under intense lobbying by counties and localities. Even when a Republican governor pledged action on growth management in 1973—one year before a reelection campaign—he was unable to get a strong bill through a Republican legislature. The Land Use Commission, however, was given some additional review powers and money to distribute to local governments for planning and technical assistance. At the same time, another new statute gave a very broad grant of authority to local governments for growth management and regulatory activities (DeGrove 1984, 291–303).

These legislative developments emphasized bolstering the capabilities of local governments rather than superimposing a new level of regulation upon local control or replacing it altogether. The Land Use Commission was often viewed with suspicion by legislators, many of whom had backgrounds in local government, and it received only small appropriations.

Interestingly, the legislature's actions had required *counties* to enact subdivision regulations (though the requirement was substantively weak), while *municipalities* were under no such obligation. According to one individual active in county politics, this leeway "has encouraged developers to play cities off against counties, and developers will play games with a particular city and work out a way in which their land can be annexed by the city to get the zoning that they want from the city government in a kind of prior commitment" (J. K. Smith, former assistant director of Colorado Counties, Inc., quoted in DeGrove 1984, 294). Thus, some developers could manipulate the situation. Others, however, felt bedeviled by the uncertainty of a system where the state and localities shared authority over land use, but where the role of each was unclear (DeGrove 1984, 316).

By the late 1970s the commission was under attack by Republicans, who controlled both legislative houses and sought to disrupt incursions into home rule by the activist governor Lamm. Since the commission had developed a reputation for political ineptness and ineffectiveness, Lamm was reluctant to push it to the forefront, and it was drastically defunded. Acting unilaterally instead, Lamm issued an executive order in September 1979, promulgating a set of so-called Human Settlement Policies to be used as guidelines for "decisions and action of all boards, commissions, and principal departments of the state government" (Judd 1986, 191). The policies were also to have been used in reviewing local applications for state and federal grants.

Lamm intended to promote clustered growth, with growth centers to be specified in regional plans. He also called for local governments to share in bearing the costs associated with new growth, such as affordable housing. Lamm claimed he wanted to "reduce our dependence upon consumptive, cost-inefficient lifestyles" (quoted in DeGrove 1984, 328). At the same time, he began a "citizen's crusade," dubbed the Front Range Project, to try to form a coalition for growth management and land-use controls. Forums with sympathetic experts and business people drew extensive participation and press coverage in 1980 (Judd 1986, 194).

But it became clear that state growth control would have consequences for the balance of power between Denver and its suburbs. As Dennis Judd notes,

> business and political leaders promoting controls tended to reside in or were identified with Denver City proper: their motivation was to prevent competition with the downtown and to promote "compatible" development outside the city. In contrast, suburban officials and developers were quite anxious to develop their own economic bases, and they cared little if this was compatible or competitive with Denver. (Judd 1986, 194)

Not surprisingly, Lamm's unilateral move led to a partisan war of words and maneuvers with the Republican-controlled legislature, which directed state agencies not to act on the policies. Under conditions of government gridlock, Lamm rescinded the Human Settlement Policies just over a year after issuing them.

Another attempt at state land-use regulation came in 1991 and 1992 in the form of a bill in the General Assembly, sponsored by the former mayor of Fort Collins. The bill was modeled on Oregon's land-use law, and aimed to steer growth into the growth areas along the Front Range, in suburban downtowns and areas served by mass transit (Wells 1991). The actual plans were to be drawn up by localities, which would need to meet stated state goals (Act for Land 1991).[34] Proponents said the goals would be general enough that municipalities could pursue their own goals within the context of the new law. A commission patterned on Oregon's LCDC was to have review power over the local plans.

Growth interests did not like the proposal. According to Steve Wilson, director of government and technical affairs for metro Denver's Homebuilders Association, "Planning proposals and regulator proposals that fly in the face of economic realities really have no success . . . in having any beneficial effect on land use. What really drives building is the economy and tax policy" (quoted in Wells 1991). Apparently taking such arguments to heart, legislators killed the bill, under lobbying pressure from local officials and shopping center developers.[35]

Thus, while a small "issue network" of information elites and sympathetic public officials has been able to put state planning on the policy agenda, it does not yet have the political wherewithal to get legislation passed. No "window of opportunity" has yet presented itself to help bring the matter to the forefront (see Heclo 1978; Kingdon 1984). Growth plan activist John Spitzer claims that public opinion would support a new initiative, pointing to a *Denver Post* poll showing more than two-thirds of respondents supporting stronger land-use planning by the state. Nevertheless, public support for something as vague as "stronger state planning" is latent at best, and is not easy to mobilize sufficiently to shake the status quo in the statehouse. Spitzer acknowledges this, saying, "The only thing that sells growth management politically is air pollution, or rapid economic growth. [People are hard to energize] when you say, 'Would you like your city to be more livable?'" (Spitzer interview). Perhaps more significant than the lack of a constituency is that Colorado, unlike Oregon, lacks much valuable, productive farmland in proximity to urban areas.

Summary

Neither Colorado nor Oregon can decide on behalf of its localities where buildings will be built. Nor does either state zone land. In this sense, most of the "action" remains at the local level, and we should thus focus primary attention on local and regional land-use regulation.

Nevertheless, Oregon's planning system clearly differs in a systematic way from Colorado's. While Colorado primarily attempts to exhort, support, and encourage "good planning" by counties and municipalities, Oregon has set some fairly strict rules, in the form of goals and guidelines, to guide local action. The presence of strong regional institutions in Portland allows that region to take a leadership role in addressing state goals and guidelines.

Organizing Urban Development in Two Regions

What were the basic institutional features that characterized these two regions in the new suburban era? In brief, Portland was marked by relatively more simple and stable political arrangements, with a substantial role given to regionwide and state institutions in guiding development. The revenue-raising system stressed the existing property tax base, and provided relatively few incentives for municipalities to seek out new commercial ratables. Special districts, while plentiful, tended to react to development, rather than cause it. And at the beginning of this period in particular, the central city was relatively dominant in territory and population. The small peripheral municipalities— generally not yet contiguous to Portland—tended to have histories and ambitions of their own, but minimal regional influence.

In contrast, metropolitan Denver developed a more complex, particularistic means of supervising suburban and fringe land-use and service provision. Through the Poundstone Amendment, the ability of the central city to respond to the locational preferences of residents and businesses was overtly restricted. Meanwhile, a number of large suburban cities had formed and were engaging in annexation patterns that would lead some to rival Denver in size. In part, this was in reaction to the use of local sales taxes. Annexations motivated by the quest for sales taxes allowed cities to augment revenues while minimizing property taxes, which represent the most visible burden of local government on its residents. Regional governance as such was almost absent, though superlocal institutions had been formed to wrestle with problems in some specific functional areas. According to the 1980 Census of Governments data, there were 223 "land-use governments" in the Denver-Boulder area, compared to 91 in the Portland-Vancouver region. Moreover, expenditure patterns were more decentralized in Colorado than in Oregon.

While the individual detail and histories of these two regions are in many cases of interest in themselves, the primary purpose of the case studies is to test and further refine the hypotheses about metropolitan political organization and land use developed in chapter 2. A secondary purpose is to illustrate the role of specific institutional arrangements in shaping the perceptions and decisions of actual developers and jurisdictions. In the theoretical section, I suggested, for example, that elected officials in small jurisdictions will pursue more particularistic agendas than those in larger jurisdictions, where mayors must worry about the vitality of the city's businesses and CBD. This conclusion also suggests that a metro area with a large-scale central city and few suburbs will be likely to have a healthier CBD. The case materials can shed light on both "halves" of this predicted relationship. In other words, while my main purpose in discussing Denver and Portland is to determine whether metro areas develop "as if" the behavioral propositions are true, I also seek to probe whether, in fact, those propositions *are* true.

5

Denver: Suburban Assertiveness, Centrifugal Development

Denver is being remade before our eyes. But people have been so caught up in the transformation that there isn't a real unified vision of where we're going.
—Phillip Burgess, executive director,
Center for the New West

The structure of government around Denver shapes urban development outcomes in a number of interrelated ways. In particular, the fluidity of suburban municipal boundaries, the constitutional restrictions upon annexation by Denver itself, the proliferation of special districts, and the reliance on local sales taxes lead to effects that can be understood within the theoretical framework outlined in chapter 2. That is, political fragmentation in metro Denver has the three predicted effects: It has weakened the center vis-à-vis other business nodes, has hastened the spread of the metropolis, and has sharpened disparities in development such as imbalances between jobs and housing.

In the first place, Denver is losing its relative position within the metro area because it has almost no influence beyond its own borders. This fixity of the city's boundaries, brought on by the Poundstone Amendment, has forced Denver's elected officials to work within the limits, literal and figurative, of the existing city. They must work with what they have—a deteriorating built environment, conflicts engendered by racial, ethnic, and class diversity—rather than being able to cushion these trends by adding more territory and residents.

Second, the institutional nexus has encouraged development at the urban fringe. The ease of creation and the independence of special-district governments, and the sales tax motivation for municipal annexation, have led repeatedly to the expansion of the urbanized area, without any consideration of the issue by an inclusive political entity. Thus, it is "the metropolis" that expands, but it is local government officials or individual development firms, rather than any metropolitan unit, that make the relevant decisions. The creation of limited-purpose highway authorities has also fueled this trend, especially given the uncertain role of regional government units and the state.

Third, the profusion of relatively autonomous local governments helps create and intensify disparities among places in the metropolis. Both progrowth and antigrowth interests are able to attach themselves to sympathetic localized institutions. Thus, some parts of the metropolis see slow, low-density growth, while other parts experience tremendous expansions in employment or population. Only in the city of Denver itself are these land-use conflicts regularly mediated and balanced with regionwide concerns such as job creation and transportation.

The implications of this case study are, first, that the Denver area lacks the governing capacity to cope with issues of regional significance, and second, that localism has organized urban growth in a distinctive way.

Adjusting to the Decline of Centrality

Prior to the Poundstone Amendment, the City and County of Denver retained a substantial degree of geopolitical flexibility. On the eve of the amendment's adoption, Denver in fact had official policy priorities that had strong implications for metropolitan organization. The stated aims included: providing services economically; retaining tax base and population; promoting a "variety of lifestyles and housing types"; seeking "balanced political representation" within the metro area; and minimizing the number of newly incorporated cities and special districts (Denver Planning Office 1974). Until Poundstone, Denver's annexation capabilities, while not unlimited, had provided a way to directly address these goals.

By the dawn of the new suburban era, however, Denver had long since lost the ability to keep up with peripheral growth, though its downtown remained unchallenged as the dominant business node in the area. New municipalities had incorporated, and existing ones had annexed extensively, beginning a process by which the city became ringed by independent jurisdictions. At the same time, developer-driven special districts had brought the possibility of urban services to new outlying subdivisions. As a result, the suburban counties began exceeding the city's growth rate in the 1950s. The outer counties of the CMSA together passed Denver in population in the 1960s. By the early 1970s they matched it in assessed property valuation. And, reflecting the tendency of the affluent to move to outlying areas, each of the five counties exceeded Denver City and County in median family income by 1970 (Denver Planning Office 1974). Denver has maintained its status as the predominant host county for employment, but the other counties have been rapidly catching up, growing much more quickly in recent decades. In the 1970s, for instance, population in the metro area grew 31 percent and the number of workers 63 percent—but the number of suburban workers increased 95 percent (Pisarski 1987, 31–32).

In that decade and the following one, huge business centers, including the Denver Technological Center, Greenwood Plaza, and Meridian Business Park, rapidly expanded in the prestigious southeast suburbs, presenting serious competition to the Denver CBD as an office magnet. The southeastern office parks compete with one another for tenants, but "the real enemy is downtown Denver" (E. Smith 1987). These two centers of commerce—the dense, concentrated CBD, and the far more dispersed and landscaped southeast corridor—account for about 60 percent of the roughly 70 million square feet of office space in the metro area. By 1991, there were 1.28 square feet of space in multitenant buildings in the CBD for every 1 square foot in the corridor. However, *if owner-occupied buildings are included, the corridor exceeds the downtown in office space.* The two areas have comparable vacancy rates and costs for office rentals (McGraw-Hill Inc. 1991, 4).

With their CBD in this difficult competitive position, Denver's leaders have been drawn into a "hands-on" policy of economic development, rearranging land uses and sometimes stoking turf conflicts as they attempt to address the diverse array of political pressures: downtown property improvement, infrastructure needs, and the need to increase the tax base to address expanding social service burdens and neighborhood quality-of-life concerns. Large and diverse jurisdictions, such as central cities, must wrestle with the full range of these issues, whereas smaller jurisdictions are apt to be driven mainly by "use value" concerns and issues of tax/service mix. In the process, Denver mayors have used three major tactics: subsidizing and otherwise supporting the "renewal" of downtown; constructing a large new airport in an attempt to attain a national leadership position in the transportation sector; and encouraging the enlargement of other business centers in the city. Each of these strategies, however, has had limitations in this diverse, geographically constrained city.

Devoting Scarce Resources to Downtown

After the Poundstone Amendment, Denver mayors perforce directed their attention inward to the CBD. The city would have to grow vertically if it could not spread over more land (Dorsett and McCarthy 1986, 323). While redevelopment had not enjoyed a sustained political commitment in earlier years, Mayor William McNichols, who served from 1968 to 1983, focused his attention on encouraging downtown investment throughout his long tenure.

Public projects in or near the CBD, including a major arts center, an arena, a stadium, and the Auraria Higher Education Complex, attempted to leverage or set the stage for private investment. The cost of these projects was not just monetary: Twenty-two blocks of homes, most of them historic Victorians, were cleared in the renewal effort for the education complex alone.[1]

After the state passed a tax increment financing law for Denver in 1968, a great deal of private redevelopment joined the public projects. During a period of growth in the energy industry from 1979 to 1983, more CBD office space was constructed than over the entire period from 1950 to 1979 (Dorsett and McCarthy 1986; Judd 1986; Peirce et al. 1983; Stanback and Noyelle 1982, 99). The Sixteenth Street Transit Mall, the capstone of the downtown redevelopment effort, opened in 1984. The mall was a public sector–led effort to revive the CBD, with heavy involvement from the urban renewal authority, the city government, and the Regional Transportation District. Meanwhile, however, suburban office growth from 1981 to 1985 was twice that of the CBD (Brazes 1986a).

Mayor McNichols rode the crest of the downtown building boom for a decade. But the economic downturn of the early to mid-1980s hastened his exit from the scene. In the recessionary atmosphere, citizens may have grown weary of the tax increases necessary to support McNichols's entrepreneurialism and the city's burgeoning social expenditures. Local per capita spending had risen from $25 in 1970 to $91 in 1980, and was to rise to $142 in 1984 (Denver Planning Office 1985). It became known, moreover, that "the city had been balancing the general fund with transfers from the capital fund for years. The recession aggravated the fiscal situation and Denver residents began to suspect that their boom town had problems" (Judd and Ready 1986, 222).

Moreover, despite the CBD's shiny new facade, it was losing ground to suburban employment sites. McNichols's successor, Mayor Federico Peña, put the matter plainly in his 1984 State of the City address, "We are in jeopardy of losing our place as the dominant center of commercial activity in the metro area" (quoted in Judd and Ready 1986, 220). Indeed, the city was forced to rely on tax increment financing for CBD retail projects in order to compete with much lower building costs in the suburbs. By the late 1980s, even sectors that were downtown Denver's traditional comparative strengths were hemorrhaging jobs to the suburbs ("Denver digs in" 1992).

Throughout the renewal era, Denver's diversity and political complexity made an exclusive focus on CBD vitality politically difficult. Developers building new business parks on outlying ranches or farmland enjoyed something of a political "blank slate." But the rebuilding of Denver, as in most other major cities, provoked distributional conflicts between downtown programs and the neighborhoods. These conflicts arose despite the relatively unitary internal structure of the city government. Historically, with a weak council, there has not been much of a "neighborhoods" lobby to counteract the CBD lobby, and the council rarely stands up to the mayor (Judd 1986; S. Moore interview 1992). Moreover, more than half the city's total tax revenue is generated by the CBD, reinforcing the downtown focus (Dorsett and McCarthy 1986, 329). Nevertheless, McNichols, and especially Peña, had to remain mindful of their constituencies in certain residential neighborhoods. They had to try to maintain a politically expedient balance in allocating benefits among residential areas with different ethnic, racial, or class constituencies, even while continually attending to the special demands of that most peculiar of neighborhoods, the CBD.

Once a Latino mayor succeeded McNichols, Denver became "a city in the process of repackaging the old downtown-growth, executive-centered coalition into a bright new wrapper more attractive to minorities and neighborhoods" (Judd and Ready 1986, 213). But if the change of administration provided the city government with a new image, it did not change the political exigencies of metropolitan development, which continued to turn Peña's attention to maintaining the CBD's competitiveness. For example, Peña's argument that the city needed a new downtown convention center, and debates about its specific location, were a source of controversy throughout much of the 1980s.[2] The 1990s even saw some proposals for a gambling resort in the Central Platte Valley, an industrial and railroad area adjacent to the CBD that is currently undergoing redevelopment.

Like many other big-city minority mayors, Peña felt compelled to collaborate with economic elites in vigorous growth boosterism while also attempting to ensure that neighborhood residents, including African-Americans and Latinos, got a piece of the action. His agenda was not limited to the downtown, which, for all its growth, clearly could not capture as much development as newer business centers. Peña also turned to Denver's aviation facilities and its secondary business districts to provide an additional motor for growth.

Constructing a New Airport

Controversy in the 1980s also revolved around the plans for a new Denver International Airport (which finally opened in 1995, far behind schedule due to mechanical glitches).[3] Among public-sector actors, the impetus and risk taking for the new airport belonged primarily to Denver, but its realization required extensive intergovernment negotiation. The issue had a high profile in the region and the outspoken support of Governor Roy Romer, who saw economic development as Colorado's foremost priority. "This airport is our one and only chance," Romer announced. "We can become the transportation hub of this country" (quoted in Koepp 1988, 52). Indeed, an economic strategy devoted to the air travel industry was part of Denver's justification for the facility. The initial motivations for a new airport, however, were the noise impact and limited size of the existing Stapleton Airport, which was sited relatively close to the central part of the city.

In abandoning Stapleton, Denver becomes the first city to simply shut down a major modern airport—and one that had overcapacity by 1990, as air traffic declined after a mid-1980s peak. The new airport is twenty-eight miles from the CBD, four times as far from downtown as Stapleton. Measuring in at an astounding forty-five square miles, it may be the world's largest (Noel 1991). Despite extensive criticism for its cost and ambitiousness, and for the high amount of risk involved, the airport became Peña's edifice, to him a tangible symbol of his effectiveness as mayor. (The airport's access road was dubbed Peña Boulevard.) The project was carried on by his successor, Wellington Webb.

After a long period of debate, studies, and vacillation, proponents of the airport settled on a location in the prairies of Adams County, significantly northeast of Stapleton. Denver, operating under the strictures of the Poundstone rule, needed the approval of Adams County voters to annex the area. In agreeing to support the airport idea and put it to a vote, Adams County commissioners extracted a number of concessions from Denver. Most notably, Adams was able to retain the lion's share of land targeted for airport-related development. Denver also agreed to build and pay for several access roads that would run through Adams, and to pay "airport impact fees" to Adams County and its school districts.

The Intergovernmental Agreement on a New Airport, signed in 1988, has a number of other specific restrictions that limit the opportunities for development that Denver can realize from the new facility. Among other provisions, the agreement required Stapleton to close upon the opening of the new airport. Denver also had to agree to limit the new airport site itself to one thousand hotel rooms, with one additional room allowed for every five built in an Adams County "hotel zone." Denver agreed to allow Adams County cities to annex across the Denver-owned transportation corridor, and also signed a separate annexation agreement with neighboring Aurora ("Intergovernmental agreement" 1988).

After the agreement was signed, additional complications arose. The parties had agreed to site the industrial uses that were accessories to the airport so as to benefit northern Adams County suburbs. But United Airlines, the dominant carrier in Denver, then attempted to convince Denver Mayor Wellington

Webb of the need to redesign the facility, placing the industrial zone to the airport's south instead. Webb's consideration of the changes provoked anger from Adams County politicians. In another conflict, Adams claimed it was not being appropriately compensated for the damage that construction vehicles were causing to its roads near the airport, and for a time summarily closed them. A leader of the regional Chamber of Commerce pleaded, "From a metro standpoint we have got to find a way to get beyond this notion that every opportunity associated with the airport is going to be judged as a win-lose proposition for Denver, Aurora, or Adams County" (quoted in Dinner 1992).

The intergovernmental politics of the new airport is too detailed and complex to discuss fully here. Nevertheless, it is fair to say that the requirements Denver has been bound to will, in effect, codify the dispersed, multicentered metropolis. Once again Denver has undertaken a project demonstrating its lead role in providing public facilities, amenities, and employment possibilities for the region. The airport may develop into the MSA's third major business node, along with the CBD and the I-25 corridor. Plans for the area include attracting headquarters and other corporate facilities. But the associated benefits will accrue disproportionately to the northeastern suburbs, not the center.

Turning Attention to Other Business Nodes Within the City

Nevertheless, Denver is a large local government, and is still able to muster resources and achieve changes that suburban governments cannot. With its politics relatively less organized around neighborhood "use values," Denver can more easily accommodate changes in land use. Most Denver rezonings are routinely approved, and the city has attempted to introduce some flexibility and speed into the approval process, at the behest of developers. Mayor Peña also founded an aggressive new economic development office, and armed it with subsidies. Denver officials have proved willing to support redevelopment and to tolerate the intensification of land uses in the city's own existing "suburban" nodes—that is, minidowntowns outside its CBD. Predictably, however, such policy sometimes meets resistance from downtown interests, which resent the city's encouragement of their potential competitors.

One outlying business district of note is the Cherry Creek district, located about three miles south of the CBD. This area saw intensified redevelopment after the opening of the upscale Cherry Creek Shopping Center in the late 1980s. One developer interviewed admired the "natural" process of "densification" occurring in the middle- to upper-income Denver neighborhoods that border the mall, and agreed that this change would have been far less likely under the same circumstances in a small, wealthy municipality (Holderith interview 1992b).[4] Old homes are being redeveloped, and some multifamily housing is being squeezed in.

City officials are also very attuned to redevelopment possibilities at two of Denver's other outlying locations. The eighteen-hundred-acre Lowry Air Force Base, which straddles Denver and Aurora, closed in 1994. Committees have been debating the disposition of the property. Proposals have included a "town center" development as well as residential units that would fit in more closely with the base's surroundings. More dramatically, the closing of Stapleton Airport presents an opportunity for redeveloping forty-seven hundred acres, with infrastructure and transportation links already in place. Unlike most potential large-scale development sites in the metropolis, Stapleton is adjacent to mixed-income, racially diverse neighborhoods. The site is planned for a mix of commercial and residential uses, and open space, in several "urban villages."

For developers, the opportunities and challenges of developing a "suburban" node within Denver itself are illustrated by the experiences of Denver-based development giant Miller-Davis Co. in developing the Regency project. Regency is a mixed-use office/commercial/hotel project just north of the mammoth suburban office park called the Denver Tech Center (DTC). (Except for a small portion, DTC is just outside Denver's border.) In 1980, Miller-Davis acquired a 50 percent interest in 335 acres that straddled I-25. The tract was chosen over others available in the area due to its good access to Routes 25 and I-225 and "because it was in the City and County of Denver" (Miller interview 1992). This jurisdictional consideration was important because the firm was the largest developer in the city and had built "good relations" with Denver's mayor and council. "There was a track record, trust" (Miller interview 1992). The land had infrastructure already in place for traffic and water, and the city was willing to help with other services. Part of the tract was zoned for industrial uses, and some was "zoned agricultural, which means it was essentially unzoned" (Miller interview 1992).

The firm produced a master plan for the property and began going through the city's zoning process. "The property had borders with Greenwood Village and Cherry Hills Village [two affluent municipalities south of Denver], and it got very involved" (Miller interview 1992). Although the zoning Denver had in place technically allowed far more intensive development than the firm proposed, numerous homeowner groups from the area rallied against the proposal. At the Denver council meeting considering the proposal, hundreds of people attended, including many who were actually residents of the villages. "The people really up in arms were Cherry Hills

Village and Greenwood Village, spearheaded by the Greenwood Village commercial property owners who didn't want any competition" (Miller interview
1992).

After an initial defeat by the council, Miller-Davis spent fifteen months
revising the master plan and rezoning package. Density was cut back slightly,
traffic impacts were studied by national consultants, and homeowner groups
were courted. Consultants were brought in to demonstrate how the project
could minimize noise and the impact on views, in one case actually doing
demonstrations with balloons to show residents that low-rise buildings would
obstruct mountain views more than high-rises.

> We did all this stuff here not because we are great people, but because we
> were forced into it. . . . For the first time in our careers, we realized you
> couldn't slam-dunk through City Hall. . . . We saved money and headaches,
> and the design changes were good for marketing the buildings. (Miller inter-
> view 1992)

The second time around, twelve residential associations supported the plan
at the council hearing, with one opposed. Accordingly, the council reversed
itself—though, mass mobilization aside, it had never been fundamentally
opposed to the development. "The people in Denver [city hall] were very
supportive. It was way out here, didn't affect them personally. . . . They wanted
the tax base and employment" (Miller interview 1992). Miller-Davis clearly
preferred the give-and-take possible in a big-city political system to the protectionism of a smaller municipality.

CBD Versus Edge City: "One More Mall" for Denver

However, a subsequent Miller-Davis proposal on this site illustrates the limits
of outlying development within the city when it competes with downtown
interests. This fight in the late 1980s and early 1990s over "one more mall" for
Denver illustrates the politics of "center versus periphery" growth when both
center and periphery are in the same jurisdiction (Miller interview 1992;
Fulcher and Leib 1990; "Showdown in Denver" 1991; "Mall wars simmer" 1992;
"Regency mall out" 1992).

The giant retail magnate Taubman Companies had recently developed the
Cherry Creek Mall, and wanted it protected from competition in nearby parts
of southern Denver. It also proposed a downtown mall. Taubman had the
backing of Denver's urban renewal authority, which controlled $50 million in
potential subsidies and could potentially have some downtown properties
designated as "blighted" to ease site assembly.

Meanwhile, Miller-Davis proposed another mall, Regency Fashion Centre,
at a location just inside Denver's southeastern boundary. Regency had some

advantages, too. It had already signed two department stores as potential anchor tenants, and one of Miller-Davis's executives previously had been Peña's chief of staff and a former deputy chief of staff to Governor Lamm (Keene-Osborne 1990). Partner Marvin Davis was a billionaire oil executive, and had long been influential in Denver. In addition, the city's 1989 Comprehensive Plan recommended working with developers to get a major retail center built in the Denver portion of DTC. On the other hand, the executive director of the city's urban renewal authority said, "We would like to see a downtown project before Regency. We have real doubts that there are enough retailers to fill both centers" ("Showdown in Denver" 1991).

The battle heated up after the real estate arm of Prudential Insurance bought the option on Regency and took over the proposal from Miller-Davis in 1991. A magazine for retailers noted that Prudential was "downtown Denver's largest landlord, with 2.3 million square feet of space worth more than $300 million," and therefore "also has plenty of political clout" ("Showdown in Denver" 1991). Regency's backers asked the city to finance a parking garage and roads for their proposed mall. But quickly, a group of opponents, headed by a downtown restaurateur, launched a petition for a referendum on the matter and, for good measure, filed a lawsuit. "We think it's bad policy to be using public funds for a center of that nature unless there's a clear need," the group's leader said. "We have to put the spotlight on downtown first" (Larry Wright, quoted in Fulcher and Leib 1990).[5]

Taubman promised financial backing to this challenge. Eventually, the Regency group, wary of controversy, withdrew the request for a $16.5 million city subsidy. Incoming mayor Webb favored the downtown project, and some speculated that he purposely held up the approval of Regency in order to aid Taubman. Prudential eventually withdrew the Regency proposal in July 1992 because the delay had caused potential financiers to back out. Thus, downtown's advocates had won this fight within the city and county.

Nevertheless, the overall metropolitan trends continued, and Denver could do little but watch. With Regency off the agenda, other developers began attempting to finance competing mall sites—in southern Aurora and northern Douglas County. In short, while the City and County of Denver has found itself with restricted geopolitical ammunition, the metro area's institutional arrangements provide favorable incentives for suburban and exurban projects. Under these circumstances, the center will not hold.

Expanding the Metropolis

According to the theoretical framework, another expected consequence of the political fragmentation characteristic of the Denver region is sprawl. This issue is particularly important in the fragile terrain of the West. With ground-water scarce, the proliferation of shopping centers and subdivisions in Den-ver's suburbs require far-flung and expensive capital projects to divert water to meet the dispersed demand. Newly extended roads and diminished air quality threaten the environment. And while initial residents of the fringe develop-ments may treasure their uncrowded surroundings, the dependence on the automobile fostered by their decentralized settlement patterns tends to in-crease congestion on regional thoroughfares. As new waves of growth begin to place "the outskirts" even farther away, these exurban residents may become just as concerned about the despoliation of the countryside as are long-time residents of the metropolis.

For many years, loose land-use regulation by rural local governments in developing areas of Colorado led to numerous "premature subdivisions," in which building lots existed on paper, but lacked the access or services to actually develop. This in turn led developers to "leapfrog" these sites, building in locations still farther away (Shultz and Groy 1986). But in the Denver area, systemic features of regional governance compound these local regulatory problems. Two examples are the construction of outer freeways and the an-nexation patterns of the city of Aurora, a municipality with a progrowth political orientation. Suburban county governments, moreover, must cope with the strains of growth in unincorporated areas such as largely rural Doug-las County.

Highways: Building Access to the Periphery

Flodie Anderson, former state highway commissioner from Golden, stated that "[Highway] C-470 links suburbs without unnecessarily routing traffic through Denver. . . . We are beyond needing additional spokes on the [freeway] wheel—the hub of which is Denver" (Leonard and Noel 1990, 275). Without much coordination, the Denver region in the 1980s undertook a de facto policy of building new freeways on land at or beyond the urban fringe. Lacking any single unit of government to address mounting metropolitan problems, the state instead has tended to create ad hoc commissions and committees to address single regional issues. But in the case of transportation, these groups primarily represent a single political perspective—the suburban progrowth coalition—rather than being broadly representative.

The primary battle over regional transportation in the 1970s concerned a proposed outer belt freeway. Governor Richard Lamm, elected on a platform of growth management, diverted federal funds from the highway proposal. Nevertheless, pressure for some form of a beltway continued, and eventually led to the construction in the late 1980s of a stretch of limited-access state highway, C-470, in the southwestern quadrant of the metropolis. It intersects I-25 in northern Douglas County, and runs northwest to I-70 near Golden—a twenty-six-mile route (DRCOG 1988b, 8). When no further federal funding was available to complete the remainder of the freeway loop, two special-purpose authorities were created to finance and build the eastern and north-western portions. Essentially, the projected path of Route 470 rings the urban-ized area, and in some cases steers well into undeveloped territory. Defenders of a completed 470 see the road accomplishing several goals: defining growth limits, providing primary access to the new airport, providing an alternative to traveling through Denver, and promoting future development that would enhance the tax base (Ferdinandsen interview 1992).

Thus, the E-470 Public Highway Authority is continuing somewhat be-leaguered efforts to build a toll road that would complete the *eastern* semicir-cle of the expressway, to run from C-470 in the south to the new airport and beyond (Patty 1992; George 1992a; George 1992c; Reed 1991a). The Authority was founded by Arapahoe, Adams, and Douglas Counties, and the city of Aurora, "with significant input from several private developers" (Buchrer 1986). About two-thirds of the land needed was to be donated by developers and landowners. Residents of the three involved counties are charged a special vehicle registration fee to support the Authority. Overall, E-470 has been estimated to cost up to $1 billion.

Through 1995, only a five-mile southeastern stretch of this toll road had been built, with traffic volumes 60 to 70 percent lighter than predicted. The E-470 Authority was hindered by its lack of authority over nearby county and local roads, some of which were built or improved, thereby creating "competi tion" for drivers who might otherwise use E-470 and pay its tolls. This prob-lem of coordination, typical of a fragmented metropolis, made it more diffi-cult for the Authority to raise the money in the bond market that would enable completion of its route. Late 1992 saw the Authority forced to seek $55 million in loans and loan guarantees from the state and local governments. In a cost-cutting effort, the Authority generated protest and lawsuits in Aurora and Arapahoe Counties by deciding to move the new road west—that is, closer to established residential areas. Nevertheless, a former executive director of the Authority predicts confidently that "development will be the name of the game again" soon, and much of it will occur in the E-470 corridor (John Arnold, quoted in Reed 1991a; see also Kelley 1995). The highway should be complete by the year 2000.

Similarly, a W-470 Authority, created in 1983, attempted to complete the *northwestern* segment of the beltway (Wood 1989; Reed 1991b; George 1995). Developers proposing huge real estate projects near the road sat on the Authority's executive committee and lobbied for interchange locations that would help their developments. A study predicted that a completed W-470 would redistribute jobs from Denver, Boulder, and inner suburbs such as Arvada to exurban locations.

But the W-470 Authority also faced repeated obstacles. Now moribund, the Authority saw its various funding proposals nixed by the General Assembly, the federal government, and then voters in a 1989 referendum. After these defeats, the Authority was propped up with donations from various interested parties, including developers, contractors, lawyers, banks, and the investment company that would have handled the sale of bonds (Chandler 1992). The city of Broomfield was left holding five thousand mostly undeveloped acres that it had optimistically annexed along the projected W-470 corridor.

These failed attempts to increase the region's transportation infrastructure illustrate the difficulties that ad hoc regional public action can face. With no clear solutions emanating from local governments or existing entities such as RTD, highway proponents used the model of special-purpose government and gained representation with the relevant public authorities. But the shaky economy, a difficult fiscal environment, and administrative foibles have thus far hamstrung the project. The city of Denver, which vowed to oppose any beltway plan unless a CBD-oriented rapid transit system was concurrently under way (Denver Planning Office 1989), has not yet lost this battle.

Nevertheless, work on the eastern leg of Route 470 is proceeding, and supporters of the northwestern segment of the beltway have renewed discussions aimed at resuscitating that project. Development patterns resulting from past highway construction provide strong clues to what will happen next if proponents of the project are successful. The metropolis will continue to spread out, as residents and firms gain easier access to larger plots of land at the fringe.

Aurora: The Sprawling Second City

The city of Aurora, which saw its growth fortunes rise spectacularly with the completion of an earlier freeway loop, I-225, provides an illustrative case of sprawl. One of the earliest true residential suburbs in the area, Aurora— originally called Fletcher—grew as Denver expanded eastward.[6] Three early developers' residential subdivisions incorporated as the Town of Fletcher in 1891, but, hampered by a serious lack of water, the tiny new municipality grew slowly over the subsequent five decades, until the area entered the auto age. East Colfax Avenue (U.S. Route 40)—early Aurora's main street—was the principal approach to the metropolis from the east until the interstate highway system was built. As a result, the town developed a commercial strip along

Colfax that for several decades formed the heart of the community. The construction of Fitzsimmons Army Medical Center farther east pulled settlement in that direction, and the strip has continued to spread.

Aurora's semiarid conditions were a perennial concern, as the city for many decades faced potential and actual water supply shortfalls. In the early decades, the city's large water-related debt, and its lack of public resources more generally, tended to cement ties between city hall and the Chamber of Commerce. Public and private elites worked together to draw extensive military employment to Aurora. Combined action was also required to overcome the Denver Water Board's stranglehold over the town's fortunes (Mehls et al. 1985). Similarly, the city turned to special districts early on, particularly for water provision, since it was unable to afford extensive infrastructure provision in advance of growth. These districts "codified the old tradition and practice of volunteerism. . . . This allowed the actual city government to remain small" (Mehls et al. 1985, 62).

The city itself, however, did not remain small. Aurora's first large-scale annexation occurred in the 1950s, when residents of unincorporated eastern residential developments petitioned Aurora to repair deficiencies in their infrastructure and services. This action set a precedent for large-scale territorial expansion by suburbs in Colorado. For Aurora, it was a sign of things to come. With an improved fiscal climate and under mounting growth pressures in the postwar era, the city became more entrepreneurial, particularly after the state granted Aurora home rule privileges in 1961. The city's repeated annexations to the south of its original area succeeded in cutting off Denver's expansion in that zone. The path of growth moved in that direction as well, and the opening of the Air Force's Lowry Field and Buckley Air National Guard bases pulled the city's center of gravity well south of Colfax Avenue.

In 1967, another major civic accomplishment allowed Aurora to consolidate its position as the emerging second city of the metropolitan area. Collaborating with Colorado Springs, Aurora completed a large water diversion project on which it had "bet the ranch." With consolidated control over its own infrastructure resources, Aurora became independent of the Denver Water Board. Today all its residents are served by municipal water, and, according to Mayor Paul Tauer, "We are in better shape than anybody but Denver" (Tauer interview 1992). Aurora estimates it has enough water capacity for an *additional* hundred thousand residents.

From a base population of a few thousand in 1940, the city's postwar growth has been truly astounding. Aurora was just under the 75,000 mark by 1970, and then more than doubled by the next census. Its 1990 population was 222,103. Interstate Highway 225, one link in the first beltway proposal for the metro area, was completed in the 1970s. Carved through areas that were then well east and south of the existing Aurora, it helped pull settlement much farther in those directions. I-225 stimulated the city's development with a number of new interchanges and quicker access to the growing office area in the southeast quadrant of the metropolis. The city's original mall, Buckingham Square, lost business to the newer and bigger Aurora Mall, completed in 1975 at a site just off I-225.

With some residents becoming nervous over Aurora's extremely rapid growth, the city at one point adopted a master plan with elements of growth control. This 1972 plan advocated focal points for the city's sprawling development, in order to instill a sense of identity for each section of the city and to alleviate congestion. But power conflicts between city council and city manager stalled action on the plan. In general, the city has not taken a "hands-on" approach to development and urban form.

Developing in rather free-form fashion, then, Aurora—unlike the typical suburb—became a city of some variety in its income mix and racial makeup. In addition to all types of rental and owner-occupied housing, Aurora hosts many areas of commercial development, particularly retail. Nevertheless, the overall orientation is still heavily residential, low- to medium-density, and auto dependent.[7] With its laissez-faire political ethos, and flat, relatively cheap land, Aurora appears to have been more reactive than proactive to developers' activities at the fringe.

For example, there has not been a sustained effort to revamp or build up Aurora's original downtown along Colfax Avenue. This small CBD has witnessed considerable decay and disinvestment.[8] Once the hub of a streetcar suburb, the commercial district lost its vitality, in both business and political terms. While enough political resources could still be mustered in the 1970s to attempt a minor urban renewal strategy for the old downtown, featuring street reconstruction and redesign, this effort lacked a long-term commitment. The business district's small presence was outweighed by the burgeoning residential and retail growth in the expanding south. Homeowner associations, with their influence over voter mobilization, and shopping center owners, who disproportionately affect sales tax revenues, received increased political attention. Thus, throughout Aurora's history, attention to the old downtown was lacking because city officials focused on maintaining the boom town image (Mehls et al. 1985). Another factor contributing to this inattention may be the district's location in a somewhat run-down residential area, where gangs have been active and the population is disproportionately poor and minority.

Mayor Tauer espouses a strategy of realism, arguing that the "original Aurora" district is not a true downtown, and that "we will never have a downtown area." The city has become progressively more control oriented regarding growth (Brazes 1986), but holds few hopes about redevelopment. This hands-off official perspective has been encapsulated by former city manager James R. Griesemer, who said, "If the economic, social, and technological forces shaping our city today don't encourage the creation of a downtown, you'd be wasting a lot of effort to build one" (quoted in Leonard and Noel 1990, 358). Mayor Tauer envisions the future Aurora as a true "twenty-first century city," marked by several activity centers: the Aurora Mall, the old CBD, a new shopping center in the southeast part of the city, and the area near the new regional airport.

With no dominant center or character, Aurora has become a collection of subdivisions, difficult to administer and unify. "By the late seventies, city government no longer managed a cohesive city, but rather attempted to control and direct the various segments of an Aurora that by 1978 sprawled over 63 square miles" (Mehls et al. 1985, 165). Aurora remains a city of parts, with a confusing, disordered physical form.

Since there is little possibility that this character can be changed, the economic development focus among city officials has remained outward, toward the open land east of the city. The city council approved a plan in 1984 for a series of huge annexations, to include 117 square miles and almost double Aurora's existing area (Mehls et al. 1985; Richardson 1990). *Regional* anti-growth forces were not heard from during this *local* decision process. The new area was to be bisected by the proposed E-470, and included a large set-aside for commercial and industrial development. Mayor Paul Tauer recalls three reasons why the council supported the annexations: "In 1985 or so it looked like we were becoming an inner ring suburb. We couldn't afford to let that happen. Second, we wanted to control the land on our side of the new airport. Third, there was all this talk about E-470; we wanted to capitalize on the new development associated with that" (Tauer interview 1992). Tauer emphasized that the annexations were "totally within the law" and that Aurora "annexed only where we were asked to." No services have been extended to these areas unless the developer pays for them. Nevertheless, there was a widespread feeling among Colorado officials (and my interviewees) that Aurora had vastly overstepped its capabilities. This sentiment led to passage of a new state law limiting annexation activity. Nevertheless, even that law is not very restrictive; Tauer maintains that Aurora's 1980s annexations were within the new law's limits.

As of 1992, Aurora had about eighty square miles of undeveloped land within a fifteen minutes' drive of the new airport. City plans call for four new commercial areas in conjunction with the facility. City officials clearly wanted to take advantage of the outlying site of the airport to generate more of a tax base by spreading the metropolis farther east. In 1992, the city council voted to appropriate whatever funds would be necessary to create a new freeway interchange near the airport before its opening. "Either we make the commitment now," warned the city's public works director, "or we stand by and watch someone else capture all the development associated with the airport" ("Aurora dreams" 1992; Richardson 1990).[9] Aurora also contributed financially to a metropolitan district formed by landowners near the airport, which will fund sewer and water construction necessary for new growth. Mayor Tauer indicated the city's strategy: "The airport area is Aurora's long-range retirement plan. But it won't happen on its own. We have to help that happen" (quoted in "Aurora dreams" 1992). In contrast to its stated policy elsewhere in the city, Aurora will extend services to the airport area in advance of development, if it appears imminent (Tauer interview 1992). A major motivation for these policies was the desperate need for a greater tax base, after the city's absorption of a great deal of condominium construction in the 1980s.

In this manner, the metropolis may become the Denver-Aurora MSA. Mayor Tauer recalls that Denver had a smaller population when he moved there as a child than Aurora has now. Forty years from now, he predicts, Aurora will be bigger than Denver. "I see an evolving Minneapolis/St. Paul type arrangement, with Denver as St. Paul: the smaller, older, capital city. Aurora is Minneapolis: progressive, growth-oriented" (Tauer interview 1992).[10]

The Unincorporated Periphery: Future Metropolis

Aurora is in the process of becoming a very large-scale government unit, a "big city" that happens to be entirely suburban. But the county governments of Adams, Arapahoe, Boulder, Jefferson, and more recently Douglas, have long been in charge of even more extensive suburban and exurban territories. They have been literally and figuratively at the frontier of growth regulation. Throughout much of the past two decades, recently rural lands were in demand by developers, who sought to build everything from small, one-shot subdivisions to multiphase, mixed-use "new communities." In the process, county officials had to consider how growth might best be accommodated, and how special districts and annexation-hungry municipalities entered the picture.

As noted in earlier chapters, counties may be expected to be less particularistic and more neutral regulators of land use than the smaller municipalities—particularly in Colorado, where counties rely on property taxes and municipalities partially on sales taxes. These expectations are generally confirmed in the Denver region. That is not to say, however, that counties such as

Adams, Boulder, and Arapahoe have taken a uniform approach to growth management. Douglas County sheds light upon the key issue of the growth "life cycle." That is, it shows that counties just beginning to experience large-scale growth pressures cannot be expected to respond in the same fashion as more urbanized counties.

Boulder and Adams Counties are pursuing land-use strategies in which growth is targeted only to the existing incorporated communities. Boulder County, a software and high-tech center, is one of a small number of counties in the country actively pursuing a strategy of contained, centered, environmentally sensitive growth. It has sought to boost the fortunes of its only true existing downtowns, those of the cities of Boulder and Longmont, while restraining fringe development. The county works in conjunction with the politically quirky city of Boulder, where slow growth is the byword.[11] Neighboring Adams County has in recent years attempted to focus its development by coordinating relations among the jurisdictions involved. The county planning staff has worked to integrate decision making with their municipal counterparts. Developers must attend a joint "preapplication conference" with both sets of planners before submitting site plans. In 1986, the county initiated annexation agreements to head off litigation and land grabs among the cities that straddle the emerging I-25 business corridor north of Denver (Coney interview 1992). In contrast, Arapahoe County, with a more conservative political orientation, has not taken overt action to manage growth. For example, it has not attempted to restrain the development of corporate offices and warehouse facilities along its exurban Arapahoe Road corridor, which is emerging as a new employment center southeast of the Denver Tech Center.[12]

It has been Douglas County's government, however, that has felt the greatest relative impact of growth in the last two decades. Its town of Parker, for instance, which incorporated in the late 1970s, grew from a population of 290 in 1980 to 5,500 in 1990, largely by extensive annexation (see table 4.4 and figure 4.4). Still, the relative share of the population living in the county's incorporated places stood at only 24 percent in 1990, meaning that the county government was the primary land-use regulator for three-quarters of the population. Not surprisingly, therefore, growth issues have dominated Douglas County's political agenda since the 1970s. Douglas is worth a brief "tour" in this analysis, since it illustrates urban growth politics in a geographically extensive, but organizationally primitive, Colorado county.

The real estate boom gave the largely rural county extreme population increases and expensive new service responsibilities. Without irrigated farmland, Douglas had been dominated by huge dry-land ranches of several thousand acres; it has a sparser population than other agricultural areas, and less ability to support small towns.[13] According to John Johnson, the county's assistant planning director, "It was a rural county with no regulations in place, no knowledge of [growth] impacts. . . . It was kind of exciting for them. . . . They were ripe for the picking" (Johnson interview 1992). At its peak, Douglas was issuing nearly twenty-five thousand residential construction permits per year.

But the high-risk real estate speculation that defined much of the home building in Douglas led to an especially severe bust by the late 1980s. Denver's oil industry recession of the mid-1980s occurred just as special districts for new communities had been created and infrastructure was being built. Among the investors caught in this extreme supply-demand imbalance was savings and loan executive Charles Keating, whose infamous Lincoln Savings and Loan had a large residential project in the county. At least six developer-spawned metropolitan districts fell into bankruptcy. At the same time, the experience of rapid growth, the burdens of higher taxes, and the influx of sophisticated, highly educated residents pushed county representatives toward a more engaged approach to growth regulation:

> In the late '70s, this was an overwhelmed rural county. But then there was a learning curve, leading to the '86 master plan, the '92 update. . . . [In recent years, developers] come in [to planning commission hearings] with an entourage of six or seven "experts" versus the two planners we have here. But we often win. It's pretty striking, compared to the old sentiment: "We're power brokers—it's fun to create another new town!" (Johnson interview 1992)

The most prominent location in the 1980s for residential growth in the county was Highlands Ranch, a planned community in northernmost Douglas, which is being developed under the direction of the massive Mission Viejo Company. In recent years Highlands Ranch has captured roughly one-quarter of the metro area's home sales. A twenty-six-thousand-acre development (with an eight-thousand-acre conservancy to its south), Highlands Ranch expects to accommodate ninety thousand residents upon its ultimate build-out ("Company of the year" 1992). The site was chosen, according to a Mission Viejo spokesman, for its vast size and single ownership, and for its attractive landscape and proximity to C-470 ("Endangered developers" 1992).

Still very heavily residential, the unincorporated community was made viable by the employment growth in the southeast part of the metropolis, and by the completion of portions of C-470. With a traditional suburban design, it has little place for pedestrians or transit. While some commercial development has occurred, Highlands Ranch is largely a collection of individual residential "communities" developed by different builders, in podlike subdivisions with looping roads. Some subdivisions feature gates and guardhouses. Although some have criticized its "engineering mentality" regarding community planning, Mission Viejo is almost inevitably a political force for the county to reckon with. Says Johnson, "They're a tough negotiator. On the other hand, we don't have to worry about them hitting the road" (Johnson interview 1992).[14]

As one drives south from Highlands Ranch, I-25 quickly plunges into virgin territory of arid, knobby hills. It is in this rugged territory, far from the jobs around Denver, that the Resolution Trust Corporation has become a major landowner. Large "new communities" here have experienced serious financial problems (Wells 1990a). The 4.2-mile-long Founders Parkway, which intersects I-25 north of Castle Rock, was intended to be the main collector street for one such community. A 1992 tour of this road revealed a smooth four-lane highway, almost completely untraveled, complete with road signs and other completed infrastructure—but not a single house, store, or other building. Founders Parkway was a significant investment in advance of future growth, an investment that was logical and easy under the rules of the game in Colorado. Unfortunately for bondholders, the future has yet to arrive. According to Johnson, these large projects failed because

> they were blobs out on the periphery, not contiguous to anything. It's a chicken/egg story. Houses and commercial development need a critical mass. The hardy souls who went out to do things forecasted selling hundreds of homes per year to retire the bonds. It takes ten to twenty million dollars of new infrastructure for a new town. This was eight or nine years ago, and there are still no houses [in 1992]. . . . Not only did the bondholders lose, it was a waste of resources. (Johnson interview 1992; see also "Suburbs' slum bering giant" 1992; Wilmsen 1992)

With its failed metropolitan districts, Douglas County saw its bond ratings lowered, because a small population of eighty thousand was carrying about $500 million in issued debt.

Meanwhile, the substantial number of homes that *were* built in the county led to fiscal dilemmas for the county's main school district. Highlands Ranch alone had an 11 percent increase in school enrollment in 1991. In this emergency atmosphere, Douglas County became the first county in Colorado to assess mandatory impact fees on developers to fund school costs—about two thousand dollars on a typical home. Questioning whether such fees are constitutional in Colorado, developers have taken the issue to court (Johnson interview 1992; "Colorado: Bonds floated" 1992).

The latest master plan for Douglas County, adopted in 1992, attempts to be both realistic and idealistic regarding future development patterns (Douglas

County Planning Commission 1992; Johnson interview 1992). It envisions maintaining separate identities for the county's remaining small towns and villages, with topography and natural features utilized to bound these places. Fundamentally, the plan recommends that new development shall be restricted to compact areas in Highlands Ranch, in the county's three incorporated municipalities, and in what are diplomatically called "separated urbanization areas"—the incomplete, remote new communities. The plan is geared toward preserving the quality of the visual landscape.

The question remains open whether the county's elected leadership will follow the master plan's growth management strategies. According to one observer, while the plan may not hold, due to political pressure from land speculators, Douglas County has "come a long way. They have the guts to say no." While some candidates for elected office voiced support for growth management, others stressed the need to create a positive atmosphere for commercial growth, in order to broaden the overburdened tax base. The vicissitudes of campaign finance provide some incentives to support the latter policy.[15] The county commission, while perennially all Republican, has had advocates both of laissez-faire and of managed growth. But it is unclear how long a single party can represent both positions. In short, as Douglas takes on the characteristics of other large and diverse metropolitan jurisdictions, its politics are becoming more complex.

Let us briefly summarize the relationship between political fragmentation and metropolitan sprawl in the Denver region. Local jurisdictions or special-purpose governments, pursuing particularistic policies such as tax base enhancement or an escalation of land values, provided an instrument to extend infrastructure and services to formerly remote sites. Highway authorities, metropolitan districts, and large-scale annexations by suburban cities all allowed development to disperse. In the case of the freeway-building authorities, the institutions were organized specifically to overcome a lack of political commitment by more unitary levels of government that would allow more traditional funding of the construction programs. Cities were quick to annex far and wide in an effort to allow sites to be developed for retail. It is probably not coincidental that an auto tour of the Denver metro area finds an inordinate number of retail complexes directly at the border between two suburbs.[16]

Larger jurisdictions have taken somewhat more complex approaches to growth. Aurora has flirted with a "growth centers" strategy and has also attempted to revitalize its small CBD, but has lacked a sustained commitment to this approach under the pressure of outward expansion. The large suburb of Lakewood has taken more of a hands-on approach to land-use intensification at a few commercial subcenters. The more diverse counties, which do not rely on sales taxes, vary in their orientation toward growth, but tend to have less clear enthusiasm for fringe development. Overall, however, there are few barriers, and a number of potential institutional resources, for those who can profit by promoting urban deconcentration.[17]

Suburban Multiplicity and Disparities in Development

Another likely reason for the spread of the metropolis has been the "capture" of some suburban jurisdictions by activists favoring slow growth. When the city of Boulder, for example, chooses to limit its annual population growth, some of its would-be in-migrants undoubtedly settle in peripheral locations with less restrictive development rules. Meanwhile, other areas whose governments support or tolerate rapid growth, as in Highlands Ranch or the Arapahoe Road corridor, attain large concentrations of housing or employment. In toto, this situation leads to disparities in development, as slow-growth and rapid-growth areas arise without overall coordination. Adding to this patchwork pattern, some of the rapid-growth places may be strictly residential, while others are almost purely employment centers. Interactions between jurisdictions and development firms shape these disparities.

The Variety of Land-Use Orientations:
Jurisdictions and Developers

With the exception of some wealthy residential enclaves, most local governments in the Denver area are interested in gaining more commercial growth to bolster their tax bases. They thus have an interest in creating a reasonably predictable environment for nonresidential developers. On the other hand, "the last thing in the world they want is residential" development, due to the unfavorable cost-benefit ratio generated by demands for schools and services (Holderith interview 1992a).

Sometimes the progrowth character of local government is known. "A project can be fast-tracked," one builder notes, "if you know approvals are forthcoming." In this way, developers can get preliminary work under way while the application is technically still being processed (Holderith interview 1992b). One developer says that in downtown Denver, where there are few residents in the "neighborhood" to express opposition, locational calculations are far less complex than in the suburbs: "The question there [downtown] is what would sell a building. Three things: location, comfort, and vertical transportation. It's a simple formula" (Miller interview 1992).

But while many Colorado cities may work to regularize development procedures *within* their domains, that is not to say that it is a quick and easy process to put up an office building. State law allows a developer's project to be overturned by referendum, even after it has cleared the necessary regulatory hurdles.[18] Developers also find that the complex structure of local government, with multiple entities having authority over land use and infrastructure issues, can make for a confusing environment. According to Steve Delva, a planner for Writer Corp., a major development firm, "There are areas of metro Denver where you have to go to some 30 different entities who all have the ability to comment on your plan" (quoted in Costas 1987). One lawyer claims his client's project was delayed six months while officials debated the type of water fountains to be required. And George Thorn, president of VRG Development Corp., a firm developing an office complex as a joint venture with the massive Denver Tech Center, complains, "The paperwork that was required for this building would be a couple of feet high if stacked—and this is the DTC. This is where it's supposed to be easy!" (Costas 1987).

In short, metro area developers work for multiple public-sector masters. This complexity is something of a double-edged sword for them. On the one hand, crafty developers can manipulate structures of public authority for their own gain. This is particularly true in the case of special districts, which allow builders to finance infrastructure provision with a minimal degree of risk, political debate, and regulatory oversight. Developers can also play jurisdictions off against one another, for example by enticing them to compete for the privilege of annexing a new retail center. On the other hand, there may be delays caused by restrictive or bureaucratized governments, or within cities that are politically divided. Negotiating separately with cities, counties, and districts may slow projects further. These delays frustrate developers, for whom time is money, since they are working with borrowed capital and must pay interest. The fragmented system of government, one developer claims,

> puts the impetus on a planner in a small municipality. If things start to heat up, he has to determine what projects are reasonable or unreasonable. So he takes the strongest tack he can [making demands on projects] to protect his butt. . . . The typical city official says, "Geez, I would like to have a bike path over here, and it has to be concrete and eight feet wide." (Anonymous interview)

Such requirements and delays can be especially overwhelming for small or new firms. On occasion, a great deal of creativity can be required of developers to operate successfully in this institutional environment.[19]

While many cities welcome new buildings that will add to the tax base, some jurisdictions have a notoriously heavy regulatory hand. This is particularly the case in cities where public opinion is oriented toward a "use value" ethos and where extensive citizen participation is the norm:

> [Boulder] County Attorney Larry Hoyt recalls "a visual impact situation" where a developer agreed to do some landscaping along the boundary of his commercial development to hide it from area residents. But the citizens worried that the trees wouldn't be taken care of and that they'd end up looking at an unsightly mess of dead limbs. So, the developer agreed to put the trees on their property, so they could look after them themselves. "Then," says Hoyt, "a big debate followed over what kind of trees to plant." (Costas 1987)

Height limitations, and requirements that so-called greenbelts surround commercial buildings, are common in suburban areas not accustomed to high-rise office buildings. Note that these policies have the effect of restricting the density of development at job sites, thereby making public transit less viable. And where neighborhood organizations are strong, developers find they must schedule meetings to warm them to new proposals. One says, "You approach the neighborhood organizations 'hat in hand' " (quoted in Costas 1987). Not surprisingly, unincorporated areas are generally considered easiest to work with for commercial development. The large-scale county governments, depending on property taxation, relatively distant from neighborhood pressures, and feeling the fiscal pinch of rapid population growth, are often seen as more accommodating and objective in their approach to development proposals. One developer says of Arapahoe County, "The county is easy to deal with—there are professionals there" (Madden interview 1992). Since county governments administer land use in unincorporated areas, they generally are not responsible for the existing business districts that might resent the new competition. "They will rush to build a WalMart even if it wrecks the downtown Ma and Pa stores a few miles away" (Holderith interview 1992b).

As for special districts, developers differ as to their merits. Some see them becoming almost mandatory for residential development—a manifestation of the suburban "pull up the gangplanks" syndrome, whereby residents who have already "made it" do not want to allow others to enter their community without paying their own way. "It's a selfish, narrow attitude. These costs should be part of general government. Now cities say, 'Screw you' " (Holderith interview 1992b). Another says, "If it were an objective city, we would prefer to work with city services. Otherwise, the special district is a necessary evil" (Madden interview 1992). Districts are also sometimes seen as another legalistic, administrative layer of government for developers to contend with. But with lenders increasingly forbidding loans for front-end infrastructure expenditure, special districts are often the only way to amortize the costs of a new project in an unserviced area. For many, therefore, "it's a great financial mechanism" (Miller interview 1992).

Jobs and Housing

These variations in the ease or awkwardness of relationships between development firms and units of government affect the differential location of employment and population in the metropolis. To be fair, much of the metro area's jobs/housing mix seems a function of the historical centrality of employment in central Denver, the scale of private landholding and financing patterns, and the organization of the development industry. But overlaid on these basic economic considerations are the motivations of local governments as they regulate land use.

Some of these motivations reflect quality-of-life neighborhood protectionism. Prestigious municipalities like Columbine Valley, which one interviewee described as "a golf course with some houses around it," almost totally exclude commercial uses. The town of Bow Mar has the appearance of a subdivision, with few connections between its looping street system and that of its neighbors; its zoning is similarly finicky. A mayor of the middle-class city of Arvada in the 1960s enlisted academic geographers, architects, and planners to design and protect "a city of homes" (Leonard and Noel 1990, 307–10). Today, Arvada has a large population but little employment.

Other cities engage in subsidies or annexation battles to promote large-scale nonresidential taxpaying entities like shopping malls or business parks. As a result of these varied approaches to land use, it is easy to encounter cases where municipal boundaries demarcate sharp differences in development patterns, such as at the border between a middle-class, mixed-use portion of southern Denver and the conspicuous-consumption, partially walled suburb of Cherry Hills Village.

Overall, the metropolitan area has about two residents for every job. But the ratio in specific places varies a great deal, as indicated in table 5.1. Denver has not lost its status as a "job-exporting" city. Given the permanent advantages and historical legacy of being the center, it should not be surprising that Denver has nine jobs for every ten residents. But the other municipalities have taken varied paths, encountered various opportunities, and pursued highly divergent strategies in regulating the use of their land. It is unlikely that randomly drawn municipal boundaries of comparable geographic size would have produced such patterns.

Older municipalities that originated as settlements with separate identities outside Denver's sphere continue to serve as business centers of varying scales.

TABLE 5.1

Ratio of Employment to Population in Municipalities and Unincorporated Areas in Urbanized Portions of the Denver CMSA

	Ratio	Total Employment
Denver six-county CMSA average	0.56	1,027,838
JOB-EXPORTING PLACES		
Lakeside	109.55	1,134
Glendale	2.11	5,182
Greenwood Village	1.82	13,812
Denver	0.90	419,665
Commerce City	0.86	14,160
Sheridan	0.84	4,159
Morrison	0.82	380
Unincorporated Boulder County	0.81	34,511
Boulder (city)	0.74	61,359
RELATIVELY BALANCED PLACES		
Unincorporated Arapahoe County	0.64	67,470
Louisville	0.63	7,831
Unincorporated Adams County	0.59	37,235
Englewood	0.59	17,305
Unincorporated Jefferson County	0.56	80,646
Golden	0.54	7,115
Wheat Ridge	0.51	15,066
Littleton	0.46	15,436
Lakewood	0.43	54,721
Brighton	0.39	5,520
Columbine Valley	0.37	397
Castle Rock	0.36	3,131
WORKER-EXPORTING PLACES		
Aurora	0.33	73,156
Longmont	0.31	16,187
Broomfield	0.27	6,675
Northglenn	0.27	7,245
Cherry Hills Village	0.25	1,333
Unincorporated Douglas County	0.24	10,990
Parker	0.21	1,169
Edgewater	0.21	991
Westminster	0.21	15,310
Bow Mar	0.19	159
Thornton	0.17	9,381
Arvada	0.16	14,417
Superior	0.14	35
Mountain View	0.10	55
Lafayette	0.08	1,134
Federal Heights	0.08	770

Source: Calculated from data in Denver Regional Council of Governments 1990, 1991b.
Note: Employment estimates are from 1988, and population data from 1990.

This includes cities such as Boulder, Golden, and tiny Morrison, which have identifiable "downtowns," however small. By contrast, the inner suburb of Lakeside, with 1,134 jobs and 11 residents, is identifiable as a separate community on paper only. As a haven for businesses, with few service obligations, Lakeside resembles places such as Industry, California, and Teterboro, New Jersey. While its institutional origins are now obscure, it is doubtful that the extreme imbalance is accidental.

Aurora has tended to be a bedroom suburb. Lakewood, in contrast, which was an unincorporated area with relatively loose building regulations until 1969, is relatively balanced. A tour of the older, eastern portion of Lakewood in particular shows a fine-grained mixture of office/commercial sites and moderate-cost housing (see Lewis 1993). Other analysts have discussed this municipal variety in socioeconomic terms. In Adams County, Stephen J. Leonard and Thomas J. Noel point out, "Competition [among cities], coupled with minimal county effort to equalize economic and social conditions, led to considerable disparity among communities. Federal Heights, in western Adams County, with many mobile homes, had 9.1 percent of its population living in poverty in 1980, while east Westminster's rate was 5 percent" (Leonard and Noel 1990, 365).

Particularly striking is the high degree of balance in the unincorporated portion of all suburban counties (except recently rural Douglas). In part, this is simply a result of the large geographic size of these areas; areas of housing and of jobs are merged into one overall ratio. But recall, too, that municipalities tend to be "entrepreneurial," whereas counties are more administrative in character. Suburban office growth, one county commissioner maintained, tends initially to take place in unincorporated county areas, where property tax (as opposed to sales tax) ratables are most sought after. Very often, these complexes are subsequently annexed by municipalities (Ferdinandsen interview 1992).

Transportation Impacts of Jobs-Housing Imbalances

These land-use disparities, along with the general growth of the population, have had a serious impact on transportation patterns. Congestion problems have been particularly pronounced in the area's freeway system. Local roads show somewhat less stressful conditions, except around some notable activity-center bottlenecks.[20] While roadway congestion has been a problem throughout the metropolis, it is suburb-to-suburb flows that have grown at the fastest pace. Vehicle occupancy continues to decline. Bus patronage and carpooling rates are steady or falling, "possibly due to a lack of incentives for auto drivers to use other modes" (DRCOG 1988b, 8). For example, the real cost of parking in metro Denver has declined in recent years.

Low-density settlement—which virtually requires frequent auto use—along with job/housing imbalances, have had predictable results. From 1960 to 1980, population density in the "urbanized area" of the CMSA fell from forty-eight hundred to thirty-five hundred persons per square mile. Vehicle-miles traveled doubled between 1971 and 1987, and an estimated 84 percent of the total takes place outside Denver's city limits (DRCOG 1988b, 14, 17). A DRCOG study found that "between 1971 and 1987, a large portion of the freeway system in the region has become congested to the point of operating at or beyond its capacity" (DRCOG 1988b, 24–25). The problems are especially acute in Aurora—for example, along I-225—with its high disproportion of housing in relation to jobs. Congestion is also very severe along much of I-25 and I-70. Overall, median home-to-work time increased from 19.3 minutes in 1971 to 23.2 minutes in 1985, a significant aggregate decline in transportation quality (DRCOG 1988b, 17). Underlying the aggregate trends are numerous decisions made by local governments and developers.

Jobs Without Housing:
The Evolution of the Denver Tech Center Area

Ten miles southeast of Denver's CBD, at and around the intersection of I-25 and I-225, rises a dramatic, albeit unfinished, skyline. Located for the most part outside Denver's boundary, the Denver Technological Center (DTC) is the region's second-largest "downtown." However, the luxury large-lot homes that border the DTC do not allow for jobs/housing propinquity for most workers. Understanding the growth dynamics of what DRCOG labels the "southeast employment area" requires knowledge of Greenwood Village—a little town with some very big houses—an awareness of the lurking presence of Denver City and County, and an appreciation for the influence of one individual.

The founder of the DTC, George M. Wallace, has been one of the most significant and complex figures in the suburban Denver boom.[21] Wallace opened an engineering office in Denver in the 1950s, suffered hard times for a few years, but in 1961 was able to buy a new, black car. A big-city hassle experienced shortly thereafter indirectly led to the DTC's development, as Wallace explains:

> Some son of a bitch with a white car had opened his door and left a big white scratch on my car. . . . I'll take credit for being the first human in orbit—I

went about 29,000 feet in a minute, I was so goddamned mad. [So I decided to] find a little piece of land outside of Denver where I'd build my own office—with a parking space 20 feet wide. . . . You can never picture exactly what will happen. I figured growth would be north to south, and that this growth would follow the Valley Highway [I-25]. In fact, I was certain of that. (Quoted in Meadow 1988)

Wallace bought the smallest tract he could find along the highway, which was forty acres of unincorporated Arapahoe County. He thought he needed one acre and planned to sell the rest. Soon, however, Hewlett Packard's David Packard approached him to purchase one and a half acres, offering $35,000. Spotting an opportunity, Wallace used the money and the land as collateral to obtain a $150,000 loan to install water, sewer, and power connections and improvements for a business park. Honeywell and Control Data occupied two more low-rise buildings by 1965. After encountering some rocky financial periods, the office center grew by leaps and bounds in the 1970s, bolstered by the completion of I-225 and other nearby arterials. Wallace entered into joint ventures with some of the nation's largest development firms, since he was unable to finance the "prestige" developments operating alone.

Although the first high-rise office building was not complete until 1980, by 1994 DTC hosted 165 buildings, about 900 firms, nearly 30,000 workers, and at least 1,100 hotel rooms (Cervero 1989, 63–65, 206–07; P. Moore 1994). Wallace sold ownership of the development in the late 1970s, but remained active as the Tech Center's CEO. DTC will be allowed to build up to a total of 22 million square feet under Greenwood Village's special "Town Center" zoning designation, and as of 1992, was developed to about half that capacity (Barnard interview 1992).

On the political side, Wallace wielded several weapons. DTC's developers established their own political action committee and gave substantial campaign contributions. Wallace and friends also created an alliance of special districts and developers functioning as a quasi government, the Joint Southeast Public Improvement Association, founded in 1982 (Buehrer 1986; Atchison 1987). Raising about $25 million in the 1980s among private parties, JSPIA, with Wallace as chair, funded key highway interchanges and internal road improvements that provide easier access to DTC and the other business parks and centers along the I-25 corridor.

In the absence of municipal control, Wallace finessed his own exclusionary mechanisms and infrastructure provision under Colorado's lenient district rules. Essentially, land-use regulation was privatized. The DTC's own Goldsmith Metropolitan District is a special district providing water and sewer connections within the complex. An architectural control committee oversees covenants and represents a quality checkpoint for new projects in the center (E. Smith 1987). These groups also have "leaned on" the Colorado Department of Transportation to widen I-25 and I-225, and pressured local jurisdictions for improved lighting and roads. One respondent said of the DTC-area districts, "Those guys know all the buttons to push politically."

The Influence of Greenwood Village

Most of the Tech Center and its neighbor, the huge Greenwood Plaza development, are now located in the small city of Greenwood Village. It is doubtful that the founding residents of that municipality, incorporated in 1950, foresaw anything like a center of commerce in their community (Barnard interview 1992; Greenwood Village Arts & Humanities Council n.d.; Greenwood Village Planning Department n.d.; Leonard and Noel 1990, 291–95). At the time, Greenwood Village was an area where some elite commuters had built homes among existing small farms, and it incorporated to retain its peace and quiet. Charles Enos, a Denver corporate attorney who had built what was initially a summer home in the area, led the drive for independence. Drawing on the model of prestigious Cherry Hills Village to the north, Enos wanted to preserve the rural aspects of the area, and specifically, to avoid "intrusions" by Denver or rezonings by Arapahoe County. Later, as Greenwood Village's first mayor, Enos presided over a town of barns and large homesteads that was initially three miles wide and one mile long. The city adopted a large-lot zoning ordinance in 1951. The roads were fashionably unpaved, discouraging through travel (some roads remain unpaved today in this original portion of the city). Upper-status subdivisions began to appear.

The next fifteen years brought rapid change to the surrounding area, as I-25 was completed and the Tech Center begun not far east of town. With Denver's interest in this developing area mounting, Greenwood Village became more assertive in the 1960s and 1970s. It undertook a series of extensive annexations, including a "flagpole" annexation across I-25 and the Cherry Creek Dam to Aurora's border. This action was taken "in order to stop Denver from coming in right on top of us," according to Rollin Barnard, a mayor in the early 1990s who had served on the planning board at the time of the annexation. This move foreshadowed the Poundstone Amendment by cutting off Denver's expansion options to the south.[22] The primary issue for Greenwood Village residents was the integrity of the prestigious Cherry Creek school district and its tax base, in the face of Denver's encroachment. The district covers much of southern Arapahoe County.

One attempt by Denver to annex Greenwood Plaza led a Greenwood Village mayor to threaten, "We will fight Denver in all ways possible like Poland did when Hitler decided he needed more land" (quoted in Leonard and Noel 1990, 293). The suburb's annexations extended the city well east of I-25, and came to include the expanding DTC—which was then hit with restrictions on its future ability to expand toward residential neighborhoods. (DTC and other lands near I-25 had been developed under county zoning allowing businesses.) Greenwood Village issued a comprehensive plan envisioning a "low-density" residential community with "commercial districts" along I-25 (Greenwood Village Planning Department n.d.).

But in 1975, after a lengthy court appeal by unhappy landowners, the Colorado Supreme Court, to the city's horror, declared all the annexations up to I-25 and beyond invalid for technical reasons. Suddenly dismembered, Greenwood Village wasted no time in responding:

> The monumental task of re-annexing the lands up to the Cherry Creek Reservoir was completed by December 28, 1975, but concessions were made in the commercial districts in order to put the City back together again. Height limitations and site-plan review no longer applied in the [DTC] town center zone east of I-25, and [business] zoning was placed on [land adjacent to Greenwood Plaza]. (Greenwood Village Planning Department n.d.)

In other words, DTC reacquired its nearly autonomous land-use control system. In the 1980s, Wallace filed a separate $850 million lawsuit against the city over its restrictions on DTC's ability to expand. "Wallace drove a hard bargain," according to former mayor Barnard. In exchange for the DTC being placed back within the village, the developer received the city's guarantee that it would permit up to 22 million square feet in a "Town Center" zoning category, to be enforced by the landowners themselves. Thus, Greenwood Village's role in land-use regulation at the DTC is limited to enforcing building codes. "A lot of people feel that was a major giveaway, but think of what the DTC provides to the city," Barnard says. He estimates that residential property taxes would be many times higher if the commercial zones had been lost.

All in all, Greenwood Village emerged from these conflicts more successfully than Poland in its fight against Hitler. It still boasts some lots of twenty to forty acres, and nearly all homes have three-quarters of an acre or more. The city's zoning is heavily single family. Greenwood Village has also acquired eighty-six acres of parks and has built many miles of bicycle paths and equestrian trails. Residents "want heavy police services, and are willing to pay for it" (Barnard interview 1992). There were 56 police officers in 1989 for a population of 7,589 (Greenwood Village Arts and Humanities Council n.d., 11, 26).

TABLE 5.2

Zoned Land Use in Greenwood Village, 1992

Zoning Classification	Total Acres (%)
Single-family housing	69.6
Multifamily housing	1.1
Mixed commercial	9.4
Office and service	3.3
Town center	16.6

Source: City of Greenwood Village, Department of Planning and Zoning, personal communication, 1993.

"Paying for it" is less burdensome than it might be because 70 percent of taxes are sales and use taxes, borne mainly by nonresidents. An "occupational privilege" levy charges employers a head tax for each worker, while a lodger's tax awaits those headed for hotels in and around the DTC. In contrast, the tax felt most by Greenwood's homeowners—the ad valorem property tax—is one of the lowest in Colorado. By itself, the mayor says, it might be "enough to keep city hall open about a week and a half per year" (Barnard interview 1992). Clearly, the little suburb has been able to extract substantial resources from the new downtown.

Local Decisions, Regional Outcomes

DTC differs in an important way from true "downtowns." Traditional central business districts have a visible density gradient around them, in which commercial services and dense residential uses cluster close to high-rise offices, while low-density, high-status housing is farther away. The zones around the DTC *that are located within Denver's city limits* basically conform to this model. An area of higher-density condominiums and apartments abuts the northern end of the office agglomeration, and provides a buffer for the single-family neighborhoods of Denver further north. Unincorporated Arapahoe County, to the south of Greenwood Village, also permits higher-density housing.

But Greenwood Village, though it has plans for eventual annexation to round off its borders, is not seeking to add any of the higher-density areas to the south. Residents, Barnard says, are "not interested in diversifying.... They want to hang on to what they've got." A Denver city planner notes that, compared with upper-income neighborhoods within the central city, Greenwood Village and Cherry Hills Village are "much more able to take care of their own self-interest" (Appell phone interview 1992).

George Wallace thus finds his empire to be something of an island surrounded by a small sea of low-density homes (and the Cherry Creek Reservoir
Recreation Area, a state park). Greenwood Village is suspicious of higher-
density building, and of change in general. J. Madden, the president of Madden Co., which developed the Greenwood Plaza complex just south of DTC,
related a number of battles with the city. The neighborhoods, he said, have an
"overzealous way of protecting boundaries. Objectivity disappears." In a city
so small, "everything becomes emotional and thereby irrational" (Madden
interview 1992). In comparison to downtown Detroit, where his firm received
a hero's welcome when it built a downtown office tower, Greenwood Village
"takes on the attitude of 'just say no' " (Madden, quoted in Raabe 1990).

When former mayor Barnard was asked what Greenwood Village would
look like if it had never incorporated, he said:

> Most developers are clearly interested in the bottom line. They can be fine
> people, quality developments. But if they can get 400 units on a piece of land
> that someone else might want one or two on, they'll do it. . . . The county
> goes right along with the densities the developers request. [So what would
> have happened if Denver had been able to annex the area?] Look and see.
> That many more houses, commercial strips. It would look like any other big
> city. [Incorporation] kept people from coming in and taking over this oasis
> in the middle of a metropolitan area.

George Wallace spotted that oasis early on, and while capitalizing on its
charms, has tried to render it "big city." It is probably as a frustrated developer,
as much as a civic leader, that he finds the Poundstone Amendment "the most
stupid thing that's ever been done, virtually destroying Denver" (quoted in
Raabe 1986). Or, as Madden puts it, "At least in Denver, the homeowners are
not the same people who run the government."

Transportation Effects

Jurisdictional orientations have an impact on the entire region. The contradictions between the municipal preservationist strategies on one hand, and
the urbanization pressures generated by the DTC and nearby complexes on
the other, have led to serious transportation problems. An island of employment sits alongside the exclusive housing of Greenwood Village and Cherry
Hills Village. The two-village area averages one household per two acres, an
exceedingly low density (DRCOG 1991a, 78). A DRCOG report on transportation problems in the southeast area also notes that "east-west travel through
Cherry Hills Village and Greenwood Village is hampered by discontinuous
streets," because the loopy road system was designed to repel through traffic
(DRCOG 1991a, 43).

At peak travel hours, many of the freeways and arterials in the area reach the highway department's lowest defined service level, which means stop-and-go travel at volumes that exceed capacity (DRCOG 1991a, 47). Many of the area's workers drive from Aurora, but journeys to and from that city are made even more difficult by the Cherry Creek Reservoir Recreation Area, which forms a natural travel barrier between the eastern portion of the metropolis and the Tech Center area. A 1990 survey of employers in the area found 50 percent agreeing that traffic congestion was a problem for their companies.[23]

The physical layout of the office-park area also makes alternatives to car commuting difficult. Staff at the Regional Transportation District bemoan the setbacks, free parking, and occasional lack of sidewalks at the southeastern complexes, which make it difficult to entice employees to ride buses. More than two-thirds of the respondents in the survey of employers stated that existing bus service was not helpful to their workers. As of the late 1980s, less than 5 percent of patrons and employees heading to DTC chose transit (Cervero 1989, 64). Cars hold an average of just 1.13 persons during peak periods.

The accessibility problems make it less likely that sites such as DTC will serve as a job option for the inner-city poor. A janitorial service company serving buildings in the area found that its largely Latino work crews had a difficult time getting to work from Denver. One developer, not involved in the southeast area, views the situation from a distance, and sums up the tensions of large-scale commercial development in the new suburbia: "DTC has a problem. . . . People have to commute from Aurora, Castle Rock, the northern suburbs. Densification there would have been nice, more apartments. But realistically, what are you going to do, put Section 8 [subsidized] housing there? You can't expect that executives are going to play with the gangs."

Incorporated Inner Suburbs: Reluctance to Change

While the DTC/Greenwood Village case is perhaps the most stark example of development disparities, it is not the only one. Suburbs around Denver show an eclectic variety of development orientations. Littleton, for example, has been trying to redevelop its old downtown, while also annexing new growth extensively. Commerce City, a lower-status community that developed around an industrial area, is now desperately trying to add housing. Citizens of the inner suburbs of eastern Jefferson and southwestern Adams Counties, many of whom are long-time, elderly residents, participate actively in volunteer causes designed to remove "adults only" businesses from their environs, and to combat decay. These areas are "both antigrowth and antitax" (Ferdinandsen interview 1992; Coney interview 1992).

While conventional theories of urban politics would lead us to suspect that upper-status towns are most likely to engage in growth controls, evidence is far from uniformly supportive (Donovan and Neiman 1992). As a rule of thumb in the Denver area, it is *older* rather than wealthier communities that tend to resist the intensification of land use. Long-time residents are familiar and comfortable with their residential neighborhoods, and tend to be dubious of engineered change. As a DRCOG study notes:

> Wheat Ridge, Englewood, Northglenn, Sheridan, Edgewater, Glendale and Mountain View all fall into the category of "first ring" suburbs surrounding the center city. Bow Mar and Morrison, though outlying, are small communities that are showing the "aging in place" phenomenon where older residents remain in the same homes where they raised their families. As time passes, they tend to have increasingly smaller household sizes as children move away. (DRCOG 1991b, 7–12)

Edgewater, with a population of forty-six hundred in an area of a single square mile, is a small-town oasis bordering Denver. Looking for sales tax revenue to supplement its long-suffering tax base, the city council created a Redevelopment Authority in the early 1980s, which then issued $11 million in bonds in order to build a strip mall on some swamp land. But the old-line citizenry was upset at this change. Council meetings grew heated, and longtime neighbors stopped speaking to one another (Mehle 1992).

Englewood, a larger municipality, illustrates the difficult position local officials find themselves in in older, inner suburbs. Early on in the region's history, the city was an independent business and population center, and developed varied land uses. But before it could capitalize very much on its independence in the modern era of suburban annexations, Englewood was beat to the punch:

> Surrounding municipalities proliferated, too, and Englewood's expansion was checked by the rise of Cherry Hills Village to the east, Littleton to the south, Sheridan to the west, and Denver to the north. Locked into 3,834 acres, Englewood saw its population peak at 33,695 in 1970 and slip to 30,021 in 1980. Residential neighborhoods vary tremendously, ranging from one-bedroom shacks on unpaved streets to an enclave of millionaires, from tar-paper boxes to Arapahoe Acres, a 1950s nest of 117 low-slung, Frank Lloyd Wright–style homes. (Leonard and Noel 1990, 286)

With no room to expand, Englewood has attempted a number of tactics. City officials have tried to retain and draw medium-sized industrial firms. Toward this end, Englewood shares a state Enterprise Zone designation with the neighboring city of Sheridan, along the somewhat run-down Santa Fe Boulevard corridor (Reed 1991a). But a plan that would have led to a major change in the cityscape close to residential areas led to a political conflict in which "the neighborhood became unglued" (Mugler interview 1992). Englewood planners sought to redevelop the declining Cinderella City Mall as a mixed-use activity center, complete with high-density apartments. In the ensuing protest, appointed city officials were ousted for trying to implement a land-use strategy at odds with residents' vision of their community.

In a centrifugal era where bigger and better malls were built ever farther into the hinterland, Englewood has found it hard to maintain its commercial tax base. Although remodeled in 1984, Cinderella City Mall generated sales tax collections in 1992 that were half the 1984 level, as beleaguered retailers began shutting their doors early in the evening. In 1990, Englewood's Urban Renewal Authority was forced to notify bondholders of its impending default on $30 million in uninsured bonds for the city's downtown retail district. When it added retail space to a glutted local market, the downtown district proved unable to compete:

> Longtime residents and businessmen took the . . . district's impending default as evidence that the blue-collar enclave south of Denver is becoming "another dying suburb." Many suggest the shopping-center approach to urban growth is partly to blame, along with Colorado's general economic slump. (Leib and Finley 1990; see also "Malls facing up" 1992)

These vignettes seem to support hypotheses that rest on the institutional model. Existing business centers are unlikely to retain their vitality where land-use regulation is highly divided and geographic spread is encouraged. Smaller jurisdictions are less able to muster the material resources and consistent political support necessary to help business districts grow and adjust. Areas of strictly residential growth coalesce. In the process, metropolitan disparities are magnified.

Attempting to Reshape Suburbia

Advocates of regionalism have not stood idly by as Denver has evolved into a radically deconcentrated shape. There have been several efforts over the past twenty years calling for stronger state or regional oversight of land use. While these campaigns have yet to achieve the results they sought, the existing regional units—DRCOG, the council of governments, and RTD, the regional public transportation agency—have also attempted to influence growth patterns. For RTD, new modes of transit have long been seen as desirable if the metropolis is to be organized more around public transportation and less around the needs of the automobile. For DRCOG, visionary land-use and transportation plans provide a model for environmentally sensitive growth.

DRCOG: Persuasion and Planning

DRCOG's political visibility is low, however, and it has been limited in its capacity to influence land-use decision making in the counties and municipalities. The council's professional staff is well versed in current planning dogma regarding the desirability of mixed-use, relatively dense suburban development, but it is unclear whether their efforts have had much impact on the local agents who actually regulate land use.

Moreover, as an entity that depends on the good will of its constituent governments, DRCOG is not in a strong political position to advocate changes in regional policy. For example, its 1976 regional plan designated twelve specific "activity centers" in the metropolis. A long debate followed about the designations, touching on issues of equity among subregions and the cross-jurisdictional impact of specific centers. After that controversy, the council's more recent plans have included only the concept of "peripheral urban centers," without an attempt to map their locations. Thus, "winners and losers" are no longer specified.

Recently, DRCOG has begun integrating its land-use planning process more closely with preparation of its transportation improvement plan. Its goal is to keep the region at the same density in 2020 as it is today. Presently, about 500 square miles of urbanized land area accommodate the metro population. Under DRCOG projections, the region would expand to 750 square miles in 2020. By comparison, local plans currently show about *1,200 square miles* zoned for urban uses.

Despite DRCOG's historical weaknesses, it is possible that the council's profile will be boosted by new federal transportation initiatives. Because the Intermodal Surface Transportation Efficiency Act (ISTEA) requires no increase in single-occupancy vehicle capacity, the region will be forced to consider alternative ways to attain transportation goals. The federal Environmental Protection Agency can sanction highway funds for regions not in compliance with Clean Air Act requirements. Given these developments, DRCOG is considering the possibility that local governments will "self-certify" that their plans are in accord with regional plans to minimize pollution. Short of a voter mandate for certification, however, this process would have to be voluntary.[24]

RTD and the Quest for Rapid Transit

Given the region's congestion problems, some residents wonder why a regional rapid transit system has not been developed to zip travelers around.

Moreover, advocates of managed growth in many metropolitan areas have long argued that a greater reliance on transit would have the positive side effect of encouraging focused, higher-density development.

In the Denver area, however, the cumulative effects of local land regulation mean that traffic problems defy any easy transit-based solution. RTD's mission to provide a viable alternative to auto use is made extremely difficult by the development patterns that local governments have permitted, and in some cases encouraged. According to RTD's manager of systems planning, "Increasingly, people want a fair share. But origins and destinations are so dispersed" (Heisler interview 1992). At informational or promotional meetings with suburban residents and workers, "We tell people, 'You have to understand when you move to your area, you're in an environment that's not supportive of transit'" (Heisler interview 1992).[25]

Like DRCOG, RTD lacks the power to punish localities whose land-use policies do not support efficient transit service. RTD has sought "densification" of land uses around suburban stations, but has few means to accomplish this. The district has had "development review" arrangements with Aurora and Arapahoe County, but these are voluntary, and sometimes pro forma (Heisler interview 1992; J. Moore interview 1992).

The impossibility of serving the new suburbia effectively became especially apparent after the RTD governing board switched from being an at-large, appointed body to a representative body elected by subdistrict. The suburban majority in the district sought a means to assert control over an entity that was seen as disproportionately tied to Denver and the CBD (Dorsett and McCarthy 1986, 275). While RTD's most visible and successful project to date, the Sixteenth Street Transit Mall, opened in downtown Denver in 1982,[26] suburban residents and elected officials watched auto traffic escalate. They wondered why this ostensibly regional transit agency, funded by a broad-based sales tax, could not accomplish more for them. But when the new elected board radically increased service levels to suburban and fringe areas, the bus system's productivity fell dramatically. The RTD board was forced to cancel its experiment.[27]

From the start, RTD studies "all indicated that buses alone, operating in mixed traffic, could not meet a significant share of the Denver metropolitan area's demand" (RTD n.d., 9). Not willing to be doomed to a bit part in the regional transportation system, RTD had spent about $15 million by 1992 planning for rapid transit projects. But until recently, little was accomplished thereby, and the effort provided a long and repeated history of false starts, overly optimistic forecasts, and unpredictable actions by Washington (RTD n.d., 4–6, 9; RTD 1992b, ii; Meyers 1990). A 1973 plan proposed an extensive, technically innovative system of "personal rapid transit" (PRT), which was estimated to cost over a billion dollars to build. Although the Urban Mass Transportation Administration at one point granted Denver status as a demonstration project for the new PRT technology, no federal funding was secured for this project.[28] After UMTA rejected a similar, but scaled-back, project in 1976, and another RTD study determined commuter rail in the region was not feasible without substantial subsidies, the district tried a different approach in 1980. A study of light rail and corridor bus systems targeted a light rail line in the southeast corridor for construction, and the RTD board put the matter on the November ballot. Uneasy about funding the project locally with a dedicated sales tax for the next fourteen years, voters killed the measure, 54 to 46 percent.

Plans continued to be generated throughout the 1980s. Under a law passed by the Colorado General Assembly in 1987, RTD was asked to develop a "Fastrack Program," which would investigate options for rapid transit in seven metro-area transportation corridors. To turn up the heat on the district, the General Assembly simultaneously created a Transit Construction Authority to develop rapid transit in the corridor between the Denver CBD and the Denver Tech Center area. The legislature was responding to pressure from development interests in the southeast office area, which had long sought a rail line that would tie their district to the CBD, so that it would not have to rely on congested I-25. However, a tax on businesses along the corridor to fund light rail proved unpopular, and the governor removed the authority's chairman—DTC developer George Wallace—for making a racial slur. The entire operation shut down a few years after it began (Walters 1988; Marsh 1988; Atchison 1987).[29]

The plans RTD developed under the state mandate were expensive, and not surprisingly, have not been fully enacted. Two specific segments have been completed, however. First, a set of high-occupancy vehicle lanes, reserved for buses, carpools, and vanpools, was constructed along the I-25 corridor north of the Denver CBD. While perhaps relieving congestion, these lanes are unlikely to affect development patterns. Second, in a greater break from the past, is the Metro Area Connection (MAC), a 5.3-mile light rail line. This project, completed in 1994, connects downtown Denver to residential areas to the northeast (including the historical center of the African-American community, Five Points) and to a new depot to the south near I-25.[30] It could have the effect of intensifying development and redevelopment near its stops.

These new projects are modest in length compared to overall transit system plans. But they clearly represent a departure from the legacy of stalled implementation efforts. While earlier plans indicated RTD's entrepreneurial ambitions in the region, the organization's lack of capacity—in terms of financial resources, intergovernment relationships, and public image—did not allow it to follow through until recently.

What changed? One immediate boost was a 1989 ruling by the Colorado Supreme Court, which held that RTD was entitled to assess a use tax on certain items (e.g., automobiles) purchased outside the district but used inside. Use tax revenues were dedicated to rapid transit development by RTD's board, and by 1991 were flowing in at the rate of $8.5 million per year (RTD 1992a, section 3, p. 3).[31] Strikingly, development of the MAC was funded *entirely* by RTD, through the use tax. Moreover, the state's creation of rival transportation agencies "gave the message to the RTD Board," according to one respondent. "It had to show the area that they were more than a bus company." Some proposals in the legislature would have dissolved RTD. Several less obvious factors also energized the organization.[32]

Overall, RTD staff clearly has high hopes for things to come, and sees MAC as an exciting chance to jump-start a full regional rapid transit system. The RTD board, however, has not been unified on this issue, and federal support is uncertain.[33] There is no doubt that RTD has become a more energized regional entity, and has set its sights on becoming a more fundamental component of the transportation system. But RTD has no authority over development patterns in the most rapidly growing parts of the region. Thus, its most visible improvements are still focused on downtown, even as intrasuburban bus routes struggle for ridership. Data from the late 1980s showed that 18 percent of work trips to the CBD were by bus, but such trips are a small minority of trips in the contemporary metropolis. Overall, less than 3 percent of total trips in the region are by transit (DRCOG 1988b, 34).[34]

In short, regional institutions such as RTD and DRCOG have not been able to make region-shaping decisions. Institutions that respond to localized pressures for growth or protection, in contrast, make decisions that collectively carry considerable weight.

Conclusion:
The Institutions of Urban Growth in Metropolitan Denver

In Colorado, the arrangements of local governance have given incentives to cities and developers to pursue particularistic strategies. These strategies, which are certainly "rational" to those who undertake them, have led in aggregate to difficult commuting patterns, metropolitan sprawl, and a relative weakening of downtown Denver and other historical business centers.

Entrepreneurship is perhaps the most notable characteristic of both local

government officials and developers, who use the possibilities of a relatively
fluid system of local governance. Municipalities are active players in locating
development. Their inducements and restrictions are an integral part of the
real estate game. Given interlocking rules regarding sales taxes and annexation
in Colorado, most municipalities both anticipate *and* follow developers—
especially those in retail. Ever in search of sales tax revenues, both Denver and
the suburbs have provided extensive subsidies for developing and redeveloping shopping centers. It may not be an accident that in 1992, Colorado had the
second-highest concentration of mall space per capita of any state.[35]

State rules have also created an environment that encourages growth entrepreneurship by private actors who can manipulate metropolitan districts and
other limited-purpose, invisible governments. DTC founder George Wallace,
who is famous for his caustic views on the inaction of self-serving elected
politicians, has perhaps been the ultimate master of this unelected sphere.
When he says, "I put deals together, I can do any goddamn thing I want to do"
(quoted in Raabe 1986), it is important to realize how much officially sanctioned "public" action has been part of those deals. The flip side of special districts is that infrastructure provision is increasingly perceived as a nonrespon-
sibility by fiscally strapped localities, which prefer to have the quasi-public
entities take the burden off their shoulders. The multiplicity of suburban
municipal governments, meanwhile, gives some neighborhoods the opportunity to opt out of the commercial growth game through restrictive zoning.

Public opinion surveys reveal that Colorado residents see growth and its
impact as the state's most important issue (Tucker 1995). But as the epigraph
to this chapter suggests, the region "lacks a unified vision" to meet these
challenges. Of course, this arises to some degree because people disagree, or
have contradictory preferences, but also because there is no visible, viable
public entity at the appropriate geographic scale that is accountable to the
public over the whole range of intertwined growth, transportation, land-use,
and environmental issues.

There is no regional "regime," in Clarence Stone's terms, to guide growth,
repair its side effects, and evaluate where it ought to go. To George Koustas, a
real estate executive, "It's just plain embarrassing [that] our local political and
business communities can't get together to solve our most pressing problems"
(quoted in Fayhee 1986). As it stands, there is a limit to what can be done by
public action on a regional scale, when action is restricted to positive-sum
policies that help some jurisdictions without hurting any. There is no coordinating entity that has the teeth to plan and enforce regional policies that may
have winners and losers.

A president of the Colorado Association of Commerce and Industry has

attributed the region's increasing congestion problems to the lack of coordination among relevant public entities and private actors (Buehrer 1986). Although RTD is a frequent scapegoat for critics of suburban mobility problems,
"the finger of failure cannot be pointed just at RTD. In fact, there's no single
entity to point the finger at, or looked at another way, there are too many—a
reality that only serves to complicate the undertaking" (Meyers 1990). Even
among the large regional agencies, relations are sometimes strained or uncoordinated. For example, RTD has expressed official uncertainty about its
service to the new airport: "The level of service provided will depend on the
level of commitment the management of the airport is willing to make to
public transit" (RTD 1992a, sec. 7, p. 3). On the issue of water supply, the
Denver Water Board, by informal agreement, asks DRCOG for comments on
requests to extend their service. But over the past decade, smaller suburban
water suppliers have done most of the extensions, and they see the service-area
question as a matter to be decided locally (Mugler interview 1992).

   Whether the new federal ISTEA requirements will bolster regionalism is an
open question. Regional governance has been a recurring topic in the circles
of civic elites, but enjoys no consistent political constituency. One planner says
it would take an emergency, for example, "two hundred people dying from air
pollution," to secure regional oversight of land development. By its own rules,
the public sector is constrained in its capacity to respond to and work with
private actors for regionwide ends.

   It is perhaps no wonder that historians Leonard and Noel are less than
charitable in their summary evaluation of the region's development: "Postwar
Denver remained a privatized metropolis. Its great achievements were sky-
scrapers, residential enclaves, shopping malls, and freeway escapes from core
city problems" (1990, 253). Similarly, some interviewees blamed a "conservative, wild west mentality" for growth problems in Colorado. But the state is
not overwhelmingly conservative. It has elected a number of progressive politicians to state and national offices, and is one of the strongholds of the
environmental movement.

   Such outcomes result not so much from ideology as from the institutional
realities of governance in the metropolitan area. As long as there is no political
mechanism to register displeasure with the negative spillovers of metro Denver's development patterns, the uncentered, spread-out growth will continue.

6

Portland:
A Regionalized Politics Shapes Growth

In Oregon, it's almost like it's one entity, one mind. In California, there are more people with different agendas.

—General manager of Oki Semiconductor, discussing the interactions with local governments involved in building his firm's new chip assembly plant in suburban Portland

Every day, I'm working for things that most of our residents would vote against if they had the opportunity.

—Planning director of a suburb near Portland, speaking anonymously to author

While Denver has found it difficult to cope with the effects of growth, Portland has been widely hailed as a livable metropolitan area, with innovative approaches to growth management. The usual spin put on such discussions in journalistic and planning articles is that Portland is simply more progressive, or has just been more careful at planning than other regions. In short, if any explanation is ventured at all, it is usually of the "Portland is smarter than the rest of us" variety (see Langdon 1992). But in a public sector that tends to be low paying and fiscally strapped, it is difficult to imagine why planners in northwest Oregon should be so much more competent than their colleagues elsewhere. And as we have seen in Denver, the "unplanned" everyday decisions regarding land use and development often have more impact than regional plans, no matter how grand. It is tempting to attribute the Portland area's initiatives to a unique "Oregon political culture," but there are few dramatic differences between Portland and Denver on this score. While Oregon has exhibited a long populist streak, so have Colorado and other western states—blending direct citizen action and environmentalism with a resistance to intrusive government and taxes. Oregon's supposed progressivism has generally not manifested itself in party politics or recent referendum votes.[1]

Other observers praising Portland's urban environment give credit to Oregon's state land-use planning laws, a notable experiment in growth management. It is certainly true, and has been persuasively demonstrated, that Oregon's state laws have had a major impact on its land values, farm and timberland preservation, and style of growth more generally (Knaap and Nelson 1992). But several other states have taken major initiatives into growth management as well, and their metropolitan areas are rarely held out as models. Oregon's planning role involves setting goals and guidelines, while much of the regulatory action remains at the local level. Moreover, metropolitan Portland has proven markedly superior to Oregon's other urban areas, such as Springfield-Eugene, Salem, and Pendleton, at meeting the state's goals and objectives (Knaap and Nelson 1992; Toulan 1994). Since these other MSAs are smaller and less complex, it is difficult to imagine why they have had a tougher time of it.

I argue instead that political organization in the Oregon portion of the Portland metropolis lends itself to regional policy activity by the public sector, and forces local political elites to consider the regional impacts of their decisions. In a PMSA where the largest suburban municipality in 1970 had a population of 18,500, the dominant central city articulated the only coherent political voice until fairly recently. And in the last two decades, the emerging regional governing institutions have directly shaped the area's orientation toward growth and the region's response to the state planning laws. Portland's distinctiveness owes less to planning genius or public opinion than to political structure.

In this chapter, I examine how this relatively unitary political system created policies that helped to preserve the viability of the central city and its downtown, to restrain growth at the metropolitan fringe, and to inhibit developmental disparities such as job/housing imbalances. Recent institutional dynamics are closely intertwined with the region's growth patterns.

Organizing the Region to Help the Center

As we have seen, a substantial political counterweight to the city of Portland did not exist in the suburban parts of the metropolis in 1970. Although the suburban counties were occasionally able to block Portland's strategic designs in this period, the lack of a municipally organized suburban presence contributed to the evolution of new governing institutions in the 1970s—the Columbia Region Association of Governments (CRAG), the Metropolitan Service District (MSD, or Metro), and the Tri-County Metropolitan Transit District (Tri-Met). Policies promulgated by those institutions during this period

worked to the city's advantage, augmenting the quality of life in inner residential neighborhoods and contributing to the centrality of Portland's downtown. They also helped inculcate an unusual areawide perspective among the
region's land-use and transportation decision makers.

The Goldschmidt Era: Making Regional
Transportation Policies Reflect Portland's Centrality

In terms of the historical and geographical setting for growth in metropolitan
Portland, advocates of the central city and its CBD proceeded uncertainly
before the new suburban era. In general, the city administration relied on
traditional urban renewal strategies.

But a transformation in the membership of the planning staff and of
elected officialdom in the late 1960s heralded a new attention to neighborhood revitalization and "use value" considerations. With federal seed money,
neighborhood organizations were created and brought into the planning process, eventually participating in small-area planning that enabled change
rather than reacting to it. A Citizens Planning Board, for example, directed
Portland's Model Cities program. Quality-of-life issues at the neighborhood
level proved a source of winning electoral strategies for the popular Neil
Goldschmidt, who succeeded Terry Schrunk as mayor in 1973. Goldschmidt
served until 1979, during the period when Portland's reputation was perhaps
rising the most; he later became United States Secretary of Transportation and
then governor of Oregon. In contrast to Denver's mayors, Goldschmidt was
able to bring together his two major priorities—livable neighborhoods and
downtown redevelopment.

Portland historian Carl Abbott, reporting a discussion with a Goldschmidt
campaign strategist, indicates that the internal institutional arrangements of
Portland's commission form of government and weak-party politics were
something of a double-edged sword at that juncture. While power appeared
slack under the previous regime, the Goldschmidt team concluded that a
dynamic leader with sufficient popular appeal would be relatively unencum-
bered in pulling together decision-making authority. In short, city government was primed for a strong dose of central direction—if an ambitious leader
like Goldschmidt were to recognize the opportunity and take charge. Abbott
finds that "Goldschmidt was eager to cut across the decision making spheres,
to find points of agreement among policy areas, and to make the necessary
deals" (Abbott 1983, 180).

Two such points of agreement concerned neighborhood quality of life and
the vitality of downtown Portland. Goldschmidt built his electoral popularity

around simultaneous attention to these two issues. To create the institutional means necessary for this effort, the mayor used his organizational prerogatives under the commission system. He reorganized the weak planning department and other relevant bodies into a new Office of Planning and Development, which reported directly to him. He also started an Office of Neighborhood Associations to coordinate the many active neighborhood groups. These groups communicated service and infrastructure needs, and testified on land-use, zoning, and budgeting concerns (Abbott 1983, 201).[2] Goldschmidt's restructuring represented an entrepreneurial way of tying together a slack, weak-party polity.

Programmatically, the mayor had been influenced by the ideas of urbanist Jane Jacobs regarding the features of livable city neighborhoods—stressing density and variety but opposing surgical reconstruction of urban space. Many Portland neighborhoods had organized to fight off freeway construction or slum clearance in the 1960s and early 1970s, a movement bolstered by Goldschmidt's reorganizations. Funds for housing rehabilitation and provisions to enable new or denser residential buildings on in-fill or redevelopment sites were part of an attempt by Goldschmidt's administration to encourage families to choose a home in the city rather than the suburbs (Lycan 1987, 117).

The mayor was able to link neighborhood living to downtown development by stressing the issue of transportation alternatives and accessibility. Using the city's relative influence within the state and region to halt suburban freeway construction and improve public transit, Goldschmidt attempted to boost the comparative attractiveness of living and doing business in the central city. In the mid-1970s, work began on a new downtown transit mall, which is a bus-only area along two major CBD streets with an attractive, pedestrian-oriented design. During the same period, city council approved a numerical limit on parking spaces in the CBD, intended to induce transit ridership, improve air quality and congestion problems, and allow parking lots to be converted to more productive uses.

These changes could have been overwhelmed by improved freeway access to suburban areas. However, the region's relationship to the interstate highway system provides a particularly interesting contrast to Denver's situation. In the 1960s, an inner freeway loop encircling central Portland was completed, well in advance of planned suburban bypass highways. This marked an important point of divergence from other metropolitan areas, where the less controversial outer loops were often finished first, fueling growth at the periphery. As Abbott reports, "The inner freeway increased the convenience of the central business district in competition with outlying towns" (Abbott 1983, 201). By demarcating a core, the highway also accomplished what urban renewal generally had not, as neglected land parcels in the area were brought into the downtown sphere.

Goldschmidt boosted his popularity by defending city neighborhoods against freeway construction. The transformations in the institutional structure of the city government during his administration helped enable inner eastside and northwest neighborhoods to be heard and taken seriously; their protests eventually killed the proposed Mount Hood Freeway and the I-505 connector in the mid-1970s. These highways had been planned in the 1960s as part of a system of spokes connecting the downtown Portland loop to suburban areas.

The Mount Hood Freeway alone would have destroyed about 1 percent of the city's housing stock and disrupted several southeast Portland neighborhoods. Instead, Goldschmidt, working with two sympathetic Multnomah County commissioners, "mobilized a movement to create a greater role for transit in the metropolitan area" (Dueker, Edner, and Rabiega 1987, 138; Abbott 1987b, 200–01). Importantly, *given the institutional environment*, they did not need to create a *mass* movement. Priority for federal grant applications would be decided by CRAG, which was the region's metropolitan planning organization before it was merged into MSD. CRAG's voting system, weighted to reflect population, allowed the city of Portland, along with Multnomah County and any one other member, to attain a majority. Since the city has always constituted a large majority of the county population, getting the Multnomah delegate's vote usually was not a problem. Moreover, the city had been developing extensive staff resources to deal with newly enacted state planning initiatives, and thus had personnel in place to examine the freeway issue carefully. CRAG technical studies on regional transportation relied heavily on Portland city staff.

Working through policy decisions by the city, its friendly county, and CRAG, Goldschmidt and his allies were able to slow down the Oregon Department of Transportation (ODOT) in its freeway construction schedule. They also pressured Governor Tom McCall, a conservationist Republican, to consider mass transit options as they publicized the environmental impact of highways. In 1975, CRAG supported a radical proposal: canceling the Mount Hood Freeway entirely and replacing it with a major new transit construction project that would link the eastern suburb of Gresham to downtown Portland.

As this new transportation initiative was formulated, Sheldon Edner and G. B. Arrington write, "The sense of known rules and procedures was intermittent" (1985, 2). Therefore, there was room for political entrepreneurship. Goldschmidt and the Multnomah County commissioners, with the eventual acquiescence of the state transportation commission, worked out a political deal in which a downsized eastern beltway loop (I-205) would be completed, and would include a right-of-way for a future transit line. The existing I-84 freeway would be improved, and the Mount Hood Freeway canceled.[3] In its place were substituted three transit corridor proposals. Immediate priority was given to one on the east side of the metro area—where the pressure for some transportation improvement, and a jobs project, was greatest. In addition, politically popular road improvements were doled out throughout the region. Ultimately, this "pot of gold" of 140 transportation improvement projects, worth $200 million, helped create the necessary political consensus behind the proposal (Dueker, Edner, and Rabiega 1987, 139).

After technical studies and considerable debate in the mid-to-late 1970s, the regional leadership settled on light rail transit (LRT) as the mode of choice for the eastside corridor. The transit district, Tri-Met, concluded that it would come closer to meeting its operating costs with light rail than the major alternative proposal—a high-capacity, reserved busway—since light rail is a less labor-intensive system.[4] At this point, Tri-Met had a very short history, having been formed in 1969, and lacked staff and political strength. But it could function as a critic of a politically uninspiring busway idea. It also looked favorably on a project that would give it a visible new role in serving the region's transportation demands. In 1978, CRAG agreed upon light rail.

LRT was recommended, too, with a focus on land-use impacts. Tri-Met anticipated that light rail, more than a busway, would facilitate dense land-use patterns that could be amenable to heavy transit usage and thus strengthen the agency's position in the region (Arrington and Edner 1985; Nelson and Milgroom 1993, 57). While the biggest impact was expected downtown, projects were feasible at many proposed stations. Planners forecast that 20 percent of all the residential development in the portion of the region east of the Willamette River would occur within a five-minute walk of the line.

Given the lack of previous relationships among ODOT, Tri-Met, and the federal transportation agencies, the process of analyzing alternative routes and technologies was largely "played by ear" (Edner and Arrington 1985, 20). Following favorable action by the Oregon legislature in 1979, the federal government approved the project the next year, after some initial delays (by which time Goldschmidt had become United States Secretary of Transportation). During the period when progress was held up, MSD demonstrated the important role of a regional government by coordinating grant proposals from local governments so as to keep the project and consensus alive. Ultimately, construction began, with the lion's share of the funding derived from the canceled Mount Hood freeway.

Portland's superior geopolitical position, as reflected by CRAG's weighted voting procedure, had allowed the transit proposal to make it to the regional agenda. In the construction phase, the city's dominance within Multnomah County also made it possible to overcome residents' preservationist instincts. MAX, as the LRT line was dubbed ("metro area express"), encountered a great deal of resistance in Gresham and unincorporated Multnomah County. Neighborhood activists had to be convinced that the LRT's positive impacts would outweigh the expectations of noise, traffic, and parking problems (Kelley interview 1993; see also Hogue 1988). In a more fragmented urban region, these opposition groups could have gained sway in municipal governments and thereby doomed the proposal.

Once opened for service in 1986, the line proved popular. The proportion of residents of the Tri-Met district saying they use transit at least twice a month rose from 17 percent to 31 percent. Support for transit allowed passage of recent referenda that temporarily increase taxes in order to add spurs to the MAX line.

The Results: Maintaining the CBD's Relative Advantages

The impact of the freeway cancellation and LRT construction have bolstered Portland's competitive position in the metro area's development market. As noted, regional elites had looked to MAX to assist in land-use goals. MSD initiated a Transit Station Area Planning Program in 1980—the first example in the United States of planning for intensive land use *prior* to the initiation of light rail service.[5] Local jurisdictions rezoned for transit-supportive development around the twenty-five LRT stations. Although it is difficult to assess the overall land-use impact of light rail, construction volume along the line was reportedly $800 million by 1993, and more is continually occurring (G. Wilson 1993). The largest share of that has been in Portland's CBD and the Lloyd district on its inner east side. Some observers credit the dramatic infusion of new construction in downtown Portland in the 1980s to MAX. But it is impossible to separate the rail line's effects—and those of the downtown bus mall—from the region's general economic boom of the mid- to late-1980s.

In the unincorporated portion of Multnomah County and in Gresham, where a fair amount of vacant land was available along the LRT route, significant increases in zoning densities were undertaken. On this portion of the line, placed along an older local arterial (Burnside Street), attempts were made to redesign a low-density suburban commercial district in order to provide a "sense of place." Development has been sparser on this easternmost end of the line, but a handful of office and commercial sites have been built near LRT stations. Planners argued that new stores should be built directly at the street side, instead of behind parking lots, in order to create an orientation toward public transit. But the market initially proved resistant. According to a Multnomah County commissioner:

> They said, "We don't do it that way in east Multnomah County!" Cluster development also happened very slowly. Offices along the MAX? That's still a head-scratcher. . . .
> Change was introduced more quickly where there was marginal housing and vacant land, because there was no counter-trend. Developers will wait until the utility of the existing stock declines. The established neighborhoods remained the same, the marginal ones changed. (Kelley interview 1993)

About a dozen multifamily developments have been built along the line, creating pockets of transit-supportive density in neighborhoods that were formerly strictly detached houses (Arrington interview 1993). Thus, east Multnomah County's traditional position as a bedroom "feeder" for inner Portland has not been altered. However, it is developing in patterns more oriented toward transit use.

In sum, accessibility to the center has been improved, but has not been associated with the cars, freeways, and parking lots that have obliterated much of the special historical character of other American downtowns. The situation stands in notable contrast to Denver. Not coincidentally, Portland's CBD has held its competitive position well since these regional approaches to governance and development began twenty years ago. The CBD actually *increased* its share of metropolitan employment in the 1960–1980 period—highly unusual in the age of American suburbanization (Abbott 1983, 227). Downtown employment has jumped from fifty-nine thousand to ninety-four thousand since 1970, with office space nearly tripling (Nelson and Milgroom 1993, 60).[6] As of 1989, the Portland metropolitan area had the lowest amount of *non-CBD* office space per capita of any major metropolitan area (4.6 square feet); its Central Business District, meanwhile, boasted 9.1 square feet per capita, a figure well above the national average.

Meanwhile, the suburbs are less heavily penetrated by interstate freeways than in most metropolitan areas. Until the I-205 bridge was completed in 1980, connecting northeast Portland to Clark County,[7] the only interstate highways running through suburban areas were I-5 and I-84, both of which serve to focus activity around inner Portland. I-5, the major north-south route, connects the area to California and Seattle. More than half of the territory it traverses inside the metro area's urban growth boundary is within the Portland city limits. I-84 connects the Portland region to Salt Lake City and points east. It runs through small portions of Troutdale, Wood Village, Fairview, and Gresham, but once again, about two-thirds of its length within

TABLE 6.1

Major Office Space Agglomerations in the Portland CMSA, 1992

	Square Feet	% of Total CMSA
Downtown Portland[a]	13,002,933	52.9
John's Landing/Barbur Blvd.[a]	1,269,005	5.2
East side[b]	982,301	4.0
Columbia corridor[b]	180,500	0.7
Clackamas Town Center/Sunnyside	515,798	2.1
Beaverton/Sylvan	1,703,056	6.9
Washington Square/Kruse Way/Lake Oswego	2,800,303	11.4
Tualatin/Wilsonville	482,070	2.0
Sunset highway corridor	186,269	0.8
Vancouver/Clark County	1,212,459	4.9

Source: Portland Metropolitan Association of Building Owners and Managers 1993, 28.

Note: Percentages do not sum to 100 percent because some office space is not located in agglomerations.
   a. Agglomerations located entirely within the Portland city limits.
   b. Agglomerations lying partially within Portland.

the urban growth boundary is inside Portland. Moreover, the freeway ends at I-5 near the CBD, and those travelers wishing to proceed further west, on U.S. 26, must first negotiate a circuitous route through central Portland.

Because of these highway configurations, the intrasuburban traffic flow is underserviced compared to Denver. Much travel is forced onto secondary roads. This situation makes these areas relatively less attractive to strategic developers and firms seeking to relocate, compared to wide-open suburban portions of other metro areas. In metropolitan Denver, four interstates cover large amounts of suburban territory, and portions of a distant ring highway have been completed. Secondary arterials in the counties around Denver tend to be six-lane boulevards laid out in a grid, in advance of development. These roads are more typically two lanes in the Portland area, where the local public sector in suburbia is less highly developed.

Because of the accessibility differences, office development patterns in Portland have proceeded in a less centrifugal manner than in Denver. Downtown Portland continues to dominate the region's market for multitenant office development (see table 6.1). Its share declined from a whopping 84 percent of the region's space in 1970 to a still exceptional 53 percent in 1992. The office submarkets in the table listed as *Downtown* and *John's Landing/Barbur Boulevard* are both located entirely within the city limits; the next two entries, *Eastside* and *Columbia River corridor*, lie partially within Portland and partially in other sections of Multnomah County.

Thus, a center-oriented decision-making network contributes to center-oriented development. But such changes required substantial political entrepreneurship; this indicates that a nonfragmented political structure is not enough. The rapid shift in transportation policy toward light rail, land-use impacts, and new decision-making structures, were part and parcel of one basic change "made possible by the emergence of a new regional political elite typified by Mayor Goldschmidt and [Multnomah] County Commission Chair Don Clark" (Edner and Arrington 1985, 29). Another key figure was Rick Gustafson, who served successively as a senior planner at Tri-Met, a state legislator, and finally as the executive officer of MSD. Only with regional institutions can such regional political elites emerge.

Real political decisions were being made by central city and areawide institutions, with very real implications for the distribution of growth in the metropolitan area. Under relatively central public-sector direction, private investment and land-use decisions have been guided to a far greater degree than in most metro areas. As Abbott summarizes the situation:

> The dry prose of planning reports has . . . concealed a conflict between the automobile suburbs and the older rings, with local suburban planners trying to avoid the costs of sprawl and metropolitan agencies trying to distribute them more evenly. More recently, the city of Portland has begun to protect inner neighborhoods and ask its newer areas to share the problems of urban change through mixed uses and higher densities. (Abbott 1983, 30)

Looking back on the 1970s, he argues that, compared to Denver and Atlanta, "the political environment in metropolitan Portland has been biased in favor of the central city" (Abbott 1987b, 198).[8]

Recent Central City Strategies: Intensified Nodes and Corridors

In the 1970s, it was expected, somewhat naively, that public transit projects would keep the region centralized. But subsequent events have made it clear that transportation investments alone will not solve the area's perceived problems (Dueker, Edner, and Rabiega 1987). As well as the center has managed to hold in the Portland metro area, and regardless of downtown's special charms and advantages, countervailing trends could not be overlooked. The issues have been ably summarized by Mark Madden, a real estate consultant: "The national trend toward the suburbs, the matter of parking (which has gone up 11 percent a year [in cost] throughout the decade), the fact that land downtown costs 10 to 15 times what prime land in the suburbs costs, plus the fact that the industries coming in are service industries, all add up to a trend to more suburbanization" (quoted in Portland Metropolitan Association 1993, 15). Macrolevel forces have strained the region's city-centered approach to growth. These pressures have led to further institutional elaborations and important policy debates in Portland city government, in regional entities, and at the state's Land Conservation and Development Commission (LCDC).

"Portland's view of the world has evolved," observes a Tri-Met official. "It's no longer so fixated on downtown" (Arrington interview 1993). The city is now trying to "densify" its residential areas, with the goal of retaining for itself 20 percent of the new growth in the metropolis. Operating with these aims, and under statewide LCDC guidelines to speed approval of permits, Portland has attempted to ease the path for land-use changes. "Portland's building director told a disbelieving audience of Seattle-area developers, planners, and local officials about her streamlined, one-stop permit center, where six city agencies coordinate their review of building permits" (Cameron 1990). The city has also encouraged mixed-use and in-fill projects by passing a pioneering parking ordinance. Under the provision, developers are offered density bonuses for mixed-use projects in which the land uses share parking areas (Cervero 1989, 206).

But the city's goal will be tough to meet. Decisions by the city's commissioners and planners to increase zoned densities in eastside neighborhoods and to allow additions on existing buildings have drawn some controversy. Some residents see row houses and "granny flats" in single-family areas as posing a threat to the established character of a neighborhood (Portland Future 1990, 26). Other community activists, however, have been socialized into the Portland approach sufficiently to give such changes a try. One neighborhood association president, who has worked with the Oregon Association of Minority Entrepreneurs in a program seeking to revitalize an area of northeast Portland, says, "I moved here four years ago from Seattle to get away from 'Pugetopolis.' . . . We'll put up with a little more density in return for keeping the land outside the urban area open and beautiful" (quoted in Perlman 1993).

More daunting than neighborhood reactions may be an indifferent response from the development market. Real estate entrepreneurs see less complex opportunities for residential development in other locations. While new row houses in close-in areas have drawn a ready clientele, more sophisticated land-use changes encounter obstacles. For example, a city planner working with a neighborhood group produced a plan to allow new two- or three-story residential additions atop existing stores on southeast Portland's Division Street. But he faced an uphill battle. "I won't touch mixed use," a local real estate broker told a neighborhood newspaper. "I don't want to tube the guy's projects; he's worked awfully hard. But the jury is out still on whether this is feasible" (quoted in "Will anybody build these?" 1993).

Another element of Portland's response to decentralization, more readily accepted by the market, is its promotion of some outlying business centers within the city limits. While continuing to promote and shape the CBD, the city has also nurtured several subordinate nodes, trying in part to head off the formation of similar business clusters in the independent suburbs. For example, John's Landing, a project in southwest Portland that mixes offices, retail, and residential uses, offers Willamette River views and close access to downtown. But it also features Class A office space that has more parking than is available for downtown tenants. This cluster grew steadily in the 1980s, with the city helping by changing zoning and by marketing the area to developers (Ashbaugh 1987, chap. 3; Mayes 1987). The Jantzen Beach shopping center and convention facility, on a resort island in the Columbia River, draws many Washington state residents to a Portland facility. Its location capitalizes on proximity to sales tax–heavy Vancouver. And the area of northeast Portland around the Portland International Airport has been a magnet for light industrial and commercial development. Much of this area is owned and marketed by the Port of Portland, and has been among the least expensive land available for "suburban" development.

The Lloyd district, located across the river from the CBD in inner northeast Portland, has long been a kind of "second downtown" within the city. The district grew up around a mall, Lloyd Center, early in the automobile era. Until recently it was still perceived as a "low-cost alternative" to the CBD, albeit a "bland, suburban-style business district" (Law 1993). The initiation of light rail MAX service through the area in the 1980s has had a clear—and carefully cultivated—impact, enabling developers and city planners to intensify development and orient it more closely to downtown, now just a brief MAX ride across the river. The public sector has promoted new investment in the area, as MSD and the city sited the Oregon Convention Center there. Meanwhile, private investors renovated Lloyd Center, and several public agencies, including MSD, occupied offices in the area. Recent years have seen the addition of several hotels and private office buildings to the surrounding area. Increases in pedestrian activity, spawned by MAX and the mall expansion, have helped reinvigorate a nearby retail area as well. In 1988, the city council passed a new Central City Plan that focused on ways to unify the business districts on the two sides of the Willamette River. One developer says, "Development of the Lloyd District makes the whole central city more competitive. The growth there would have gone to the suburbs, not downtown" (quoted in McCloud 1991; see also Friedman 1993, 169).

Summary

Portland's mayors and planners have been able to use the city's leading position in metropolitan decision making to cement policies that reinforce the advantages of living and doing business in the center. Most notably, the transportation policy changes accomplished in the 1970s resulted in a transit program that appears to have funneled new development downtown, rather than outward along new freeways. Portland has also been more advanced than Denver in shaping its secondary business nodes such as those at Lloyd Center, the airport, and along the Willamette River. In part, this results from its control of a greater proportion of "suburban" territory.

Beyond these self-contained strategies, the city continues to lobby for regional reform, realizing how vital this process has been to its successes thus far. The strategic plan of the Portland Future Focus Policy Committee concluded in 1991 that "the Portland region needs a government that is equipped to deal with urban needs on a regionwide basis" (quoted in Friedman 1993, 170). Illustrating this attitude, in 1992 departing Portland mayor Bud Clark, a proponent of consolidating some city and county services, half-facetiously threatened to run for county commissioner, saying, "I'd eliminate the job" (Friedman 1993, 128).

Limiting Fringe Growth:
State Growth Management Using Regional Institutions

While the new regional approach to transportation was taking shape, a more fundamental restructuring of the rules and responsibilities of land regulation was under way. The state of Oregon, seeking to conserve farmland, took the initiative and set the major parameters for local rule changes. Its main requirement for each of Oregon's urban areas is for an urban growth boundary, enclosing a land area sufficient to accommodate the growth expected over the next twenty years. Thus, the approach to fringe development in the Portland area can be discussed more succinctly than the situation in Denver. Oregon's requirement of a UGB eliminates most of the possibilities for large-scale peripheral development of the type that Colorado has seen. Nevertheless, it is important to stress the key intermediate position of Portland's regional government in shaping the UGB process.

Regionwide Institutions Shape Portland's Response

Planning scholars Knaap and Nelson argue that the UGB process helps inspire intergovernmental coordination, and does so more effectively than voluntary local agreements on growth boundaries. With state input, "urban growth boundaries in Oregon are more circumspect than they would have been if local governments had drawn them on their own" (Knaap and Nelson 1992, 66–67). Moreover, the state's rules have generally given most discretion in any given urban area to the general-purpose jurisdiction with the largest geographic focus. Thus, where county and special-district plans differ over how extensive infrastructure provision should be, LCDC (and state courts) have presumed the county to be better able to make the determination and thus guide service extensions. Counties review municipal plans and identify conflicts, while drawing up their own comprehensive plans. Not surprisingly, counties lobbied the legislature in support of Senate Bill 100, while Oregon's League of Cities was opposed to it. Since the suburban cities in metropolitan Portland were so small in the mid-1970s, the counties were especially instrumental in the comprehensive planning process (Seltzer interview 1993b).

More important, however, the state legislation gave the Portland area's most territorially extensive government—MSD (initially CRAG)—the power to coordinate county and local plans. Primarily, this involved drawing a UGB for the entire metro area. Rather than having three counties bicker about the line, the state decided that the metro government was a convenient planning entity that could avoid local jealousies.

But MSD, as "the new kid on the block," was not yet prepared to do serious battle with powerful local jurisdictions on a matter of policy (Kelley interview 1993). In particular, Washington County's earlier progrowth decision to extend sewer service across much of the county affected the UGB process there. Sewer construction had put the county in serious debt, and as one respondent describes the situation, "You can't very well tell a farmer he can't sell when he's gone into so much debt" (Seigneur interview 1993a). Therefore, Washington County pushed regional officials for a generous UGB. While the Portland area in the late 1970s had 220 square miles of urbanized land, the original boundary proposed by CRAG would have included 367 square miles.[9]

In 1979, the recently reorganized MSD decided to stick with CRAG's boundary proposal. After considerable hand-wringing at LCDC, court actions, and compromises, a Portland-area UGB of 334 square miles was approved in 1984 (Poulsen 1987, 88). The 1000 Friends of Oregon environmental lobby opposed the planned UGB, contending that it included much more than twenty years' worth of vacant land. Indeed, LCDC had accepted MSD's request to include 15 percent "excess vacant land" in an attempt to control land price shocks, with provision for an inner "interim" growth boundary for the first ten years. Local plans in the Portland area have had to specify conversion of agricultural lands within the UGB so as to prevent leapfrog growth.

Perhaps the boundary was overgenerous. But MSD officials, just beginning to establish working relationships with local governments, were in no position to force a tighter UGB on mayors and county commissioners:

> As a newly created public agency, it needed to win public approval and would soon have to seek continued funding from the three counties and 27 cities within its jurisdiction. . . . Rightly or wrongly, MSD said, local governments had been planning around the proposed UGB for more than two years, and thousands of public and private investments had already been made in anticipation of the boundary. (Leonard 1983, 104)

This emphasizes the importance of perceptions of regularity and predictability in the economic environment, which are essential to steady economic development (North 1981).

LCDC's position was difficult, because the agency was reluctant to interfere, given the stable context. All parties involved had made difficult compromises, and LCDC was under criticism from the state legislature for its general lateness in acknowledging local plans. Thus, when LCDC approved MSD's urban boundary with few major modifications, "everyone agreed the decision was baldly political, but LCDC thought the decision necessary to avoid the political consequences that might ensue if the MSD proposal were rejected. . . . The commission felt it could not afford to alienate nearly half the voters of the state in a single decision" (Leonard 1983, 103). Whatever its faults, the line has by and large held. To date, about thirty expansions have been approved, most of them insignificant. The current boundary delineates about 350 square miles within which metropolitan Portland's growth is to be contained. In 1989, MSD conducted a review of the area's UGB, attracting hundreds of area citizens to its forums. Overall, the regional government has been an important instrument in setting and enforcing limits on the geographic expansion of the Portland area.

Regional Governance:
Guiding Suburban Development to Achieve Balance

While canceled freeways and the growth boundary may have kept development from spreading thinly, Portland was belatedly experiencing the new suburban era by the late 1980s. Probably the last obstacle to Portland fully joining the process that was long under way in the rest of the country was the delay in completing I-205, the region's final interstate highway. Once finished in 1984, the area had a major freeway that connected suburbs with suburbs and bypassed central Portland (though the city was in the process of annexing lands up to and beyond the highway). Meanwhile, both the prosperity and pain of urban change were being felt in the suburban jurisdictions, as urban ills such as gang activity and toxic waste disposal problems began to appear there. One example of the rapid changes in suburbia: The 1990 Census found that nearly one in four residents of the city of Beaverton had moved to the metro area in the last five years (Friedman 1993, 111).

In contrast to the isolationism that marks municipal pockets of metro Denver, the Portland area has seen the costs and benefits of growth spread more evenly. In particular, fewer disparities in development, such as jobs/housing mismatches, have appeared. In suburban growth areas, workers find they can secure moderately priced housing relatively close to their workplace, if they so choose. And the older business districts of the suburbs generally have held their own. The regional transportation and land-use decision process has helped shape these results, by making it difficult for local growth interests to "go it alone."

Transportation Planning with Teeth: Institutionalizing a Regional Process

In the midst of the chain of events that led to the area's first light rail line, voters empowered MSD by merging it with CRAG. During the process of freeway cancellation and LRT development, the regional government served as a common table for the area's jurisdictions. While MSD was not directly in charge of building light rail, the forum it provided helped avoid cumbersome interlocal consultations, according to one account:

> Used or abused by the participants, the MPO [metropolitan planning organization] has become a common meeting ground for the resolution of policy and program differences. Without it, and its technical capability, there is sufficient justification to question whether the process would have found the necessary mechanisms for integrating the diverse jurisdictional interests. (Edner and Arrington 1985, 76)

As an elected government rather than a voluntary council, MSD was much more systematic than Denver's DRCOG in requiring consistency in transportation planning as a condition for federal grants to localities. As one participant put it, "You played ball with the region or you didn't get transportation funds" (Seltzer interview 1993b). MSD formed a seventeen-member advisory committee of local politicians and representatives from state and federal agencies, the Joint Policy Advisory Committee on Transportation (JPACT).[10] An analogous *technical* committee of local, state, and federal staffers was created as well. These committees were formed to meet federal transportation planning rules, which required that all MPOs provide advisory representation for local governments as units; the MSD council, since it was elected by district, did not meet those requirements. Moreover, the MSD council was reluctant to force through its own views, since it did not want to put its legitimacy on the line at such an early stage (Kelley interview 1993). However, the MSD council did cast the final votes on transportation plans. In essence, this created a double-veto system in which MSD's final decisions on transportation improvement priorities could first be grounded in necessary political deal making among county and local officials on the transportation committees. At the JPACT level, "there was a concerted effort to balance the projects out [geographically]," according to Multnomah County's top planner. "You had to get cooperation, build a consensus." The presence of the technical advisory committee "added a technocracy element," and eventually "refined it into a pretty sophisticated political-technical process" (Pemble interview 1993).[11]

In these regular advisory committee meetings, the participants discussed development trends in all parts of the metropolis and eventually came to the realization that population and employment patterns were driving their transportation needs (Pemble interview). Moreover, the group came to see, transportation facilities were being developed to support the land-use planning being done by twenty-six jurisdictions. Seeking to get beyond this vicious cycle—road improvements create more growth, which creates more demand for road improvements—MSD staff began producing pioneering analyses and models to tie together projections of land use and transportation demand. In short, by the mid-1980s the regional dialogue had reached a level of sophistication that anticipated current academic research.

In the process, Metro developed as much, or more, staff competence than the Oregon Department of Transportation (ODOT) on these issues. This has created "an undercurrent of tension," because ODOT is responsible for serving the entire state with transportation, but Metro is by far the most well-organized geographic entity. ODOT must react to Metro's many initiatives (Seltzer 1993b). With its unusually large and sophisticated planning staff, MSD (now Metro) has been responsible throughout for modeling planned highway and transit projects, rather than leaving the task to highway agencies or Tri-Met. In fact, ODOT contracts with Metro to provide transportation planning for the area. When G. B. Arrington, Tri-Met's transit construction czar, discussed this arrangement at a meeting in Washington with representatives from the Urban Land Institute and the Federal Transit Administration, "they couldn't believe it—that a transportation agency would let an MPO do the modeling" (Arrington interview 1993).

But Portland's suburbs have come to see advantages in ceding these responsibilities to the metropolitan government. As Abbott writes, the process "creates a level playing ground and agreed rules for dealing with city-suburban and intersuburban conflicts. To some degree, it mitigates the heavy-handed role that Portland played in transportation planning in the early and middle 1970s." The priorities among transportation projects that Metro sets, Abbott notes, "are treated as contracts" (Abbott 1994, 218). This elimination of uncertainty is a valuable political commodity.

Taken together, the regional decision process for transportation has developed a regularity that has advanced its legitimacy. According to policy analyst Sy Adler, two challenges to the region's system of contractual agreements on priorities have emerged in the last few years. First, progrowth coalitions in outlying business centers "sought transport projects that would facilitate autonomous, locally-oriented growth" (Adler 1994, 125). Second, a group of architects, urban designers, and advocates of downtown Portland pushed a plan that would have changed the route of I-5 through the central part of the city, removing it from the east bank of the Willamette to promote waterfront recreation and development. "Taken together," Adler writes, "these contextual elements called into question the formal and informal arrangements through which participants in land-use and transportation planning had related to each other" (1994, 127).

It appears, however, that both the downtown boosters and the would-be suburban development "regimes" have been beaten back in the name of regional comity. Highway proposals for Washington and Clackamas Counties have been scuttled or granted low priority at Metro. And in 1990, the Portland City Council, despite heavy pressure, decided not to press ahead with the plan to relocate I-5. Cost estimates had run to $300 million, which would have involved substantial reallocation from other projects across the region. The council was unwilling to risk disrupting a regional process that the city had labored hard to create (Abbott 1994).

In sum, the particularistic growth politics of the Denver region is not found in Portland. As the regional transportation planning process has gained credibility and legitimacy, it has been given the teeth to ensure that perceived regional needs outweigh the project goals of local groups. The result has probably been to reinforce existing patterns of employment concentrations, since participants in the planning process have incentives to improve access to existing business centers, rather than promoting new ones near the fringe.

Keeping Land Uses Balanced: The Metropolitan Housing Rule

Another policy in which the regional government took a lead role involved promoting lower-cost housing near areas of suburban job growth. As with the

UGB process, the regional government played a mediating role in the state land-use program. The issue arose because every Oregon city with a population over five thousand—except Portland—had the housing component of its comprehensive plan rejected on first submission to LCDC. With the exception of the inclusive central city, municipalities were reluctant to zone for the apartments or high-density housing that would provide more affordable shelter, whether because of tax/service calculations or their residents' resistance to density.

MSD attempted to overcome this logjam in 1979 by enacting an Areawide Housing Opportunity Plan. This program doled out federal assisted-housing funds in relation to each jurisdiction's needs. However, the program soon disintegrated when funding for housing programs was significantly reduced in the Reagan years.

At this point, LCDC was in a showdown with the recalcitrant city of Lake Oswego. The prestigious suburb had made statements supportive of affordability in the text of its comprehensive plan, but kept actual zoned densities low in order to maintain "community character." Troubled by what it saw as contradictions such as this, LCDC issued a new regulation for the Portland metro area called the Metropolitan Housing Rule (MHR), which drew upon the original MSD plan. The MHR required a mix of at least 50 percent multi-family or attached single-family housing within MSD's boundaries. It also established a "ten-eight-six" formula, under which the metro area's largest municipalities, along with unincorporated Multnomah County, were required to zone for an average density of at least ten dwelling units per buildable acre. Nearly all the remaining cities were given an eight-unit-per-acre requirement, except for five tiny jurisdictions, where the quota was set at six per acre.

The rule is relatively inflexible, and critics say it lacks a coherent technical rationale.[12] The attitude of some suburban officials was summed up by a Tigard council member, after her city was forced into adopting a smaller minimum lot size. "I think LCDC should go suck an egg. . . . We can't be all things to all people. If people moving to Tigard don't like what we've got, let them move to Beaverton" (quoted in Leonard 1983, 112–13). Similarly, in tiny Happy Valley, near the biggest growth area of Clackamas County, city officials wished to preserve "rural character," while LCDC ordered upzoning from 2.4 to 6 dwelling units per acre. Mayor James Robrett said the decision violated the spirit of state planning by allowing "special interests to force development that local residents don't want" (quoted in "Oregon's first land-use order" 1982). From a regionwide perspective, of course, it might be Happy Valley's affluent residents who are perceived as a special interest.

Despite such objections, the zoning changes were made, forced by the state but overseen by MSD. "In calling for such coordination, LCDC comes as close as it can to mandating a lesser form of regional development planning" (Toulan 1994, 106). The metropolitan government is given responsibility to ensure that housing needs are being met in areas with rapidly growing employment, which had already been the goal under its original Areawide Housing Opportunity Plan. The results are dramatic:

> Pursuant to these state goals and assisted by regional planning agency (Metro) guidelines, each jurisdiction in the Portland area has accepted fair share responsibility for affordable housing. The average vacant single-family lot in the twenty-seven Portland metropolitan jurisdictions has decreased through rezonings from 12,800 to 8,500 square feet, and land zoned for multifamily housing has quadrupled to over 25 percent of net buildable acres. (Bollens 1992, 461)

For example, Washington County, unlike other "prestige" suburban areas in the United States, has seen a spate of apartment building to accompany its employment growth. As of 1991, zoning of all vacant land within the Portland-area UGB allowed for 54 percent multifamily units, with some suburban jurisdictions, notably Beaverton, significantly exceeding the required fifty-fifty mix. In two of the region's suburban employment areas, the apartment market was actually considered "overbuilt" in 1992, despite a population influx to the area (B. Gordon 1988; Friedman 1993, 218; Metro 1991b).

An empirical study released jointly by 1000 Friends of Oregon and the Metropolitan Homebuilders found housing to be two to three times more affordable in Portland than in such comparable MSAs as San Diego, Sacramento, and Seattle. Some Portland-area jurisdictions saw more apartments developed in the report's five-year study period (1985–1989) than their *twenty-year* plans would have allowed in the days before MHR.[13]

Evaluating the Relationship Between Regionalism and State Growth Management

The state program has created a state-regional-local nexus of land use regulation, and has increased awareness of urbanization and conservation issues. By approaching these topics in a regional manner, it has forced local elected officials to consider the regional impact of local decisions, especially since LCDC has costly sanctions at its disposal. Finally, the state program energized the metropolitan government at a key time, shortly after its creation, making it a politically relevant unit with a clear focus. In terms of policy effects, the requirement for relatively dense housing in areas with increasing employment has helped prevent wide jobs/housing disparities. In recent years, school overcrowding has made some local electorates restless about the housing mandates, but no slow-growth ordinances have yet materialized.[14]

There are often complaints about the constraints cities face, given state and Metro oversight. But ironically, conflicts with higher levels of government may amount to a symbiotic relationship for local officials who would *like* to be able to act more like trustees than delegates. As Leonard writes, "Although they sometimes have genuinely disagreed with LCDC policies, in many cases the local governments simply lack the political will to carry through policies unless LCDC 'forces' them to do so. Similarly, 1000 Friends has made LCDC appear more reasonable when it has taken some tough actions against local governments" (Leonard 1983, 127).[15]

Since the regional government's role has been less visible than that of the state government, which initiated the administrative rules, it is difficult to evaluate what independent effect Metro has had on the success of the UGB and jobs-housing balance. It is certainly reasonable to hypothesize that having a sovereign entity at a middle level, between state technocrats and local politicians, has made state planning easier politically. Parochial jealousies can be resolved within the region before they are played out at the state level. There, regulators must walk a fine line if they do not wish to be seen as technical overlords. Scott Bollens, who has analyzed several state land-use programs, discusses this pattern of implementation and enforcement as a form of "conjoint federalism." He cites evidence that metropolitan Portland has gone further toward realizing the state goals than other urban areas in Oregon, which lack a metropolitan government. For example, one study found that about 95 percent of Portland-area growth took place within its UGB, while three other areas examined allowed 24 to 57 percent of their growth to escape the urban boundary (Bollens 1992, 461).

Several of my interview respondents supported the idea that Metro was responsible for the Portland area's better performance. A few others claimed there was simply a cultural predisposition in favor of planning in their part of the state. Part of the explanation for divergent outcomes may be that county commissioners are given the coordination responsibility in the rest of the state. They may resist imposing restrictions on outlying development because they are sensitive to farmers' desires to maintain their land values. But in the Portland PMSA, Metro officials lack such a bias, since there are relatively few farmers within the agency's boundaries. Moreover, the sustained experience with regional institutions has made the interrelationship of localities clearer to elected officials than in many other urban areas.

The Clackamas Town Center Area: An Emerging Mixed-Use Node

While the state and Metro programs may restrain centrifugal forces, they have had neither the purpose nor the effect of preserving Portland as the metro

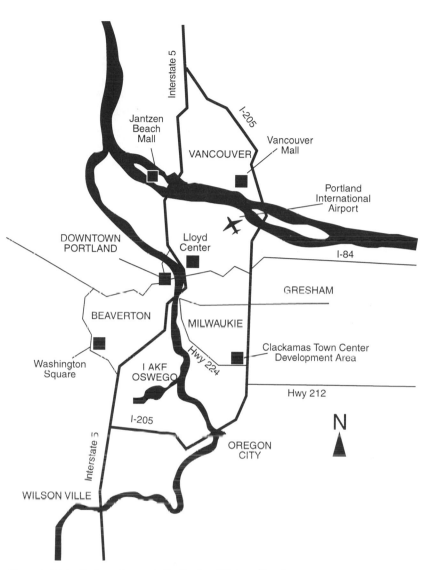

Figure 6.1 Major Business Centers in the Portland Metropolitan Area

area's sole center of significant commerce. Several suburban nucleations—developing under the watchful eyes of public-private booster groups—emerged in the 1980s. The major outlying activity centers in the metropolitan area are the Washington Square mall area in eastern Washington County, the Vancouver Mall area in unincorporated Clark County north of Vancouver, the Portland Airport industrial area in northeast Portland, and the area around the Clackamas Town Center mall in unincorporated Clackamas County. While none of these "edge cities" have cutting-edge planning or design ideas, the Oregon nodes have avoided the disparities displayed by such developments as the Denver Tech Center.

Political dynamics in the Clackamas area are interesting to examine in some depth, since they present both similarities and contrasts to Denver's edge cities. Heavily reliant on timber, Clackamas County was deeply affected by the recession of the early 1980s. The county commission experienced a total turnover in membership, as three business persons promising economic development and job growth were elected. Barry Cain of Gramor Development, which was to undertake several projects in the county in the 1980s, recalls: "They decided, 'Let's sell the area.' They were very cooperative, so long as it was high-quality development. . . . They said, 'Let's not try to over-interpret the zoning code, but rather look at the big picture'" (Cain interview 1993). The Clackamas County Development Agency (CCDA), in conjunction with a booster group known as the Sunnyside 205 Corridor Association, formed a nascent development "regime," in Stone's terms. Established as the county's urban renewal district and business recruitment arm, CCDA concluded that the conditions for a suburban multiuse center were emerging, and that to develop to its full potential, it required a public "custodian" (Seigneur interview 1993a). The agency did marketing research to determine which users the area would appeal to, and settled on a strategy emphasizing retail development, distribution, institutional and medical uses, and high-density apartments. The node now hosts the largest single concentration of suburban retail space in Oregon: 1.2 million square feet in the mall and at least 2.3 million square feet nearby.

The county government used tax increment financing as a tool in building up the area around the Clackamas Town Center mall, spending $8 million for land assembly. Urban renewal policies administered by CCDA rivaled big-city redevelopment schemes in scale and complexity. An area of single-family housing abutting the shopping center was rezoned to allow commercial and industrial uses; this zone change required that land in the zone be sold in parcels of three acres or more. When residents of this seventy-one-acre subdivision complained that their tax assessments had skyrocketed after the rezoning, the county commissioners suggested the residents band together to sell their properties collectively.

Painstaking negotiations ultimately resulted in a developer buyout of 112 homeowners, whose lives had been changed because they stood in the way of redevelopment (L. Hill 1987, 23; Clackamas County n.d.; Brock 1992). While the original developer proposal for this tract after the sale called only for retail, the county development agency held out for more variety. "We wanted mixed use," CCDA director David Seigneur said. "The county still wanted to diversify its employment base—not just eat the orange and throw away the peel" (quoted in L. Hill 1987). A larger development firm took over the property and had a complex mixed-use proposal approved.

Sunnyside 205 and CCDA have actively cultivated the area as a growth center and nurtured its emergence by lobbying the state, county, and Tri-Met for transportation improvements. According to CCDA director David Seigneur:

> Most suburban centers appeared to just happen. There was no caretaker. Clackamas County was maybe a little different: We recognized what was beginning to happen and made a decision to cultivate the center into something as big as possible through a tax increment financing district, and tried to get as much revenue as possible out of it. (Seigneur interview 1993b)

Seigneur's perspective is that the county had the advantage, in promoting the area, of being less parochial than a city. Cities are "too narrow-minded to be custodians. They're not capable of really studying their community—where it's been and where it can go." Certainly, elected officials in a typical suburban municipality would have found it much harder politically to endorse such a thoroughgoing land-use change.

With centralized county direction, less proactive special districts, and a Metropolitan Housing Rule operating in the Portland area, this activity center shows clear differences from the Tech Center zone in Denver. Many high-density apartments and single-family subdivisions are close by, and there is a balanced mixture of jobs and housing. Within five minutes' travel time, the job/population ratio is 0.42; within fifteen minutes, 0.65.[16] Moreover, varied types of employment—retail, office, warehouse, and institutional uses—can be found in the Town Center cluster.

As of yet, however, the fine-grained mix of uses required to support walking, biking, and transit at high levels has not emerged. At the microlevel, county stewardship has not been enough to overcome the limitations of project design (nor has the CCDA tried to do so). The Sunnyside 205 group has lobbied for a light rail connection to the area, and proposed LRT corridors have been protected from encroachment. But the node would require substantial retrofitting in order for it to work with, rather than around, light rail. Sunnyside 205 argued that Tri-Met could have built a light rail corridor along I-205 at a fraction of the cost of its forthcoming westside route. But the transit agency saw an I-205 line as essentially serving only as an economic development project without any major effect on the region's mobility. Tri-Met thus anticipated having trouble getting federal approval, and MSD's JPACT made the westside route its first priority (Freeman 1987).

Nodes in the Western Part of the Metro Area

Other suburban business centers are on the west side of the metro area. Kruse Way, also in Clackamas County, is a new thoroughfare that features several office parks along and around it. The corridor runs east for about a mile and a half from the intersection of I-5 and Oregon 217, and features 1.26 million square feet of office space, along with residential, hotel, and commercial uses. The area is currently unincorporated, but draws on the prestige of neighboring Lake Oswego and that city's executive housing. Like many business parks, its growth was largely developer-driven, and made possible by simple land-ownership patterns—in this case, a heavily wooded tract owned by the Church of Jesus Christ of Latter-Day Saints.[17] Massive oak trees surround the office buildings and make the area one of the most desirable suburban office settings in the region. While not closely intermixed, several single- and multifamily developments have gone up in the area, providing a reasonable jobs/population balance. The job/population ratio is 0.62 within a five-minute travel radius, and 0.83 within a fifteen-minute radius.

Just four miles northeast along Route 217 is an edge city centered around the Washington Square mall. This node was developed in an unincorporated area of Washington County, and later annexed by Tigard. The large mall, and several smaller shopping centers nearby, have been joined by at least ten modern office buildings and two hotels; by 1989, the area had about 1 million square feet of offices and 1.7 million square feet of retail. While precise job/population breakdowns are not available in this case, a quick driving tour of the activity center's surroundings makes it clear that housing is available in large quantities. In fact, one apartment complex directly adjoins the mall.

All together, Robert Cervero delineates a "large-scale office growth corridor" of over thirty square miles on the west side, along Routes 217 and I-5. In 1989 this larger area included "around 32,000 employees, and an even larger number of housing units; accordingly, it has a fairly even jobs-housing balance. A mixed bag of business campuses, industrial parks, warehousing districts, retail complexes, and tract housing populate the corridor's landscape" (Cervero 1989, 99). The Tualatin Valley Economic Development Corporation, drawing members and contributions from private sources and local governments, watches over the corridor.

The most highly touted business area in the west suburbs, however, is a widespread, low-density area of high-tech firms along the "Sunset Corridor."

(The name refers to the portion of U.S. 26 west of Portland, long dubbed the Sunset Highway.) As delineated by its booster business group, it includes roughly nine thousand acres. The corridor still has far more housing than employment, as the area grew from 22,500 residents in 1970 to 62,000 in 1983, and from 5,000 to 11,000 jobs. But it is famous because of its well-known corporate residents: Epson, Fujitsu, NEC, and other high-tech firms, and the headquarters of Nike. With thirty technology firms that employ one hundred or more workers, it is the ninth-largest concentration of the sector in the country (Portland Metropolitan Association 1993, 10). Yet, a Canadian newspaper reports,

> the 3,600 hectares spread on both sides of the highway are not just another string of high tech industrial parks. It's essentially a mixed-use community of industry, commerce, and residences set in a landscaped, low-density, campus-like environment where 80 percent of employees live within a kilometre of their workplace. (D. Smith 1992; see also Benner 1984)

Again, a lobby group—the Sunset Corridor Association—has taken on a major role.

Summary

A mature regionalism combines with state rule making in the Portland area to shape suburbia in a way that contrasts sharply with the patchwork pattern of metro Denver. Through the transportation planning process and the Metropolitan Housing Rule, the area has managed to have suburban growth without massive jobs/housing disparities or an escalation of sprawl and dispersal. In the several cases where progrowth suburban elites have coalesced to promote new business nodes—generally acting through the less provincial county governments—the resulting job centers have not been distant from affordable housing. In addition, the small existing downtowns in several of the older suburbs have generally managed to hold on to their viability, due in part to public policy.[18]

Institutional Elaborations and the Continued Shaping of Growth

To the naked eye, Portland's suburbia does not *appear* vastly different from American suburbia generally. Some land-use activists and regional officials have voiced interest in consciously shaping the form of suburban growth on a more "micro" scale. A set of institutional changes in the late 1980s and early 1990s altered somewhat the political context of development policy. A number of policy changes related to these institutional shifts may portend a new era for the regulation of metro Portland's growth. These changes may help create urban development patterns that look quite different from the standard suburban model in the United States. The degree of proactive policy shaping suburban form in Portland is clearly more advanced than the halting efforts of RTD and DRCOG in the Denver area—even though there is no groundswell of popular support for such initiatives.

Reevaluating the Roles of Counties and Cities

One relatively straightforward change in the rules of the game that will affect development concerns service delivery. Multnomah and Washington Counties are in the process of handing over much of their service roles to municipalities.

Portland officials had long urged various forms of consolidation of city and county services in Multnomah, given the great degree of overlap. But it was a financial crisis at the county level that spurred an unprecedented decision. A large unincorporated portion of Multnomah County had been making do with septic and cesspool systems for decades, in the process becoming one of the largest unsewered urban areas in the country. When the state Department of Environmental Quality ordered the installation of sewers in the early 1980s, county commissioners decided they could not ask the rest of the county to subsidize expensive new infrastructure provision for the area. At the same time, unincorporated residents were in danger of losing their homes if they had to pay for the huge project themselves (Kelley interview 1993; Poulsen 1987, 95).

The county used this opportunity to reevaluate its role as a service provider. As Thomas Poulsen describes the decision:

> Prompted by financial pressures, it announced in early 1983 that it would reduce to minimal rural levels its police protection, planning, parks and recreation, and other activities. In effect it terminated the county service district that had itself been created to reduce the tangle of special districts on the urban fringe.
>
> Residents affected by the change in county policy were encouraged to meet their service needs by annexation to an existing incorporated city. (Poulsen 1987, 96)

In effect, the county decided to put itself out of business as a provider of "primary" urban services, i.e., those normally taken on by cities (Metro 1991b, 69; Abbott 1987b, 54).[19] The city of Portland agreed to build the necessary sewer system if residents of the area signed a waiver promising they would not protest annexation by the city. These rapid institutional changes—and the fear of higher taxes if annexed by Portland—"angered some, who thus tend[ed] to cling to Gresham" (Seigneur interview 1993a). Some residents of the un-sewered area also attempted to create a new city, to be called Columbia Ridge. But the Metropolitan Boundary Commission ruled that such a city would be unable to meet the financial obligations necessary to provide urban services. Meanwhile, Multnomah County worked out annexation agreements with the cities of Portland, Gresham, and Troutdale, designating spheres of influence that would guide future annexations. In the 1990s, the unincorporated pock-ets between the cities are gradually disappearing. The county will be the primary local government only in its rural easternmost portion, most of which is part of the Mount Hood National Recreation Area and is thereby limited in development potential.

The disappearance of unincorporated territory has been something of a shock to accepted institutional norms of service delivery in Multnomah County (Harris 1993). The annexation agreement certainly has given more territorial might to Portland. After holding steady at about 375,000 persons from 1950 to 1980, despite adding land here and there, the city again went on the offensive in the 1980s and 1990s. About 66,000 persons were added through annexation in the 1980s (Friedman 1993, 92). Portland's annexations may be made easier politically because the newly amalgamated residents gen-erally remain in their former school districts. Thus, while the Portland Public Schools serve over 55,000 students—easily the largest system in a tri-county area with fifty-three districts—some Portlanders are in districts that were set up for unincorporated areas. Students in a small portion of west Portland actually attend the Beaverton school district (Friedman 1993, 225).

To the west, Washington County has also attempted to rationalize service provision and lessen double taxation by crafting agreements with cities on annexation. Its plans assume that all unincorporated urban land will even-tually be annexed to a city. The county has told residents of unincorporated areas that if they want neighborhood street repairs or urban levels of police protection, they must vote for special bonds, with amortization localized to their areas. Under these circumstances, large areas have been annexed to Hillsboro, Beaverton, and Tualatin, adding both population and major em-ployment centers to those cities.

But the geopolitical issues are more complex in Washington County, which contains twelve cities along with a small slice of west Portland. Metro has provided mediation between Portland and Beaverton, seeking to iron out ser-vice provision and annexation plans in an unincorporated area located be-tween the two cities. Residents of the area seem less than enamored with tak-ing on Portland's tax and service levels, but the city has nevertheless pushed a proposal that would divide the area along neighborhood boundaries and geographical features (Bodine 1993; "Beaverton council" 1993). In notable contrast to litigation-oriented metro Denver, neither city has tried to take over the area unilaterally, and Metro's mediation process has been respected as legitimate (Abbott, personal communication to author).

The ultimate outlook is for a handful of full-service municipalities dominating the region territorially. Once the unincorporated areas dwindle, the several tiny municipalities, which generally contract with their bigger neighbors for services or rely on special districts, may find the pressure turned on them. As the Portland Future Focus Committee articulates the philosophy:

> Smaller cities which cannot provide a full range of municipal services should eventually be merged with their larger neighboring cities. The remaining cities should be assigned full authority and responsibility for planning, financing, and delivering all municipal services. . . . The cities should also take over small service districts. Larger regional service districts might be retained. (Portland Future 1991, 123)

The Regional Government Matures

Not only do local services determine where future growth will locate, but the transportation priorities of a metropolitan area are also of key importance. In Portland, a continued desire among regional elites to integrate transportation planning and other forms of leverage over development has led to a rethinking of the very role of regional government.

As noted earlier, in the 1980s MSD and its transportation committees had come to the conclusion that they should no longer respond to congestion merely by planning for new transportation facilities. Rather, a process was needed in which the participants would "sit down and talk about where growth *should* go" (Pemble interview 1993). MSD's initial response in 1988 was to begin work on a set of "regional urban growth goals and objectives" in close consultation with local officials; the unwieldy acronym was RUGGOs. The RUGGOs were to be something of a regional constitution for land-use decisions, to accompany the state's goals and objectives. They would form the basis of a series of regionwide plans for such functions as transportation, sewerage, water, and open-space acquisition (Metro 1991c; Glick 1993, 78).

However, some observers of and participants in the process became dissatisfied with the RUGGOs, which were adopted in 1991. As the Multnomah planning director describes the function-by-function approach to regional development, "It got confused and redirected. We realized it needed vision, a three-dimensional texture" (Pemble interview 1993). The Metropolitan Homebuilders expressed the fear that the RUGGOs process would mire regional decisions on growth policy in local turf battles. Moreover, after a decade of Metro in its elective form, by 1990 many were calling for a reevaluation of the agency. For land-use planning activists like the members of 1000 Friends, "We feel it has more authority under state law than it has said it does. We feel they have the role of overseeing local plans" (Kasowski interview 1993).

Under such prodding, a Metro Charter Committee was appointed by state, local, and Metro representatives to propose a new "constitution" for the regional government (Law 1991b). The group rocked the boat by spelling out a significant expansion in MSD's authority. Mayor Gussie McRobert of Gresham was one of a number of suburban officials expressing dismay at the extensiveness of the charter's language, complaining that it "throws out two and a half years of work" on RUGGOs, during which time Metro had collaborated and consulted with local governments. Despite such reservations by defenders of municipal prerogatives, voters in a 1992 referendum approved the charter, which affirmed regional planning as the agency's foremost responsibility. The charter's preamble states:

> We, the people of the Portland area metropolitan service district, in order to establish an elected, visible and accountable regional government that is responsive to the citizens of the region and works cooperatively with our local governments; that undertakes, as its most important service, planning and policy making to preserve and enhance the quality of life and the environment for ourselves and future generations; and that provides regional services needed and desired by the citizens in an efficient and effective manner, do ordain this charter for the Portland area metropolitan service district, to be known as Metro.

The charter gave Metro jurisdiction over "matters of metropolitan concern," which, in an open-ended interpretation, are deemed to include "powers granted to and duties imposed on Metro by current and future state law and those matters the council by ordinance determines to be of metropolitan concern" (Metro 1992, 1). In other words, Metro has become a home rule government, not subject to the whims of the state legislature. The charter even allows it to assume Tri-Met's transit responsibilities (and its taxing authority), after seeking advice from JPACT and passing an ordinance. Metro also received authority to levy $12.5 million per year in new local taxes, not subject to voter approval. The regional government has been studying its options in raising these new revenues (Oliver 1993). The charter also changed the composition of the Metro council, made effective in 1995. The thirteen-member council was reduced to seven, plus a full-time executive officer with veto powers.

The Metro council, under the terms of the charter, was obliged to adopt a regional "Future Vision" by July 1995. "The Future Vision is a long-term, visionary outlook for at least a 50-year period," including "how and where" to accommodate new growth. It is the initial step in a multistage process prescribed by the charter. The next step involves a "regional framework plan" in 1997, covering specific functional areas like the UGB, urban design standards, parks, and water supply. "To encourage regional uniformity, the regional framework plan shall also contain model terminology, standards and procedures for local land use decision making that may be adopted by local governments" (Metro 1992, 2–3). The framework plan must be acknowledged by LCDC, and will represent the basis for coordinating county and municipal comprehensive plans, which will be binding one year after the Framework Plan is adopted.

In short, Metro has the potential to make substantial further inroads into localism in land-use regulation. In the foreseeable future, it could become the region's primary land-use actor. Metro launched into these new responsibilities with a process it called "Region 2040," involving citizens, public officials, and private interests in a discussion of what the region should optimally look like in 2040.

Restricting Freeways and Focusing Growth

Actually, Region 2040 is but the latest in a number of instances in which land-use elites and activists have begun to reflect on the overall current and future shape of development in the metropolitan area. Indeed, events converged in the late 1980s and early 1990s to force such reflection. It was again the issue of highways that drew Portland's regional elites to what may prove to be a critical juncture in evaluating the region's future. Suburban boosters in Multnomah and Clackamas had been pushing for two new limited-access routes, the so-called Sunrise Freeway and the Mount Hood Parkway. But the most tendentious debate was over a planned north-south route through Washington County, a proposal called the Western Bypass (Adler 1994; Tri-Met 1992; Tri-Met 1993; Portland Metropolitan Association 1993, 60; Kirkland 1989; various interviews).

Washington County's growth has spawned a great deal of intersuburban travel. However, much of the county still relies on routes designed as farm-to-market roads. Seeking additional economic development in the county, some elites argue that these conditions are intolerable, and note that the heavily traveled State Route 217 is currently "the only four-lane north-south highway west of Portland and east of Japan . . . in an area where 260,000 new people are expected in twenty years" (Tobias interview 1993). As traffic in this growth zone increased, traffic engineers proposed a twenty-mile Western Bypass. The highway's route would run from I-5, south of its intersection with I-205, toward the northwest, eventually intersecting with the Sunset Highway. Investors quickly bought up land along the proposed route.

When the state's Land Use Board of Appeals ruled in 1989 that building the road would violate LCDC farmland preservation provisions, growth management activists in Portland used the delay in the process to air alternative proposals. According to 1000 Friends' Kevin Kasowski, "Our problem with [the bypass] is that if you build it, they will come. A lot of those lands are rural, and the pressure for UGB expansion would be inevitable. But we should propose an alternative, because growth is inevitable" (Kasowski interview 1993). The group therefore drafted a competing land-use and transportation plan, relying on consultants Peter Calthorpe and Cambridge Systematics. Calthorpe is nationally known in planning circles for his concept of "pedestrian pockets": areas of medium- to high-density development featuring mixed uses, pedestrian features, and transit, rather than cars and parking lots. This alternative to the bypass became one of the options evaluated by the state transportation department. While the bypass is still under study at this writing, Metro officials have indicated they are unlikely to include the highway among the region's priorities for transportation funding.

The Calthorpe study went beyond the immediate question of the bypass to address another problem: While jurisdictions in the west suburban area have accepted a share of commercial development that helps balance jobs and housing opportunities, the microlevel patterns of land use rarely depart from traditionally suburban, auto-dependent forms. A map by Metro of the region's composite zoning pattern shows that the vast bulk of commercial zoning in the western part of the metropolis has been concentrated along six or seven major arterial roads. The situation can be contrasted with the older suburbia of Portland's east side, where commercial development lines nearly every well-traveled thoroughfare in the grid, and housing fills in the interstices.[20]

In other words, suburban officials generally have not attempted to shift their regulation and infrastructure policies away from the types of development patterns that have been tested and accepted time and again. Suburban cities must accommodate all forms of development—apartments, stores, industry, and single-family residences. But as of yet they have been loath to break the mold of the marketplace by trying to *mix* these uses, except in the occasional redevelopment project.

As it has become more and more clear to urban planners that segregated land-use patterns tend to induce heavy reliance on the automobile to the exclusion of other modes, regional, state, and even local elites have begun to articulate a new approach challenging "business as usual" in suburban development. Metro and the city of Portland have promoted the concept of intensive, mixed-use centers, and higher-density suburban corridors, looking to the Toronto area for inspiration.[21] Several Portland-area jurisdictions are also encouraging developers to experiment with the "urban village" or neotraditional town planning model ("Local developers" 1992; Grillo interview 1993).[22]

The major impetus for revised notions of land use, however, has not been a positive planning vision but a new state sanction. LCDC's Transportation Planning Rule, drawn up in 1991 with input from 1000 Friends and the Oregon Department of Transportation, requires a 20 percent reduction in per capita vehicle miles traveled over the next thirty years, with benchmark goals along the way. Once again, Metro was asked to provide oversight, by designing a Transportation System Plan for the region that will provide a framework for local ordinances. In a review of the origins and implications of the Transportation Planning Rule, Adler concludes, "DLCD and ODOT, urged on by environmental activists, have woven a tightly fitting garment for local and regional planners to wear" (Adler 1994, 143).[23] In combination with federal ISTEA regulations, the rule has created pressure for action in metro Portland.

Using Transit as the Hub of New Development

This pressure created a window of opportunity for Tri-Met, which was simultaneously planning its new westside light rail line. (Metro had ultimate responsibility for deciding on the route.) The transit agency knew it was engaged in a riskier enterprise by routing the LRT into the new suburbia of the west, as opposed to the more traditional development it encountered on its earlier eastside line. With the realization that the west side's existing growth patterns would not support mass transit, Tri-Met and Metro chose not to run the LRT along the east-west highway corridors in Washington County—the Sunset Highway or Oregon Route 8. These two strips were already low- to medium-density, with many large parking areas surrounding businesses.

Instead, the rail planners sought to set the stage for new, dense forms of growth by starting fresh. The two agencies decided to utilize an abandoned rail corridor that is contiguous to large tracts of vacant land. About 60 percent of the sites chosen for transit stations are "greenfield" locations—that is, predominantly open space (Kasowski interview 1993; Arrington interview 1993).[24] The state agreed to provide half the required "local match" for constructing the new line, provided that the affected jurisdictions reach an agreement to intensify land uses around MAX stations.

Under the leadership of Washington County, Tri-Met, and Metro, the suburban cities have made such transit-oriented development plans. Influenced by Calthorpe's ideas, these feature zoning minimums of fifteen units per acre for residential and thirty jobs per acre for commercial buildings within a half-mile radius around each station. "Many of the concepts embodied in transit supportive development reflect the design character of Portland's original streetcar neighborhoods, but are tailored to work with today's lifestyles and market practices" (Tri-Met 1993, 16). The county's director of land development services views the situation as precedent-setting:

> Light rail is beginning to crystallize all these [land-use] issues. If they build it [mixed-use station-area developments], will they come? Who will build it first? Who will lend them the money? It alters the rationale of why people come to suburbia. (Grillo interview 1993)[25]

Portland is already doing significantly better than Denver in shaping the metropolis to the needs of transit, and vice versa. Bus, rail, bike, and walking account for 40 percent of commutes to Portland's CBD, where the parking limit poses serious disincentives for drivers, and the Transit Mall makes that mode user-friendly. Looking at the entire PMSA, public transportation accounts for 9.2 percent of the work trips, compared to 6.1 percent in Denver's PMSA. Portland (as of the mid-1980s) also had about one-third more transit trips per capita, and a far lower operating cost per passenger. Per capita vehicle miles traveled, a measure of auto use, is 20 percent lower in metro Portland than in Denver.[26] A comparison of the mode split for work trips in some comparable cities in the two metro areas clearly favors Portland—though some of the transit riders appear to be drawn from the ranks of would-be carpoolers (see table 6.2).

Still, Tri-Met's average weekday ridership of about two hundred thousand will have to increase substantially if a dent in traffic congestion is to be achieved. The MAX rail line, according to one report in the late 1980s, was responsible for removing only three thousand cars per day from the region's roads; the rest of the riders were former bus commuters. At a capital cost of $214 million, that amounts to seventy-one thousand dollars per removed vehicle, and "unfortunately, many of those 3,000 automobiles are still driven to a park-and-ride lot" (Rutherford 1989).[27] MAX ridership, in comparison to the region's 4 million auto trips per day, seems skimpy.

But Tri-Met is pressing on to make transit a viable alternative to driving on additional routes. It is proceeding with steps that will eventually extend a Portland-centered light rail network throughout the metropolitan area. Early arguments from executives in the high-tech industry that intrasuburban transit was a more pressing need for investment have by and large been brushed aside, and work on the westside LRT is proceeding, with 75 percent federal fi-

TABLE 6.2

Comparing Transit Use Among Commuters in
Similar Denver and Portland Municipalities
(in percent)

Residents of	Denver Area Jurisdictions			Portland Area Jurisdictions		
		Mass Transit	Carpool		Mass Transit	Carpool
Central city	Denver	8.0	13.1	Portland	11.0	12.9
Large residential municipality	Arvada	2.9	12.0	Gresham	5.6	13.0
	Aurora	3.9	13.0			
	Westminster	3.4	13.7			
Large mixed municipality	Englewood	4.2	12.6	Beaverton	4.9	10.9
	Lakewood	3.5	11.6			
	Littleton	2.5	10.4			
Medium, rapid-growth municipality	Wheat Ridge	4.1	12.6	Tigard	4.2	11.6
Small, wealthy, residential municipality	Bow Mar	1.0	4.9	Happy Valley	2.4	11.0
	Cherry Hills Village	0.5	7.5	King City	4.3	6.9
				Rivergrove	0	6.5
	Columbine Valley	2.1	4.2	West Linn	2.4	9.8
Executive housing, with office employment near central city	Greenwood Village	1.9	7.9	Lake Oswego	3.0	8.6
Large outlying town	Golden	2.7	10.7	Hillsboro	3.5	15.2
Small Outlying town	Brighton	0.6	17.3	Cornelius	4.1	20.7
	Morrison	0.6	8.6	Wood Village	4.2	15.8

Source: Bureau of the Census, 1990 Census of Population and Housing: Summary Social, Economic, and Housing Characteristics, 1992.

Note: Figures are percentages of total work trips by residents of each municipality.

nancing. The overall cost will weigh in at close to 1 billion dollars. Metro is also planning a major north-south light rail spine, which will connect Clackamas County to downtown Portland, and then proceed north. Voters in Clark County, Washington, nixed a sales tax increase that would have helped pay to extend the LRT line into their state, so for now the route is expected to terminate in Portland.[28]

Looking to the Long-Term Future

Meanwhile, numerous public forums and working groups of public officials met to initiate Metro's Region 2040 process. This effort tied together the disparate strands of activity: neotraditional developments, the Western Bypass study, Portland's city strategies, and Tri-Met's station-area planning. This is particularly true since Metro has final say on the framework and functional plans that will emerge from the Region 2040 "visioning," and can require compliance by counties and cities. The debate has been simplified to one basic question: Should the hundreds of thousands of new residents and jobs expected in the region by 2040 be accommodated by an additional spread of the urbanized area (perhaps by expanding its UGB), or by emphasizing recentralization and greater densities? This debate over "growing up" versus "growing out" is an umbrella issue, with repercussions for local and county zoning. Metro commissioners unanimously voted in late 1994 for a Region 2040 plan that minimizes expansion of the UGB to about fifteen thousand acres, while focusing new growth along transit lines and at six regional centers (Law 1994; see also Metro 1993).

Not surprisingly, the political elites and activists who formed the heart of the dialogue on Region 2040 did not choose to accommodate new growth by expanding the UGB. Thus, Bing Sheldon, the former chair of the Portland Planning Commission, has predicted, "In the coming decade, Portland's city and suburbs will look more alike" (quoted in Portland Metropolitan Association 1993, 14). Such an attitude is resisted by some suburban officials who point out the variety of lifestyle options that suburbia includes. "It's a real advantage, and we don't want to lose that," argues the former mayor of Sherwood. "We can if we go too much to centralized planning and central city dominance" (Tobias interview 1993). Nevertheless, even as a critic of past Metro policies and a self-described conservative Republican, she participated actively in Metro's Region 2040 process. For those seeking to influence future growth patterns, this regional forum was the main game in town.

Challenges to Maintaining the Portland Approach

As Portland area officials attempt to maintain and enhance the region's distinctive approach to land use, two roadblocks are beginning to appear. Both may be by-products of some of the very initiatives viewed as innovative. First, the city-county annexation agreements may result in the rise of "supersuburbs." Second, where developers are reticent to build in the Portland area be-

cause of the constraints of the UGB or other regulations, some growth may be
deflected to some small peripheral towns to the south, and to Clark County,
Washington, to the north.

The Enlargement of Suburban Cities

The recent agreements to phase out county service provision in Multnomah
and Washington Counties, while ostensibly decreasing fragmentation in the
delivery of services, could make the geopolitical situation more complex.
LCDC rules requiring contiguous service provision have also encouraged
cities to stake claims to future expansion into unincorporated areas. A third
factor providing incentives for the future expansion of suburban cities is
Oregon's new tax limitation rule, Measure 5. Under the strictures of this
referendum, local taxes are capped, and many residents of unincorporated
areas are for the first time finding it a "bargain" to annex themselves to a city
and receive its services (Kelley interview 1993). Thus, while Portland itself is
still growing, the suburban municipalities, once tiny, can be expected to grow
at a faster rate.

It remains true that suburban cities, in line with my theoretical predictions
in chapter 2 and with the Denver findings, pursue more particularistic growth
agendas than the counties. Knaap and Nelson find that the sharpest increases
in zoned densities under the provisions of the Metropolitan Housing Rule
have been in unincorporated Washington and Clackamas Counties (Knaap
and Nelson 1992, 82). This should not be surprising, given the inclusive nature
of county governance. Washington County, one respondent says, "has a view
of itself, not necessarily shared by the cities, that it must take a longer-term,
larger-picture view. It wants to exert leadership, to have a Washington County
approach" (Arrington interview 1993; see also Metro 1991b, 71). Thus, enforcement of state goals may be more difficult if suburbs annex unincorporated
areas before they develop.

As of yet, there are no supersuburbs in metropolitan Portland. To former
Metro official Ethan Seltzer, this is important, because a suburban jurisdiction
of 150,000 or more "has the resources to do real damage" to regional development patterns (Seltzer interview 1993a). However, some municipalities—
notably Beaverton, Gresham, and Hillsboro—now expect to be taken seriously as voices discussing the region's future. Hillsboro, for example, where
the longtime city manager was a growth entrepreneur, steadfastly and aggressively grew from a largely agricultural community of eight thousand in
1960 to reach thirty-eight thousand in 1990. The city increased in area from
just over three to about twenty square miles, and its sites are highly sought-

after by industrial developers. Population projections for the year 2000 are sixty thousand or more (Potter 1991, 25). And in the case of Multnomah's annexation agreements, as Abbott puts it, Portland "created two problems for itself. . . . First, a bigger and better Gresham emerged. Second, it was annexing outer voters who don't share the agenda of the CBD and inner east side" (private conversation with author, July 9, 1993). Tax-conscious, and feeling unrepresented, these residents resent Portland's emphasis on rejuvenating its downtown and older neighborhoods.

If such changes in the composition of cities continue, Portland's municipal dominance in the region could be challenged. The larger suburbs might demand a reassessment of their influence in metropolitan decisions. In responding to these strains, the region's elites could reopen old debates about transportation and land-use policy.

Rural Cities and Clark County—Escape Valves?

A second concern is not that suburbs will gain large populations, but that potential new residents or businesses will bypass the entire area. As conditions for large-scale growth become more stringent within the Portland urban growth boundary, one danger is that developers will increasingly turn to lesser-known peripheral cities for industrial and residential development (Rose 1993; Seigneur interview 1993). Within distant commuting range of parts of the PMSA are small rural cities such as Estacada and Sandy, which are circled by their own urban growth boundaries. With few historical links to the metropolitan area and its values, these cities have generally proven far less disciplined at setting development standards.

Closer yet is Wilsonville in Clackamas County, with a 1990 population of 7,075. This city has established its own freestanding, generously sized UGB just a few miles from the Metro UGB. Wilsonville is advantageously located, spanning I-5 just south of the developed area. Incorporated in 1969, and beginning as a retirement haven, the city has recruited several corporate complexes and many distribution and warehouse businesses. In the process, it became the only municipality in the metro area to accumulate more jobs than residents—though the absolute numbers remain small.

With industry, orchards, strip shopping centers, and trailer parks abutting one another, Wilsonville has a helter-skelter appearance. Not surprisingly, it has sparked the ire of regionalists. They are angered by, among other things, that city's decision to withdraw from the Tri-Met district in an attempt to avoid the transit agency's payroll tax. Mostly, the city lacks bedrooms for its workers. The decision of a large high-tech firm to locate in Wilsonville in the early 1990s was one of the events that energized land-use activists to lobby for the new Metro charter, with its strengthened provisions for overseeing development.

Metro has begun to set policy that attempts to avert premature urbanization at the periphery. It has discussed the concept of "urban reserves," which would designate future urbanizable land outside the UGB. Urban reserves would be those areas contiguous to existing urban growth that can be serviced efficiently. It is theorized that, with these properties planned for development well in advance and held in reserve, the land market could anticipate future growth. In this way, the price of land in the reserves would be bid up, preventing premature absorption of peripheral land for large-lot estates, and thereby preserving the possibility of higher-density settlement later.

Metro, however, lacks jurisdiction outside Oregon, and that is where growth has recently accelerated. The completion of the I-205 bridge made Clark County, Washington, more proximate to the Portland International Airport than is most of the Oregon portion of the region. The freeway opened a traffic bottleneck, while also helping break down the "emotional barrier" separating the Vancouver- and Portland-area commutersheds (Hart 1985; Kirkland 1988). With this connection established, Clark County has become something of an escape valve for the types of developments hindered in Oregon. The county's extensive infrastructure has opened large areas to growth. "It's true that the big parcels are lacking under the current UGB," says developer Cain. "Those kinds of developments are being pushed up into Washington state" (Cain interview 1993). At the intersection of I-205 and Washington Route 500, a low-density "edge city" has begun to emerge around the Vancouver Mall, in an unincorporated area. By 1989, about 275,000 square feet of offices and 1.35 million square feet of retail had been built in on 1,230 acres in or around the mall.[29]

Taxes are another factor leading many in-migrants to the Portland area to chose a home in Clark County. The state of Washington lacks personal and corporate income taxes, in contrast to Oregon, and property taxes are roughly 60 percent lower on the northern side of the Columbia as well. On the other hand, Clark County's high sales tax drives retail consumers to the Oregon side, where no sales tax exists. Thus, if Oregon ever enacts a state sales tax (a prospect widely discussed), then retail development, too, could mushroom in Clark County (Shaw 1993). Overall, in 1990 about forty thousand workers in the CMSA crossed state lines to commute to Oregon, ten thousand to Washington.

To summarize, then, peripheral, semirural cities in Oregon, along with nearby areas of Washington, create escape hatches for developers who seek different styles of land-use regulation. In addition, the suburban cities around Portland, which have the governments least oriented toward accounting for the spillovers of growth, are expanding geographically at a relatively rapid pace. These two factors may limit the leverage and impact of regionalists in shaping the Portland metropolis.

Conclusion:
The Institutions of Urban Growth in Metropolitan Portland

Lewis Mumford, speaking before the Portland City Club in 1938, stated:

> I have seen a lot of scenery in my life, but I have seen nothing so tempting as a home for man in this Oregon country. . . . You have here the basis for civilization on its highest scale, and I am going to ask you a question which you may not like. Are you good enough to have this country in your possession? Have you got enough intelligence, imagination and cooperation among you to make the best use of these opportunities? Rebuilding our cities will be one of the major tasks of the next generation. . . . In providing for new developments you have an opportunity here to do a job of city planning like nowhere else in the world.

Despite the new challenges facing it, many planners, academics, journalists, and visitors have concluded that Portland has indeed "done a job like nowhere else"—or at least, like few other metropolitan areas in the United States. But was this because its citizens had greater "intelligence, imagination, and cooperation"? Or did unusually integrative political institutions allow political values other than localism, boosterism, and exclusionism to be included in the debate?

Institutions and Development Outcomes

I have argued that the second explanation is a more persuasive account of the distinctive Portland approach. At the opening of the new suburban era, the PMSA was characterized by a large central city government with few viable competitors, and was adding new institutions that addressed regional issues— institutions which may have *over*represented the center.[30] This constellation of forces led to policies that departed from the typical approach to metropolitan transportation, stressing modal choice and environmental considerations over auto-oriented mobility.

In a subsequent stage, this emerging organization of politics in the metropolis helped shape the response to state land conservation mandates. While MSD may have underemphasized agricultural preservation in drawing the UGB (hardly unexpected from a *metropolitan* government), it resolved a potential standoff between localists and state technocrats. It also helped develop, and later enforce, housing requirements to ensure that the supply of affordable shelter was adequate in places that were experiencing employment growth.

Finally, recent institutional developments have cemented the notion of regional oversight and the synoptic approach to transportation and land use. Specific policy manifestations of this approach—station-area planning at light rail stops, for example—may or may not prove appropriate in an economic environment that still makes auto-oriented, low-density living less costly in the perceptions of most Americans. The point is not the relative wisdom of Portland's policies, but the fact that innovations and departures from convention have been seriously considered and found favorable, and that they are being implemented. Such holistic approaches to metropolitan land use are unlikely to be pursued in the prototypical fragmented metropolis, or indeed in Denver.

Elites and Governance

The Portland area's distinctive governing structures lend themselves to these approaches, even in the new suburban era. Ethan Seltzer adeptly sums up the way the city of Portland's role has changed:

> It was not that long ago that the "metropolitan" economy was confined to Portland, with a handful of little towns around. No one was very conscious of them. Portland was big enough to call the shots. All the employment was there, the locally owned corporations. "Portland" meant the region. . . . Now, Portland can't go it alone. It needs strategic alliances in the legislature. Suburbs can stop something now, but they're not in a good position to create anything. Portland can start the process, but it needs help to complete it. (Seltzer interview 1993b)[31]

In this situation, the empowered Metro fills a useful role. With maturing regional institutions, metropolitan Portland has the potential to pursue urban development strategies that remain mere fairy tales for land-use activists in other urban parts of the country. Insulated from day-to-day localism and popular pressure on land-use policy, planners in Portland have an enviable position in the governing structure. In the words of Gary Eisler, a real estate writer, "Metro may be Portland's secret weapon in dealing with the future, depending on how much area residents want to entrust their future to it" (Eisler 1993, 16).

Indeed, that *if* could yet be put to the test. Despite the positive charter vote, Metro lacks an immediate constituency that might defend it if its specific land-use strategies are ever challenged at the ballot box. As Seltzer sees it,

Metro, still the region's newcomer, "can go to the mat maybe once" to push an unpopular policy against parochial interests: "Right now its most organized constituents are local governments. They're uncomfortable about Metro, but they hate each other, and they're nervous about their counties" (Seltzer interview 1993b). To fully implement the charter's provisions, therefore, it is important that Metro take care to maintain and enhance its political credibility.[32]

Institutional patterns have helped create an unusual opportunity structure for politicians interested in land-use reforms. As an example of the expert networks operating to affect regional policy, consider the career pattern of Charles Hales. Formerly staff vice president of the Metropolitan Home Builders, Hales was a forceful voice against suburban exclusionism, often teaming up with 1000 Friends to lobby for mutual goals. "The power base of a suburb is single-family homeowners," Hales complains (quoted in Langdon 1992). He went on to be appointed to the Metro Charter Committee, which in 1991 proposed Metro's expanded powers and home rule charter. Shortly thereafter, he was elected a Portland city commissioner.

Through the efforts of such regional political elites, Portland possesses a process for weighing transportation improvements and land-use changes, a process that forces local decision makers to consider regional impacts. In Denver, George Wallace and associates could restructure the geography of the metropolitan job market by forming a special district, bargaining with and suing a small municipality, and influencing state transportation agencies. In Portland, would-be suburban development regimes that seek improvements to promote their outlying business centers find themselves dependent upon geographically large, demographically inclusive governments.

For example, the Sunnyside 205 Corridor Association felt compelled to purchase a multipage ad in the February 1989 *Oregon Business*, to issue a "white paper" on metropolitan growth. The group argued:

> Some observers note that our transportation spending policies reflect pre-
> war, industrial urban area concepts which are inappropriate in our postwar,
> post-industrial urban development. . . . The health of the inner city is depen-
> dent upon the orderly development of its suburban activity centers. The is-
> sues which face county commissions and suburban city councils demand a
> place on the agendas of the Portland City Council and the state and federal
> governments.

However, the Portland region has an insulated, elite process for guiding road improvements and light rail connections, and Sunnyside could not force its way past that. (Indeed, neither could the urban design zealots in central Portland, who sought to remove I-5 from the east-side riverfront.) In a section pointedly called "Who Speaks for the Suburban Activity Centers?" Sunnyside 205 addresses the entities it hopes will look kindly upon its vision of the metropolis:

> The Sunnyside 205 Corridor Association calls for new agendas of responsibil-
> ity for our suburban activity centers on the part of the Metropolitan Service
> District, Tri-Met, the Oregon Department of Transportation, county govern-
> ments, Portland city government, local municipalities, and service districts.

The order in which these governments is listed gives a sense of their relative influence.

Despite pretensions of citizen participation, the land-use and transporta-tion planning system has by and large been an elite process. While the region's residents know they want to avoid the growth problems that plague southern California, there are indications they would prefer a "no growth" approach, rather than the managed growth visions of Metro, Tri-Met, or the City of Portland (see Metro 1991a, 40–45). There is also little evidence that the Region 2040 alternatives were widely discussed among people who are not planners, public officials, or land-use activists.[33] If anything, what people in the suburbs know most is that they "don't want more people on small lots, lots of apart-ments," according to one source who spent much time campaigning door-to-door during a recent election season. "It's mentioned even above taxes, and pretty consistently" (Tobias interview 1993).[34] However, these latent politi-cal preferences are not easily expressed through the metro area's relatively unified institutional system. It is precisely this deflection of the more localistic public opinion that has enabled metro-area officials to proceed with unusual approaches.[35]

The Political Culture Thesis

Again, doubt is cast on the proposition that the Portland region does things differently because its residents are somehow cut from a different cloth than other urban Americans. A 1991 article in *The Economist* argues that Portland's successes are particularly due to being "settled by New Englanders, who brought with them a cautious attitude to unbridled economic growth and a sense of high-minded civic duty" ("America's holy trinity" 1991). Carl Abbott has made a more extended and nuanced argument in this vein. "There is a strong reservoir of support for land use planning in Oregon," Abbott claims, "because both the concept and the processes fit with the underlying political culture and values of the state" (Abbott 1994, 205).

There is a certain amount of circularity to this argument, however. First, Portland is seen as having achieved better or more well-planned development patterns than similar regions. In the absence of obvious differences from other political systems, this outcome is attributed to a distinctive political culture. But the presence of that political culture is deduced from the region's willingness to undertake communally oriented land-use programs.

I argue, rather, that the lack of a separate suburban institutional interest has shaped Portland's political response to growth. These political arrangements have attenuated the particularistic, neighborhood-level manipulation of land regulation for local advantage. It is possible, of course, that at some level, a distinctive "political culture" may have contributed to Oregon's initial *choice* of institutional arrangements. Nevertheless, one would have to count institutions as the more proximate, visible cause than an ill-defined, probably unmeasurable "culture" (Elkins and Simeon 1979). In short, the methodological problem with a political culture argument in this case is that it is not falsifiable.

The comparison between Oregon and Colorado in chapter 4 failed to demonstrate a convincing difference in political ethos between the two states. In fact, one can easily find contradictory evidence to the argument about Pacific Northwest "values" supporting Portland's unique land-use policies. Migrants from the same basic "moralistic" tradition founded sprawling Seattle, as well as numerous undistinguished urban areas in the northern tier of the country. (For that matter, New England, the spawning ground of American "moralism," has had its own problems with suburban growth and central city disinvestment.) Moreover, mass opinion in Portland has not always impressed local observers as moralistic. Consider historian E. Kimbark MacColl's cataloguing of the ethos of Portland as of 1950:

> Portlanders considered the rights of private property to be sacred.
> Portlanders were rurally oriented.
> Portlanders had a deep-seated Anglo Saxon bias.
> Portlanders viewed their city as a center of problems: Crime, rising taxes, minorities, and welfare recipients.
> Portlanders wanted above all else to keep their neighborhoods familiar and unchanging.
> Portlanders wanted to improve their lives by moving on.
>
> (MacColl 1979, 655)

These are hardly the ingredients for a groundswell of populistic support for unprecedented state and regional planning interventions—especially ones designed to advantage the central city and restrict residents' ability to escape to the urban periphery.

Abbott argues, however, that such social conservatism may be consistent with Portland's land-use process. "In a conservative and moralistic state, land use planning has allowed Oregonians to be community-minded and 'good' without being revolutionary" (Abbott 1994, 210). This statement evokes a picture of a policy-making system fulfilling an electorate's deep cultural longings. As such, it approximates the discredited sociological approach of "structural functionalism." Abbott probably attributes too much purposiveness and farsightedness to the myriad policy makers who set various policies in motion at the city, regional, and state levels.

If we leave aside the state program for the moment, it is not even clear that it is "planning" rather than politics that has determined, for example, the accessibility advantages of the center as opposed to the periphery. It does seem true that Portland policy makers have been more inclined to *listen to* suggestions of planners—for example, in revitalizing the transit system, in emphasizing pedestrian street life in downtown Portland, or in sketching the alternatives for the Region 2040 process. But it is easier to attribute this to the dominance of large, relatively technocratic government units—the city of Portland, Metro, Tri-Met, and the state, as opposed to individual suburbs—than to the cultural predilections of the general public. Simply put, a centralized, insulated policy-making system is more susceptible to "issue networks" and expertise than a system that is closer to local public opinion.

Land Markets and Land Politics

Finally, the Portland experience again suggests the ambiguity of the concept of a "free market" for land. Whether through fragmentation or a more unitary regulatory system, the development market in any urban area is guided by public actions and omissions.

Portland now faces a challenge as it begins an ambitious attempt to "force" the market to devote more attention to the circulation of pedestrians and transit rather than cars. According to the former mayor of Sherwood, "Most local officials are concerned about how far we can 'push the envelope' of government controls, in the interest of the greater good or planning theory" (Tobias interview 1993). For goals like neotraditional town planning and station-area zoning, the question may be the following: Are there sufficient outlets for profit-making development, given the area's small-scale development industry? Judging by the support developers have shown for the regulatory system to date, profit opportunities appear to have been sufficient in the past two decades. The public sector in the region has set some quite specific rules for players in the land-use game, but then allowed them to operate within that framework in a fairly unfettered fashion.

However, where land-use regulation constrains conventional development and encourages the unconventional, the anticipated vision may take time to materialize. This was certainly the case along the suburban portion of the original eastside MAX line, where developers were slow to respond. On the other hand, there is far greater demand for commercial, office, and residential sites in Washington County today than there was for sites in somewhat run-down older areas of Multnomah County in the 1980s. Perhaps the profit motive will be powerful enough to induce developers to give experimental station-area projects a try.

Despite the Portland region's relative centralization of goals, guidelines, and procedures for development, it may be viewed as a more "free"—or at least, more *neutral*—political-economic land market than Denver, where pro-growth elites and antigrowth interests seek out or even create institutions that will accommodate their specific visions. Certainly, Portland's process has become just as "natural" to participants there as Denver's. As one respondent put it, "It's hard to evaluate it because we're so used to it. It doesn't become clear until you go somewhere else" (Arrington interview 1993).

7

Conclusion:
Political Economy and Metropolitan Growth

Urban development is in important ways a political phenomenon. That much has long been apparent in the literature on central city politics and CBD renewal. The theories and case studies examining power and influence in the downtown context, however, took as their subject matter a skewed and relatively small sample of American urbanization. By examining urban development with a regionwide lens, one can better illustrate the systemic political forces and incentives at work in the process of growth and change. From infrastructure financing to annexation rules, taxation mechanisms to state/local relations, American urbanization is patterned in distinct and relatively predictable ways by the political institutions operating at the local, metropolitan, and state levels.

Even if we assume that developers, elected officials, and residents each have motivations and goals that are similar across urban America, variations in metropolitan institutions are likely to lead to variations in strategies and actions on the part of these key players. In turn, the decision makers effect land-use outcomes that vary across metro areas, allowing for the growth rate, size, age, income, and socioeconomic characteristics of each area. These differences result, I have suggested, because of the ways in which political arrangements organize interests geographically, provide decision rules for development politics, and filter citizens' perceptions of politics, places, and growth impacts. The political structure of an urban area, therefore, plays a key intervening or mediating role in the translation of economic forces and interest-group pressures into changes in the landscape.

Of particular importance is the degree of complexity or fragmentation of the public sector in the metropolis. The more divided that governance is within an urban area, the more likely commerce will be drained away from its old core and growth will spread farther across the landscape and occur in a patchwork fashion.

In this chapter, I offer some concluding observations on the politics of land-use policy making and discuss the relationship between this project and existing strands of research on the political economy of the metropolis. I also offer guidance to those interested in changing public policies or institutional arrangements in order to reshape urban growth. Finally, I reconsider the nature, origins, and impact of urban governing institutions.

Land-Use Policy Making: A Profoundly Political Process

In most cases, there are political costs involved when a traditional "bedroom" suburban area becomes an "edge city" of new jobs and commerce. To be sure, new tax ratables may be gained, employment may locate closer to home, and a few landowners may get rich. But many other residents are likely to feel that their toes are being stepped on, and will turn on local government in frustration. For these citizens, the amenities that drew them to the periphery are being compromised by growth that seems to alter the character of their community. Clearly, then, accommodating nonresidential growth in suburbia requires some political adjustment.

The mayor of Aurora, an unusually extensive suburb in the Denver area, has provided an instructive description of the pull-and-tug process by which opposing interests are reconciled in large-scale jurisdictions like his:

> The rural-type developments have the assumption that nothing will ever change. But it will. . . . To a degree there's an always-understood [political] pressure in favor of new projects, pressure from the parties that stand to benefit. They become more vocal if it looks like the project won't occur due to opposition. If it's really necessary, a balancing will come about; the project will be approved in return for the mitigation of impacts, reduction of its scale, and so forth. (Tauer interview 1992)

In smaller suburbs, the "balancing" that Mayor Tauer alludes to may not emerge. In such municipalities—for example, Cherry Hills Village or Edgewater in the Denver area, Lake Oswego or Happy Valley near Portland—the "parties that stand to benefit" have fewer political claims on elected officials than in larger or more balanced jurisdictions. Developers who operate in a complex, multijurisdictional environment must therefore often "satisfice," picking locations that are somewhat suboptimal from a purely economic standpoint, in order to avoid long and costly battles over sites (see Clawson 1971, chaps. 5–6).

This capsule description of the decision-making process involved in the development of suburbia illustrates the manner in which *politics rations land*. Local politicians, assessing market demand, the characteristics of their jurisdictions, local public opinion and interest-group pressures, and their own interests, have resources at their disposal to help determine the rate, scale, and character of community growth. Through zoning codes, subdivision requirements, litigation, subsidies, annexations, infrastructure investments, and many more informal means, they can determine the intensity and type of development on a given property. In this sense, urban growth as a process is intrinsically political.

Critics might claim, perhaps fairly, that my argument has been overdrawn. There is no denying that market demand, technology, demographic changes, growth trajectories, and even historical accident all play major roles in determining the physical layout of urban areas. I have stressed the public regulation of land in order to make it clear that political arrangements play a systematic role in the allocation of space. Metropolitan areas, rather than converging toward some preordained market or urban-systems "equilibrium," experience significant differences in their patterns of residential and commercial location. Metropolitan travel behavior, by and large, results from these location decisions. Therefore, institutional arrangements are also a partial determinant of traffic congestion and air pollution—and similarly, of concentrations of poverty and affluence, the aesthetic character of suburban growth patterns, and many of the other facets of "the urban problem."

Political institutions, then, need to take their place beside economic and sociocultural factors as a systematic part of the process by which the metropolitan landscape is shaped. There are certainly precedents for emphasizing the impact of politics on the urban built environment. Aristotle's *Politics* (7.11) conceived of the structure of ancient cities as reflecting political, military, and constitutional values, along with social and economic characteristics. In Lewis Mumford's magisterial history of urban life (1961), the city is often interpreted as an artifact of the politics of the era. Even in Sam B. Warner's *Private City* (1968), the layout of Philadelphia is seen as a reflection of public values in the early American "commercial republic."

In contemporary social science accounts of urban structure, however, most economists, geographers, and sociologists proceed without incorporating the political variable, or else relegate it as "noise" to the error term of their model. Sometimes, historians and even political scientists do so as well. Part of the problem has been the difficulty of neatly summarizing "politics" quantitatively, because the focus has been on group power and newspaper headline politics, not its everyday framework of rules. It is possible, however, to move toward a more precise measure of metropolitan political arrangements, a measure that appears to have a telling statistical association with certain indices of urban structure.

The political framework is also often missed as a potential cause of urban outcomes because Americans tend to be most familiar with their own region's government structure, which seems "natural." As one Denver-area source maintained, "I think people generally assume that whatever you have right now *is* the 'free market system'" (Spitzer interview 1992). Thus, it is not surprising that some analysts tend to reach for "political culture" explanations of urban differences, even where there seems little basis for making sharp distinctions in political culture.[1] I have argued that political culture cannot fully account for the different orientations of elected officials and developers in Denver and Portland, for example. Rather, as one planner told me, Colorado and Oregon "are both fairly conservative states, but the expression of that conservatism differs greatly" (Rutsch interview 1992).

The institutional system, like the man-made physical environment of an urban community, becomes "second nature" to its residents, to use historian William Cronon's incisive term (Cronon 1991). Just because a given set of political arrangements is accepted, expected, or "invisible" to us in our everyday actions, does not mean it is unimportant. Indeed, such assimilation of the political system into our subconscious indicates the extent to which it permeates and influences our environment for action.

But this invisibility very likely hinders effective responses to the nation's urban problems. For example, the increasing congestion problems of a suburban area are typically diagnosed as due to excessive migration to the area, or to an insufficient highway capacity—rather than a result of compartmentalized land uses that reflect the multiplicity of jurisdictions. Thus, local moratoria on residential growth, or the expansion of highways, are frequently offered as "solutions" to congestion, even though they may only intensify the problem. More perniciously perhaps, the lack of employment among inner city residents may be perceived as the result of a lack of effort by those residents, rather than as the result of political and economic patterns that create incentives for business creation or expansion at the urban periphery.[2] Central city politicians, then, who are virtually the only elected officials held accountable on this issue, typically look to the traditional ameliorative policy options: place-based development programs or social expenditure subsidies from the state and federal governments. In contrast, regional transportation or land-use reforms (such as a dispersal of subsidized housing, an easing of suburban zoning barriers, or nodes of transit-accessible development) are not seriously considered. Such policies have little payoff for politicians whose constituencies are emphatically local. And in any event, such policies are politically unfeasible in a fragmented metropolis.

In interpreting the consequences of fragmentation for urban land use, we must issue a word of caution. High levels of political integration, as in a regional city arrangement, are not a guarantee that the costs and benefits of land-use changes will be rationally accounted for. It is not my aim to show that a regional city always *tries* to achieve a suburban jobs/housing balance. But unitary political arrangements present *fewer obstructions* to natural market processes by which such a balance may be achieved than do fragmented arrangements. Similarly, it is not that a large-scale jurisdiction necessarily will *prevent* suburban business centers from forming, if the market is leaning in such a direction—though it may, as in the case of the proposed Regency Fashion Centre in Denver. Rather, the point is that unitary governance does not create the nonmarket *incentives* to allow an outlying area to be overloaded with commercial development without a consideration of costs.

Nor does a regional city guarantee a healthy downtown. But its CBD will not be *forced* into a noncompetitive position because of a deprived fiscal environment. The latter outcome is far more likely when the central city accounts for a small portion of the metropolitan population.

In other words, relatively low levels of fragmentation in a metropolitan area—and in particular, an extensive central city—may be a *necessary* condition for shaping suburban growth and alleviating regionwide problems and growth disparities. But unitary government is not a *sufficient* condition for such policy action.[3] In the Portland region, for example, the emergence of entrepreneurial politicians and appointed officials, notably Mayor Neil Goldschmidt, was key in bringing about regional light rail transit and other inner city–oriented policies. Earlier elected elites, such as Goldschmidt's predecessor, Terry Schrunk, were typically content to maintain a "housekeeping" approach to governance, or were fearful of stirring unpredictable opposition from voters if they strayed too far from established norms of policy making. Once Goldschmidt was elected, however, the mechanisms of the metropolitan government, along with the extensive scale of the city of Portland, enabled him to attain his regional policy objectives. Had a similar figure emerged in the city and county of Denver, he or she would almost certainly have lacked the institutional leverage to alter regional development patterns.[4]

Urban planners often claim that the geographical scale of a planning jurisdiction will correlate with its success. Some I spoke to about my research found it an unremarkable truism that units of government with more extensive physical size would plan better. But planners may take this position because they value extending their command-and-control techniques over a wide area. Government structures that are insulated from localistic concerns give greater voice to "rational" technocrats like themselves. My argument, however, is based not on planning but on politics. Different institutional arrangements are congruent with different types and levels of interest articulation.

Planners themselves may be thought of as representing a particular political interest (Altshuler 1965; Judd and Mendelson 1973). Planning doctrines and fads—like political or bureaucratic reform efforts—can often be characterized as "solutions looking for problems, ideologies looking for soapboxes, pet projects looking for supporters, and people looking for jobs, reputations, or entertainment" (March and Olsen 1989, 82).[5] A metro area with a relatively insulated institutional structure may make it more likely that planners espousing such ideas will be able to formulate and articulate policies and project them onto a political agenda, without being seriously challenged by other political values.[6] In Portland, for example, planners have been far more important to central city and regional policy development than they have in Denver. Nevertheless, the wisdom of the planners' recommendations should not be taken as self-evident, nor as the necessary source of "progressive" land-use regulation in northwest Oregon. The point, rather, is that the regionalized political process in the Portland area has the *capacity* to weigh such holistic designs against more localistic political interests.

Simply put, there are neighborhood political values and metropolitan political values. One might make a distinction between a "local majority" and a "latent majority" in urban development politics. A local majority takes shape because of a geographically immediate issue, an issue that has a direct and easily perceived effect on residents of a small area. In contrast, a latent majority may be expected to support certain positions on regional issues that have a widely dispersed impact. For example, there are latent majorities in favor of increasing the employment options of a region (which will serve, at the margins, to increase the wages of the MSA's residents) and of reducing certain negative externalities of uncoordinated growth (such as traffic on regional thoroughfares, housing costs, or air pollution).

A polity that approximates the metropolis in size has the potential to grapple with such issues. At the same time, it may deal with the more neighborhood-level values, depending upon its rules of representation. But *under almost no circumstances will neighborhood-sized polities deal with metropolitan values.* Thus, latent majorities essentially lack political representation in highly fragmented metro areas. This effect is in addition to the basic potential representational bias of any preference-aggregation system made up of smaller decision-making parts—for example, the United States Electoral College (see Ordeshook 1992, 140–43).

The situation can be summarized with reference to James Q. Wilson's well-known two-by-two matrix explaining the politics of policy-making episodes.

Wilson categorizes policies (and potential policies) according to whether their costs and benefits are narrowly concentrated or widely diffused. Land-use regulation in a fragmented metropolis is likely to respond to narrow or concentrated interests. Thus, in Wilson's typology, zoning battles or subdivision regulations in a small municipality can typically be characterized as either *interest-group* politics (costs and benefits both narrowly concentrated) or *clientelistic* politics (costs dispersed, benefits narrowly concentrated). The beneficiaries in a given case may be local homeowners or favored developers. By contrast, large-scale jurisdictions such as states, big cities, or urban counties are more likely to witness either *majoritarian* politics (dispersed costs and benefits) or *entrepreneurial* politics (concentrated costs, dispersed benefits) over land use. At this geographic scale, wider ("majoritarian") political debates about rapid growth versus managed growth, or environmentalist versus laissez-faire regulatory philosophies, can find expression. Similarly, an energetic public entrepreneur is more likely to score political points by taking on established sectional interests in a large-scale jurisdiction. In the Portland area, for example, Goldschmidt and the managed growth activists were able to thwart highway builders and growth coalitions that represented particular segments of suburbia (see Wilson 1980, 367–72).[7]

In sum, ample room exists for a true political science of urban regional development. Such analysis departs in important ways from current approaches to urban political economy.

Reconsidering the Study of Urban Political Economy

How does my theoretical framework and empirical analysis square with existing strands in this literature? While popular paradigms of urban political economy cast some useful light on metropolitan development, the research reported here suggests possible shortcomings or extensions of each.

If one examines urban development through the lens of footloose firms and single jurisdictions, one is likely to exaggerate the limitations of local political systems in shaping growth. This is the weakness of the "city limits" perspective (see Peterson 1981; Schneider 1986). In a regional context, the public sector does in fact have a significant impact upon development patterns. In toto, local governments' orientation toward various types of development shapes metropolitan growth—though any individual suburb's efforts may not appear significant.

The "city limits" perspective derives its most basic assumptions from the Tiebout hypothesis (Tiebout 1956). Primarily, however, the work of Charles Tiebout and his followers concerns the efficiency of *public service delivery* in a static, "given" urban area. In the Tiebout world, political fragmentation allows mobile residents and firms to move to the jurisdiction that best matches their tastes for services and tax rates; local officials must continually strive for efficiency. More realistically, we might entertain the thought that the development of the urban area itself is first shaped by the institutional configuration of that area's governance. Land-use regulation may not be analogous to local public services like garbage collection or police protection, in that "efficient" solutions may be least likely to emerge in a highly fragmented context. Each jurisdiction's immediate local tastes may be satisfied, but externalities are large and unpriced. Ultimately, then, the problem is political, rather than economic.[8]

Public choice analysts might conceivably argue that my critique can be answered by designing the proper "catchment area" for land-use planning, viewed as a public service (Ostrom, Tiebout, and Warren 1961). But the Tiebout model cannot survive this redesign, for two reasons. First, the removal of land-use control to a regional level of government would necessarily alter the logic of local decisions that attempt to balance property tax ratables against a desired level of public services. Second, the intrajurisdictional homogeneity that Tiebout posits as a basis for efficient public service choices would not exist were land-use authority not in local hands. In short: There can be no tax/service mix that efficiently responds to the demands of mobile citizens unless each jurisdiction has the capacity to recruit and zone for development.

Two other approaches to urban development take a more explicitly political perspective. Logan and Molotch's "growth machine" framework examines the incentives and organization of real estate elites, locally oriented businesses, and other interests that can generate rents from an intensification of local land use. The growth machine school, however, overemphasizes these elites, and underplays the role of public-sector actors with independent interests. In Molotch's view, "exchange value" elites are hegemons of local political systems (Molotch 1988). Logan and Molotch occasionally note that inequalities are organized along jurisdictional lines (1987, 14), but they assume incorrectly that the "growth machine" game is played out in miniature in each municipality. Normally, in a metropolis, growth elites are organized *regionally*, and citizen and government interests *locally*, which sets the stage for varied patterns of interaction among key players in the development process.

Growth machine theory admits that the occasional affluent residential suburb may be able to deflect development, and thus present a rare victory of "use values" over "exchange values." But in fact, empirical studies do not show a significant link between municipalities' class or socioeconomic characteristics and their proclivity to support slow- or no-growth policies (Donovan and

Neiman 1992). Rather, "antigrowth policy entrepreneurs" may be the force behind such policies (Schneider and Teske 1993). Surely, if such entrepreneurs are the key (which seems plausible), they should find municipal governments easier to "capture" in a fragmented suburban region than in a more unitary, bureaucratized region.

The other analytic framework offering itself as an explicitly political approach to urban development is the "urban regime" perspective, closely associated with Clarence Stone (Stone 1989; Stone and Sanders 1987). Stone argues that cities are given most of the responsibility, but only some of the resources, needed to effectively govern their area. Because of this limitation, mayors and other elected officials form governing coalitions—"regimes"—with private actors who hold useful resources or wield important decision-making capabilities. In central cities of the type Stone and his followers have studied, these governing coalitions generally do not correspond closely, in a demographic or representational sense, to the electoral coalitions that put the mayor and council members in office. Elected officials' attempts to reconcile the claims made on them by their electoral supporters with the wishes of "regime" members—who tend to be downtown business elites—make up the fundamental tensions of city politics.

From my standpoint, there is less that is overtly objectionable in this approach than in the others. If one were to carry the regime perspective to the level of the metropolis, instead of focusing on one city, one could (at least theoretically) determine the composition of governing coalitions and electoral coalitions for each jurisdiction.[9] This knowledge could be used to help explain the land-use decisions and infrastructure investments undertaken by each unit of government (or by a sample of jurisdictions). The composite effect of each jurisdiction's policy could then presumably be seen in the MSA's development patterns.

What is apparent, however, is that parsimony would never be a strength of the regime approach on the metropolitan level. Regime analysis seems impractical except for in-depth, individual case studies. The institutional framework suggests that the set of boundaries, rules, and formalized procedures guiding the actions of local decision makers are at least as important in shaping choice and delimiting options as almost any other political factor. In short, institutional arrangements play a major role in *constituting* the governing coalitions that Stone stresses.

Therefore, none of the major existing theoretical approaches in urban political economy seems sufficiently robust to contribute to a systematic understanding of governance and growth at the metropolitan level. Institutional analysis is more practical for comparative research on the political environments that are relevant to most urban Americans. The institutional approach, moreover, raises important questions about the processes by which urban growth might be *re*shaped.

Some Tentative Implications for Public Policy

An urban-oriented political scientist is wise to show restraint in offering reform proposals or wide-ranging policy critiques. The reason for this trepidation is the long tradition of urban analysts who have offered sweeping recommendations for government structure that were based more on reformist biases, unexamined public administration dogmas, and assumptions about how the world *should* operate, than on empirically supported analysis (see Herson 1957; and Ostrom 1972). I have tried to organize my research around theory and evidence, rather than pet proposals.

Therefore, I offer only two clusters of policy recommendations. These are aimed at preserving the range of choice of location options for urban residents and firms (and expanding such options for those ill served by the current state of affairs), expanding transportation options, and attempting to ameliorate some of the major collective costs of individual choices. I also try to maintain a sense of political realism.

Separated Land Uses and Overreliance on the Automobile

The first set of policy issues relates to the development disparities emerging in suburbia, and the transportation difficulties these land-use patterns create. It would be desirable to offer a wide range of housing choices within close commuting range of suburban employment clusters. Situations like the Denver Tech Center, where many workers have virtually no alternatives to driving alone to work along congested freeways, are intolerable, particularly when residential zones nearby are so spacious. As suburban job nodes take shape, one would expect the market to respond by building apartments and other attached housing in proximity to the work sites. Real estate analyst Christopher Leinberger argues that increases in density and "retrofitting" are the logical route toward rationalizing land use in the suburban era:

> According to a recent poll by the American Institute of Architects, "densification of the suburbs" will be the number one development trend of the 1990s. . . . Sophisticated developers or institutional owners of existing office buildings and shopping centers in suburban cores will lead this urbanization process by developing on land now used for surface parking. . . . *This process depends on convincing surrounding neighborhoods to accept increased density.* (Leinberger 1990, 7, emphasis added)

In many cases, however, developers are likely to have a hard time convincing nearby residents. If those residents' neighborhoods form a substantial portion of a municipality, then an intensification of land uses is likely to be precluded from the beginning.

But the new suburbia need not be high density in design.[10] To accommodate these to evolving trends in employment and transportation, there must be a tolerance for varied land uses (including lower-cost housing) within any subregion of the metropolis. This implies a medium-density pattern that intermingles many types of land use. Should such a policy be sought, more unitary political arrangements are likely to have more success. Elected officials in a fragmented metropolis have few incentives to pursue such diversification.

However, comparable gains in land-use efficiencies could be gained through state or national policies that place an increased price on automobile usage. Presently, the large externality costs of driving—in terms of air pollution, congestion, safety, and the disruption of the physical fabric of the metropolis— remain unpriced by and large. If gasoline prices were to triple or quadruple, or if there were a long-term disruption in fuel supply, developers and relocating firms and residents would feel incentives to locate in a more compact fashion. High gasoline taxes could have a similar effect. At the least, such cost factors would dampen the motivation to develop at the exurban frontier.[11]

Related to these transportation deficiencies is the need for better circulation *within* new and existing office and commercial projects in suburbia, and among adjacent properties. In many cases, the automobile is the only practical or safe option for travel, even for extremely short distances. Pedestrian and bicycle circulation and transit accessibility are issues that deserve increasing emphasis as policy makers in urban areas seek to reduce solo automobile use. The actions required of developers would generally be minor in cost. Again, however, most individual municipalities have few incentives to undertake such microlevel design ordinances, which would only put them at a disadvantage compared to their competitors in attracting commercial taxpayers.[12] Inclusive units of government, such as states or metropolitan entities, would be more likely to draft such guidelines (and probably more successful at doing so).

These policy instruments, however, do not represent a frontal attack on local land-use control and neomercantilist or slow-growth zoning. Efforts to erode local controls (as in the movement to "open up the suburbs" to low-income housing) generally suffer from extreme collective action problems and lack any visible political constituency (Danielson 1976); only "latent majorities" would benefit, while "local majorities" would be opposed. But as the nation's economy becomes increasingly suburban, local land-use control is likely to see sustained attention from a new group of critics who focus on the costs of doing business, rather than on social goals. As William Fischel summarizes the implications of local growth controls:

> The long-run effect of this is a lower standard of living. People will commute more than they otherwise would, which reduces their real incomes unless they enjoy commuting. Dispersion of residences and jobs promotes more automobile travel and longer trips, creating more congestion and pollution . . . and eventually requiring more highway construction. The more subtle loss from inefficiently dispersed homes and businesses is the loss of agglomeration economies for firms. (Fischel 1990, 56–57)

In this last sense, fragmented suburban areas seem ill equipped to duplicate the fertile business climate of downtowns. If this reasoning is well circulated among suburban business elites, some pressure may emerge for relaxation of strict local autonomy.

Open Space Preservation

A second set of policy considerations concerns the rapid disappearance of open spaces in and around metropolitan areas. With green spaces increasingly claimed for development, voters in metropolitan areas are likely to react favorably to proposals that government acquire extensive tracts of the remaining undeveloped land for urban and suburban parks and nature preserves. Typically, this would take the form of a ballot measure regarding the issuance of bonds for acquiring open spaces. Such a policy can mitigate some of the losses due to today's extensive patterns of development (in which "open space" of a sort exists more than ever—but in the form of private backyards and corporate lawns). Regional planning advocates also argue that tracts of open space can be used to help shape and provide cohesion to the areas that *are* developed for urban uses (Whyte 1968).

What about the pace of development on open lands at the edge of the metropolis? It is these areas, with large-scale landownership patterns and increasingly good highway access, that have been in heavy demand by developers in many MSAs. The Oregon urban growth boundary rule, while apparently an effective device to control sprawl, is unlikely to be adopted in such a strong form elsewhere.[13] However, it is conceivable that other regions can slow down peripheral sprawl, if they so desire, by erecting what might be thought of as a UGB by default: Under this approach, no major new extensions of roadway, water, or sewer infrastructure to outlying areas would be funded without careful study and regional debate. With increasing pressure on capital budgets, and growing environmental objections to highway construction and water diversion, political sentiment is less favorable toward urban expansion policies than at any time in the recent past. In-fill growth will become a more acceptable proposition to developers if their options are limited at the periphery.[14]

Institutional Prerequisites

Both these clusters of policy recommendations have significant implications for institutional arrangements in MSAs. The idea of regional park acquisition or deliberations on infrastructure extensions presupposes that some political unit exists to give voice to issues of regional ("latent majority") concerns. For example, restrictions on urban fringe expansion are unlikely to come about if most relevant decision-making authority is in the hands of outlying municipalities or special districts. While these issues can usefully be pursued at the state level in many cases (particularly in states that are geographically small and heavily metropolitan in character), some metropolitan overlay unit of government will probably need to be up and running to promote such policies in some MSAs. In the form of metropolitan service authorities, councils of governments, or large-scale urban counties, numerous options already exist that could incrementally take on such a role.

Sympathetic state legislators could put such an existing regional unit "in business" by assigning it one or more responsibilities that would be perceived in positive-sum terms by local residents and elected officials. The tasks I have in mind are those that remove burdens from local governments or provide regionwide benefits that are beyond the reach of individual towns and cities. Such activities might include park acquisition, the operation and development of cultural or entertainment facilities, and solid waste planning and disposal. Not coincidentally, these are some of the functions assigned to Portland's Metro. As in Portland, a regional government could add more controversial and weighty responsibilities, such as transportation and regional planning, once it had demonstrated its viability. If federal air quality legislation continues to require coordinated transportation decision making, such regional units would be hard to ignore as potential policy-making venues.[15]

In contrast, the wholesale merger of municipalities into massive "cities without suburbs" (Rusk 1993) is not only politically impossible, but dubious from the standpoint of policy analysis. For reasons of efficient service delivery alone, such mergers have little justification (see Ostrom, Tiebout, and Warren 1961). However, the strengthening of regional units of government is justified. Some public issues currently have no relevant polity in which policy decisions can be formulated without extreme externalities. Moreover, a major shortcoming of urban America, reflected in the go-it-alone policy making that currently prevails in many MSAs, is the lack of a sense of community or interdependence among residents of metropolitan areas. The region, along with the neighborhood, would seem to be a natural geographic basis for such shared affinity—as identification with regional sports franchises, civic groups, and cultural institutions illustrates. If a viable unit of government that corresponded to such a geographic level existed, it could promote such a consciousness.

As a starting point, states like Colorado would be well advised at least to try to remove some of the obstacles to greater political integration that currently exist in state law or constitutional provisions. Annexation restrictions that single out central cities, lenient provisions for the incorporation of new municipalities, organizational and budgetary restraints on urban counties, and nearly automatic approvals of new special-district governments are examples of "rules of the game" that promote fragmentation and need to be reevaluated. Circumscribed central city boundaries, in particular, set the entire process of decentralization in motion, as the allocational debate between those favoring new public investments at the fringe and those touting the improvement of existing areas disappears. And in the case of special districts, Kathryn Foster has argued that the political perspectives that tend to be voiced in the insulated decision making of districts are those in favor of spending money on new development and infrastructure projects. In short, she finds, the world of special districts is disproportionately a world of special interests (Foster 1993).[16]

In highly fragmented areas, public confidence in local government is likely to erode if municipalities and counties continue to prove unable to deal with growth's spillovers. A regional-scale government would be better able to match wits—in either the cooperative or competitive sense—with a sophisticated development industry. A regional government could also represent the "countervailing power" that citizens may need to interact effectively with powerful private organizations (Schattschneider 1960).

Public choice analysts, attuned to the study of urban service delivery systems, may still argue that decentralized political institutions provide for a closer fit between preferences and government outputs. They might even argue that voluntary interlocal cooperation can be expected to mitigate some of the negative regional consequences of local decisions (Friesma 1970; Ostrom 1972; Ostrom 1983)—even though the conditions that Elinor Ostrom associates with the voluntary solution of common-pool resource problems are largely absent (Ostrom 1990, esp. 88–102).[17] Writers who have stressed the virtues of decentralization and government fragmentation in the provision of local services are understandably nervous about the potential of knee-jerk calls for government consolidation. For example, Donald Chisholm, who has studied cooperation among the multiple providers of public transit in the Bay Area, calls for a "least common denominator" approach to coordination among local units: "Use the minimum mechanisms necessary to achieve a satisfactory level of coordination" (Chisholm 1989, 63).

Working in accordance with such precepts has been a new organizational form emerging in many suburban regions that are buffeted by congestion and air pollution problems: Transportation Management Associations (TMAs). These groups, generally funded by member governments, firms, and development interests, have assisted and helped manage programs promoting ride sharing and alternative transportation arrangements, have helped to coordinate parking procedures, and in some cases have even provided day care to employees (Hartshorn and Muller 1992, 154). While undoubtedly useful in remedying some of the problems of local development disparities, TMAs are nevertheless a response that does not fundamentally affect the root causes of suburban congestion. TMAs do not, for example, increase housing opportunities near suburban job corridors, or alter the low-density, transit-unfriendly patterns of business parks. Like interlocal agreements, TMAs are reactive, not proactive, responses to the pressures of growth in the new suburban age.[18]

Rethinking Urban Institutions

Cautions such as those from Chisholm should be taken seriously. But public-private cooperative ventures like TMAs do not really achieve policy coordination. Popular control, in the case of urban development and its related issues, may require a different approach:

> Control of policy is not achieved simply by electing officials on the smallest scale possible, but rather by having a vote for or against the officials who will have sufficient scope of authority to make the important decisions. (Doane, Wall, and Winter 1993, 11)

Moreover, fragmented decision rules may advantage elites, as James G. March and Johan P. Olsen describe it:

> Indications are that the more complex and conditional are a set of rules, the fuzzier the distinctions between responsibilities of agencies, and the greater the effort to map the complexity of the world onto the institutional structure, the greater the political advantage of persons possessing economic or intellectual resources. . . . In this way, modern developments of complicated institutional rules with many conditions . . . counter important principles of democracy. (1989, 28)

To be sure, those attempting to simplify suburban governance and land-use policy making should be aware that there may be severe repercussions for economic development in a region if institutional arrangements are seriously destabilized. Certainty is important in making economic decisions, and developers have lobbied for decision systems that they see as offering less arbitrary, more predictable outcomes. The possibility that there will be rules changes, boundary manipulations, or the creation or elimination of local governments creates the potential for unknown and disruptive changes in property rights. This instability may lead developers, or businesses looking for sites, to discount the future benefits of some locations. Thus, there are notable virtues in institutional stability, regardless of the particular political arrangements that an urban area may feature. But experimentation and choice are also prized values of American state and local government, and thus the temptation to suggest rigid or uniform decision-making systems for all MSAs should be avoided.

Indeed, the variety of local institutional arrangements is one of the characteristics that makes the politics of urban growth in the United States such a rewarding research laboratory. One might say, however, that a focus on the effects of institutions begs a major question. How did urban governing institutions take shape? What explains their varied form across metropolitan areas? Are there underlying factors, manifested in institutional structures, that better explain urban development outcomes?

Although the literature examining urban political institutions as a "dependent variable" has not been well developed, political scientists have posited a wide variety of explanations for the origins of contemporary political arrangements. To some, the answer comes easily. For neo-Marxists such as Patrick Ashton, urban government structure reflects the mischief of economic elites, who benefit from it directly:

> Capitalists have very astutely used the political fragmentation inherent in the proliferation of suburbs to maximum advantage. They have used the competition for capital among suburbs to extort tax breaks, special services, and investments, and other highly profitable arrangements from the privileged suburbs in which they have located their investments. (Ashton 1984, 73)

The fiscal problems, traffic congestion, and other negative results of this process, which less clearly serve the needs of elites, are then found to represent the contradictions inherent in capitalist development.

In a quite different type of analysis, Gary Miller has used game theory, along with a case study of the Los Angeles region, to examine the creation of local governments. Miller concludes that expansions of choice through the formation of new municipalities (though they may be viewed as favorable for efficiency reasons) are typically undertaken by groups of homeowners or firms seeking windfall gains (Miller 1981).[19] Nancy Burns, who has undertaken

what is probably the most comprehensive study of American local government formation, argues that groups of citizens with a variety of motives create
a *potential* basis for new institutions. To solve the collective action problems
inherent in getting new local units up and running, political entrepreneurs
and small groups of strategic actors—typically developers and property interests—have devoted concentrated efforts to the creation of municipalities and
special districts (Burns 1994).

For other writers, more telling than economic or interest-group motivations has been the context of state rules and constitutional requirements that
establish the provisions and conditions for local government formations,
annexations, and autonomy. Since this is largely the world of the "old institutionalism," so to speak, its study has generally been neglected in recent political science, and satisfactory comparative accounts of state rules on this subject
are virtually nonexistent. Nevertheless, this lost world of scholarship is important, as Alvin Sokolow emphasizes:

> Lurking in the background, as the controlling factor for these local inter-
> governmental games, are the rules established by state government. . . . By
> unevenly assigning different powers and responsibilities among the various
> forms of local government and by establishing procedures for changing
> boundaries, revenue levels, and representation, the rules allocate respective
> advantages and disadvantages. Thus they structure the local intergovernmen-
> tal arena. (Sokolow 1993, 55)

However, it appears that autonomous choices about government structure are
not thoroughly stripped from the residents of a region by these constitutional
factors. For example, within the general rules for local governance in Texas,
there has been a substantial difference in the historical evolution of local
government formation in the Houston and Dallas metropolitan areas.[20]

This small but emerging body of research on local political structure is
promising, but provides no clear evidence of an underlying "hidden hand" of
institutional change. My reading of this nonconsensual literature, along with
detailed consideration of the experiences of metropolitan Portland and Denver, suggests a more complex, "path-dependent" mechanism at work.[21] Many
forces appear to be involved, including historical accident and incidents, constitutional choices of generations past, politically motivated institutional elaborations such as the Poundstone Amendment, persistent pressures for greater
autonomy by local majorities, and incremental reforms that attempt to overcome the inadequacies of existing structures. In a typical metropolis, the
overall patterns of governance probably change very slowly over time. However, longitudinal research, perhaps using a political fragmentation measure
and data set like the one I have employed, is clearly needed.

The likelihood of historical path dependence suggests again the futility of the "scrap-the-system-and-start-over" approach to government structure in the metropolis (see Harrigan 1993, chap. 11). Would-be reformers need to think about how their desired alterations might evolve (or be coaxed) from the present circumstances of their region, given a window of opportunity for change.

As it now stands, there is reason to doubt that many Americans are getting what they seek from the governing structures that have grown up in urban areas. Chisholm, the advocate of decentralization, concludes that "*organizational arrangements should be judged by their results, not by their apparent rationality*" (1989, 192, emphasis in original). This is a sensible recommendation. Those who originally crafted the institutions that now organize urban development probably made what were for them eminently rational choices. The contemporary results of these past decisions, however, may reasonably be challenged.

Appendix 1
Metropolitan Areas in the Data Set

All observations are for metropolitan areas as of 1980. The units of analysis are SMSAs, or Standard Metropolitan Statistical Areas, as defined by the United States Census Bureau. This concept is generally equivalent to the current Metropolitan Statistical Areas used by the bureau. In New England states, for reasons of comparability, New England County Metropolitan Areas (NECMAs) are used in place of SMSAs. Land-use governments are those with some authority over land regulation or infrastructure that can shape growth. Land-use governments include counties or parishes, townships or towns, municipalities, highway districts, housing and community development districts, sewerage districts, water supply districts, transit districts, and districts that provide both sewer and water services. "Local spending per capita" refers to the total per-capita expenditures during 1980 by these land-use governments. *PFI* is the political fragmentation index. For more discussion of the measurement of political fragmentation, see chapter 3.

SMSA	Population	Number of Land-Use Governments	Local Spending Per Capita	PFI
Akron, Ohio	660,328	67	$ 706	0.562
Albany, N.Y.	795,019	104	856	0.750
Albuquerque, N.M.	454,499	13	592	0.169
Allentown, Pa./N.J.	635,481	172	487	0.452
Atlanta, Ga.	2,029,710	132	901	0.787
Austin, Tex.	536,688	48	1,280	0.299
Baltimore, Md.	2,174,020	23	1,257	0.897
Baton Rouge, La.	494,151	21	599	0.245
Birmingham, Ala.	847,487	102	*	*
Boston, Mass.	3,662,830	295	1,384	1.314

(continued)

SMSA	Population	Number of Land-Use Governments	Local Spending Per Capita	PFI
Bridgeport, Conn.	807,143	51	1,109	1.011
Buffalo, N.Y.	1,242,830	66	1,385	1.017
Charlotte, N.C.	637,218	37	1,137	0.843
Chicago, Ill.	7,103,620	440	832	0.715
Cincinnati, Ohio/Ky./Ind.	1,401,490	177	696	0.565
Cleveland, Ohio	1,898,830	141	1,012	0.863
Colorado Springs, Colo.	317,458	45	1,161	0.462
Columbus, Ohio	1,093,320	148	802	0.556
Corpus Christi, Tex.	326,228	31	723	0.448
Dallas/Ft. Worth, Tex.	2,974,800	245	659	0.579
Davenport, Iowa/Ill.	383,958	105	597	0.522
Dayton, Ohio	830,070	107	686	0.555
Denver/Boulder, Colo.	1,620,900	223	926	0.763
Des Moines, Iowa	338,048	72	770	0.513
Detroit, Mich.	4,353,410	221	*	*
El Paso, Tex.	479,899	12	475	0.212
Fort Wayne, Ind.	382,961	89	*	*
Fresno, Calif.	514,621	51	970	0.488
Gary, Ind.	642,781	59	627	0.539
Grand Rapids, Mich.	601,680	62	674	0.571
Houston, Tex.	2,905,350	375	739	0.527
Indianapolis, Ind.	1,166,570	167	573	0.302
Jackson, Miss.	320,425	20	685	0.389
Jacksonville, Fla.	737,541	23	1,132	0.240
Jersey City, N.J.	556,972	26	1,399	1.078
Kansas City, Mo./Kans.	1,327,110	196	771	0.656
Knoxville, Tenn.	476,517	35	1,448	0.954
Las Vegas, Nev.	463,067	10	986	0.430
Lexington, Ky.	317,629	27	429	0.219
Lincoln, Nebr.	192,884	20	1,297	0.418
Los Angeles/Long Beach, Calif.	7,477,500	118	1,292	0.978
Louisville, Ky./Ind.	906,152	156	531	0.406
Madison, Wisc.	323,545	64	1,074	0.683
Memphis, Tenn./Ark./ Miss.	913,472	48	1,674	0.754
Miami, Fla.	1,625,780	31	1,156	0.481
Milwaukee, Wisc.	1,397,140	97	1,140	0.927
Minneapolis/ Saint Paul, Minn./Wisc.	2,113,530	325	1,076	0.987
Nashville, Tenn.	850,505	80	1,399	0.776
Newark, N.J.	1,965,970	149	1,041	0.936

SMSA	Population	Number of Land-Use Governments	Local Spending Per Capita	PFI
New Orleans, La.	1,187,070	19	758	0.462
Norfolk, Va./N.C.	806,951	9	*	*
Oklahoma City, Okla.	834,088	90	610	0.490
Omaha, Nebr./Iowa	569,614	122	*	*
Paterson, N.J.	447,585	25	964	0.748
Philadelphia, Pa./N.J.	4,716,820	510	876	0.616
Phoenix, Ariz.	1,509,050	23	815	0.571
Pittsburgh, Pa.	2,263,890	458	*	*
Portland, Ore./Wash.	1,242,590	91	661	0.562
Providence, R.I.	865,771	61	876	0.813
Raleigh, N.C.	531,167	26	1,007	0.797
Richmond, Va.	632,015	11	1,211	0.814
Rochester, N.Y.	971,230	125	*	*
Sacramento, Calif.	1,014,000	42	990	0.667
Saint Louis, Mo./Ill.	2,356,460	355	509	0.428
Salt Lake City, Utah	936,255	82	573	0.484
San Antonio, Tex.	1,071,950	49	1,105	0.431
San Diego, Calif.	1,861,850	44	834	0.606
San Francisco/ Oakland, Calif.	3,250,630	132	1,213	1.041
San Jose, Calif.	1,295,070	24	1,150	0.777
Seattle, Wash.	1,607,470	110	818	0.615
Shreveport, La.	376,710	30	588	0.387
Spokane, Wash.	341,835	21	497	0.294
Syracuse, N.Y.	642,971	98	1,231	0.889
Tampa/Saint Petersburg, Fla.	1,569,130	48	724	0.604
Toledo, Ohio	791,599	135	711	0.559
Tucson, Ariz.	531,443	5	849	0.430
Tulsa, Okla.	689,434	129	*	*
Washington, D.C./Md./Va.	3,060,920	80	2,021	1.613
Wichita, Kans.	411,313	109	762	0.508
Worcester, Mass.	646,352	119	1,006	0.884

Sources: U.S. Census Bureau Publications, including State and Metropolitan Area Data Book, and the Census of Governments.
* not available due to missing expenditure data for some local governments.

Appendix 2
Denver: The Setting

Founded in 1858 and incorporated in 1861, Denver was a rough-hewn, up-start mining camp in the 1860s. It soon passed several competing boomtowns to attain dominance as the center of commerce in Colorado and the sparsely settled, mountainous states surrounding it. Denver's leap to the top arose not entirely from natural geographic advantages, but from unsurpassed boosterism, political cunning, and intergovernmental lobbying (Judd 1986; Leonard and Noel 1990). Its status as a transportation hub, for example, was largely a function of the careful negotiations city fathers carried on with railroad elites in one era, and with President Dwight Eisenhower in another. These consultations enabled transcontinental transportation links—rail in the first period, interstate highways in the second—to be routed through the "Queen City," rather than Cheyenne or some other suitor.

Another key development in transportation was the early completion of a major airport located on an eastern site convenient to the downtown, despite lukewarm public support. Undertaken at the prodding of Mayor Ben Stapleton's administration in the late 1920s, "Stapleton's folly" became one of America's leading sites for landings and takeoffs—the nation's fifth-busiest as of 1986 (DRCOG 1988b, 44). (In 1995, it was replaced by a new facility at the northeast periphery of the metropolis.) With Stapleton Airport's status as a major air traffic hub, Denver boosters were better able to promote their city, initially as a tourism center and later as a logical site for regional or national corporate headquarters (Stanback and Noyelle 1982, 100).

Another strategy for Denver's boosters was an emphasis on environmental amenities, and particularly air quality, which marked the area early in the century. In an era rife with tuberculosis and other respiratory ailments, the ability to draw "lungers" to a big-sky environment of dry, clean air was a serious economic development strategy (Leonard and Noel 1990, 120). Tourists and retirees were also attracted to Denver. City officials and business leaders refrained from recruiting "smokestack" firms in the industrial era, in an attempt to preserve the area's environmental allure. Although the days of pristine air are long gone, the quality-of-life orientation to economic development remains strong in what one local academic observer labels "the first postindustrial city" (S. Moore interview 1992). Not coincidentally, the manufacturing sector is seriously underrepresented in metro Denver in comparison to the United States as a whole.

The seekers of health and recreation early in the century had fewer ties to downtown Denver's commerce than did previous residents. Thus many settled at some distance from the CBD's haphazard collection of loft businesses and offices. In doing so, some joined earlier settlers in satellite suburban communities such as Arvada, Littleton, Englewood, and Aurora (then the town of Fletcher). These settlements supplemented the existing outlying towns of Golden and Boulder, which had gotten their start in the same period as Denver. Originally quite independent of Denver in their economic character, Golden and Boulder were gradually drawn into its sphere when transportation technology improved, allowing Denver's economy to penetrate outlying areas.

Both Boulder and Golden, however, remain distinct communities that do not blend inconspicuously into the wider suburban sprawl. Golden, which lies at the western edge of Denver's urbanized area, sits in a recessed area surrounded by mesas and sharp hills near the foot of the Rockies. Severe topography prevents suburban development from extending continuously to Golden. About twice as far from Denver, the city of Boulder lies northwest of the core city, about a 35 minutes' drive up U.S. Highway 36. With a sizable university community and a thriving downtown, Boulder has always been a destination of its own, rather than a poor cousin to Denver. Politically distinctive, and surrounded by publicly acquired open space, Boulder remains enough of a separate realm to be considered apart from the Denver metropolis.[1]

Entrepreneurs built rail and streetcar links to connect Denver to the surrounding communities in the last two decades of the nineteenth century. As elsewhere, the advent of relatively inexpensive streetcar transportation spurred the residential deconcentration of the Denver population into new subdivisions of detached suburban houses, and allowed commercial corners and strips to take shape along the numerous radials that led outward from the city center (see Leonard and Noel 1990, chap. 6; Meyers 1990; Warner 1978; Jackson 1985: chaps. 5–6). The Denver Tramway Company, founded in 1886, was a powerful entity in the region's politics in the first half of this century. It developed a virtual monopoly over public transit, and was responsible at its peak for 156 miles of electrified lines. The company survived in vestigial form as a bus operator until 1970, when it sold the remainder of its equipment to the City and County of Denver for $6.2 million, having been driven to virtual extinction in the automobile era (Leonard and Noel 1990, 443).

A Weak Economic Order

By the 1930s, Denver was a "city prematurely grey." Historian Carl Abbott notes the commonality of Denver with other slow-growing Sun Belt cities in this period:

> Local bankers and capitalists were largely interested in finding a safe haven for money earned by a previous generation in south Texas ranching and farming, Colorado mining, or trade in Oregon timber and wheat. As a result, San Antonio, Denver, Portland, and Norfolk each grew by only 10 to 13 percent during the 1930s with annual increments of three to five thousand residents. (Abbott 1987b, 41)

The authors of the preeminent history of Denver agree, noting that money to finance Denver's postwar growth was put up to a large degree by eastern financiers. "Moreover, Denver's elderly elite tried to discourage potential rivals" (Leonard and Noel 1990, 240).

In the context of the national depression, these lending practices did not generate dynamic urban development. When world-famous megadeveloper William Zeckendorf came to the city in 1945 to consider some downtown projects, he found a

> town that time forgot. . . . [Denver was] too spread out to be quaint and too ugly to be pleasant. . . . Boosters told you Denver was a growing city, but the growth was in the suburbs. Denver, like so many other cities, was decentralizing so rapidly that its dry-rotted core had begun to fall in on itself. (Quoted in Leonard and Noel 1990, 247)

Denver's nascent city planning establishment did not seek to reverse this trend, calling instead for road improvements and decentralization. In the interwar years, a planning commission president had commented, "It is easier to travel long distances to and from work, easier to build a new home amid cleaner surroundings than to put forth the effort to bring old neighborhoods up to the rising standards of American residential requirements" (Leonard and Noel 1990, 266). Along the same lines, an elite commission evaluated the potential for rapid transit and found it too expensive a prospect, recommending that Denver emphasize car and bus travel.

Also at midcentury, physical improvements beyond the city limits, some undertaken with money from the new federal grant pipeline, helped set the structure of the evolving metropolis. The development of the grand Denver

Mountain Parks provided facilities for and access to the foothills west of the city—at least for those who could make the auto trip. Sixth Avenue, a major east-west thoroughfare, was converted to a freeway that plunged well into the (then unincorporated) western suburbs. Tolls quickly paid for a new Boulder-Denver Turnpike (now U.S. 36), which opened areas northwest of Denver to large-scale development. And in the 1950s, plans were underway for major interstate highways that would enable brisk north-south and east-west travel (I-25 and I-70, respectively).

Denver was slower to take advantage of federal subsidies for downtown redevelopment. After much disagreement, the city began a massive urban renewal program only in the 1960s. With Seventeenth Street's bankers reluctant to open the city to outside intervention, it took significant mayoral prodding and out-of-state financing to get the renewal machine running. Eventually, however, office-tower canyons came to line downtown's streets, particularly in the wake of the oil boom of the 1970s.

An Ecological Sketch of Metropolitan Denver

To make sense fully of the analysis of contemporary Denver, we need to take a brief tour of the built environment of the metropolitan area, considering its appearance and economic structure. Here I exclude its political structure, concentrating instead on pure description of development patterns in each county in my study area. (Readers will find it useful to refer to the maps in chapter 4.)

As the central and original settlement of the region, *Denver City and County* is of course far older and denser than the rest of the region, and it retains a significant Central Business District in its northwestern quadrant, a few miles southwest of the I-70/I-25 interchange. The downtown consists largely of newer office structures, disproportionately holding communications and public utility firms; finance, insurance, and real estate concerns; and regional headquarters, particularly of energy companies. A large government and civic center is located just south of the CBD. The white-collar work force is also prominent in the south-central portion of the city, where smaller office agglomerations occur where I-25 intersects major arterial streets.

Neighborhoods consisting largely of small single-family structures mark much of the city, with large African-American populations in the area east of the CBD, Latinos to the northeast and northwest and abutting the CBD, and middle-class whites to the south. The small, brick "Denver bungalow," a distinctive architectural style, can be found in areas ranging from the racially diverse neighborhoods near Stapleton Airport to the sleepy middle-class sections near Washington Park. Wealthier areas include the east-central, south-east, and extreme southwest portions of the city. Many neighborhoods have small shopping districts, ranging from the chic to the tawdry.

The area of Denver abutting Adams County and paralleling I-70 (east of I-25) is disproportionately oriented toward heavy industry and transportation. In addition, a section known as lower downtown, between the CBD and the South Platte River, is composed of warehouses and old loft industrial structures dating back to the turn of the century and before. Neglected for decades, the area boasts classic architecture and close proximity to downtown, which has helped begin a gentrification process bringing restaurants, young adults, and renovation. Much of the land along the South Platte, which is flood-prone, remains vacant or has been converted to recreational purposes.

Adams County is situated directly north of Denver, with its extreme south-western portion very close to Denver's CBD. That portion has become a transportation hub, due to its central location and its access to the South Platte, rail lines, highways, and airports. From early on, Adams County ab-sorbed some of the industrial growth associated with Denver's expansion. Its leading employment sectors are retail and services, buoyed by the population base in the north I-25 corridor. The southern crossroads portion of the county contributes to Adams's disproportionate emphasis on transportation, com-munication, public utilities, and wholesale trade.

As historians Leonard and Noel write,

> Adams has been a dumping ground for whatever other communities did not want—a dog track, feed lots, hog farms, junkyards, massage parlors, and the Metropolitan Denver Sewage Disposal District treatment plant; mobile home courts, oil refineries, rendering plants, striptease bars, and sand and gravel quarries. (Leonard and Noel 1990, 345)

Most recently, the county gave up a large tract of land for the site of the new Denver airport, which promises to provide economic development benefits. North and east of Adams County's flat southern industrial section lies an area that has been more attractive for home builders and subdividers. Here, the county contains all or parts of the largely residential, moderate-income cities of Thornton, Northglenn, Westminster, and Broomfield.

The county grew by 7.8 percent in the 1980s, attaining a population of 265,038 at decade's end, but that was due solely to natural increase, as the county experienced net out-migration throughout the decade (DRCOG 1991b, 5). Of the suburban counties, it remains the most tied to Denver's employment base and the most susceptible to economic downturn and unemployment.

West of Adams and Denver, *Jefferson County* is by and large a hilly area, and is characterized by lower residential densities and higher incomes as one moves west toward the mountains. Small office and service firms are mixed among the residences in the older eastern portion, and five large shopping malls serve the large population of this county. The most significant sector, however, has been manufacturing, based primarily on a small number of large plants performing military contract work. In the freestanding western city of Golden, office, commercial, and government employment mixes with residences, with the large Coors plant nearby. The eerie-looking Rocky Flats nuclear weapons plant, always controversial, is a large fenced-in compound northwest of Arvada, near the Boulder County line.

Arapahoe County was the focus of a great deal of residential, commercial, and office growth in the 1970s and 1980s. Dominated by plains except in the hillier southern areas of the county, Arapahoe includes most of Aurora, which is largely residential; some established, older suburban areas of mixed character, south of Denver; and expanding newer suburbs of more prestigious character southeast of Denver. Arapahoe's employment base is centered in clusters of offices along the I-25 and Arapahoe Road corridors, offices housing both regional and national firms. This southeast sector of the metropolis was host to about 336,000 residents and 151,000 jobs by 1990, with 38,500 of those jobs clustered in a small area around I-25 south of I-225. More than one-fifth of travel in the CMSA occurs in this southeast area (DRCOG 1991a: 1–2, 24).[2] Arapahoe also boasts several large shopping centers. Its leading sectors are services and retail, with a burgeoning finance/insurance/real estate sector.

To the south of Arapahoe, *Douglas County* remains largely rural. But as the county between the Denver and Colorado Springs metropolises, it has long been targeted as a future site for extensive suburbanization. In the 1980s Douglas increased its population from 25,153 to 60,391, and 84 percent of that gain was due to in-migration, as opposed to natural increase. Its heavy emphasis on employment in the construction industry relative to the rest of the region, therefore, rests on rapid growth rather than the location proclivities of that industry. While some business parks are located in the extreme northern part of the county, the suburban portions of Douglas County are still overwhelmingly residential.

Appendix 3
Portland: The Setting

Like Denver and most western cities, Portland's early growth in the late nineteenth century was driven by access to and processing of natural resources (see Abbott 1983; Abbott 1987b; MacColl 1979; Poulsen 1987; O'Donnell and Vaughan 1976; Dodds and Wollner 1990). In Portland's case, timber rather than gold or minerals was the product in demand. Portland also parallels Denver in that its early days saw it competing with rival cities in its immediate area before assuming precedence. Just upstream on the Willamette River, the cities of Milwaukie and Oregon City were competing ports, until Portland entrepreneurs gained competitive advantage in the 1850s by constructing a road over the jagged hills west of the river. Platted in 1845, the city incorporated in 1851, and welcomed its first rail connection in 1883.

There were notable booms in the city's population after the 1905 Lewis and Clark Exposition displayed Portland's attractions to the nation, and again during the shipbuilding years of the two world wars. The city reached a population of 200,000 by 1910, and 300,000 two decades later. Like Denver, Portland had conservative public leadership and bank lending practices at midcentury. But military employment during World War II created a bustling economy and rapid population growth. Many of the in-migrants left again after the war, but others stayed, and the city grew to 373,628 in 1950.

For many years, the city's deep-water port primarily served as a staging point for exports of wood from Oregon's mighty forests. Various wood products and paper industries also flourished. But timber has been a declining force in the Portland-area economy throughout the twentieth century, especially since a devastating timberland fire in 1933 (Nelson and Milgroom 1993, 13). Thus, Portland mimicked Denver in being forced to diversify from a resource-based economy.

Development in the Central City

Portland has always been oriented along the north-south Willamette River, which bisects the city. Indeed, the first distinction many Portlanders make in introducing visitors to the metro region is to distinguish between the areas west and east of the Willamette. "Portland is generally flat on the east side . . . with a strong grid street pattern. Bordering the CBD to the west, the Tualatin mountains form a strong physiographic barrier and rise to an elevation of approximately 1,000 feet" (Dueker, Edner, and Rabiega 1987, 137). The west side includes Portland's downtown and oldest structures, with newer and more prestigious homes nearby in the "west hills," and middle-class houses and office buildings farther southwest. Much of northwest Portland is taken up by Forest Park, a hilly "urban wilderness."

Since topographical constraints initially cordoned off growth west from the river, the city's early suburban neighborhoods were directed east, and connected to the CBD by several bridges. Today, the vast majority of the city's population resides on the east side. Aside from an industrial area along the river, frame houses on small lots typify this area. "A popular east side style, now known as the Old Portland, is a small bungalow home, with an open floor plan and big front porch" (Friedman 1993, 208). Inner eastside Portland still has some extremely viable neighborhoods. Most notably, several planned subdivisions that date to the turn of the century, such as Laurelhurst and Ladd's Addition, were and continue to be more prestigious and architecturally unified than the marginal surrounding areas.

As in Denver, "suburbanization," in the days before mass auto ownership, took place mainly within Portland's city limits. The year 1912 may have been the apogee of the streetcar era, when a city of just over a quarter million generated almost 90 million rail trips. There were no competing options for most travelers (Dueker, Edner, and Rabiega 1987, 137).[1] In the auto era, infrastructure improvements to the east side and road improvements through the west hills led inevitably to the appearance of new retail nodes in outer portions of the city, striking more of a balance with downtown (See Abbott 1983, 120).

In this manner, the part of Portland east of the Willamette gradually took on the shape it continues to have: medium-density housing in well-defined neighborhoods, with ribbons of commercial development along the busier thoroughfares spaced within the street grid. Eastside Portland is an extension of the streetcar suburb pattern, comparable to the outer portions of Denver and inner Lakewood and Englewood in Colorado. The eastside pattern lends itself to accessibility among homes, jobs, and shopping opportunities—often by bus, bicycle, or foot. By the 1920s, eastside Portland's numbered street grid was well populated as far east as 82nd Avenue—or roughly to today's Interstate 205. After a slack period during the Depression, the city's frontier of continuous development expanded at an accelerated pace (O'Donnell and Vaughan 1976, 135).

Given Portland's extensive geographic scale, its *city* planning in the first two-thirds of this century was essentially *metropolitan* planning. According to Carl Abbott's excellent historical monograph, Portland's planners saw their fortunes wax and wane depending upon the convenience of their ideas to organized downtown interests and to elected leaders. During World War II, when shipbuilding and other military activities pumped astounding amounts of money and numerous new residents into a sleepy Portland economy, the elected city leadership bypassed the slow-moving planning commission altogether, relying instead on ad hoc pragmatic fixes for a housing shortage and other land-use problems. These strategies were propounded most notably by shipyard tycoon Edgar Kaiser, who was prospering mightily from the wartime buildup.

The Portland Area Postwar Development Committee, an elite group of private and public leaders, met regularly to plot the future of highways, arterials, and public facilities in the postwar metropolis. There is evidence that details of their proceedings, including consultations with the state Highway Commission, were passed on to influential builders. One especially notable builder was retail magnate Fred Meyer, who dotted the metropolis with his combination supermarkets and department stores in the following decades (MacColl 1979, 586). Later, one of the nation's most powerful civil servants, New York's Robert Moses, was recruited by the downtown business leadership to write a regional plan, which focused in typical Moses style on radically improving the infrastructure (particularly highways) and public facilities of Portland. Where the city's planning staff seemed inadequate or unsupportive, CBD leaders repeatedly commissioned outside consultants to issue studies responding to their specific concerns.

But if Portland's leaders made business expansion easy in outer areas of the city, they also noted with alarm the decline of the CBD and the adjoining neighborhoods. As the city grew, the downtown business community and its on-again, off-again partners, the mayor and council, searched for ammunition against the widely feared decentralization of residential and economic vitality. Professional planning, in the form of hired consultants and city (and later regional) planning staff, offered at various times two seemingly contradictory paths toward balanced growth, involving large-scale and small-scale plans for land use and services. While often more striking in their appeal to elites, comprehensive plans and grand urban renewal schemes came at the cost of the everyday "use value" concerns of a substantial proportion of Portland's populace. For instance, planners in the 1950s and early 1960s applied traditional ecological and trickle-down assumptions, and concluded that neighborhoods within three miles of the city center were not viable. They attempted to rationalize the changing land uses in these areas with slum clearance projects. Meanwhile, the working-class and middle-class neighborhoods east of the Willamette were slated for a form of enforced suburbanization. Planners wanted them kept single use, with lower densities and highways bounding them, in accordance with the assumed auto orientation of the middle class.[2] For more forceful implementation of the redevelopment agenda, a powerful and semiautonomous renewal agency, the Portland Development Commission, was created in 1958.

A transformation in the membership of the planning staff and elected officialdom in the late 1960s heralded a new attention to neighborhood revitalization and "use value" considerations. Subsequent changes in planning strategy are discussed in chapter 6.

An Ecological Sketch of Metropolitan Portland

Portland's CBD and oldest, most high-density residential area are just west of the Willamette River. Its inner areas on the east side of the river contain both industry and a wide variety of residential neighborhoods, as well as the Lloyd District, a major office and retail hub. Areas of the city farther east, heavily residential except along through streets, are newer and more automobile oriented, with homes set farther back from the road. Moving east from Portland's boundary, the remainder of *Multnomah County* appears as almost an extension of the city. It is characterized by working- and middle-class residential areas, and traditional strip commercial development along main traffic arteries (Abbott 1983, chap. 1; Dodds and Wollner 1990; MacColl 1979; Friedman 1993; Seltzer interview 1993).

Thus, the metro area's east side roughly approximates the "concentric circles" model of urban development proposed by University of Chicago social scientists in the 1920s. Residential districts fan out in rings of decreasing density, from an industrial-commercial center. An exception to this pattern is the strip of land along the Columbia River, which is devoted to industrial and distribution activities. This corridor is anchored by the Portland International Airport and some facilities of the Port of Portland. A regional rather than truly national hub, Portland International—which had 7.2 million passengers going through in 1992—draws only a fraction of Denver's airport activity. The Port of Portland exports more tonnage than any other west coast facility. Overall in Multnomah County, the sectors of transportation, communications, and public utilities; finance, insurance, and real estate; services; and government are overrepresented relative to the PMSA as a whole.

To the south of Multnomah, *Clackamas County* has long been divided between a timber-dependent rural south and a suburban north. The suburban section itself includes several varied cities and a large unincorporated area, and is notable for its metals manufacturing and warehousing activities. The cities are distinctive. For example, Milwaukie blends an older downtown area with later suburban tract housing; Happy Valley is a small, isolated suburb of wealthy homeowners and is surrounded by hills; and historic Oregon City, one of the poorer municipalities in the PMSA, is a hillside community centered around its old industrial waterfront. The new business heart of Clackamas County is the unincorporated area that spans I-205, from the Portland border south to Highways 212/214. This area boasts a major shopping mall as well as smaller retail facilities, medical and education centers, apartment complexes, and a small amount of high-quality office space. With lower-quality soils, a hillier terrain, and more of a "hardscrabble legacy" than Washington and Multnomah Counties, Clackamas County has tended to be localistic and buffeted by intracounty conflict. Historically, its lands close to Portland were not much more than "stump farms." They were smaller and more quickly subdivided for suburban housing than the lush agricultural fields of Washington County. Two of Clackamas County's cities, however— Lake Oswego and West Linn—are west of the Willamette River and nestled among the Tualatin Mountains. They are among Portland's most prestigious suburban residential areas—particularly Lake Oswego, where real estate interests worked early to create an elite housing community, in part by engineering the formation of a lake. Indeed, it is important to keep in mind the variety that characterizes Clackamas.[3] Its other new hub for development has been the city of Wilsonville, along Interstate 5, which began to grow with the location there of an upper-status retirement community. The small city has branched out to include corporate campuses, distribution centers, and townhouses.

West of the hills that rise above the Willamette, suburban *Washington County* has always been rich in agriculture, until recently its predominant activity. The county had a population of just 39,194 in 1940, but grew to 312,000 by 1990. Today it is quite self-contained economically, and this "west side" of the metropolis is generally considered highest in status. As Abbott writes, "The east side of the SMSA can claim several prestige neighborhoods that are known to eastsiders, but an address almost anywhere from Portland

Heights west to Hillsboro and south to Wilsonville carries the cachet of respectability" (Abbott 1987a, 79). While manufacturing is heavily overrepresented in Washington County, it tends to be of the light, clean, and high-tech variety. Two new highways allowed growth to penetrate this area in the late 1960s.

Medium-density residential neighborhoods, office buildings, and commercial strips, built mostly in the last twenty years, huddle close to west Portland in Washington County cities such as Tigard, Tualatin, and Beaverton. To the west of Beaverton is the Tualatin River Valley, which has evolved into a prosperous node of major suburban development, and is largely auto dependent. North and northwest of Beaverton, "Silicon Forest" companies employ thousands of electronics workers. The plants and offices of these firms are hidden behind the lush vegetation off the Sunset Highway (U.S. 26), and tend to be low density. Accordingly, over 90 percent of employees in this area commute by driving alone. Many workers, however, live close by in the new subdivisions and apartment complexes near the highway. This area blends into the city of Hillsboro at the western fringe of the urbanized area. Hillsboro is the county seat and also features an attractive, small downtown, kept alive by workers and visitors at the Washington County offices located there.

Notes

Chapter 1. Shaping the New Suburbia: An Introduction

1. For an excellent exploration of the role of urban political boundaries in shaping patterns of segregation, see Weiher 1991.

2. In a more bald dichotomy, Cervero defines *suburban* areas as anything outside the CBD. While I am not comfortable with this definition, I agree with Cervero's complaint about the more conventional classification: "In many cases, political boundaries are used to distinguish suburbs from central cities, though activities on both sides of the boundary may be virtually identical" (1989, 15). Historian Carl Abbott employs a more careful measure of "suburbanness" in his study of postwar Sun Belt cities. It relies on the average age of the housing stock in census tracts (1987b, chap. 3).

3. Other parts of his five-part criterion for edge cities include: 600,000 or more square feet of retail space; jobs in excess of bedrooms; newness; and a requirement that the area be perceived as a single place. Of course, it is easy to debate this or any other definition of suburban business centers.

4. For a discussion of changes in firms that may lead to office decentralization, see Rhodes and Kan 1971, 6–7.

5. Garreau ultimately argues that the old downtowns have been buoyed, not drained, by the new development on their peripheries. But the weight of scholarly argument is stacked against him. For one such view, see Kenneth Jackson's review (1991) of *Edge City*.

6. In the recessionary atmosphere of the early 1990s, "build-to-suit" office buildings became far more common relative to speculative development. However, this trend still did not prescribe what sites developers would choose.

7. For details on this process and its pervasiveness, see Linowes and Allensworth 1973.

8. In a study testing the influence of municipal fiscal and service expenditure policies in attracting firms, Schneider (1986, 38) concluded that "the general policy options available to local governments in their attempts to attract retail trade [are severely restricted]. The items most under the control of local governments do not seem to be the items of interest to retail firms." But Schneider's policy measures may not be the proper ones to test a "dependent municipality" hypothesis. Indeed, local taxation and expenditure patterns probably would tell us even less about *office* location, given the recruitment of firms as tenants by developers. In part, the different policy emphases are simply a matter of whether the analyst wishes to address the impact of politics on local *economic development* or on the broader question of regional *urban development patterns*, which I take up.

9. Note that there are no value judgments associated with my use of the word *creative*. It merely denotes government action that enables, rather than simply rendering a verdict.

10. For an analysis of suburban growth conflicts based on survey data, see Baldassare 1986. For cases of specific regions, see for example, Dowall 1984 (on the Bay Area); Miller 1981 (Los Angeles); Danielson and Doig 1982, chaps. 3–4 (New York region); Thomas and Murray 1991 (Houston).

11. Lynch (1960) masterfully analyzes the aspects of urban "imageability," that is, the role of a city's visual form in providing behavioral (dis)orientation to its residents. Discussions of suburbia relevant to this theme include Langdon 1988, 39; Calthorpe 1993; Rowe 1991.

12. Typical criticisms include the following: that public choice does not recognize that the costs of migration are proportionally far greater for labor than for capital; that cities' competitive strategies for attracting business are often ineffective; that biased political processes internal to jurisdictions can structure opportunities for potential "migrants" along class lines; and that the politics of development is not "unitary" but conflictual. See Logan and Molotch 1987; Stone and Sanders 1987.

13. William Riker (1980) saw them, rather, as "congealed preferences." The ways in which the institutions of urban political economies correspond to these views of institutions will be explored in chapters 2 and 7.

14. This is seen as the case under local Labor councils in Britain and Communist city governments in Italy.

15. Logan and Molotch (1987, 10) note that under the neo-Marxist logic, "suburbia developed merely to provide capital with a new realm in which to invest and to stimulate additional demand for consumer goods. This verges on a Marxian version of functionalism, a 'fudging' that avoids working through how human activities actually give social structures their reality."

16. My overall argument here follows the perceptive analysis of Tony Smith 1979.

17. "It has not even been apparent from much of the scholarship of urban social science that place is a market commodity that can produce wealth and power for its owners, and that this might explain why certain people take a keen interest in the ordering of urban life," especially land use (Logan and Molotch 1987, 50).

Chapter 2. Actors, Preferences, and Political Institutions

1. Perhaps the most groundbreaking scholar in the tradition of "positive political economy" is Douglass C. North; see esp. North 1990.

2. Following Ruth Lane, my approach might be labeled "concrete theory," which "borrows the logical rigor introduced by the rational choice theorists," but employs "methods and assumptions . . . both more flexible and more deeply empirical." Concrete theory is marked by its "concern with the environment and institutions within which choice occurs" and attempts "to bridge the gap between behavioral and institutional approaches" (1990, 927–28).

3. These are actually two somewhat different preferences. But empirical studies have shown that consumers capitalize their expected future tax burdens into the price they are willing to pay for a house (Yinger et al. 1988). Thus I will make no analytical

distinction between the two goals at this stage. For the purposes of the current model, higher than expected inflation in a homeowner's property value and an unexpected increase in the service/tax ratio would both represent a windfall gain.

4. This is true even though such goals may in the end conflict with one another. One analysis incorporates this trade-off by positing an "implicit market for environmental quality" among jurisdictions, where "fiscal dividends act as a shadow price for environment" (Erickson and Wollover 1987, 26).

5. At its most noble, use value is associated with the social life of urban neighborhoods, as discussed in Jane Jacobs 1961. At its lowest level, use value can be equated with knee-jerk reactions of NIMBY ("not in my backyard"). Recent research indicates that residents will withstand roughly a 15 percent income loss in order to remain in a valued place. See Bartik 1991, 64–66.

6. An increase in jobs at a rate exceeding the increase in adult population raises employment and wages almost by definition (assuming no increase in workforce participation among previously inactive groups). Other potential tactics for improving these indices, such as unionization or transfers from higher levels of government, are normally beyond the purview of local politics and are therefore not considered here.

7. In New Jersey's suburban growth corridors, for example, only one-seventh of the work force lives in the municipality where it works (Sternlieb and Schwartz 1986, 65).

8. "Zoning is . . . permissive in small, rural jurisdictions in which the majority of voters are farmers or people otherwise allied with owners of undeveloped parcels, who do not want the disposal of their major assets constrained by regulations" (Fischel 1992, 171–77).

9. A survey of Kentucky mayors finds suburban mayors far less interested in additional industrial and commercial growth than their counterparts in core cities and nonmetropolitan towns. See Maurer and Christenson 1982.

10. As more communities limit growth, "the lower the average density of the metropolitan area, and the larger the territory its built-up areas must occupy to accommodate a given population" (Downs 1992, 125).

11. Hochschild (1984) shows that central elites are more capable of egalitarian actions than local elites.

12. One need not argue at this point that such an inclusive decision process will necessarily produce "better" land-use outcomes. The regional city's decision will also be the outcome of its internal decision mechanisms, which may themselves be highly fragmented. (Consider, for example, the case of a city with council members selected by ward, and a "unit-veto" rule among council members. Such was the case in physically extensive Yonkers, New York, for decades, and led to a highly inequitable distribution of subsidized housing.) Riker's argument about the nonexistence of any "true" or "neutral" social choice or "general will" is still operative. Even where the regional city makes a truly "inclusive" choice, it may be a poor one. Participation does not ensure intelligence.

13. On paper, the closest thing to a regional city is Honolulu, which controls all relevant local expenditures on the island of Oahu. In Hawaii, however, the state government holds a unique and special role with respect to land use. Otherwise, even America's "metro reform" cities are not nearly unitary actors. In most cases, independent suburbs have ringed the cities' once-extensive boundaries. And without exception, special-purpose governments with land use influences, such as sewer or water districts, exist within or overlap the city boundaries.

14. Similarly, Pelissero and Fasenfest hypothesize that "suburban government offi-cials' orientations toward, and policies for, economic development will vary depending upon their perceptions of the community's development orientations, needs, and the development policies of neighboring governments" (1989, 303). See also Danielson and Wolpert 1991; Fleischmann and Pierannunzi 1990.

15. In fact, Weiher attributes causality in this stratification process to political bound-aries themselves. Boundaries are held to be efficient transmitters of information to potential migrants. I would instead argue that stratified outcomes arise because political advantage and disadvantage is encapsulated in the structure of municipal power in each metropolitan area. My position stems from a conception of local polities as power-political, neomercantilist territorial units; Weiher's stance relies on a social psychology model of information processing.

16. For a Texas case study and some theoretical analysis, see Perrenod 1984. One journalist writes that "to a large extent, suburban growth is shaped by where water and sewer agency officials decide to put the pipes. The further out they go and the more pipe they lay, the bigger their multimillion-dollar bureaucracies grow and the more connec-tion fees they collect from developers, so they tend to encourage and provide the plumbing for increasing sprawl" (Downie 1974, 91).

17. Bellevue (a sizable and sophisticated suburb) and the region's transit provider negotiated a system whereby Bellevue was granted additional "transit-hours" of service as rewards for instituting parking restrictions and increasing employment and popula-tion densities. See Noguchi 1982.

18. For perspectives on the role of central city "boundedness" in contributing to the relative economic health of the city, see Jackson 1972; Zeigler and Brunn 1980. For an extensive portrait of the politics of growth and annexation in several Sun Belt cities, see Abbott 1987b.

19. Although the classic Sun Belt pattern is of at-large governing bodies, rather than ward-based councils, this has been changing. Under Justice Department pressure re-garding alleged dilution of minority voting strength, several Sun Belt cities have in recent years switched from at-large to mixed or district electoral systems.

20. Especially notable in instilling and communicating the "state of the art" is the Urban Land Institute, a well-funded think tank and information clearinghouse that publicizes ambitious projects, documents emerging trends, and voices public policy concerns through its magazine *Urban Land* and other publications. Specialized real estate trade journals are also numerous.

21. For a fascinating collection of "the laws" of development among key actors in "edge city," see Garreau 1991, chap. 13.

22. In Canada, a relative handful of banks, operating coast to coast, dominate the national financial sector; in the United States, there are thousands of separately orga-nized financial institutions, many with only one or two branches. In her explanation of the leadership role assumed by Canadian developers in the 1970s, Goldenberg (1981) emphasizes the developers' ability to secure creative and large-scale financing.

23. The only efforts I am aware of to apply regime analysis to suburban development are DiGaetano and Klemanski 1991; Kerstein 1993. Again, however, each article discusses a single jurisdiction's development politics. The effort is more satisfying in Kerstein's article because the jurisdiction in question is a large county covering a substantial portion of an urban region.

24. Such an argument might point to the expanded options for social and economic choice, the lower level of bureaucratic overhead and pathology, and the potential for fueling unpredicted economic growth that would not take place under a more "planned" environment. (Burgeoning young industries, for example, might get their chance for a start through the availability of relatively cheap land and buildings in outlying areas.)

Chapter 3. Political Structure and Urban Outcomes

1. Hawkins 1971 and R. Hill 1974 count the total number of governments in each metro area. O'Dell 1973 uses a categorical variable in which metropolitan areas are classified as having "few," "several," or "many" governments.

2. A wide variety of such measures is deployed by Bollens 1986; Hawkins 1971; R. Hill 1974; Zeigler and Brunn 1980.

3. As Paul E. Peterson reports, "In some cities [municipal] governmental units not only are responsible for routine housekeeping functions such as police and fire protection but also are the managers of health, welfare, and educational systems. In other cities the state has assigned just the basic housekeeping functions to municipal governments and has reserved for itself or assigned to counties or special districts the responsibility for hospitals, schools, parks, and welfare. All sorts of combinations can be found" (1981, 10). See also Liebert 1976; Clark, Ferguson, and Shapiro 1982.

4. For a different version of a dispersion measure of political fragmentation, which I find unsatisfactory, see Dolan 1990. Dolan, whose sample consists of Illinois local governments grouped by county, is on the right track when he focuses on expenditure data. But he inexplicably chooses to measure dispersion by calculating the standard deviation of expenditures across government units. This does not show how a county's expenditure "pie" is divided, but instead determines how unequal the levels of expenditure are among local governments. See George A. Boyne's methodological criticism (1992).

5. The little-known world of township government is particularly poorly explored in the scholarly literature. The functions of townships vary widely, but generally include some transportation and land-use activities. And in several states, towns or townships serve as primary local governments, essentially as municipalities. The variety and importance of township governments is catalogued in Stephens 1989.

6. Critics charged that the separation of Nassau and Suffolk Counties (which have no central city) from the larger New York metropolitan area in 1970, and the carving of new metropolitan areas out of older, larger ones in the 1980s, rested more on political considerations than demographic reasoning. See Harrigan 1989, 19. Nevertheless, these designations of new metropolitan areas of regions that would normally be considered entirely "suburban" in character merely give official sanction to the growing economic force of these realms. The phenomenon of relatively centerless new metropolitan areas has been especially prevalent in southern California, where, for example, Anaheim-Santa Ana-Garden Grove has joined the ranks of MSAs.

7. The Census Bureau redesignated what had been Standard Metropolitan Statistical Areas (SMSAs) as Metropolitan Statistical Areas (MSAs) in 1983, but these two concepts differ only in minor technical respects.

8. Unless otherwise noted, all data are drawn from Census Bureau sources—the *State and Metropolitan Area Data Book*, *City and County Data Book*, or *Census of Population*.

9. Urban scholars will recognize my cases, therefore, as either freestanding metro areas, or, in larger agglomerations, what are now generally the "primary" portions (PMSAs) of "consolidated" metro areas (CMSAs). For example, my sample includes what is now termed the Philadelphia PMSA, rather than the entire Philadelphia/Wilmington/Trenton CMSA.

10. In part, this is because the District of Columbia stands in for a state government as a provider of some services.

11. For a discussion of this test, see Gujarati 1988, 223–26.

12. I thank Dr. Hughes for giving me her network centralization data, making possible the analysis below (personal communication 1993).

13. Groups at particular risk of long-distance commutes to such centers are skilled workers coming from elsewhere in the suburban ring and low-wage service and clerical workers commuting from the inner city or from the rural fringe. See Hartshorn and Muller 1991, 153.

14. Low commuting times may also be indicative, of course, of a regional roadway system that is relatively well designed, given housing and employment locations. In reality, however, development patterns tend to respond to the transportation system, rather than the reverse. Other critics might argue that some metropolitan areas with low commuting times have an overcapacity of transportation infrastructure (for example, because interstate highways were built prematurely and penetrate deep into the hinterlands, or were rammed through bulldozed city neighborhoods). This criticism is less easy to answer. However, keep in mind that most of the interstate network was completed in the 1960s, with plenty of time for the development market to adjust to the new capacity by 1980; certainly, few neighborhoods have been razed to make way for highways since the late 1960s. And although some western metropolises have more highly developed highway systems than their eastern counterparts, western residents seem to have responded by choosing residences more distant from their workplace. Altshuler 1979, 324–25, reports that Los Angeles, with its highly developed freeway system, has average trip times about the same as those in dense Boston, which developed largely before the auto age. Los Angeles residents can travel faster on their roadways, but drive nearly twice as far per trip. In short, people throughout the country appear to have very similar "expenditures" of time they are willing to make for daily travel. The current model seeks to explain how SMSAs depart from this norm.

15. Planners' ideals to the contrary, public transit tends to be less convenient than the automobile, and transit use pushes average commute times upward.

16. The classical economic models of the city, on the other hand, assume all employment is located at the center.

17. My reasoning is that in the recessionary atmosphere of the early 1990s, some of the "emerging" edge cities have emerged at far smaller sizes than expected, and many "planned" edge cities have remained on the drawing board.

18. It may seem counterintuitive that suburban areas with fragmented political structures can amass sufficient resources to enable significant agglomerations of commerce. The results here imply, however, that developers can choose from among the larger "menu" of jurisdictions in fragmented areas to bring about more edge cities. The infrastructure-providing capacities of special-district governments may be crucial to this relationship.

19. Textbooks in urban economics also provide brief introductions to this literature.

20. Note that the equation can be rewritten as $ln(d_x) = ln(d_o) - bx$, which may make the b variable easier for some readers to interpret. It is essentially the slope of the density curve.

21. Macauley's principal concern is with alternative methods of calculating b. I use what she regards as the most reliable of these, the "Mills/Ohta" method.

22. In the monocentric urban model, rising incomes imply more decentralization of residences, as residents allocating a fixed proportion of their income to housing consumption can afford to buy more land.

23. Plane refers to the impact of political fragmentation in Phoenix, which is actually one of the less fragmented regions in the sample ($PFI = 0.571$).

Chapter 4. The Institutional Context for Development in Two Regions

1. Interviews ranged in length from thirty minutes to two hours, averaging about seventy-five minutes; a few were conducted by telephone. I did not seek a random sample of respondents, attempting instead to explore how relevant actors perceived their political and economic environment. Interviews were also used to acquire additional factual detail on events. While no tape recorder was used, I took notes on each interview, and "wrote up" the conversation immediately afterward. I am confident that the quotations I use here are very close indeed to the vocabulary and speech patterns of the interviewee. Interview sources are identified in the text, with rare exceptions. For example, in some cases I was asked not to attribute particular information, while in a few cases I suspected that identifying the source could pose negative personal or professional repercussions for that person. A list of "on-the-record" interviews appears at the end of the bibliography. Discussions of elite interviewing that I found to be useful guides include the appendix in Fenno 1978 and Wildavsky 1989.

2. The Census Bureau now includes Yamhill County, Oregon, as part of the PMSA, because a significant component of Yamhill's small population (sixty-five thousand in 1990) commutes to work in the urbanized area. However, Yamhill is still a predominantly rural county that is not viewed as metropolitan in Oregon. It is not included in any of the regionwide institutions operating in the Portland area, and is well outside the area's legally defined urban growth boundary.

3. The army and air force bases near Denver, and the naval shipbuilding yards of Portland, both drew from nationwide labor forces that included significant numbers of minorities. When Portland's "city" of temporary housing for shipyard workers, called Vanport, was destroyed in a 1948 flood, the city was directly confronted with the issues of race and housing, since many of Vanport's residents were African-Americans. Most of those who stayed in the region after the flood were relegated to the run-down Albina neighborhood in inner eastside Portland. Vanport was apparently the world's largest settlement of wartime housing. See the account in MacColl 1979.

4. Such residential decisions have only secondary effects on the patterns of commercial and office growth with which this study is most concerned, however.

5. For example, see the map in MacColl 1979, 657. It is undated, but given the absence of the city of Tigard (incorporated 1964), it must predate that year.

6. Originally, annexation required a triple majority: a majority of voters, property owners, and owners of a majority of assessed valuation. The rules have been eased to require only the first two majorities.

7. On two occasions when Portland seemed to pose more of a threat, incorporations and suburban annexations ensued. The first (early 1960s) was a period of active annexation after a long hiatus; the second was a ballot measure proposing a unified City-County of Portland-Multnomah in 1974. The measure was defeated. See Abbott 1987b, 199–202.

8. See the description of the concentric circles or zones of the metropolis in Abbott 1983, 23–30.

9. Still 20 percent less dense in 1980, Portland lost its advantage in the following decade when Denver annexed territory for its new airport. For a discussion of the competitive advantages to cities of lower densities, see Rusk 1993.

10. See the portraits of the city council at work in Abbott 1983; MacColl 1979.

11. Denver's suburban era was registered in state and national politics as well. See the maps of Colorado's congressional and General Assembly districts in Greater Denver Chamber of Commerce 1991. Reapportionment of the Assembly in the 1960s under the Supreme Court's new "one person, one vote" rules eliminated rural bias, but did more to increase suburban representation. See Furniss 1973. On political unity in the southern suburbs, see Reed 1991.

12. Municipalities will sometimes "cherry pick," or annex along a narrow right-of-way to an outlying commercial development.

13. This feature is apparent in touring the region by auto, where in most municipalities signs direct the motorist to the "City Center."

14. Just west of the study area are the cities of Cornelius and Forest Grove, which share their own freestanding urban growth boundary. Both predate 1900. See Metro 1991b.

15. For example, a small neighborhood in unincorporated Multnomah County incorporated as Maywood Park in 1969, in an attempt to block the progress of the proposed I-205 freeway through the area. Durham came into being to try to keep out a proposed truck assembly plant, Johnson City was a mobile home park in search of state revenues, and the incorporation of Happy Valley was seen by its residents as a way to "protect the community's exclusively residential character" (Paulsen 1987, 91).

16. The only full-time local elected officials outside Portland are Beaverton's mayor, the Clackamas and Multnomah County commissioners, and the chair of the Washington County commission.

17. Symbolic of the emerging importance of counties is the giant government complex in Golden, a 193-acre project that hosts Jefferson County's government operations. The visually striking main building, nearly as big as the state capitol, has acquired the nickname "Taj Mahal."

18. MSDD can issue bonds with a majority vote of the electorate in the district. It pays off its operating costs and debt via contracts with its constituent units. See Greater Denver Chamber of Commerce 1991; Furniss 1973; Mugler 1992.

19. The unified district served 250,000 persons in 1980. Studies have found lower average connection fees and a shorter time required for permits in the unified district. Territory covered by the district appears to spawn more and higher-density growth than comparable areas of the PMSA with fragmented sewer provision. See Knaap and Nelson 1992, 110–18; Kamara 1987, 116.

20. RTD's proposals for new transit modes and projects will be discussed in chapter 5.

21. More recently, DRCOG appointed a "Metro Forum" of twenty-five community leaders in 1990. The forum deliberated on regional governance, concluding by calling for a combination service authority and regional planning agency.

22. As in Denver, regionalism developed slowly, beginning with a Metropolitan Planning Commission (1957–1966), which did little beyond providing planning data and assistance to local governments. To meet the regional planning requirements of the federal highway program, a Portland-Vancouver Metropolitan Transportation Study met from 1959 to 1967; this group became the basis of a regional council of governments. For details, see Abbott 1983; Harrigan 1993, 389–90; Vars 1994.

23. The Port of Portland owns about a quarter of the available industrial land in the metropolitan area, and has developed a number of business parks. These are tied to activities at Portland International Airport and two smaller airports, all owned and managed by the Port of Portland. See Hamilton 1987, 185.

24. An exception is in Clackamas County, where the Clackamas County Development Agency has been vested with industrial recruitment authority.

25. Calculated from the Census Bureau's *1991 state and metropolitan area data book*.

26. The national average for SMSAs was 11.6 percent. Calculated from U.S. Census Bureau's *1982 state and metropolitan area data book*. Multnomah County is alone among the three counties in having a business income tax. In addition, the central city has established its own Portland business license fee. These small totals account for the area's "gross receipts" taxes. At the state level, there is a relatively high income tax due to the lack of sales tax revenues.

27. Voters also may approve a "serial levy." This is an additional property tax, collected for a fixed time period and dedicated to a specific purpose.

I am providing only the simplest sketch of a highly unusual tax system. See Portland Future 1990. The same "tax base" rules operate for the separate levies gathered by school districts. For an analytical discussion of the tax base system in Oregon in the context of school budgeting, see Romer and Rosenthal 1979.

28. Supported by some as a means to force more equitable school funding across Oregon, Measure 5 has generated extreme changes in the state budgeting process. Oregon is obligated to find massive replacement funds to make up for much of the local school cuts.

29. Puzzlingly, Elazar characterizes Oregon as a localistic state with tendencies toward centralization, and Colorado as the reverse—despite tables showing that state government bears a greater proportion of school and welfare costs in Oregon than in Colorado (1972, 198–204). As noted earlier, direct expenditure is much more heavily controlled by localities in Colorado.

30. Both states receive the lowest score in Mayhew's exhaustive study of "traditional party organization" in the American states (1986, 175–78, 188–89). Morehouse's indices of professionalism, industrialization, welfare effort, and other contextual variables consistently show the two states clustered near the middle of the pack. Morehouse identifies Colorado as a strong party, weak interest group state, with Oregon as the reverse, but finds elections in both to be competitive in partisan terms (Morehouse 1981, 59, 117, 513–14). More recently, Brace and Straayer (1987) have cast substantial doubt on Morehouse's classification of Colorado.

31. Readers interested in more depth may refer to the substantial literature on state

land-use planning in Oregon. The best place to start is the text and references of Knaap and Nelson 1992, which summarizes a large body of literature on the topic in planning and urban economics journals, much of it by the authors themselves. Other useful sources for this account are Leonard 1983; DeGrove 1984, chap. 6; Rohse 1987; Abbott, Howe, and Adler 1994.

32. The Willamette Valley, which contains over three-quarters of Oregon's population, is a 120-mile-long north-to-south corridor that ranges from 20 to 50 miles wide. There was widespread concern among residents of the valley that its farmland was disappearing at a rapid rate. In 1973 alone, 2 percent of the valley's acreage was converted from rural to urban uses. Knaap and Nelson conclude that state planning is likely to be more effective where there is such "spatially concentrated political power" (1992, 5). Former Oregon governor Tom McCall, a populist Republican, was a fervent supporter of the measure. For details, see DeGrove 1984.

33. The everyday staff work on these activities is performed by the LCDC's staff arm, the Department of Land Conservation and Development (DLCD). Thus, LCDC has legislative and quasi-judicial powers, while DLCD is an administrative bureaucracy. By law, DLCD must be notified of any local plan change, and where it deems necessary, it can appeal these changes to LCDC. The legislature also created a Land Use Board of Appeals, which functions as a specialized court for land-use cases. The state courts have determined that land-use decisions such as rezonings are quasi-judicial rather than legislative: they apply law to persons rather than making law. Oregon's local governments are highly limited in their quasi-judicial authority, and therefore must justify rezonings to the state's satisfaction. See *Fasano* v. *Washington County Board of Commissioners* 264 Or. 574, 507 P2d 23 (1973); and the discussion in Rohse 1987, 99–100, 184–85.

34. The state's planning goals were to include the following: "Urban growth areas should be compact, have concentrated employment centers, and provide opportunities for people to live in a variety of housing types close to where they work. Development densities should be sufficient to protect open space, natural features and parks; promote affordable and varied housing; and promote transit[;] . . . ensure the siting of . . . public facilities, so that each county and its municipalities accepts their fair share . . . and no county is overburdened[;] . . . reduce proliferation of special districts to reduce sprawl and create more efficient government services."

35. Another factor was the generally slow state of the Denver economy. " 'Killing a spirit of entrepreneurship' was the bogeyman for this plan" (Spitzer interview 1993b).

Chapter 5. Denver

1. As in many cities, the urban renewal period saw more housing destroyed than constructed in downtown Denver. See Judd 1986, 179; Dorsett and McCarthy 1986.

2. The convention center managed to gain a recommendation from the Denver Regional Council of Governments, which Denver used to convince the state of the areawide benefits of the new center. The facility became financially viable only after the legislature authorized funds to purchase the land in question. It opened in 1990. See DRCOG n.d.; 9; Dorsett and McCarthy 1986, 331–33.

3. Scott Moore prepared an extensive study of the organizational and intergovernment politics of this venture. See S. Moore 1994.

4. The *1989 Denver comprehensive plan* envisions new mixed-use city subcenters at the Central Platte Valley, Cherry Creek, and the former Stapleton Airport.

5. Technically, the subsidy would have been in the form of sales tax increment financing.

6. Except where noted, the chronology in this historical sketch draws on Mehls et al. 1985.

7. Without a dominant CBD, residents patronize stores in strip shopping centers and "shopettes" that line the major arterials and collector streets. In this sense, the visual landscape of Aurora is prototypically suburban. Wide streets are bordered by low-rise shopping areas, set far back from the curb, with a great deal of off-street parking. There are also two regional shopping malls.

8. One tell-tale sign is provided by a pamphlet intended to promote shopping and business in the "original Aurora" business district. Among the enterprises listed by the brochure are Waste Management of Aurora, a police substation, Aurora Rehabilitation Authority, the Colorado Drug Education Service, Plasma Services of Denver, two thrift shops, and seven pawnbrokers.

9. The city arranged a special contract with the Colorado Department of Transportation so that the Buckley interchange could be constructed on time.

10. City officials have also considered the viability of forming a City and County of Aurora. This was motivated in part by the fact that Aurora is split between Arapahoe and Adams Counties—an administrative nightmare. Such a city-county reorganization would place Aurora on true parity with Denver, though the odds for passage of such a measure—which would require ballot approval statewide—seem slim. Interestingly, achieving city/county status would make Aurora like Denver in another way: Under the Poundstone Amendment, it would effectively be trapped within its boundaries—extensive though they now are.

11. In the 1970s, the city instituted an annual growth "cap" of 2 percent, while encouraging redevelopment and mixed uses downtown. (The city controls residential growth by licensing new water taps.) Growth management agreements between the city of Boulder and the county ensure that proposals for development at the city's periphery undergo a cumbersome four-party review process: Proposals must be approved by the city council and planning board as well as the county commission and planning commission. Having acted to limit population growth, the city and its periphery now show a serious excess of jobs in relation to housing; apartment rents are significantly higher than in the Denver portion of the CMSA. See Thomason 1986; Reed and Atkins 1989; Pochna 1992.

12. Residential development was restricted in this area for many years, due to noise impacts from a nearby corporate-oriented airport. Because there is little housing close to the employment sites, one developer in the area sells clients on the "country atmosphere: no high-density, no traffic congestion" (quoted in Brazes 1986c). However, many employees must commute from afar on crowded highways. Moreover, in a tour of the area I noticed that employees in an exclusive, architecturally refined office park walked through high grass and along roads that lacked sidewalks, in order to get to a humble hot dog vending truck parked at one building. Such behavior is understandable, since the single-use character of the area ensures few other lunchtime options.

13. Only one municipality, the county seat town of Castle Rock, existed when the market began heating up in the 1970s. Parker and the small south-county town of Larkspur were incorporated shortly thereafter.

14. Another public official in the region complained to me that "the land-use plan looks like a big subdivision. They're not planning for creating a community, but for building more houses."

15. In 1992, a Republican candidate for county commissioner from the Highlands Ranch district, who had opposed school impact fees on developers, recorded collecting at least eleven campaign contributions of $250 or more from developers or real estate personnel as of two months before the election. For a low-information campaign in a relatively small county, such funding represents a significant advantage. The candidate had amassed a $20,791 campaign chest by the September 10 reporting date; her Democratic opponent, who favored impact fees and growth management, collected about $700. See Bangs 1992a; Bangs 1992b.

16. Locating commercial facilities at municipal boundaries is also convenient for city officials because it allows them to externalize some of the negative "neighborhood effects" of these projects, such as traffic, petty crime, or visual blight.

17. The major barrier to fringe growth for many decades was the availability of water. This restraint has eased as suburbs such as Aurora and Thornton developed water supplies independent of the Denver Water Board, and the DWB itself undertook new water diversion projects that allowed it to expand its domain.

18. State rules also require that commercial real estate be assessed at more than twice the percentage of market value as residential real estate. Greater Denver Chamber of Commerce 1992.

19. For an interesting example involving an office project developed near the boundary between Denver, Aurora, and unincorporated Arapahoe County, see "Waterpark" 1987.

20. Throughout most of the study area, multilane arterial roads are arranged in a grid of north-south and east-west routes, generally spaced a mile or two apart. The system of nonhighway arterials and thoroughfares appears more extensive than in many comparable metropolitan areas, and can act as something of a relief valve for crowded highways.

21. Wallace's long career involves both private work and service as consultant and committee member in public bodies. Among other exploits, he helped design the hub system organizing air travel in the United States, and as an engineer, invented an important copper extraction process and designed sophisticated medical instruments. In suburban Denver, he also developed Meridian International Business Center in northern Douglas County, and was a major force behind the opening of a corporate airport in southern Arapahoe County. A member of several public commissions, Wallace also chaired the state's Transit Construction Authority. Wallace is thus something of a Robert Moses figure in Denver, though he operates more from a private- than a public-sector perspective. His bloodlines for such a role are strong: interestingly, his father was construction superintendent on the Holland Tunnel. Biographical material is drawn from Raabe 1986; Meadow 1988; Cornwell 1995; and interviews.

22. The architect of the amendment, Freda Poundstone, lived in Greenwood Village, where she served as mayor in the 1980s.

23. More revealing in some ways were individual open-ended comments in the survey, including the following: "The long commutes frustrate employees." "Employees who live farthest away want to work early hours." "Many employees are moving closer to work." "Entry level positions are difficult to fill in the Tech Center because of the long commute for some prospective employees," and "poor RTD service to northwest and northeast Denver affects our ability to attract minority employees." See DRCOG 1991a, 111–22.

24. The San Diego region, from which DRCOG borrowed this approach, did receive referendum approval that made the process binding (Broderick interview 1992).

25. RTD staff noted that many suburban mall owners do not like buses entering their property. The buses' weight is tough on parking lots, and they are seen as bringing in "undesirables."

26. The mile-long downtown mall provides continuous free shuttle bus service at close intervals along the downtown's major retail street. The project is funded as a special assessment district for affected property owners.

27. While bus miles increased 27 percent between 1983 and 1986, mostly in low-density areas, ridership increased only 8 percent (DRCOG 1988b, 29). On the difficulties of providing transit in suburbia, see also DRCOG 1991a.

28. Personal rapid transit would use a fleet of small vehicles on a fixed guideway, with service responding to demand, and no onboard operators. It was hoped that the system would be in place for the 1976 Winter Olympics; after a referendum canceled Colorado's participation in the Olympics, the Department of Transportation killed the PRT demonstration project.

29. In 1989, the legislature tried again, creating a new Metropolitan Transportation Development Commission to come up with a financing plan for the area's transit and highway needs. However, the MTDC never succeeded in finding a funding source for its $3.2 billion construction agenda.

30. The route is called Metro Area "Connection" because it is designed to collect and distribute passengers for the entire proposed regional rapid transit system. It replaces the final segment of bus routes running to the CBD from the south.

31. By way of comparison, RTD sales tax receipts amounted to $92.5 million in 1991, while fares and other operating revenue brought in $27.1 million.

32. In 1990, the state required transit construction projects to be submitted to DRCOG for approval. For RTD, this has meant hundreds of meetings before local civic groups, and has provided valuable experience in consensus building. In addition, experience with the elected board became somewhat more stable, and a board chair shifted away from a position as an anti-light rail zealot.

33. Staff members allegedly withheld a highly critical Federal Transit Administration report about MAC financing from the elected board. In November 1992, three RTD Board incumbents were defeated by challengers who expressed doubts about RTD's justification for MAC. In 1995, controversy revolved around whether MAC should be viewed as a demonstration project to test light rail's support, or whether to go forward with additional rail lines. See Flynn 1992; George 1992b; Schamp 1995.

34. The policy of Denver City and County emphasizes maintaining a "hub-and-spoke" transit system. See Denver Planning Office 1989.

35. Colorado has 26.2 square feet of mall space per person. The national average is 18.2. Without enough buying power to support all the new retail activity, the smaller, older malls have fallen on hard times. See Parker 1995.

Chapter 6. Portland

1. Most notably, recent referenda have resulted in a strict property tax limitation, and, in some cities and counties, have sought to limit the legal protection of gays and lesbians. (A similar measure was passed in Colorado in 1992, but later struck down in court.)

2. A number of subsequent mayors, city council members, and county commissioners in Portland had their political roots in the neighborhood movement.

3. The decision was hardly consensual, even within the city of Portland. The freeway cancellation was an active issue for years. Billboards in the 1976 mayoral campaign carried the message, "If you had taken the Mount Hood Freeway you would be there by now" (Edner and Arrington 1985, 17–18).

4. The projection was correct. By the early 1990s, Tri-Met's light rail line generated 51 percent of its operating costs from fares, compared to a ratio of 30 percent for Tri-Met buses.

5. MSD administered this program for the three jurisdictions involved (Portland, Gresham, and Multnomah County), employing a group of planners, architects, and economists. See Glick 1993.

6. Another source puts the employment figures at fifty-six thousand in 1975 and eighty-six thousand in 1993 (Portland Metropolitan Association 1993, 16).

7. The southern portion of the I-205 freeway, connecting it to I-5 at Tualatin, was not finished until 1984.

8. Abbott places less emphasis than I do on the relative size and configuration of the jurisdictions involved, and more on the lack of political credibility of the suburban city governments (certainly a related issue).

9. Meanwhile, in Clackamas County, not much periphery was included in the proposed UGB. Wealthy homeowners living in existing small subdivisions adjacent to berry farms wished to be placed outside the UGB, maintaining that they lived in the "country." Rather than fight, the county decided to label their developments "exception areas" within farm-use zones. These have remained "dysfunctional areas" for planners, and the county now lacks large, vacant parcels within its UGB area. Unincorporated Washington County contains 28 percent of the vacant buildable land within the UGB, compared to only 9 percent in unincorporated Clackamas. Portland is the second-leading jurisdiction, with 14 percent. A number of interviewees gave this interpretation of the politics of the UGB process; for data on buildable land, see Metro 1991b.

10. JPACT's membership consists of local elected officials, three MSD councillors, and representatives of the Oregon and Washington Transportation departments, Tri-Met, the Port of Portland, Clark County, and the Oregon Department of Environmental Quality.

11. "There were winners and losers, but the locals accepted the structure because it represented what were new bells and whistles going off: the political atmosphere of environmentalism. Also, there were dollars on the table after the [Mount Hood] freeway was decommissioned." Pemble interview 1993.

12. One suburban anti-LCDC activist argues, "Urban sprawl is always portrayed as terrible, without any studies of actual impacts" (Potter interview 1993).

13. However, the study warned that two-thirds of all *single-family* developments were built at lower densities than plans permitted, raising talk that minimum densities should be required. (Comprehensive plans establish maximum densities, but allow less intensive uses within zones.) See 1000 Friends 1991.

14. The wealthy city of Lake Oswego is probably the most restrictive development environment in metro Portland, but it is somewhat anomalous, according to developer Barry Cain: "Lake Oswego is very arbitrary. They see themselves as a cut above everything else. . . . But it's the oddball case. There are relatively few roadblocks put in the way of development elsewhere" (Cain interview 1993).

15. As a recent LCDC chair put it, "Our feeling is that we're trying to strike the right balance between nudging the local government to do things and providing some backbone that they can use" (William Blosser, quoted in Metro 1991a, 44).

16. Job/population statistics in this section are based upon marketing data acquired by CCDA from private vendors. No ratios are available for municipalities in the Portland area.

17. Brigham Young University had originally acquired the site as the possible future campus of a junior college. When that plan fell through, the church, operating under a single master plan, made most of the site available to developers, while building a massive temple on the remainder of the tract. See Law 1990. The juxtaposition of the huge Mormon shrine and nearby office buildings in the midst of towering woods makes for a very unusual visual panorama.

18. In addition to enhanced transit serving these older business districts, loosened state rules enabled a much wider array of projects to qualify for tax increment financing in the 1980s. As a result, suburban jurisdictions turned to their own versions of "urban" renewal. Beaverton, Hillsboro, Lake Oswego, and Oregon City were among the cities employing renewal districts in attempts to revitalize and modernize older business districts. However, the law was also used to help redevelop new-style nodes like the Clackamas Town Center and the city of Wilsonville. Tualatin's renewal agency has attempted a hybrid policy, with a mixed-use project in a central area of this relatively new suburb, in effect attempting to create a downtown. However, future redevelopment projects of this type will be difficult, both in the suburban municipalities and in Portland. The region's fiscally conservative voters have indicated uneasiness with the urban renewal agenda. In a 1993 vote (previewed by several local referenda), Oregon voters chose to include urban renewal bond repayments in the cap on local property taxes. This subjects redevelopment policy to a tougher fiscal calculation by public officials.

19. The county maintains a large role in traditional county functions such as social services and the judicial system.

20. As Ethan Seltzer puts it, despite the region's seemingly "unbelievable" institutional structure—a regional government, unified UGB, all comprehensively planned, with minimum zoning densities—"it's still not enough to forestall some kinds of decentralization, congestion, and patterns of zoning," particularly the absence of all commercial activity from suburban neighborhoods. "This in particular is [the problem] we have in common with other places" (Seltzer interview 1993b).

21. The Municipality of Metropolitan Toronto directs growth to regional subcenters, using transit and public facilities to shape it; for corridor development, it encourages medium-rise, streetside buildings along roads that can appropriately serve as community centers. On Metro's ideas, see Law 1991a.

22. Joseph Grillo, director of Land Development Services, Washington County, views these experiments as particularly important in testing whether financiers can be persuaded to underwrite unconventional developments. Grillo interview 1993.

23. The rule also mandates a 10 percent reduction in the per capita parking ratio over that time period. The rule is set out in Oregon Administrative Regulations Chapter 660, Division 12 (1991).

24. The LRT is also being linked to the urban renewal–based redesign of Beaverton's old downtown.

25. Grillo notes that it can be "an uphill battle to get a different design" at the undevel-

oped tracts that will host MAX stations. This is because some of the properties had already had preliminary plans for development approved under previous zoning. In some cases, chain stores that would be expected to rent the retail sites at station-area developments have balked at the absence of spacious parking lots and auto-oriented design.

26. Data drawn from the U.S. Census Bureau's *1986 state and metropolitan area data book*; and DRCOG 1988b, 36–37.

27. Rutherford's figures were based on a weekday ridership of 19,000 in 1988—a number that had risen to 24,100 per weekday in 1993. Before it was constructed, planners projected weekday ridership for the line of 42,500 by 1990.

28. Voters on the Oregon side of the metro area approved a supplemental property tax to pay for their share of the local funding of the LRT. The southern terminus of the line is expected to be the Clackamas Town Center shopping mall. See Steward 1993; Ryll 1995.

29. In the process, the old Vancouver CBD was drained of commerce. For a time it turned to limited stakes card gambling to lure more visitors. This effort failed, but a small comeback is now under way.

30. Certainly, being the major part of Multnomah County has been advantageous to Portland. It can use the county government as a lever to wield even greater institutional authority. Also, compared to Denver City and County, Multnomah serves to strip away some of Portland's responsibilities for welfare, social service, and criminal justice expenditures.

31. Seltzer continues: "But there are still more professional personnel in Portland than in most of the state agencies."

32. In 1992, Metro's executive officer, Rena Cusma, put forth a ballot measure (later withdrawn under intense opposition) to consolidate Metro, Tri-Met, and the three counties into a single unit of government, with savings promised to taxpayers. It can be argued that pouring energy into an unrealistic scheme such as this, on the heels of an earlier reorganization, is a poor use of Metro's limited political capital. Metro owes many of its accomplishments thus far to its incremental approach. Regional governance demonstrated its political strengths and avoided directly usurping the powers and offices of more local units.

33. Metro was pressured by citizen complaints to consider a slow-growth alternative to its Region 2040 "visions." In a brochure, it felt compelled to remind the public that United States constitutional law forbids placing restraints on citizens who wish to move from one state or region to another.

34. Barry Cain says, "Let's face it, people don't move here to live at high densities."

35. A survey of eight hundred residents of the tri-county area finds little support for centralized authority. Respondents rated special districts as both the most efficient and the most responsive units of government, with Tri-Met, counties, and cities ranked lower, and Metro rated last. See Western Attitudes, Inc. 1993.

Chapter 7. Conclusion

1. It is interesting to note that comparisons of cities in the United States and Canada sometimes fall into the same rut. But there, the clearer differences between the two nations' systems for governing urban areas are typically obvious enough to be brought to the fore. See "Toronto and Detroit" 1990, 17–20.

2. Clearly, there are many forces at work creating high unemployment among inner city workers, and political-institutional arrangements need not assume explanatory precedence. Nevertheless, the link between political fragmentation and the "spatial mismatch" separating poor people's housing from entry-level work, is likely to be significant—and often overlooked.

3. For a suggestive case study of the limitations of Columbus, Ohio, in this respect, see Workman 1994.

4. In fact, Denver's Mayor Peña, who put together a new, "progressive" electoral coalition, was a likely candidate for such entrepreneurship. Because of the constrained environment in which he operated, however, he chose to leave his mark on the region with huge infrastructure investments such as the new airport and downtown convention center.

5. In that sense, planners are at the nexus of a particular type of "issue network" or "policy community," seeking windows of opportunity to promulgate favored ideas. See Kingdon 1984.

6. "The claims of planners often seem to be in conflict with those of politicians. Both claim a unique ability to judge the overall public interest. The politician's claim rests on his popular election, his knowledge of the community, his sensitivity to human needs, and his personal wisdom. The planner's claim is one of professionalism and research. If it seems somewhat devoid of human warmth, it also sounds more authoritative, more precise, more modern" (Altshuler 1965, 303).

7. There are some limitations in applying this framework to a geographic context, for reasons alluded to throughout this book. That is, interests that appear "narrow" or "concentrated" when viewed from a regionwide standpoint may appear broadly representative or "majoritarian" within the context of a particular jurisdiction.

8. This is made especially clear by the deductive finding that there exists a degree of "monopoly supply" over land by municipal officials, and therefore excess property taxes cannot be "competed away." This means that Tiebout's economic approach must be tempered by politics if one is examining land use. See Epple and Zelenitz 1981.

9. As I have suggested, this exercise is likely to show that business elites of the type influential in declining central cities are less important to governing coalitions in many other types of localities.

10. Although high density suburban development may make public transit a more viable, attractive option, the associated increases in congestion are likely to be even greater. See Lewis 1993. For alternative perspectives of various kinds, regarding the redesign of urban areas and the relationship of such designs to transportation, see Downs 1994; Transportation Research Board 1991; Barnett 1989.

11. Some states, particularly those affected by nonattainment under the Clean Air Act, have discussed instituting sizable annual motor vehicle fees or excise taxes that would be based on mileage driven. This policy would have an effect similar to high gasoline taxes.

12. Those cities and towns more interested in deflecting new growth, conversely, could use case-by-case design review procedures to drag out the planning approval of new developments. Indeed, this already occurs in many cases, though from an effort more to insulate neighbors from change than to improve circulation and reduce car use in new projects.

13. Oregon's conservation activists, riding the first wave of environmentalism, were able to push through the state land-use program in large part because of an unusually

supportive and popular Republican governor. The cause was also aided by the fact that farmland in the Willamette Valley is among the most productive and valuable in the country. These conditions are unlikely to be duplicated elsewhere.

14. This policy, of course, offers little immediate consolation to regions like Denver that already have substantial excess infrastructure capacity at the urban rim.

15. The direct election of representatives to such a metropolitan unit would seem to bolster its legitimacy. In particular, a visible, elected executive officer or "regional mayor" would lend some accountability and visibility to a metropolitan government. If local governments are represented as units, as in councils of governments, then weighted voting procedures should be used. One-vote-per-government mechanisms of the type used by DRCOG appear to violate the constitutional requirements of equal protection.

16. Foster mentions Colorado as one of the states with a very high concentration of infrastructure districts (1993, 257–58).

17. It is actually quite difficult to make an analogy between the cases that Ostrom describes and the circumstances relevant in metropolitan areas. In the context of metropolitan development, units of government rather than individuals are the relevant decision-making actors; and the "common-pool resources" are multiple and complex (roadway space, clean air, open space, etc.).

18. An exception is the attention some TMAs give to "flex-time" arrangements for work hours, which can serve to spread some of the peak-hour use of roadways over a longer period.

19. In Miller's Institutional Bias Game (1981, 164–67), a change in the parameters of the game leads to a better equilibrium outcome for one player (i.e., a suburban neighborhood that incorporates), but a worse outcome for the other (the central city). Unlike the Prisoner's Dilemma, the structure of the Institutional Bias Game means that cooperation cannot lead to real gains for both players (without side payments).

20. "Examining the origin of local government complexity enables us to challenge the conventional wisdom that 'states create local governments.' . . . That notion is too simple. Tracing the evolution of local governments shows local choices exercised within the state's general legal framework" (Thomas and Boonyapratuang 1993).

21. "Path dependence is a way to narrow conceptually the choice set and link decision making through time. It is not a story of inevitability in which the past neatly predicts the future" (North 1990, 98).

Appendix 2

1. My analysis of Denver in chapters 4 and 5 does not include Boulder County, focusing instead on the contiguous urbanized area within the counties of Denver, Adams, Arapahoe, Jefferson, and Douglas.

2. The "southeast area" includes small portions of Denver and Douglas Counties, but is almost entirely composed of territory in Arapahoe.

Appendix 3

1. Portland had the nation's third most extensive electric rail system in 1915 (MacColl 1979, 103).

2. The planning commission said it aimed at "restructuring our residential sections into secluded units protected from the encroachment of conflicting land uses" (Abbott 1983, 188, and chap. 9).

3. For an intriguing depiction of the appearance and culture of Clackamas County, which unfortunately misses this variety, see Orlean 1994.

Bibliography

Abbott, Carl. 1983. *Portland: Planning, politics, and growth in a twentieth-century city.* Lincoln: University of Nebraska Press.

——. 1987a. The everyday city: Portland's changing neighborhoods. In *Portland's changing landscape*, ed. Larry W. Price. Portland: Portland State University.

——. 1987b. *The new urban America: Growth and politics in sunbelt cities.* Rev. ed. Chapel Hill: University of North Carolina Press.

——. 1987c. The suburban sunbelt. *Journal of Urban History* 13:275–301.

——. 1990. Southwestern cityscapes: Approaches to an American urban environment. In *Essays on sunbelt cities and recent urban America*, ed. Robert B. Fairbanks and Kathleen Underwood, 59–86. College Station: Texas A&M University Press.

——. 1994. The Oregon planning style. In *Planning the Oregon way*, ed. Carl Abbott, Deborah Howe, and Sy Adler. Corvallis: Oregon State University Press.

An Act for Land Conservation and Development. 1991. July 23. Typescript of proposal.

Adler, Sy. 1994. The Oregon approach to integrating transportation and land use planning. In *Planning the Oregon way*, ed. Carl Abbott, Deborah Howe, and Sy Adler. Corvallis: Oregon State University Press.

Advisory Council on Intergovernmental Relations. 1987. *The organization of local public economies.* Washington, D.C.: GPO.

Altshuler, Alan. 1965. *The city planning process.* Ithaca: Cornell University Press.

Altshuler, Alan, et al. 1979. *The urban transportation system: Politics and policy innovation.* Cambridge: MIT Press.

America's holy trinity. 1991. *Economist*, October 26.

Armstrong, Regina B. 1972. *The office industry: Patterns of growth and location.* A report of the Regional Plan Association. Cambridge: MIT Press.

——. 1979. National trends in office construction, employment, and headquarter location in U.S. metropolitan areas. In *Spatial patterns of office growth and location*, ed. P. W. Daniels. New York: John Wiley and Sons.

Arrow, Kenneth. 1951. *Social choice and individual values.* New York: Wiley.

Ashbaugh, James. 1987. Portland's changing riverscape. In *Portland's changing landscape*, ed. Larry W. Price. Portland: Portland State University.

Ashton, Patrick. 1984. Urbanization and the dynamics of suburban development under capitalism. In *Marxism and the metropolis*, ed. William Tabb and Larry Sawers. 2d ed. New York: Oxford University Press.

Atchison, Sandra. 1987. He's been working on the railroad in Denver. *Business Week*, June 8.

Aurora dreams tied to airport. 1992. *Denver Post*, June 28.

Babcock, Richard. 1966. *The zoning game*. Madison: University of Wisconsin Press.

Baerwald, Thomas J. 1978. The emergence of a new "downtown." *Geographical Review* 68:308–18.

———. 1982. Land use change in suburban clusters and corridors. *Transportation Research Record* 861:7–12.

Baldassare, Mark. 1986. *Trouble in paradise: The suburban transformation in America*. New York: Columbia University Press.

———. 1989. Citizen support for regional government in the new suburbia. *Urban Affairs Quarterly* 24:460–69.

Bangs, Richard. 1992a. Candidates address efficiency in county government. *Douglas County News-Press*, October 21.

———. 1992b. Cooke defends campaign contributions. *Douglas County News-Press*, October 21.

Barnett, Jonathan. 1989. Redesigning the metropolis: The case for a new approach. *Journal of the American Planning Association* 55:131–35.

Barrett, Katherine, and Richard Green. 1992. A special report. *Financial World*, February 18.

Bartels, Larry M. 1988. *Presidential primaries and the dynamics of public choice*. Princeton: Princeton University Press.

Bartik, Timothy. 1991. *Who benefits from state and local economic development policies?* Kalamazoo: Upjohn Institute.

Beaverton council to consider policy for urban boundary. 1993. *Oregonian*, July 9.

Bell, Daniel. 1973. *The coming of post-industrial society*. New York: Basic.

Benner, Susan. 1984. Life in the silicon rain forest. *Inc.*, June.

Berry, Brian J. L., and Frank E. Horton. 1970. *Geographic perspectives on urban systems*. Englewood Cliffs, N.J.: Prentice-Hall.

Birch, David L. 1975. From suburb to urban place. *Annals, AAPSS* 422:25–35.

Bodine, Harry. 1993. Portland, Beaverton still drawing the line. *Oregonian*, June 28.

Bollens, Scott. 1986. A political-ecological analysis of inequality in metropolitan areas. *Urban Affairs Quarterly* 22:221–41.

———. 1992. State growth management: Intergovernmental frameworks and policy objectives. *Journal of the American Planning Association* 58:454–66.

Bonner, Ernest. 1978. Portland: The problems and promise of growth. In *Personality, politics, and planning*, ed. Anthony Catanese and W. Paul Farmer. Beverly Hills: Sage.

Booth, Michael. 1988. Texas-based Leede Oil and Gas moving to Denver. *Denver Business Journal*, May 2.

Boyne, George A. 1992. Is there a relationship between fragmentation and local government costs? A comment on Drew Dolan. *Urban Affairs Quarterly* 28:317–22.

Brace, Paul, and John A. Straayer. 1987. Colorado: PACs, political candidates, and conservatism. In *Interest-group politics in the American west*, ed. Ronald Hrebenar and Clive Thomas. Salt Lake City: Utah State University Press.

Brazes, Jane. 1986a. Downtown Denver readies battle plans. *Denver Business*, August.

———. 1986b. An employment base grows in Aurora. *Denver Business*, September.

———. 1986c. The south I-25 corridor. *Denver Business*, December.

Brimberg, Judith. 1991. Employment growth on fast track: Suburbs put metro area first in U.S. *Denver Post*, September 2.

Brock, Kathy. 1992. Sisters of Providence plans doctors' offices in Clackamas area. *Business Journal—Portland*, December 21.

Buehrer, Judi. 1986. No exit? *Denver Business*, October.

Bureau of the Census (U.S. Department of Commerce). 1982. *Census of governments, 1982 finance statistics* (computer file). Washington, D.C.: U.S. Department of Commerce, Bureau of the Census (producer); Ann Arbor: Inter-University Consortium for Political and Social Research (distributor).

———. *Census of population* (various dates and reports). Washington, D.C.: Bureau of the Census.

———. *City and county data book* (various dates). Washington, D.C.: Bureau of the Census.

———. *State and metropolitan area data book* (various dates). Washington, D.C.: Bureau of the Census.

Burns, Nancy E. 1994. *The formation of American local governments: Private values in public institutions.* New York: Oxford University Press.

Calthorpe, Peter. 1993. *The next American metropolis.* Princeton: Princeton Architectural Press.

Cameron, Mindy. 1990. A good land-use bargain in Oregon. *Seattle Times*, December 9.

Cardoso, Fernando, and Enzo Faletto. 1979. *Dependency and development in Latin America.* Berkeley: University of California Press.

Caro, Robert. 1974. *The power broker: Robert Moses and the fall of New York.* New York: Vintage.

Castells, Manuel. 1976. Is there an urban sociology? In *Urban sociology: Critical essays*, ed. C. G. Pickvance, 33–59. New York: St. Martin's.

Cervero, Robert. 1989. *America's suburban centers: The land use-transportation link.* Boston: Unwin Hyman.

Chandler, David. 1992. Look who's not talking. *Westword* (Denver), October 21–27.

Chisholm, Donald. 1989. *Coordination without hierarchy: Informal structures in multiorganizational systems.* Berkeley: University of California Press.

Clackamas County Development Agency. n.d. Promotional packets.

Clark, Don. 1990. Oregon grows a new industry. *San Francisco Chronicle*, August 20.

Clark, Terry. 1985. Fiscal strain: How different are snow belt and sun belt cities? In *The new urban reality*, ed. Paul E. Peterson. Washington, D.C.: Brookings.

Clark, Terry, Lorna Ferguson, and Robert Shapiro. 1982. Functional performance analysis. *Political Methodology* 8:187–223.

Clarke, Susan E. 1987. More autonomous policy orientations: An analytic framework. In *The politics of urban development*, ed. Clarence Stone and Heywood Sanders. Lawrence: University Press of Kansas.

Clawson, Marion. 1971. *Suburban land conversion in the United States.* Baltimore: Johns Hopkins University Press.

Colorado: Bonds floated to aid ailing school districts. 1992. *American Political Network Daily Report Card*, January 7.

Company of the year: Real estate and construction—Adolfson and Peterson, Inc. 1992. *Colorado Business*, August.

Cornwell, David. 1995. 50–40–10, my friend. *Colorado Business*, May.

Costas, Suzanne. 1987. Paper wait: Bureaucrats threaten developers' budgets—and sanity—at every turn. *Denver Business*, June.

Cronon, William. 1991. *Nature's metropolis: Chicago and the Great West*. Chicago: W. W. Norton.

Daniels, P. W., ed. 1979. *Spatial patterns of office growth and location*. New York: John Wiley and Sons.

Danielson, Michael N. 1976. *The politics of exclusion*. New York: Columbia University Press.

Danielson, Michael N., and Jameson W. Doig. 1982. *New York: The politics of urban regional development*. Berkeley: University of California Press.

Danielson, Michael N., and Paul G. Lewis. 1996. City bound: Political science and the American metropolis. *Political Research Quarterly* 49: 203–20.

Danielson, Michael N., and Julian Wolpert. 1991. Distributing the benefits of regional economic development. *Urban Studies* 28:393–413.

Davis, Judy S., and Sheldon M. Edner. 1993. Refining estimates of double taxation: Lessons from law enforcement in a suburban county. *Urban Affairs Quarterly* 28: 593–616.

Davis, Mike. 1990. *City of quartz: Excavating the future in Los Angeles*. New York: Verso.

DeGrove, John. 1984. *Land, growth, and politics*. Chicago: APA Planners' Press.

Denver digs in. 1992. *Colorado Business*, August.

Denver Planning Office (Denver City and County). 1974. Denver, the core city. Pamphlet.

———. 1985. Denver data. Pamphlet.

———. 1989. *1989 Denver comprehensive plan*. Denver: Denver Planning Office.

Denver Urban Observatory. 1975. *Denver metropolitan area: Why citizens are moving in and out of Denver and the suburban ring*. Denver: University of Denver.

Denver Water Department. 1990. *Annual report*. Denver: Denver Water Department.

DiGaetano, Alan, and John S. Klemanski. 1991. Restructuring the suburbs: The political economy of economic development in Auburn Hill, Michigan. *Journal of Urban Affairs* 13:137–58.

Dinner, P. J. 1992. The economic turnaround and beyond. *Accent Aurora*, October 21–27.

Doane, Robert, David Wall, and Bill Winter. 1993. Birth of a region. Presented at the Annual Meeting of the Urban Affairs Association, Indianapolis.

Dodds, Gordon, and Craig Wollner. 1990. *The silicon forest: High tech in the Portland area, 1945–1986*. Portland: Oregon Historical Society.

Dolan, Drew. 1990. Local government fragmentation: Does it drive up the cost of government? *Urban Affairs Quarterly* 26:28–45.

Donovan, Todd, and Max Neiman. 1992. Community social status, suburban growth, and local government restrictions on residential development. *Urban Affairs Quarterly* 28:323–36.

Dorsett, Lyle W., and Michael McCarthy. 1986. *The queen city: A history of Denver*. 2d ed. Boulder: Pruett.

Dotterrer, Steve. 1987. Changes in downtown Portland. In *Portland's changing landscape*, ed. Larry W. Price. Portland: Portland State University.

Douglas County [Colo.] Planning Commission. 1992. *Douglas County master plan executive summary*. Castle Rock, Colo.: Douglas County Planning Commission.

Dowall, David. 1984. *The suburban squeeze*. Berkeley: University of California Press.

Downie, Leonard. 1974. *Mortgage on America*. New York: Praeger.

Downs, Anthony. 1967. *Inside bureaucracy*. Boston: Little, Brown.

———. 1992. *Stuck in traffic*. Washington, D.C.: Brookings.

———. 1994. *New visions for metropolitan America*. Washington, D.C.: Brookings.

DRCOG (Denver Regional Council of Governments). 1980. *Industrial land and development in the Denver region*. Denver: DRCOG.

———. 1988a. *An approach to regional services: The Colorado Service Authority Act*. Denver: DRCOG.

———. 1988b. *Mobility*. Denver: DRCOG.

———. 1990. *Employment estimates by sector, 1988*. Denver: DRCOG.

———. 1991a. *Mobility—the southeast area*. Denver: DRCOG.

———. 1991b. *Population change in the Denver metro region, 1980–90*. Denver: DRCOG.

———. 1992. *1960–1990 population and household data by 1990 Census tract boundaries*. Denver: DRCOG.

———. n.d. *Off the drawing board*. Denver: DRCOG.

Dueker, Kenneth, Sheldon Edner, and William Rabiega. 1987. Transportation planning in the Portland metropolitan area. In *Portland's changing landscape*, ed. Larry W. Price. Portland: Portland State University.

Edner, Sheldon, and G. B. Arrington. 1985. *Urban decision making for transportation investments: Portland's light rail transit system*. Washington, D.C.: U.S. Department of Transportation.

Eisler, Gary. 1993. Coping with the future. In Portland Metropolitan Association of Building Owners and Managers, *1993 metropolitan office guide*. Portland: PMABOM.

Elazar, Daniel. 1972. *American federalism: The view from the states*. New York: Harper and Row.

Elkin, Stephen L. 1985. Twentieth century urban regimes. *Journal of Urban Affairs* 7:11–28.

———. 1987. *City and regime in the American republic*. Chicago: University of Chicago Press.

Elkins, David, and Richard Simeon. 1979. A cause in search of its effect, or, what does political culture explain? *Comparative Politics* 11:127–47.

Endangered developers resurge. 1992. *Colorado Business*, June.

Epple, Dennis, and Thomas Romer. 1989. On the flexibility of municipal boundaries. *Journal of Urban Economics* 26:307–19.

Epple, Dennis, and Allan Zelenitz. 1981. The implications of competition among jurisdictions: Does Tiebout need politics? *Journal of Political Economy* 98:1197–1217.

Erickson, Rodney A. 1986. Multinucleation in metropolitan economies. *Annals, Association of American Geographers* 76:331–46.

Erickson, Rodney A., and David Wollover. 1987. Local tax burdens and the supply of business sites in suburban municipalities. *Journal of Regional Science* 27:25–37.

Fainstein, Susan, et al. 1986. *Restructuring the city: The political economy of urban redevelopment*. Rev. ed. New York: Longman.

Fayhee, M. John. 1986. Water: A critical issue in Colorado's economic future. *Denver Business*, March.

Feagin, Joe R., and Robert Parker. 1990. *Building American cities: The urban real estate game*. Englewood Cliffs: Prentice Hall.

Fenno, Richard. 1978. *Home style: House members in their districts*. Boston: Little, Brown.

Financial World. 1991. February 18.

Finley, Bruce. 1992. New aim: Keep water in hills. *Denver Post*, October 20.

Fischel, William A. 1985. *The economics of zoning laws: A property rights approach.* Baltimore: Johns Hopkins University Press.

———. 1990. *Do growth controls matter? A review of empirical evidence on the effectiveness and efficiency of local government land use regulation.* Cambridge: Lincoln Institute of Land Policy.

———. 1992. Property taxation and the Tiebout model: Evidence for the benefit view from zoning and voting. *Journal of Economic Literature* 30:171–77.

Fishman, Robert. 1987. *Bourgeois utopias: The rise and fall of suburbia.* New York: Basic.

———. 1990. Megalopolis unbound. *Wilson Quarterly* (Winter): 25–45.

Fleischmann, Arnold, and Carol A. Pierannunzi. 1990. Citizens, development interests, and local land-use regulation. *Journal of Politics* 52:838–53.

Flynn, Kevin. 1992. RTD staff withheld critical report on light-rail project. *Rocky Mountain News*, October 21.

Form, William H. 1954. The place of social structure in the determination of land use: Some implications for a theory of urban ecology. *Social Forces* 32:317–23.

Foster, Kathryn A. 1993. Special districts and the political economy of metropolitan service delivery. Ph.D. diss., Princeton University.

Freeman, Douglas. 1987. Light rail expansion plans uncertain. *Business Journal—Portland*, October 5.

Friedman, Elaine S. 1993. *The facts of life in Portland, Oregon.* Portland: Portland Possibilities, Inc.

Friesma, Paul. 1970. Interjurisdictional agreements in metropolitan areas. *Administrative Science Quarterly* 15:242–52.

Fulcher, Michelle, and Jeffrey Leib. 1990. Foes sue to stop Regency Mall. *Denver Post*, June 13.

Fulton, William. 1986. Silicon strips. *Planning* 52 (May): 7–12.

Furlong, Tom. 1991. A messy cleanup program. *Los Angeles Times*, June 28.

Furniss, Susan. 1973. The response of the Colorado General Assembly to proposals for metropolitan reform. *Western Political Quarterly* 26:747–65.

Gans, Herbert J. 1962. Urbanism and suburbanism as ways of life: A reevaluation of definitions. In *Human behavior and social processes*, ed. Arnold Rose. Boston: Houghton Mifflin.

Garn, Harvey, and Michael Springer. 1975. Formulating urban growth policies: Dynamic interactions among people, places, and clubs. *Publius* 5:25–49.

Garreau, Joel. 1991. *Edge city: Life on the new frontier.* New York: Doubleday.

George, Mary. 1992a. Plan avoids putting E-470 traffic on Tower Road. *Denver Post*, October 27.

———. 1992b. Light rail faces new scrutiny after 3 on RTD board ousted. *Denver Post*, November 5.

———. 1992c. Local E-470 funding expected. *Denver Post*, November 6.

———. 1995. Suburban parkway debated. *Denver Post*, February 13.

Giuliano, Genevieve. 1986. Land use impacts of transportation investments. In *The geography of urban transportation*, ed. Susan Hanson. New York: Guilford.

Glick, Fred. 1993. Light rail transit and effective land use planning: Portland, Sacramento, and San Diego. *Transportation Research Record* 1361: 75–80.

Goldenberg, Susan. 1981. *Men of property: The Canadian developers who are buying America*. Toronto: Personal Library.

Gordon, Britta. 1988. Washington County enjoying apartment boom. *Business Journal—Portland*, January 25.

Gordon, Peter, Ajay Kumar, and Harry W. Richardson. 1989a. Congestion, changing metropolitan structure, and city size in the United States. *International Regional Science Review* 12:45–56.

———. 1989b. The influence of metropolitan spatial structure on commuting time. *Journal of Urban Economics* 26:138–51.

Gordon, Peter, and H. L. Wong. 1985. The costs of urban sprawl: Some new evidence. *Environment and Planning A* 17:661–66.

Gordon, Steven C. 1988. Urban growth management Oregon style. *Public Management* 70:9–11.

Gottdiener, Mark. 1977. *Planned sprawl: Private and public interests in suburbia*. Beverly Hills: Sage.

———. 1983. Understanding metropolitan deconcentration: A clash of paradigms. *Social Science Quarterly* 64:227–46.

Gottdiener, Mark, and George Kephart. 1991. The multinucleated metropolitan region: A comparative analysis. In *Postsuburban California*, ed. Rob King, Spencer Olin, and Mark Poster. Berkeley: University of California Press.

Gottman, Jean. 1979. Office work and the evolution of cities. *Ekistics* 46:4–7.

Greater Denver Chamber of Commerce. 1991. *Government action guide, 1991–1992*. Denver: Greater Denver Chamber of Commerce.

———. 1992. Metro Denver quick facts. Pamphlet.

Greene, David L. 1980. Urban subcenters: Recent trends in urban spatial structure. *Growth and Change*, January: 29–40.

Greenwood Village, Colo., City of, Arts and Humanities Council. n.d. *The Greenwood Village history quilt*. Greenwood Village: City of Greenwood Village, Colo.

Greenwood Village, Colo., City of, Planning Department. n.d. History of Greenwood Village. Typescript.

Gujarati, Damodar. 1988. *Basic econometrics*. 2d ed. New York: McGraw-Hill.

Hall, Peter. 1986. *Governing the economy: The politics of state intervention in Britain and France*. New York: Oxford University Press.

Hamilton, F. E. Ian. 1987. Silicon forest. In *Portland's changing landscape*, ed. Larry W. Price. Portland: Portland State University.

Harrigan, John. 1993. *Political change in the metropolis*. 5th ed. New York: Harper Collins.

Harris, Craig. 1993. District 10 may revive fire brigades. *Oregonian*, June 30.

Hart, Paul. 1985. Clark County has its advantages for business. *Business Journal—Portland*, June 10.

———. 1976. *Metropolis in Georgia*. Cambridge: Ballinger.

Hartshorn, Truman. 1973. Industrial/office parks: A new look for the city. *Journal of Geography* 72:33–45.

Hartshorn, Truman, and Peter O. Muller. 1991. The suburban downtown and urban economic development. In *Sources of metropolitan growth*, ed. Edwin Mills and John McDonald. New Brunswick, N.J.: Rutgers Center for Urban Policy Research.

Harvey, David. 1989. From managerialism to entrepreneurialism: Urban governance under late capitalism. Paper delivered at the Vega Symposium, Stockholm.

Hawkins, Brett W. 1971. *Politics and urban policies*. Indianapolis: Bobbs-Merrill.

Heclo, Hugh. 1978. Issue networks and the executive establishment. In *The new American political system*, ed. Anthony King. Washington, D.C.: American Enterprise Institute.

Hedrick, William, and L. Harmon Zeigler. 1987. Oregon: The politics of power. In *Interest-group politics in the American west*, ed. Ronald Hrebenar and Clive Thomas. Salt Lake City: University of Utah Press.

Herson, L. J. R. 1957. The lost world of municipal government. *American Political Science Review* 51:330–45.

Hill, Luana Hellman. 1987. Buying a neighborhood. *Oregon Business*, October.

Hill, Richard Child. 1974. Separate and unequal: Governmental inequality in the metropolis. *American Political Science Review* 68:1557–68.

Hochschild, Jennifer L. 1984. *The new American dilemma: Liberal democracy and school desegregation*. New Haven: Yale University Press.

Hogue, Kendra. 1988. Ex-mayor wheels into Tri-Met post. *Business Journal—Portland*, July 18.

Holden, Matthew. 1964. The governance of the metropolis as a problem in diplomacy. *Journal of Politics* 26:627–47.

Hughes, Holly L. 1993. Metropolitan structure and the suburban hierarchy. *American Sociological Review* 58:417–33.

Intergovernmental agreement on a new airport. 1988. Agreement made at Denver. Typescript, April 21.

Irwin, Michael D., and Holly L. Hughes. 1992. Centrality and structure of urban interaction. *Social Forces* 71:17–51.

Jackson, Kenneth. 1972. Metropolitan government versus suburban autonomy: Politics on the crabgrass frontier. In *Cities in American history*, ed. Kenneth Jackson and Stanley Schulz, 442–62. New York: Knopf.

——. 1985. *Crabgrass frontier: The suburbanization of the United States*. New York: Oxford University Press.

——. 1991. Review of *Edge City*. *New York Times Book Review*, September 22, 11.

Jacob, Philip E., and Henry Teune. 1964. The integrative process. In *The integration of political communities*, ed. Philip E. Jacob and James V. Toscano. Philadelphia: Lippincott.

Jacob, Philip E., and James V. Toscano, eds. 1964. *The integration of political communities*. Philadelphia: Lippincott.

Jacobs, Jane. 1961. *The death and life of great American cities*. New York: Vintage.

Johnson, Dirk. 1991. After boom and bust, Denver enters big leagues. *New York Times*, June 12.

Jonas, Andrew. 1991. Water and sewerage, and schools: The "failure" of metropolitan political reform in Columbus. Presented at the Annual Meeting of the Association of American Geographers, Miami.

Jones, Bryan. 1989. Why weakness is a strength: Some thoughts on the current state of urban analysis. *Urban Affairs Quarterly* 25:30–40.

Judd, Dennis R. 1986. From cowtown to sunbelt city: Boosterism and economic growth in Denver. In *Restructuring the City*, by Susan Fainstein et al. New York: Longman.

——. 1988. *The politics of American cities: Private power and public policy*. Glenview, Ill.: Scott, Foresman.

Judd, Dennis R., and Robert Mendelson. 1973. *The politics of urban planning.* Urbana: University of Illinois Press.

Judd, Dennis R., and Randy L. Ready. 1986. Entrepreneurial cities and the new politics of economic development. In *Reagan and the cities,* ed. George Peterson and Carol Lewis. Washington, D.C.: Urban Institute.

Kale, Steven, and Patrick Corcoran. 1987. Economy of the Portland area. In *Portland's changing landscape,* ed. Larry W. Price. Portland: Portland State University Press.

Kamara, Sheku G. 1987. Effect of local variations in public services on housing production at the fringe of a growth-controlled multi-county metropolitan area. *Urban Studies* 24:109–17.

Kasowski, Kevin. n.d. Oregon's fifteen years of land use planning. *Developments* 1, 1:6–8.

Katzenstein, Peter. 1985. *Small states in world markets.* Ithaca: Cornell University Press.

Keene-Osborne, Sherry. 1990. Leadership past, future leaders. *Colorado Business,* January

Kelley, Guy. 1995. E-470 moves from courthouse to prairie. *Rocky Mountain News,* May 22.

Kerstein, Robert. 1993. Suburban growth politics in Hillsborough County: Growth management and political regimes. *Social Science Quarterly* 72:614–30.

Kingdon, John W. 1984. *Agendas, alternatives, and public policies.* Boston: Little, Brown.

Kirkland, John. 1988. The tug-of-war with Vancouver, U.S.A. *Oregon Business,* April.

——. 1989. Avoiding gridlock. *Oregon Business,* January.

Kling, Rob, Spencer Olin, and Mark Poster, eds. 1991. *Postsuburban California.* Berkeley: University of California Press.

Knaap, Gerrit, and Arthur C. Nelson. 1992. *The regulated landscape: Lessons on state land use planning from Oregon.* Cambridge, Mass.: Lincoln Institute of Land Policy.

Knudson, Thomas. 1987. Western cities move aggressively to clear up smoggy skies. *New York Times,* November 24.

Koepp, Stephen. 1988. Gridlock: Congestion on America's highways and runways takes a grinding toll. *Time,* September 12, 52.

Lane, Ruth. 1990. Concrete theory: An emerging political method. *American Political Science Review* 84:927–40.

Langdon, Philip. 1988. A good place to live. *Atlantic Monthly,* March: 39.

——. 1992. How Portland does it. *Atlantic Monthly,* November: 134–41.

Langfur, Hal. 1989. Colorado's water fight. *New Leader,* July 25

Law, Steve. 1990. Controversial Lake Oswego developer bails out. *Business Journal—Portland,* May 7.

——. 1991a. Metro approves bold new blueprint for future growth. *Business Journal—Portland,* October 28.

——. 1991b. Metro charter panel emphasizes more regional planning. *Business Journal—Portland,* November 25.

——. 1992. Henry Richmond: Land-use guru finds developers adding to Oregon's 1000 Friends. *Business Journal—Portland,* January 6.

——. 1993. Dursts, Pacificorp may revive Lloyd District deal. *Business Journal—Portland,* February 8.

——. 1994. Region 2040 will be born, but will it have any teeth? *Business Journal—Portland,* November 4.

Leib, Jeffrey, and Bruce Finley. 1990. Englewood retailing faces challenge. *Denver Post,* April 14.

Leinberger, Christopher B. 1990. Urban cores: Development trends and real estate opportunities in the 1990s. *Urban Land*, December, 4–9.

Leinberger, Christopher B., and Charles Lockwood. 1986. How business is reshaping America. *Atlantic Monthly*, October, 43–52.

Leonard, Jeffrey. 1983. *Managing Oregon's growth: The politics of development planning.* Washington, D.C.: Conservation Foundation.

Leonard, Stephen J., and Thomas J. Noel. 1990. *Denver: Mining camp to metropolis.* Niwot, Colo.: University Press of Colorado.

Lewis, Paul G. 1993. Suburban activity centers as public policy? Putting first things first. Working Paper 93–1, Center of Domestic and Comparative Policy Studies, Princeton University.

Liebert, Roland. 1976. *Disintegration and political action: The changing functions of city governments in America.* New York: Academic Press.

Linowes, R. Robert, and Don T. Allensworth. 1973. *The politics of land use: Planning, zoning, and the private developer.* New York: Praeger.

Local developers experiment with "urban village" concept. 1992. *Business Journal—Portland*, October 26.

Logan, John. 1978. Growth, politics, and the stratification of places. *American Journal of Sociology* 84:404–15.

Logan, John, and Harvey Molotch. 1987. *Urban fortunes: The political economy of place.* Berkeley: University of California Press.

Logan, John, and Mark Schneider. 1982. Governmental organization and city/suburb income inequality, 1960–70. *Urban Affairs Quarterly* 17:303–18.

Logan, John, and Todd Swanstrom, eds. 1990. *Beyond the city limits.* Albany: State University of New York Press.

Long, Norton E. 1958. The local community as an ecology of games. *American Journal of Sociology* 54:251–61.

Lycan, Richard. 1987. Changing residence in a changing city. In *Portland's changing landscape*, ed. Larry W. Price. Portland: Portland State University.

Lynch, Kevin. 1960. *The image of the city.* Cambridge, Mass.: MIT Press.

Macauley, Molly K. 1985. Estimation and recent behavior of urban population and employment density gradients. *Journal of Urban Economics* 18:251–60.

MacColl, E. Kimbark. 1979. *The growth of a city: Power and politics in Portland, Oregon, 1915–1950.* Portland: Georgian Press.

Malls facing up to ravages of age. 1992. *Denver Post*, May 18.

Mall wars simmer below surface as Regency faces hurdles. 1992. *Denver Business Journal*, July 3.

Manners, Gerald. 1974. The office in metropolis: An opportunity for shaping metropolitan America. *Economic Geography* 50:93–110.

March, James G., and Johan P. Olsen. 1989. *Rediscovering institutions: The organizational basis of politics.* New York: Free Press.

Marsh, Steve. 1988. Graebner: Lot of shaking needed to get rapid transit moving. *Denver Business Journal*, March 7.

Martin, Roscoe, Frank Munger, and associates. 1961. *Decisions in Syracuse.* Bloomington: Indiana University Press.

Masotti, Louis, and Jeffrey Hadden, eds. 1973. *The urbanization of the suburbs.* Beverly Hills: Sage.

Maurer, Richard C., and James A. Christenson. 1982. Growth and nongrowth orienta-
    tions of urban, suburban, and rural mayors: Reflections on the city as a growth
    machine. *Social Science Quarterly* 63:350–58.
Mayes, Steve. 1987. North Macadam area could get big facelift. *Business Journal—Port-
    land*, October 26.
Mayhew, David. 1974. *Congress: The electoral connection*. New Haven: Yale University
    Press.
———. 1986. *Placing parties in American politics*. Princeton: Princeton University Press.
McCloud, John. 1991. In Portland, Ore., rivals prosper in unity. *New York Times*, Au-
    gust 25.
McCoy, William, and Michael Gallis. 1993. Regional approaches: The Charlotte region.
    Presented at the Annual Meeting of the Urban Affairs Association, Indianapolis.
McDermott, Terry. 1991. Post-modern politics: Oregon asks what works. *Seattle Times*,
    November 17.
McDonald, John F. 1989. Econometric studies of urban population density: A survey.
    Journal of Urban Economics 26:361–85.
McGraw-Hill, Inc. 1991. *Black's office leasing guide: Metro Denver office space market*. Red
    Bank, N.J.: McGraw-Hill, Inc.
Meadow, James B. 1988. P.E., B.M.E.—and S.O.B? *Denver Business Journal*, January 18.
Mehle, Michael. 1992. Fighting to keep small-town image. *Chicago Tribune*, Apr. 25.
Mehls, Steven F., et al. 1985. *Aurora: Gateway to the Rockies*. Evergreen, Colo.: Cordillera
    Press.
Metro (formerly Metropolitan Service District, Portland). 1991a. *Building a liveable
    future*. 1991 Regional Growth Conference Proceedings. Portland: Metro.
———. 1991b. *Community profiles*. Portland: Metro.
———. 1991c. *Regional urban growth goals and objectives*. Ordinance 91–418B.
———. 1992. *Metro Charter*. Portland: Metro.
———. 1993. 2040: Decisions for tomorrow. Pamphlet.
———. n.d. Resourceful renovation. Pamphlet.
Meyers, Glenn R. 1990. Colorado's mass transit odyssey. *Colorado Business*, October.
Miller, Gary J. 1981. *Cities by contract: The politics of municipal incorporation*. Cambridge:
    MIT Press.
Mills, Edwin S. 1992. The measurement and determinants of suburbanization. *Journal of
    Urban Economics* 32:377–87.
Mills, Edwin S., and Wallace E. Oates, eds. 1975. *Fiscal zoning and land use controls: The
    economic issues*. Lexington, Mass.: D. C. Heath.
Mollenkopf, John. 1983. *The contested city*. Princeton: Princeton University Press.
Molotch, Harvey. 1988. Strategies and constraints of growth elites. In *Business elites and
    urban development: Case studies and critical perspectives*, ed. Scott Cummings. Al-
    bany: State University of New York Press.
Moore, Paula. 1994. Who owns the Tech Center? *Denver Business Journal*, January 28.
Moore, Scott T. 1994. Between growth machine and garbage can: Determining whether
    and where to expand the Denver airport, 1982–88. Presented at the Annual Meeting
    of the Southern Political Science Association, Atlanta.
Morehouse, Sarah M. 1981. *State politics, parties, and policy*. New York: Holt, Rinehart,
    Winston.
Mueller, Dennis. 1979. *Public choice*. New York: Cambridge University Press.

Muller, Peter O. 1981. *Contemporary suburban America*. Englewood Cliffs: Prentice Hall.

Mumford, Lewis. 1961. *The city in history*. New York: Harcourt, Brace, World.

Neiman, Max. 1975. *Metropology: Toward a more constructive research agenda*. Beverly Hills: Sage.

Nelson, Arthur C., and Jeffrey H. Milgroom. 1993. The role of regional development management in central city revitalization. Working Paper 6, National Center for the Revitalization of Central Cities, University of New Orleans.

Nice, David C. 1983. An intergovernmental perspective on urban fragmentation. *Social Science Quarterly* 64:111–18.

Niskanen, William. 1971. *Bureaucracy and representative government*. Chicago: Aldine, Atherton.

Noel, Thomas J. 1991. Unexplored western skies: Denver International Airport. *Journal of the West* 30:90–100.

Noguchi, Tomoki. 1982. Shaping a suburban activity center through transit and pedestrian incentives: Bellevue CBD planning experience. *Transportation Research Record* 861: 1–6.

North, Douglass C. 1981. *Structure and change in economic history*. New York: W. W. Norton.

——. 1990. *Institutions, institutional change, and economic performance*. Cambridge: Cambridge University Press.

Oakey, R. P., and S. Y. Cooper. 1989. High technology, agglomeration, and the potential for peripherally sited small firms. *Regional Studies* 23:347–60.

O'Dell, Doyle. 1973. The structure of metropolitan political systems: A conceptual model. *Western Political Quarterly*, March, 64–82.

O'Donnell, Terence, and Thomas Vaughan. 1976. *Portland: A historical sketch and guide*. Portland: Oregon Historical Society.

Oliver, Gordon. 1993. Up front: Taxes for Metro. *Oregonian*, June 30.

Olson, Mancur. 1965. *The logic of collective action*. Cambridge: Harvard University Press.

The once and future transportation plan (with sidebar articles). 1992. *Governing* (April): 65–71.

1000 Friends of Oregon and Home Builders Association of Metropolitan Portland. 1991. *Managing growth to promote affordable housing: Revisiting Oregon's goal 10*. Executive summary. Portland: 1000 Friends.

Ordeshook, Peter C. 1992. *A political theory primer*. New York: Routledge.

Oregon's first land-use order to create growth issued by LCDC. 1982. UPI distribution, June 2.

Orlean, Susan. 1994. Figures in a mall. *New Yorker*, February 21, 48–63.

Ostrom, Elinor. 1972. Metropolitan reform: Propositions derived from two traditions. *Social Science Quarterly* 53: 474–93.

——. 1983. The social stratification-government inequality thesis explored. *Urban Affairs Quarterly* 19:91–112.

——. 1990. *Governing the commons: The evolution of institutions for collective action*. New York: Cambridge University Press.

Ostrom, Vincent, Charles Tiebout, and Robert Warren. 1961. The organization of government in metropolitan areas: A theoretical inquiry. *American Political Science Review* 55: 831–42.

Parker, Penny. 1995. Dinosaur malls. *Denver Post*, February 6.

Patty, Mike. 1992. Arapahoe snubs more tax money for E-470. *Rocky Mountain News*, October 20.

Peirce, Neal R., et al. 1983. Politics is not the only thing that is changing America's big cities. *National Journal*, November 26, 2479.

Pelissero, John P., and David Fasenfest. 1989. A typology of suburban economic development policy orientations. *Economic Development Quarterly* 3:301–11.

Perlman, Lee. 1993. Planning Bureau looks for neighborhood to test plan. *Oregonian*, June 30.

Perrenod, Virginia. 1984. *Special districts, special purposes*. College Station: Texas A&M University Press.

Peterson, Paul E. 1981. *City limits*. Chicago: University of Chicago Press.

——. 1985. Introduction: Technology, race, and urban policy. In *The new urban reality*, ed. Peterson. Washington, D.C.: Brookings.

Pisarski, Alan. 1987. *Commuting in America*. Westport, Conn.: Eno Foundation.

Plane, David A. 1986. Urban transportation: Policy alternatives. In *The geography of urban transportation*, ed. Susan Hanson. New York: Guilford.

Pochna, Peter. 1992. City votes to sue county over a new development. *Colorado Daily*, October 22.

Portland Bureau of Water Works (City of Portland). 1989. *Annual report*. Portland: Portland Bureau of Water Works.

Portland Future Focus Committee (City of Portland). 1990. *Environmental scan*. Portland: Portland Future Focus Committee.

——. 1991. *Strategic plan*. Portland: Portland Future Focus Committee.

Portland Metropolitan Association of Building Owners and Managers. 1993. *1993 metropolitan office guide*. Portland: Portland Metropolitan Association of Building Owners and Managers.

Potter, Connie. 1991. We made it happen. *Public Management* 73:25.

Pouslen, Thomas M. 1987. Shaping and managing Portland's metropolitan development. In *Portland's changing landscape*, ed. Larry W. Price. Portland: Portland State University.

Private water scheme proposed for Denver. 1991. *Englewood News-Record*, March 11.

Raabe, Steve. 1986. "A little building for my people" grew into Denver Tech Center. *Rocky Mountain Business Journal*, May 12.

——. 1990. Denver developer leaves mark on Motor City. *Denver Post*, April 16.

Rae, Douglas. 1967. *The political consequences of electoral laws*. New Haven: Yale University Press.

Rebchook, John. 1992. Builders come to Colorado from across the nation. *Rocky Mountain News*, October 20.

Reed, Carolyn, and Linda Atkins. 1989. Boulder County: A fertile soil for small business. *Colorado Business*, September.

Reed, Carson. 1991a. South metro Denver. *Colorado Business*, Feb.

——. 1991b. The northwest parkway. *Colorado Business*, June.

Regency Mall out, downtown retail center in? 1992. *Denver Post*, July 16.

Reich, Robert. 1992. *The work of nations*. New York: Vintage.

Rhodes, John, and Arnold Kan. 1971. *Office dispersal and regional policy*. Cambridge: Cambridge University Press.

Richardson, Glen. 1990. DVX Aurora: Cleared for takeoff. *Denver Business*, November.

Riethmayer, Leo. 1971. Colorado. In *Rocky Mountain urban politics*, ed. JeDon Emenheiser. Logan, Utah: Utah State University.

Riker, William. 1980. The implications of the disequilibrium of majority rule for the study of political institutions. *American Political Science Review* 74: 1235–47.

———. 1986. *The art of political manipulation*. New Haven: Yale University Press.

Rohse, Mitch. 1987. *Land-use planning in Oregon*. Corvallis, Ore.: Oregon State University Press.

Romer, Thomas, and Howard Rosenthal. 1979. Bureaucrats vs. voters: On the political economy of resource allocation by direct democracy. *Quarterly Journal of Economics* 93:563–87.

Rose, Michael. 1993. Development edges into tiny town of North Plains. *Business Journal—Portland*, January 25.

Rowe, Peter G. 1991. *Making a middle landscape*. Cambridge, Mass.: MIT Press.

RTD (Regional Transportation District, Denver). 1992a. *1993–1997 transit development program*. Denver: RTD.

———. 1992b. *RTD rapid transit planning history*. Denver: RTD.

———. n.d. *RTD: A history, 1969–1982*. Denver: RTD.

Rusk, David. 1993. *Cities without suburbs*. Baltimore: Johns Hopkins University Press/ The Woodrow Wilson Center.

Rutherford, G. Scott. 1989. Light rail: Heavy politics. *Pacific Northwest Executive*, October.

Ryll, Thomas. 1995. Arguments on both sides of the track. *Columbian* (Vancouver, Wash.), January 29.

Schamp, Caroline. 1995. The pains of transportation whiplash. *Denver Post*, January 20.

Schattschneider, E. E. 1960. *The semi-sovereign people*. New York: Holt, Rinehart, Winston.

Schiesl, Martin. 1991. Designing the model community: The Irvine Company and suburban development. In *Postsuburban California*, ed. Rob King, Spencer Olin, and Mark Poster. Berkeley: University of California Press.

Schmenner, Roger. 1982. *Making business location decisions*. Englewood Cliffs: Prentice Hall.

Schneider, Mark. 1986. The market for local economic development: The growth of suburban retail trade, 1972–82. *Urban Affairs Quarterly* 22:24–41.

———. 1989. *The competitive city: The political economy of suburbia*. Pittsburgh: University of Pittsburgh Press.

———. 1992. Undermining the growth machine: The missing link between local economic development and fiscal payoffs. *Journal of Politics* 54:214–30.

Schneider, Mark, and Paul Teske. 1993. The antigrowth entrepreneur: Challenging the "equilibrium" of the growth machine. *Journal of Politics* 55: 720–36.

Shaw, Larry. 1993. Oregon sales tax could help Clark County merchants. *Oregonian*, July 6.

Shefter, Martin. 1985. *Political crisis/fiscal crisis: The collapse and revival of New York City*. New York: Basic.

Showdown in Denver: Developers vie to build one more mall. 1991. *Chain Store Age*, executive edition, September.

Shultz, Michael M., and Jeffrey B. Groy. 1986. *The premature subdivision of land in Colorado*. Cambridge, Mass.: Lincoln Institute of Land Policy.

Simon, Herbert. 1955. A behavioral model of rational choice. *Quarterly Journal of Economics* 69:99–118.

Smith, David. 1992. Seeding the silicon forest. *Vancouver [B.C.] Sun*, September 26.

Smith, Eric. 1987. The southeast corridor: Denver's fountain of growth. *Colorado Business*, December.

Smith, Michael P., and Joe R. Feagin. 1987. *The capitalist city*. New York: Basil Blackwell.

Smith, Michael P., Randy L. Ready, and Dennis R. Judd. 1985. Capital flight, tax incentives, and the marginalization of American states and communities. In *Public policy across states and communities*, ed. Dennis R. Judd, 181–201. Greenwich, Conn.: JAI.

Smith, Rogers M. 1992. If politics matters: Implications for a "new institutionalism." *Studies in American Political Development* 6: 1–36.

Smith, Tony. 1979. The underdevelopment of development literature: The case of dependency theory. *World Politics* 31: 247–88.

Sokolow, Alvin. 1981. Local politics and the turnaround migration. In *Population redistribution in the Midwest*, ed. Larry Whiting. Ames: Iowa State University Press.

——. 1993. State rules and the city-county arena: Competition for land and taxes in California's Central Valley. *Publius* 23: 53–69.

Stanback, Thomas M. 1991. *The new suburbanization: Challenge to the central city*. Boulder: Westview.

Stanback, Thomas M., and Thierry Noyelle. 1982. *Cities in transition*. Totowa, N.J.: Allanheld, Osmun.

Stephens, G. Ross. 1989. The least glorious, most local, most trivial, homely, provincial, and most ignored form of local government. *Urban Affairs Quarterly* 24: 501–12.

Sternlieb, George, and Alex Schwartz. 1986. *New Jersey growth corridors*. New Brunswick, N.J.: Rutgers Center for Urban Policy Research.

Stewart, Bill. 1993. Light-rail examination combined for Portland, Vancouver. *Oregonian*, July 9.

Stone, Clarence N. 1987. Summing up: Urban regimes, development policy, and political arrangements. In *The politics of urban development*, ed. Clarence Stone and Heywood Sanders. Lawrence: University Press of Kansas.

——. 1989. *Regime politics: Governing Atlanta, 1946–88*. Lawrence: University Press of Kansas.

Stone, Clarence N., and Heywood T. Sanders, eds. 1987. *The politics of urban development*. Lawrence: University Press of Kansas.

Suburbs' slumbering giant stirs. 1992. *Denver Post*, June 21.

Swanstrom, Todd. 1993. Beyond economism: Urban political economy and the postmodern challenge. *Journal of Urban Affairs* 15:55–78.

Tax Supervising and Conservation Commission of Multnomah County. 1993. Summary of valuations, annual budgets, property tax levies, tax rates, and indebtedness for local governments in Multnomah County. Pamphlet.

Taylor, Leon. 1991. The race to build: Infrastructure competition among communities. *Economic Development Quarterly* 5:60–63.

Teaford, Jon C. 1979. *City and suburb: The political fragmentation of metropolitan America, 1850–1970*. Baltimore: Johns Hopkins University Press.

Teske, Paul, et al. 1993. Establishing the micro foundations of a macro theory: Information, movers, and the competitive local market for public goods. *American Political Science Review* 87: 702–13.

Thomas, Robert, and Suphapong Boonyapratuang. 1993. Local government complexity: Consequences for county property-tax and debt policies. *Publius* 23: 1–18.

Thomas, Robert, and Richard Murray. 1991. *Progrowth politics: Change and governance in Houston*. Berkeley: IGS Press.

Thomason, Sharon. 1986. Suburban sprawl: How counties cope. *American City and County*, July, 58–64.

Townslee, Tom. 1985. Land use planning brings high tech to Oregon. UPI distribution, March 23.

Tiebout, Charles. 1956. A pure theory of local expenditures. *Journal of Political Economy* 64:416–24.

The top ten cities. 1992. *Fortune*, November 2, 50.

Toronto and Detroit: Canadians do it better. 1990. *Economist*, May 19, 17–20.

Toulan, Nohad. 1994. Housing as a state planning goal. In *Planning the Oregon way*, ed. Carl Abbott, Deborah Howe, and Sy Adler. Corvallis: Oregon State University Press.

Transportation Research Board. 1991. *Transportation, urban form, and the environment*. Washington, D.C.: National Research Council and Transportation Research Board.

Tri-Met (Tri-County Metropolitan Transportation District, Portland). 1992. *Strategic plan*. Discussion draft two. Portland: Tri-Met.

——. 1993. *Planning and design for transit*. Portland: Tri-Met.

Tucker, Jill. 1995. Focus on metro growth. *Denver Post*, April 30.

Tufte, Edward R. 1970. Improving data analysis in political science. In *The quantitative analysis of social problems*, ed. Tufte. Reading, Mass.: Addison-Wesley.

Vance, James Jr. 1977. *This scene of man: The role and structure of the city in the geography of western civilization*. New York: Harper's College Press.

Walters, Dennis. 1988. Denver's rail project gets back on track with naming of financial advisory team. *Bond Buyer*, July 21.

Warner, Sam Bass, Jr. 1968. *The private city: Philadelphia in three periods of its growth*. Philadelphia: University of Pennsylvania Press.

——. 1978. *Streetcar suburbs*. 2d ed. Cambridge: Harvard University Press.

Waterpark: From drainage problems to liquid assets. 1987. *Urban Land*, March, 30–31.

Weiher, Gregory R. 1991. *The fractured metropolis: Political fragmentation and metropolitan segregation*. Albany: State University of New York Press.

Weiss, Marc A. 1987. *The rise of the community builders: The American real estate industry and urban land planning*. New York: Columbia University Press.

Wells, Garrison. 1990a. Castle Pines real estate struggling to get back on course. *Denver Business Journal*, August 6.

——. 1990b. RTD's staff, board sabotaged rail plan in secret meetings. *Denver Business Journal*, August 20.

——. 1991. Land-use planning for Colorado? *Denver Business Journal*, December 20.

Western Attitudes, Inc. 1993. Government operations and organization in the tri-county area. Executive summary of survey. Lake Oswego, Ore.: Western Attitudes, Inc.

Whyte, William H. 1968. *The last landscape*. Garden City, N.Y.: Doubleday.

Wildavsky, Aaron. 1989. *Craftways: On the organization of scholarly work*. New Brunswick, N.J.: Transaction.

Will anybody build these? 1993. *Southeast [Portland] Examiner*, July.

Williams, Brett. 1988. *Upscaling downtown: Stalled gentrification in Washington, D.C.* Ithaca: Cornell University Press.

Williams, Oliver. 1971. *Metropolitan political analysis: A social access approach*. New York: Free Press.

Wilmsen, Steven. 1992. Haney again seeks Meadows project. *Denver Post*, October 22.

Wilson, Geordie. 1993. Portland, Oregon, MAX has made public transit almost trendy. *Seattle Times*, January 21.

Wilson, James Q., ed. 1980. *The politics of regulation*. New York: Basic.

Wirt, Frederick M. 1985. The dependent city? External influences upon local control. *Journal of Politics* 47: 83–112.

Wirt Frederick, et al. 1972. *On the city's rim: Politics and policy in suburbia*. Lexington, Mass.: D.C. Heath.

Wirth, Louis. 1938. Urbanism as a way of life. *American Journal of Sociology*, July, 1–24.

Wood, Christopher. 1989. Developers vow to continue W-470 projects. *Boulder County Business Report*, March.

Workman, T. Christian. 1994. Assessing the effects of urban annexation policy on city planning and development. Senior thesis, Princeton University.

Yinger, John, et al. 1988. *Property taxes and house values*. Boston: Academic Press.

Zeigler, Donald J., and Stanley D. Brunn. 1980. Geopolitical fragmentation and the pattern of growth and need: Defining the cleavage between sunbelt and frostbelt metropolises. In *The American metropolitan system*, ed. Stanley D. Brunn and James Wheeler. New York: Wiley.

Zoning and regulations are homebuilder's biggest headache. 1988. *Urban Land* (Feb.): 28.

Interviews

Appell, Gordon. 1992. Denver Planning Office. Phone interview, September 25.

Arrington, G. B. 1993. Director of Transit Development, Tri-Met, in Portland, June 28.

Barnard, Rollin. 1992. Mayor of Greenwood Village, in Greenwood Village, October 30.

Broderick, Bill. 1992. Denver Regional Council of Governments, in Denver, October 26.

Cain, Barry. 1993. Vice President, Gramor Development, in Clackamas, June 28.

Coney, Robert D. 1992. Director of planning and development, Adams County, in Commerce City, October 28.

Ferdinandsen, Rich. 1992. Former commissioner, Jefferson County, in Golden, October 20.

Grillo, Joseph. 1993. Director of Land Development Services, Washington County, in Hillsboro, June 29.

Heisler, Jennifer. 1992. Manager of systems planning, RTD, in Denver, October 30.

Holderith, Emeric R. 1992a. President, The Summit Group, Inc, October 13. Phone conversation.

——. 1992b. In Lakewood, October 21.

Johnson, John W. 1992. Chief planner, Douglas County, in Castle Rock, Colo., October 23.

Kasowski, Kevin. 1993. Member, 1000 Friends of Oregon, June 29.

Kelley, Sharron. 1993. Multnomah County Commissioner, and former Metropolitan Service District councillor, in Portland, July 1.

Madden, J. 1992. President, John Madden Co., at Greenwood Village, November 4.

Miller, James H. 1992. Executive vice president, Miller/Davis Co., in Denver, November 2.

Moore, Jared. 1992. Transportation planner, RTD, in Denver October 30.

Moore, Scott T. 1992. Associate professor of political science, Colorado State University, in Denver, November 5.

Mugler, Larry, 1992. Director of development services, Denver Regional Council of Governments, in Denver, November 2.

Pemble, R. Scott. 1993. Planning director, Multnomah County, in Portland, July 1.

Potter, Herman. 1993. Resident of Tigard, Ore., June 28. Phone interview.

Rutsch, Randall. 1992. Denver Regional Council of Governments, September 18. Phone interview.

Seigneur, David. 1993a. Director, Clackamas County Development Agency, in Oregon City, July 2.

——. 1993b. June 22. Phone interview.

Seltzer, Ethan. 1993a. Former land use coordinator, Metropolitan Service District, and currently director, Institute for Portland Metropolitan Studies, Portland State University, June 21. Phone interview.

——. 1993b. In Portland, July 7.

Spitzer, John. 1992. Attorney, Boulder, October 22.

Tauer, Paul. 1992. Mayor of Aurora, at Aurora, Colo., October 29.

Tobias, Mary. 1993. President of Tualatin Valley Economic Development Corp., and former mayor of Sherwood, in Tualatin, July 9.

Index